Computer Graphics and Multimedia

Express Learning Series

Computer Graphics and Multimedia

Express Learning Series

ITL Education Solutions Ltd.
Research and Development Wing
New Delhi

Pearson

ISBN 978-81-317-8591-1

First Impression

Published by Pearson India Education Services Pvt. Ltd, CIN: U72200TN2005PTC057128

Head Office: 1st Floor, Berger Tower, Plot No. C-001A/2, Sector 16B, Noida – 201 301,Uttar Pradesh, India.

Registered Office: Featherlite, 'The Address' 5th Floor, Survey No 203/10B, 200 Ft MMRD Road,Zamin Pallavaram, Chennai - 600044
Website: in.pearson.com; Email:companysecretary.india@pearson.com

Digitally printed in India by Trinity Academy for Corporate Training Ltd, New Delhi in the year of 2024.

Contents

Preface

Computer graphics involves producing, manipulating, and storing images and animations on computers. The last decade has experienced enormous growth in the field of computer graphics and multimedia. Developments in computer graphics have revolutionized the world of entertainment by enhancing the quality of animations, movies and video games. The special effects created with the help of computers look so real that it sometimes becomes almost impossible to distinguish live action from computer-generated effects. New specialized software and hardware have given more power to graphic designers to create the kind of images that would have been impossible earlier. The magic touch of computer graphics is evident in those three-dimensional images and animated graphics that keep popping up during television commercials and movie shows. In a nutshell, there is no area untouched by computer graphics and multimedia whether it is engineering, science, medicine, mathematics, business, government, entertainment, education, advertising, and so on.

Keeping in mind the importance of computer graphics, almost all the universities have integrated the study of computer graphics and multimedia in B. Tech., MCA, BCA and B.Sc. courses. The book in your hands, Computer Graphics and Multimedia, in its unique easy-to-understand question-and-answer format directly addresses the need of students enrolled in these courses. The questions and corresponding answers in this book have been designed and selected to cover all the fundamentals that one must learn in order to pursue virtually any endeavour in the field of computer graphics. The main objective is to teach the concepts of computer graphics to people who will be the end users and to those who need some insight into it. The organized and accessible format allows students to quickly find the questions on specific topics. In simple words, reading this book will benefit anyone who wishes to arm themselves with substantive graphical skills.

The book Computer Graphics and Multimedia is a part of series named *Express Learning* which has a number of books designed as quick reference guides to important undergraduate and postgraduate courses.

Unique Features

1. Designed as a student-friendly self-learning guide. The book is written in clear, concise and lucid manner.
2. Easy-to-understand question-and-answer format.
3. Includes previously asked as well as new questions organized in chapters.
4. All types of questions including MCQs, short and long questions are covered.
5. Solutions to numerical questions asked at examination are provided.
6. All ideas and concepts are presented with clear examples.
7. Text is well structured and well supported with suitable diagrams.
8. Inter-chapter dependencies are kept to a minimum.

Chapter Organization

All the questions and answers are organized into 12 chapters.

- *Ch.1* provides an overview of computer graphics concepts and its applications and discusses the importance of computer image processing and virtual reality systems.
- *Ch. 2* is a detailed account of various input and output devices used by graphics systems and also provides the solved numericals to elaborate the practical concepts.
- *Ch.3* introduces the scan conversion of important graphic primitives such as straight lines, circles and ellipses and explains various polygon filling algorithms. It also describes how fonts can be stored in computers.
- *Ch.4* is about the various attributes associated with output primitives. These include line attributes (such as line width, line color, line type), curve attributes, area-fill attributes (fill styles, fill patterns), character attributes (text attributes and marker attributes).
- *Ch.5* is about the underlying theory to transform and view objects in 2D. It also describes the concepts of homogeneous coordinates and various types of 2D clipping such as line clipping, polygon clipping, curve clipping and text clipping.
- *Ch.6* explains how various tools can be used to view 3D objects. It also discusses different types of projections along with 3D viewing and clipping.
- *Ch.7* takes the reader to various ways of representing three-dimensional objects include polygons, quadratic surfaces, spline curves and surfaces, fractals and octree encodings.
- *Ch.8* tells about the basic concepts of primary colors. Different illumination and color models are also discussed at length.
- *Ch.9* deals with the hidden-surface elimination techniques and surface-rendering methods. These techniques and methods are used to generate three-dimensional scenes containing three-dimensional objects.
- *Ch.10* gets the reader started with writing graphics programs in OpenGL and VRML. It discusses the basic primitives used in OpenGL and VRML. It also describes how to draw 3D objects and 3D scenes using the primitives provided by these two languages.
- *Ch.11* provides a broad grounding in multimedia. It explains the basic building blocks of multimedia system, types of multimedia systems and application areas of multimedia. It also introduces the architectural framework for multimedia system. It also gives a brief overview of technological advancements in multimedia such as multimedia databases, video on demand, virtual reality, etc.
- *Ch.12* introduces the reader about the basic concepts of animation and throws lights on various animation techniques and languages.

Acknowledgements

- Our publisher Pearson Education, their editorial team and panel reviewers for their valuable contribution towards content enrichment.
- Our technical and editorial consultants for devoting their precious time to improve the quality of the book.
- Our entire research and development team who have put in their sincere efforts to bring out a high-quality book.

Feedback

For any suggestions and comments about this book, please free to send an e-mail to itlesl@rediffmail.com.

Hope you enjoy reading this book as much as we have enjoyed writing it.

ROHIT KHURANA
Founder and CEO, ITL ESL

1

Introduction to Computer Graphics

1. Define computer graphics.

Ans. Computer graphics is the process of producing, manipulating and storing images and animations on computers. Earlier, it started with the display of data on hard copy plotters and cathode ray tube (CRT) monitors, but now its use has become widespread. Today, there is no such area where computer graphics is not in use whether it is engineering, science, medicine, mathematical, architectural, business, government, entertainment, education, advertising and so on. However, in earlier times, computer graphics was not a popular field, because of the expensive hardware and limited graphics-based application programs. Thereafter, personal computers with in-built raster graphics were developed, and also the use of Apple Macintosh and IBM PC have significantly helped in popularizing the use of **bitmap graphics** for user–computer interaction. Soon after the bitmap graphics became accustomed, many cost-effective graphics-based applications started following. All these graphic-based applications helped large number of users to control different low-cost application programs, such as word processors, spreadsheets, and drawing programs. People who do not even use computers in their daily work still encounter computer graphics in television commercials and cinematic special effects. Thus, we can say that computer graphics is no longer a rarity.

2. Explain interactive and non-interactive computer graphics.

Ans. The **interactive computer graphics** involves a two-way communication between computer and a user. Here, creation and manipulation of the picture is done on the computer with the help of input devices which are operated by the user to get the simulated pictures on the screen. For example, ping pong video game. It is a tennis sports game, in which two people with the help of a pair of input devices separately turn on and position a 'paddle' to hit the ball back and forth across the screen. The aim is to defeat the opponent by earning a higher score than other player where the points are earned when one player fails to return the ball back to another player. On receiving signals from the input device, a computer can alter the displayed picture accordingly. It may appear to a user that picture is changing constantly in response to his entered commands.

On the other hand, the computer graphics in which observer does not have any control over the images is termed as **non-interactive computer graphics**. It involves one way of transmission of information. A common example of non-interactive graphics is the logo of a channel shown on TV. This image is usually a static stored program that works only on the instructions given in the program. In other words, the image is controlled completely by the program instead of the user/observer.

3. What are the advantages of interactive computer graphics?

Ans. Interactive computer graphics provides an efficient way of interacting with the computer and is being widely used in producing pictures since the invention of photography and television. It not only aims at producing highly developed two-dimensional (2D) and three-dimensional (3D) images of the real world objects, but also of abstract and synthetic objects such as complex mathematical surfaces in four-dimensions (4D), development of a human face from childhood through old age, survey results, and so on. With the advancement in interactive computer graphics, we are not confined to static images now. Though, static images usually provide better and good means of communicating information, but dynamically varying images have gone a step further in providing information, especially in time-varying phenomena such as the deflection of an aircraft wing in supersonic flight, in abstract visuals like population growth in India or nuclear energy use in the United Kingdom. A movie can now show changes over time more graphically than can a sequence of slides. Moreover, a sequence of frames which are displayed on a screen at the rate of more than 15 frames per second can display smooth motion or change in the form far better than a jerky sequence, having several seconds between individual frames. The use of dynamics can be put up to best use when the user can himself control the animation by manually adjusting the speed, the amount of detail shown, geometric relationship of the different objects in the scene with one another, and so on. Therefore, most of the interactive graphics technology constitutes hardware and software for user controlled *motion dynamics* and *update dynamics*. With **motion dynamics**, objects can be moved with respect to stationary observer or objects can remain stationary and observer can move around them. The typical examples of motion dynamics are flight simulators and video games where the user can control the movement of the objects. In most of the cases, the objects and camera both are moving. However, in some cases, the camera can be held fixed and the objects in the scene are moved relative to it. For example, linkage on a steam engine can be animated by moving all the parts appropriately. The **update dynamics** on the other hand, is the actual change of the shape, color, or other properties of the objects being viewed. The deformations of an airplane structure in flight or the state changes in a block diagram of a nuclear reactor in response to the user's manipulations are examples of update dynamics.

Another advantage of interactive computer graphics is that it permits extensive and high bandwidth user–computer interaction. This in turn enhances our ability to understand data, to perceive trends, to visualize real or imaginary objects, etc., in much precise form.

4. List and explain the applications of computer graphics?

Ans. In the earlier days, use of computer graphics was limited to only certain special capabilities such as implementing straight lines, cones, circles, ellipses, fulfilling the requirement of drafting, and so on. With the passage of time, these graphics tasks were increased to include transformations, geometrical modifications, variations of line thickness, editing, etc. As the graphics features developed, more and more uses were found for them in non-drafting areas. Now, in present scenario, computer graphics is used in numerous fields ranging from routine daily activities to specialized areas in different fields such as research, advertising, etc. Some of the major application areas of computer graphics are described as follows:

- **Presentation graphics:** This deals in generating graphical representation of information by making use of graphs and charts. It is commonly used to summarize statistical, financial, mathematical, scientific, and economic data for making managerial reports, research reports, consumer information bulletins, etc. A variety of workstation devices and service bureaus are available for converting screen displays into films or slides so as to effectively provide training sessions. Nowadays, the graphs and charts are also displayed as 3D figures to provide additional information. 3D graphics help in providing more attractive presentation of data relationships. Some of the examples of presentation graphics include pie charts, surface graphs, bar charts, etc.
- **Drawing and art:** Computer graphics methods are widely used in fine art and commercial art applications. There are numerous computer methods and tools, symbolic mathematics programs, animation systems, etc., that help in designing object shapes and specifying objects motions. For example, the paintbrush program also uses the artist to paint electronically on a graphics tablet (also known as **digitizer**) by using a stylus, which tends to simulate various brush strokes, brush widths, and colors. These pictures are displayed on the screen of a video monitor. A variety of other computer technologies such as combination of 3D modelling packages, texture mapping, drawing programs, and CAD software are used by fine artists for creating images.

  Apart from producing electronic images in fine arts, these methods can also be substantially used in commercial arts for generating logos, designs, page layouts, TV advertisements, and so on. The most common graphics method used in various television commercials is **morphing**. In this, one object is transformed into another; for example, transforming one person's face into another, oil can into automobile engine, and so on.
- **Entertainment:** Today, the use of computer graphics in entertainment has reached quite far and wider than before. It has been widely used in producing motion pictures, music videos, TV shows, games, and cartoon movies. Many a times, objects in graphics are mixed with live scenes for creating a powerful entertainment environment and sometimes, graphics are displayed by themselves. There are numerous award winning movies where graphics have played a key role, such as Jurassic park, Titanic, Star trek, etc. Similarly, developers use combination of graphics, sound, and animation to develop variety of games. The children can enjoy these games, by having real experiences of driving cars of different models, playing musical instruments, flying aircrafts, and so on.
- **Education and training:** Computer-generated models of physical, financial, and other systems have revolutionized the whole process of education. Currently, the classrooms, libraries, and museums are utilizing such models to make education much more interesting. Unlike recorded television shows, Computer Aided Education (CAE) and Computer-Based Training (CBT) packages are making learning much more interactive. Several models of physical processes, physiological functions, or population trends, such as color-coded diagrams help trainees to effectively learn the operation of system. In many specific training applications, specialized systems called **simulators** are designed to train ship captains, aircraft pilots, and air traffic control personnel. This simulated environment helps a person to get comfortable with the system, before he/she is allowed to operate on a real system. Although simulators can be used as training systems, they are also commonly employed to study the behaviour of drivers in critical situations.
- **Computer aided design (CAD):** It is probably the biggest factor which is responsible for significant use of computer graphics in design processes, especially in engineering and architectural systems. Moreover, CAD methods are widely used in design of automobiles, aircraft, spacecraft, buildings, bridges, highways, textiles, computers, and many other products. For some design applications, objects are displayed in a wireframe outline form which gives the overall shape and

internal features of objects. This helps designers to view the effects of interactive adjustments in designing different shapes without waiting for the object surfaces to be fully generated. Animations are often used in CAD applications for testing the performance of a vehicle or system displayed in the wireframe outline form. Wireframes displays of the system allow the designer to view the interior of the system and also watch the behaviour of different components present inside the system during motion.

- **Graphical user interface (GUI):** Nowadays, almost every application software comes with a graphical interface. Its major component is a window manager which permits a user to display multiple window areas. Each area either contains graphical or non graphical information which can be made active by simply clicking on that area using a pointing device such as mouse. A typical graphical interface consists of a window manager, menus, and icons. Menus and icons are used for fast selection of processing options or parameter values.
- **Cartography:** Computer graphics is also used to produce accurate and schematic representation of geographical maps, oceanographic charts, weather maps, contour maps, population density maps, and relief maps.

5. State the importance of computer image processing. Explain in detail the image synthesis and image analysis.

Ans. Image processing (also called **picture processing**) deals with manipulating and interpreting the existing pictures such as photographs, TV scans, etc., rather than developing and creating them. It is one of the important aspects in many areas such as education, science, medicine, entertainment, etc. A picture is usually first converted into digital form in order to apply image processing methods on it. Thereafter, digital methods can be applied to rearrange picture parts, to enhance the quality of shading or to provide optimum color separations. Such techniques are widely used in commercial art applications where retouching and rearranging of parts of an image is carried out extensively. It is also used in analyzing satellite pictures of the earth and galaxies. Medical applications also make wide use of image processing techniques for image enhancements, in simulations of operations and also in tomography. **Tomography** is a technique of X-ray photography where cross-sectional views of physiological systems are displayed. Both types of tomography, namely, *computed X-ray tomography (CT)* and *position emission tomography (PET)* make use of projection methods for reconstructing the cross sections from the digital data. Image processing techniques are also used to monitor the internal functioning of the body as well as to show cross sections at the time of surgery. There are three important sub areas of image processing, which are as follows:

- **Image enhancement:** It deals in improving the quality of picture by either removing noise or by enhancing contrast.
- **Pattern detection and recognition:** It deals in detecting and clarifying standard patterns from the picture. Moreover, it helps in finding deviations or distortions from these detected patterns.
- **Scene analysis and computer vision:** It allows scientists to construct a 3D model of a scene from different 2D images.

Image synthesis is the process of creating new images from a sequence of activities that gradually creates the required effect. This contrast with the image processing method as in this case the starting point is an image whose properties need to be explored. There is not lot of difference between images which are created by process of synthesis than those which are created by an artist itself. That is, an artist first requires to choose the arrangement of objects or a scene to be displayed and then creates an image in a selected medium and manner for creating a representational image or sculpture. While on the other hand, synthesis aims at building a conceptual model of objects which are then depicted by a chosen method. Thus, it can be said that images in synthesis is built in two stages where the first stage is called **modelling** and second stage is known as **rendering**.

Image analysis is mainly concerned with extraction of meaningful information from images which are necessary for higher-level scene analysis methods. The techniques in image analysis include computation of perceived brightness and color, complete recovery of 3D data in the scene, location of discontinuities corresponding to objects in the scene, and characterization of properties of uniform regions in the image. Image analysis is widely used in many important areas such as, slow-scan television images of moon or of different planets obtained from space probes, aerial surveillance photographs, television images taken from an industrial robot's eye, major X-ray images, fingerprint analysis, computerized axial tomography (CAT) scans, etc.

6. Is there any difference between computer graphics and image processing?

Ans. Though the methods used in computer graphics and image processing overlap, the two fields deal with completely different operations. Computer graphics is all about synthesizing a new image from geometry, lighting parameters, materials, and textures. Image processing, on the other hand, applies techniques to manipulate, interpret, or enhance the existing images acquired through some devices such as scanners, medical equipments, etc. In computer graphics, one begins with knowledge of different shapes and features of an object and then gradually works on it to form a 2D or 3D image. However, while applying the image processing methods, we first digitize a photograph or any other picture into an image file. Digital methods are then applied on this image to improve and enhance the image quality.

However, both image processing and computer graphics methods are often combined so as to be used in various applications such as, in multimedia for producing stunning visual effects, in medical applications for study of physical functions, to plan and practice surgery, and to design artificial limbs.

7. What do you mean by scientific visualization? Explain.

Ans. The data produced by performing numeric simulations on supercomputers generally contain thousands and even millions of data values. In the same way, the data files generated from satellite cameras and other sources are also very large in size. Scientists, engineers, and medical personnel often need to analyze such large amounts of information to determine the trends and patterns or to study the behaviour of certain processes. However, scanning these large sets of numbers is a tedious and ineffective process. To make the scanning process an effective and comparatively simple task, the data are converted to a visual form so that the trends and patterns become immediately apparent. This process of producing graphical representations for scientific, engineering, and medical data sets and processes is known as **scientific visualization**.

Data values collected from numeric simulations can be scalar values, vectors, high-order tensors, or any combination of these data types. In addition, data sets may be 2D or 3D in nature. Depending on the characteristics of the data, many different kinds of effective visualization schemes can be used. Some of the most commonly used visualization techniques are color coding, contour plots, graphs and charts, surface renderings, and visualization of volume interiors.

8. Explain how virtual reality systems can be used in design applications.

Ans. Virtual reality systems represent a realistic simulation and visualization environment that enables us in creating a real-time experience of an environment. With the continuous use of animations in computer graphics, it has become easier to use virtual reality systems in various design applications. Almost, every real-time animation uses wireframe displays on a video monitor, which are useful in testing the performance of a vehicle or system virtually. When the objects are not displayed with their surfaces on the monitor, they tend to allow fast calculations for every segment of an animation in producing a smooth real-time motion on the screen. Another important aspect of using wireframe displays is that it helps a designer to view the interior of the object (such as interior of the vehicle, skeleton of a human body, etc.) and also to observe the behaviour of inner components while in motion. Another technique used in virtual reality system is known as **Stereoscopic viewing**. It is used in representing 3D objects where users can step into a scene and interact with the environment. In this technique, a user wears a headset which contains an optical system for generating the stereoscopic views. This headset is most commonly used in conjunction with interactive input devices in order to locate and manipulate the objects in the scene. The headset is equipped with a sensing system which keeps track of the viewer's position, so that front and rear positions of the objects can also be seen with the movement of the viewer. However, an interactive virtual reality environment can also be viewed with stereoscopic glasses and a video monitor, rather than a headset. It usually aims to provide a low-cost virtual reality system.

MULTIPLE CHOICE QUESTIONS

1. ________ is the process of producing, manipulating and storing images and animations of objects.

   (a) Computer graphics (b) Bitmap graphics
   (c) Interactive graphics (d) Non-interactive graphics

2. Which of the following are the applications of computer graphics?

   (a) Presentation graphics (b) Entertainment
   (c) CAD (d) All of these

3. ________ applies numerous techniques on the images to edit, manipulate and modify to improve their overall quality.

   (a) Computer graphics (b) Image processing
   (c) Visualization (d) Interactive graphics

4. CAD stands for ________

   (a) Common Aided Design (b) Commercial Aided Design
   (c) Computer Aided Design (d) Computer Animation Design

5. ________ is the process of creating new images from a sequence of activities that gradually creates the required effect.

   (a) Image analysis (b) Image synthesis
   (c) Image processing (d) None of these

Answers. 1. a 2. d 3. b 4. c 5. b

2

Overview of Graphics Systems

1. List some standard input and output device hardware used by graphics systems.

Ans. The two main elements required by graphics systems for displaying pictures with fast response time are *hardware* and *software*. **Hardware** is the electronic device which is capable of computing and manipulating information, whereas **software** is responsible for controlling, integrating, and managing the hardware components of a computer. Hardware can be further categorized into input devices (which allow the user to feed into the computer) and output devices (which convert machine-readable into human-readable form). Some standard input device hardware for graphics systems includes keyboards, light pens, mouse, digitizing tablets, etc., while output device hardware includes plotters, printers, and graphics display on the monitor. The monitors are based on cathode ray tubes (CRT), direct view storage tubes (DVST), liquid crystal display (LCD), plasma, and other more techniques. On the other hand, software of computer graphics includes integration of the man-machine interface, packages, programming languages, and operating system in modular form.

2. With the help of a suitable diagram explain the working of CRT.

or

With a neat cross-sectional view explain the functioning of CRT devices.

or

Explain the construction and functioning of typical CRT display device.

Ans. The basic operation of CRT is similar to that in television sets. Figure 2.1 illustrates the basic components of a CRT.

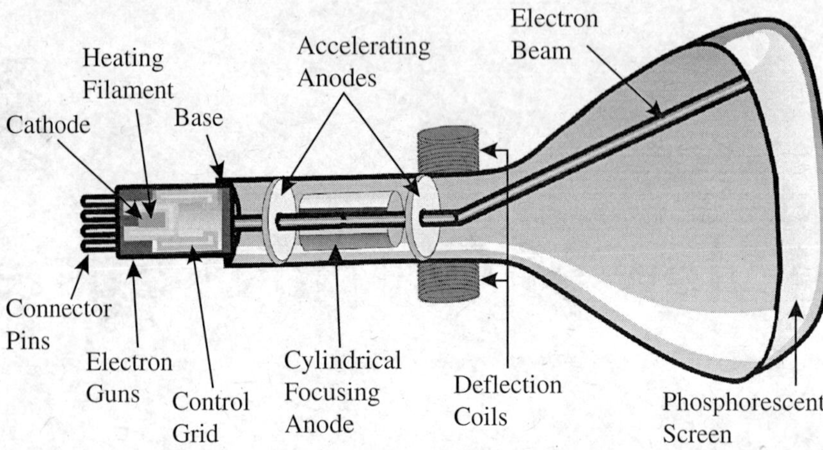

Figure 2.1 Components of CRT

A beam of electrons (cathode rays) emitted by an electron gun passes through focusing and deflection systems that direct the beam towards specified positions on the phosphor-coated screen. The phosphor then emits a small spot of light at each position contacted by the electron beam. Since the light emitted by the phosphor fades very rapidly, some method is needed for maintaining the screen picture. One way to keep the phosphor glowing is to redraw the picture repeatedly by quickly directing the electron beam back over the same points. This type of display is called a **refresh CRT**. The primary components of an electron gun in a CRT are the heated metal cathode and a control grid. Heat is supplied to the cathode by directing a current through a coil of wire (called **filament**) inside the cylindrical cathode structure which causes electrons to be 'boiled off' the hot cathode surface. In the vacuum inside the CRT envelope, the free, negatively charged electrons are then accelerated towards the phosphor coating by a highly positive voltage. The accelerating voltage can then be generated with a positively charged metal coating on the inside of the CRT envelope near the phosphor screen, or an accelerating anode can be used, as shown in Figure 2.1. Before reaching the phosphor-coated screen, the electrons have to be passed through the monitor's focusing system. The focusing system is initially set up to focus the electron flow into a very thin beam and then in a specific direction. Focusing can be accomplished either by electric or by magnetic fields. When the electrons in the beams collide with the phosphor coating, their kinetic energy is absorbed by the phosphor. Some of this energy is converted into heat while rest of the energy causes the electrons in the phosphors to move up to the higher energy levels. After this, when these electrons begin to return to the ground state, they emit light at certain frequencies. These frequencies are proportionate to the energy difference between the higher state and the ground state. As a result, the image, which we see on the screen, is the combination of all the electron light emissions.

3. What do you understand by refresh rate of a monitor and how do you measure it?

Ans. Refresh rate refers to the number of times per second the pixels are recharged so that their glow remains bright. Generally, screen pixels are made from phosphor and they need to be refreshed periodically because the phosphors hold their glow for just a fraction of a second. The refresh rate for a monitor is measured in Hertz (Hz) and varies from 60 to 75 Hz. A refresh rate of 60 Hz means that image is redrawn 60 times a second. The higher the refresh rate, the more solid the image looks on the screen, that is, it does not flicker.

4. Describe the term persistence in reference to CRT.

Ans. CRT uses different kinds of phosphors which are different in terms of their persistence (that is, for how long it continues to glow). In technical terms, **persistence** is defined as the time it takes the emitted light from the screen to decay to one-tenth of its original intensity. However, different phosphors are used for different purposes depending on their persistence. A low-persistence phosphor is used for animation and it requires high refresh rates in order to maintain its steadiness; whereas a high-persistence phosphor is used for displaying static and highly complex pictures.

5. What is meant by the resolution of a video display unit?

Ans. Resolution refers to the number of pixels (points per centimetre) that can be plotted in the horizontal and vertical directions on the screen. It can be of two types, namely, *medium resolution graphics* (where pixels are large) and *high-resolution graphics* (where pixels are small). Nowadays, most video display units operate on the basis of standard CRT design. With reference to CRT, resolution refers to the number of points which can be displayed on it without being overlapped. The average CRT resolution is currently 800 × 600 or 1024 × 768. However, resolution of high-quality systems (also known as **high-definition systems**) is 1280 × 1024. Large number of dots, or screen points result in sharper image. Therefore, a resolution of 1280 × 1024 will produce sharper images (for example, smaller icons and more information) than one of 800 × 600.

6. What do you mean by an image's aspect ratio?

Ans. Aspect ratio is the ratio of the width of the display screen to the height, that is, the ratio of vertical points to the horizontal points necessary to produce equal length lines in both directions on the screen. Generally, computer displays have an aspect ratio of 4:3. It means that a vertical line plotted with three points has the same length as a horizontal line plotting with four points.

7. What is the main difference between interlaced and non-interlaced monitor?

Ans. The main difference between these two monitors (or video modes) is that interlaced monitor tends to produce more flicker images with low resolution and quality as compared to a non-interlaced monitor. This is because a non-interlaced monitor uses only single pass or sweep of the electron gun to display an image, while on the other hand an interlaced monitor uses two passes to produce that same image. In simple terms, a non-interlaced monitor is one in which scanning lines are done sequentially whereas an interlaced monitor is one in which all the odd lines are scanned first followed by all of the even lines.

8. Explain the two techniques for producing color displays with CRT.

or

Explain how colors are generated on the screen.

Ans. A CRT monitor displays color pictures by using a combination of phosphors that emit different colored light. By combining the emitted light from the different phosphors, a range of colors can be generated. The two basic techniques for producing color displays with CRT are as follows:

- **Beam-penetration:** This method is commonly used with random scan displays where two layers of phosphor (usually red and green) are coated on the inner side of the CRT screen. The displayed color depends on how far the electron beam penetrates into the phosphor layers. A beam of slow electrons excites only the outer red layer while a beam of very fast electrons penetrates through the red layer and excites the inner green layer. At intermediate beam speeds, combinations of red and green light are emitted to show two additional colors, orange and yellow. The speed of the electrons, and the screen color at any point, is controlled by the beam-acceleration voltage. Beam-penetration is an inexpensive way to produce color in random scan monitors. However, with this method, only four colors are possible, and the quality of pictures is not as good as compared to other methods.

- **Shadow-masking:** This method is commonly used in raster scan systems because it produces a much wider range of colors than the beam-penetration method. A shadow-mask CRT has three phosphor color dots at each pixel position. One phosphor dot emits a red light, another emits a green light, and the third emits a blue light. This type of CRT has three electron guns, one for each color dot, and a shadow-mask grid just behind the phosphor-coated screen. These electron beams are deflected and focused as a group onto the shadow mask, which contains a series of holes aligned with the phosphor-dot patterns. When the three beams pass through a hole in the shadow mask, they activate a dot triangle, which appears as a small color spot on the screen. The phosphor dots in the triangles are arranged so that each electron beam can activate only its corresponding color dot when it passes through the shadow mask.

9. Write a short note on working of raster scan display system.

or

Describe raster display system with the help of a neat diagram.

Ans. Raster scan display system is the most common graphic monitor which employs CRT and it is based on television technology. In this system, the electron beam is swept across the screen, one row at a time from top to bottom (see Figure 2.2). As the electron beam moves across each row, the beam intensity is turned ON and OFF to create a pattern of illuminated spots. The picture definition is stored in a memory area called the **raster refresh buffer** or **frame buffer**, which holds the set of intensity values for all the screen points. These values are then retrieved from the refresh buffer and 'painted' on

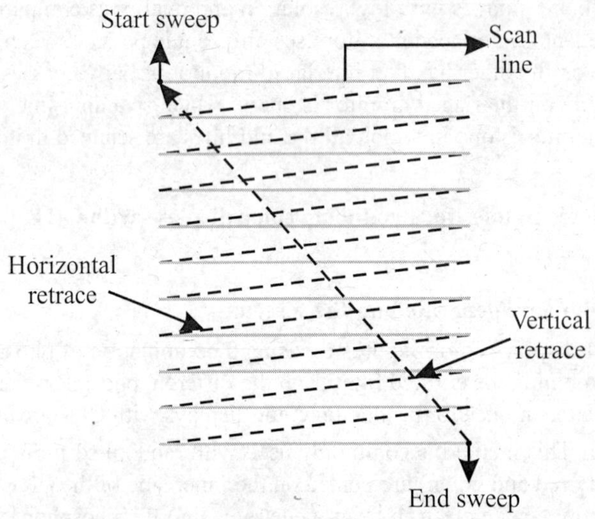

Figure 2.2 Raster Scanning

the screen one row (*scan line*) at a time. Each screen point is referred to as a **pixel** or **pel** (shortened form of **picture element**). At the end of each scan line, the electron beam returns to the left side of the screen to begin displaying the next scan line. The return to the left of the screen, after refreshing each scan line, is called the **horizontal retrace** of the electron beam. At the end of each frame, the electron beam returns to the top left corner of the screen to begin the next frame. This is known as **vertical retrace**. On some raster scan systems, each frame is displayed in two passes using an interlaced refresh procedure. In the first pass, the beam sweeps across every other scan line from top to bottom. Then after the vertical retrace, the beam sweeps out the remaining scan lines. Interlacing of the scan lines in this way allows us to see the entire screen displayed in half the time it would have taken to sweep across all the lines at once from top to bottom. This is an effective technique for avoiding flicker providing that adjacent scan lines contain similar display information. Raster scan systems are well suited for the realistic display of scenes containing subtle shading and color patterns. Some systems such as television sets and printers make use of raster scan methods.

10. How the size of frame buffer pixel and resolution are related to each other?

Ans. More the number of pixels required to control the intensity of screen positions and higher the resolution of the system, then more storage area will be required in the frame buffer for holding the intensity values for all screen points. For example, a system with 24 bits/pixel and having a resolution of 1024×1024 requires atleast 3 megabytes of storage for the frame buffer.

11. How the different color or gray levels are incorporated in raster refresh display tube?

Ans. A frame buffer is the most common method for implementing a raster CRT graphics device. Usually, in the raster there is one memory bit for each pixel which is known as **bit plane**. This means that the picture is built up in the frame buffer one bit at a time. As memory bit represents only two states, that is, 0 and 1, thus a single-bit plane yields a black-and-white (or monochrome) display. Since frame buffer is a digital device and raster CRT is an analog device, a digital to analog converter (DAC) is required to convert digital information from the frame buffer into an analog signal so that it can be displayed on the raster CRT graphics device. Hence, it can be said that each pixel in the frame buffer must be accessed and converted before it is visible on the raster CRT.

However, for incorporating different color or gray levels into a frame buffer raster graphics device, additional bit planes need to be used. The schematic representation of an N-bit-plane gray level frame buffer is shown in Figure 2.3. Pixel intensity on the CRT is controlled by the corresponding location of pixel in each of the N bit planes. As each N-bit plane will represent a binary value (0 or 1) therefore, each value will be loaded into the corresponding position in a register. This resulting binary number is then interpreted as an intensity level between 0 (dark) and 2^N-1 (full intensity). Finally, DAC will convert such binary values into an analog voltage between 0 and the maximum voltage of the electron gun. Thus, a total of 2^N intensity levels are possible. However, to increase the number of available intensity levels, the concept of lookup table is used (see Figure 2.4 for $N = 3$). After reading the bit planes in the frame buffer, the resulting number is used as an index into the lookup table. That is, lookup table also contains 2^N entries, where each entry is W bits wide. When W becomes greater than N, then 2^W intensities become available. However, at a single time, only 2^N different intensities would be available. Thus, to get additional intensities, the lookup table must be reloaded.

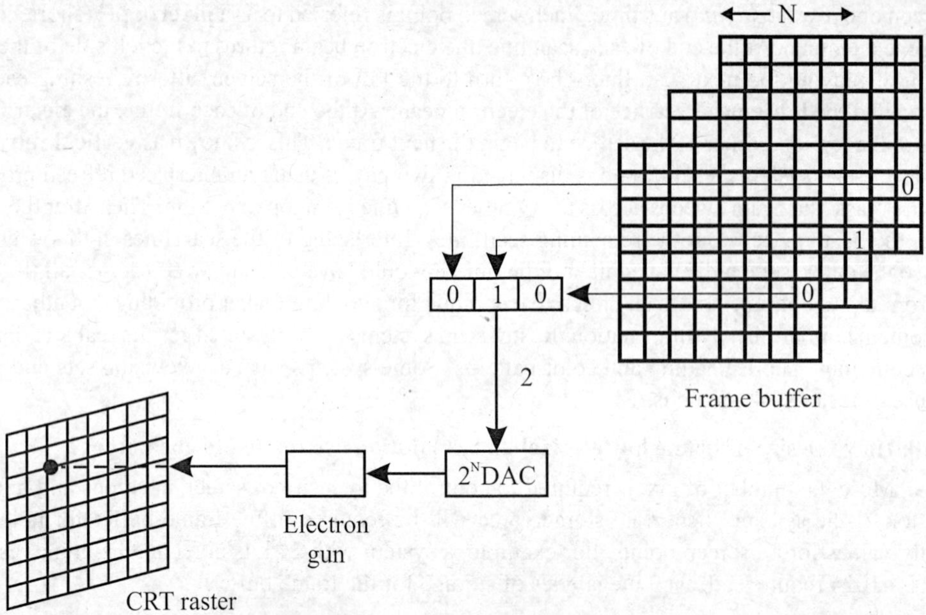

Figure 2.3 An N-bit Plane Gray Level Buffer

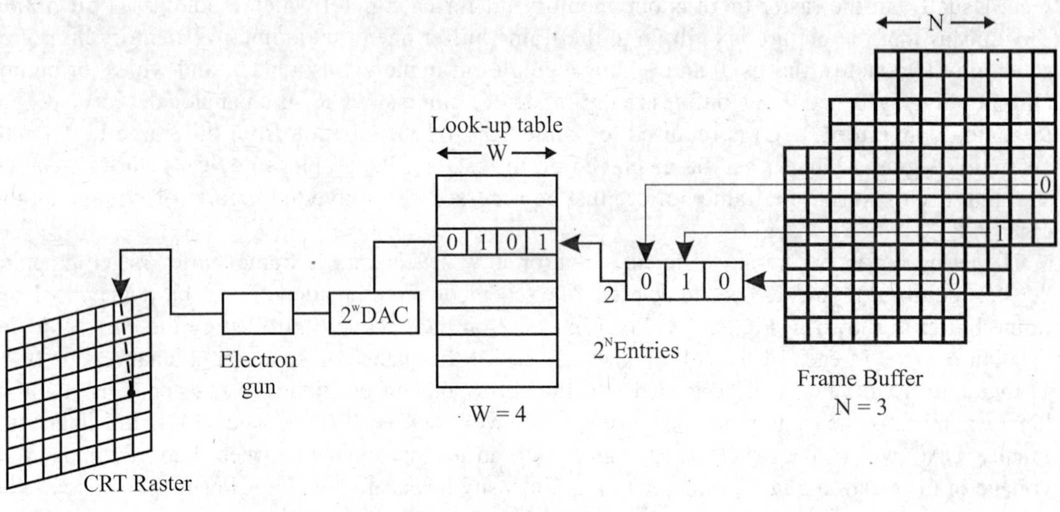

Figure 2.4 An N-bit Plane Gray Level Frame Buffer, with a W-bit Lookup Table

An implementation of simple color raster frame buffer is shown in Figure 2.5. It consists of three bit planes, one for each primary color (red, green, and blue). These three colors are combined at the CRT to yield eight colors, which are listed in Table 2.1.

Table 2.1 Simple 3-bit Plane Frame Buffer Color Combinations

	Red	Green	Blue
Black	0	0	0
Red	1	0	0
Green	0	1	0
White	1	1	1
Cyan	0	1	1
Yellow	1	1	0
Blue	0	0	1
Magenta	1	0	1

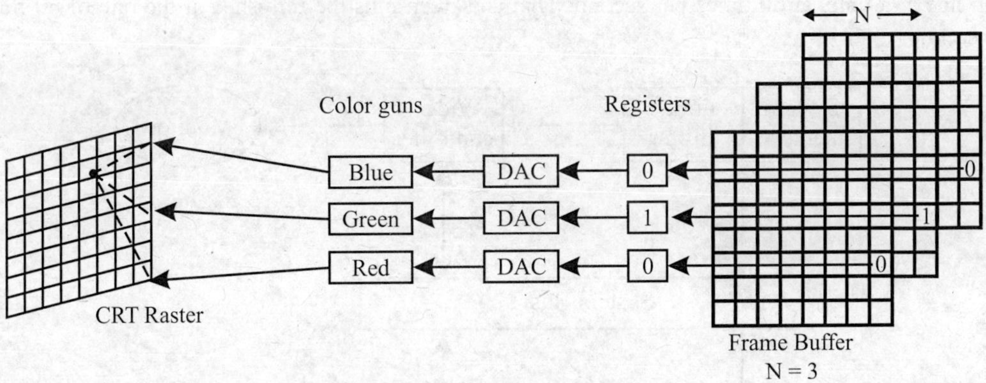

Figure 2.5 Simple Color Frame Buffer

12. Explain the architecture of a simple raster graphics system.

Ans. The organization of a simple raster graphics system is shown in Figure 2.6. In addition to the central processing unit (CPU), another special purpose processor, known as **video controller** or **display controller** is also used to control the operations of the display device. Here, the relation between system memory and the CPU is exactly the same as in a non-graphic computer system. In this architecture, the frame buffer may be stored anywhere in the system memory, and the video controller accesses the frame buffer via the system bus to refresh the screen.

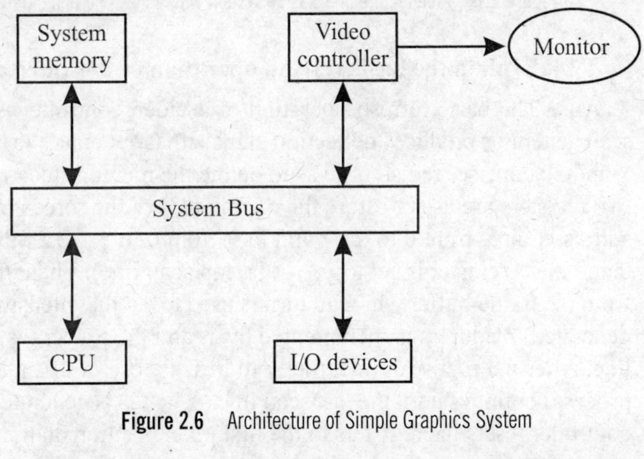

Figure 2.6 Architecture of Simple Graphics System

13. Explain the architecture of raster display system with a fixed portion of the system memory reserved for the frame buffer.

Ans. This is the most common organization of a raster display system where a fixed area is reserved for the frame buffer in the system memory, and video controller is given direct access to the frame buffer memory rather than making use of the system bus. To accomplish this, system memory is made as dual-ported and a separate access port is provided to the video controller. Such architecture is shown in Figure 2.7. In this, the location of the frame buffer and the corresponding screen position are addressed in Cartesian coordinates. The origin of the coordinate system is usually specified in the lower left corner of the screen. In a 2D system, the surface of the screen is represented as the first quadrant with positive x (values increases to the right) and y (values increases from bottom to top) coordinates. Scan lines are marked from the top of the screen (labelled as y_{max}) to the bottom (zero). Along these scan lines, screen pixel positions are marked from zero to the right corner of the screen (labelled as x_{max}). Here, the video controller cycles through the frame buffer, one scan line at a time, at 60 times per second. That is, screen must be refreshed at the rate of 60 frames per second.

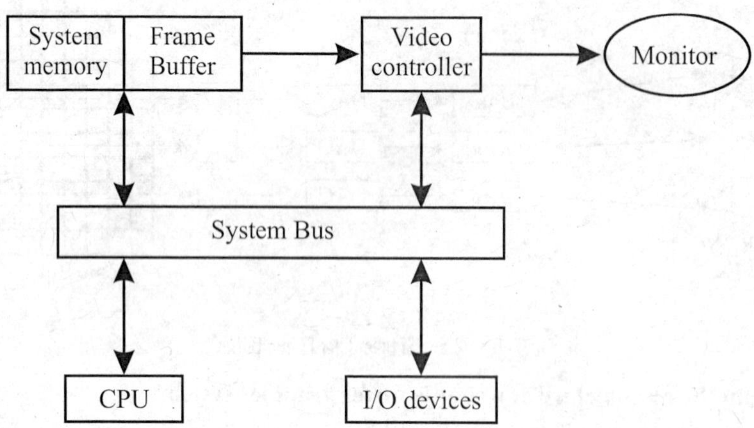

Figure 2.7 Architecture of a Raster System with a Fixed Portion of the System Memory Reserved for the Frame Buffer

14. Explain the basic refresh operation of the video controller.

Ans. The basic refresh operation of a video controller is shown in Figure 2.8. Initially, the raster scan generator produces deflection signals that generate the raster scan. The generator also controls the X and Y addresses registers so as to define the memory location which needs to be accessed next. These two registers are used to store the coordinates of the screen pixels and it is assumed that frame buffer is addressed in x from 0 to x_{max} and in y from 0 to y_{max}. At the start of refresh cycle, X register is set to 0 and the Y register is set to y_{max} (the top scan line). Then, the value for this pixel position is retrieved from the frame buffer which in turn is used to set the intensity of the CRT beam. As the first scan line is generated, X address is incremented by 1, and the process is repeated for the next pixel on the top scan line. After the first scan line, the X address is reset to 0 and the Y address is decremented by one. The process continues until the last scan line ($y = 0$) is generated. After going through all pixels, the video controller resets the registers to the first pixel position on the top scan line and the refresh process starts over again.

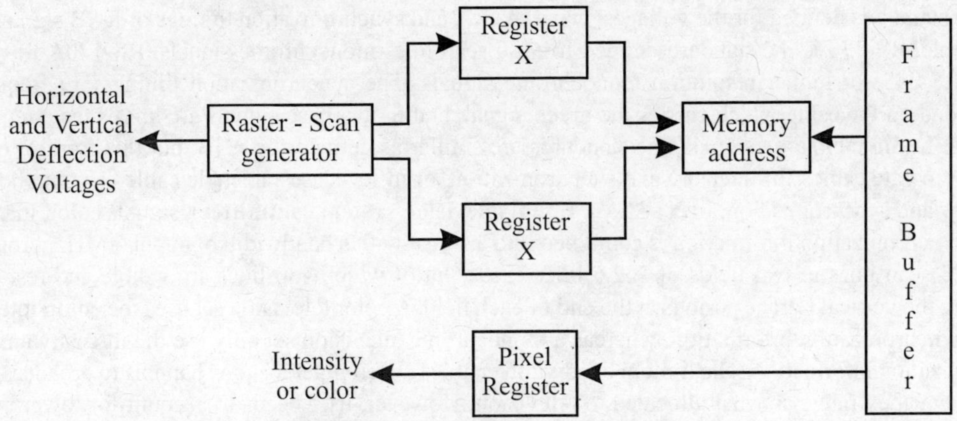

Figure 2.8 Basic Video Controller Refresh Operation

Normally, screens are refreshed at the rate of 60 frames per second for a display of resolution 640×480 pixels. Therefore, the cycle time available for displaying a single 1-bit pixel is 54 nanoseconds(ns) (1/480*640*60). As, the RAM chips have cycle time of around 200 ns, so the procedure illustrated in Figure 2.8 cannot support such chips. Thus, to speed up pixel processing, the video controller must retrieve multiple pixel values from the refresh buffer in one memory cycle. That is, video controller need to fetch 16 bits in one memory cycle, hence using 864 nanoseconds of refresh time (16 pixels*54 ns/pixels = 864 ns). These multiple pixels are stored in a separate register which are then used to control the CRT beam intensity for a group of adjacent pixels. While these groups of adjacent pixels are being processed, the next pixel block of pixel values is retrieved from the frame buffer.

15. Give some operations performed by the video controller. Explain all the forms in which output of a video controller can be seen.

Ans. In addition to the basic refresh operation, the video controller also performs a number of other important functions. It is capable of recovering pixel intensities from different memory areas on different refresh cycles. In case of high-quality systems where two frame buffers are provided, one buffer can be used for refreshing while the other is used for filling intensity values. These frame buffers can switch their roles to provide a fast procedure for generating real-time animations. This is possible because different views of moving objects can be successively loaded into the refresh buffers. In addition, the video controller can perform some transformations such as screen area can be reduced, enlarged, or moved to another location during the refresh cycles. Moreover, the video controller may contain a **lookup table** (an array or matrix of data that contains items to be searched) to provide a fast method for changing screen intensity values. The lookup table contains as many entries as pixel values, so the pixel values will access the lookup table instead of controlling the CRT beam intensity directly so as to speed up the process of changing screen intensity values. In some systems, the video controller is also allowed to mix the frame buffer image with an input image captured from a television camera or other input device.

The output of the video controller can be seen in any one of the three forms, namely, *RGB*, *monochrome*, and *NTSC*. In **RGB (red, green, and blue)**, separate cables are used to carry the three signals (red, green, and blue) which controls the three electron guns of a shadow-mask CRT, and another cable is used to carry the synchronization which signals the start of vertical and horizontal retrace. There are some standards defined for the voltages, wave shapes, and synchronization timings of RGB signals. For example, RS-170 is the standard defined for 480 scan lines monochrome signals, RS-170A for color, and RS-343 for higher resolution monochrome signals. The synchronization timings are frequently included on the cable which carries the green signal, and in that case signals are known as **composite video**. In **monochrome** signals, the standards are similar as defined for RGB, but this form of output uses separate cables for intensity and synchronization, or in few cases, a single cable carrying both intensity and synchronization. In **NTSC** (**national television system committee**), signals color, intensity, and synchronization information is combined into a signal with a bandwidth of about 5 MHz, broadcast as 525 scan lines in two fields of 262.5 lines each. Out of which 480 lines are visible and rest occur during the vertical retrace periods at the end of each field. A color television set uses the color, intensity, and synchronization information, whereas a monochrome television set only use the intensity and synchronization information. The limit in bandwidth enables different television channels to broadcast over the frequency range as what allocated to television. However, user needs to account for lower picture quality to an effective resolution of about 350 × 350.

16. Discuss the disadvantages of simple raster display system architecture.

Ans. Though simple raster display system architecture is not costly to build, but still has some disadvantages which are as follows:

- In such systems, scan conversion in software is slow. For example, in this architecture, one needs to calculate (x,y) address of each pixel on a line, which must be then translated into a memory address consisting of a byte and bit-within-byte pair. Such steps are repeated many times which thus slows down the overall pace of the user interaction with the application. Hence, creating user dissatisfaction.
- As the refresh rate of the display increases, the number of memory accesses made by the video controller also increases. This results in the decreasing the number of memory cycles available to the CPU and thus, leading to the slowing down of CPU.

17. Explain the architecture of raster display system with peripheral display processor.

Ans. This architecture helps to overcome the disadvantages of simple raster display system architecture by introducing a separate display processor (also called **graphics processor** or **display coprocessor**) with a separate processor memory area and frame buffer as shown in Figure 2.9. The purpose of a display processor is to free the CPU from the graphics tasks; while frame buffer helps in performing image refreshing functions. A major task of such processor is to digitize a picture definition given in an application program into a set of pixel-intensity values so that it can be stored into the frame buffer. This digitization process is known as **scan conversion**. Graphics commands specifying straight lines, curved lines, and polygon outlines, and other geometric objects are scan converted into a set of discrete intensity points. Scan conversion of straight line, for example, is performed to locate the pixel positions closest to the line path and to store the intensity for each position in the frame buffer. As shown in Figure 2.9, this architecture contains two processors, namely, *CPU* and *display processor*. It also includes three memory areas, which are as follows:

- **System memory:** It contains data as well as programs which execute on CPU such as application programs, graphics package, and operating system.
- **Display processor memory:** It contains data and programs which are executed scan-conversion and raster scan operations.
- **Frame buffer:** It contains images to be displayed and are created by the scan-conversion and raster operations.

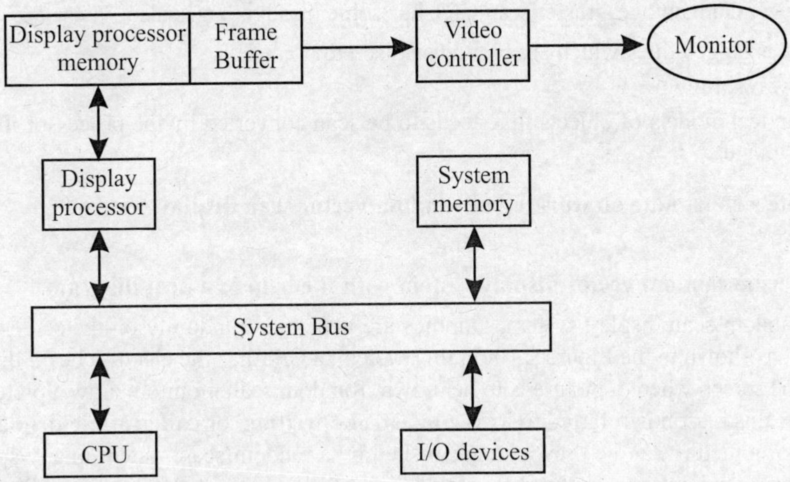

Figure 2.9 Architecture of a Raster System with a Peripheral Display Processor

18. Discuss the additional display-processor functionality.

or

What all functionalities can display processor provide?

Ans. The simple display processor is able to perform only few graphics functionalities which can be easily implemented. The system designer desires to offload the main CU more and more by adding functionalities to the display processor. The display processor can be deigned to perform several additional operations, which are as follows:

- It can be designed to generate various line styles such as dashed, dotted, or solid, to display color areas, and to perform certain transformations and manipulations on displayed objects.
- It can be designed to act as an interface with interactive input devices, such as mouse.
- Local segment storage (also called **display list storage**) can also be maintained in the display-processor memory to store the display instructions. These instructions are basically grouped into named segments having unclipped integer coordinates. The local segment storage permits the display processor to operate more autonomously from the CPU. Storage of named segments helps the display processor to transform, redraw, and drag segments to new locations. It also allows the display processor to create, delete, and edit the segments, and make them visible or invisible on the screen.
- Window-manager operations such as close, scroll, push, and pop can also be implemented if all the displayed information is represented in a segment data structure.

19. Give some merits and demerits of raster scan CRT.

Ans. Some of the advantages of raster scan CRT are as follows:

- It has gained popularity due to less memory cost and is being widely used by computer monitors and TVs.
- High degree of picture quality (or realism) is achieved with the aid of advanced shading and hidden surface techniques.
- Its refresh rate is not dependent on the complexity of an image.

Apart from several advantages, raster scan CRT has some disadvantages also. These are as follows:

- It produces jagged lines which are plotted as discrete point sets.
- It has low resolution.
- Mathematical models of objects first needs to be scan converted by the processor in order to produce an image.

20. Write a short note on working of random/vector scan display system.

or

Describe random/vector display system with the help of a neat diagram.

Ans. In random scan display system, graphics are generated randomly on the screen according to the user input as shown in the Figure 2.10. In this system, a CRT has the electron beam directed only to the parts of the screen where a picture is to be drawn. Random scan monitors draw a picture one line at a time and for this reason is referred to as **vector, stroke-writing**, or **calligraphic displays**. The component lines of a picture can be drawn and refreshed by a random scan system in any specified order. Refresh rate on a random scan system depends on the number of lines to be displayed. Picture definition is stored as a set of line drawing commands in an area of memory referred to as the **refresh display file** (also known as **display list, display program**, or **refresh buffer**). To display a specified picture, the system cycles through the set of commands in the display file, drawing each component line in turn. After all line drawing commands have been processed, the system cycles back to the first line command in the list. Random scan systems are mainly designed for line drawing applications and are not suitable for displaying realistic shaded scenes.

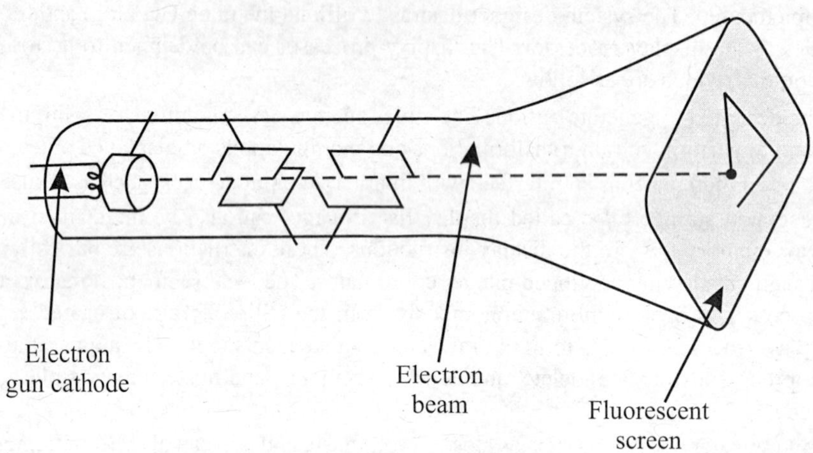

Figure 2.10 Random Scanning

21. Explain the architecture of simple random scan display system.

Ans. The organization of a typical random display system is shown in Figure 2.11. It is generically similar to the architecture of raster display system with peripheral display processor. Here, an application program is input and stored in the system memory along with a graphics package which is then executed on CPU. Graphics commands of the application program are translated by the graphics package to create a display program (or display file) which is stored in the system memory. This program is then executed by the **display processor**, also known as **display processor unit (DPU)** or **graphics controller**, to refresh the screen. The program is executed until stopped by the graphics package. A JUMP instruction at the end of program transfers control back to the start and cycles through each command once during every refresh cycle without CPU intervention.

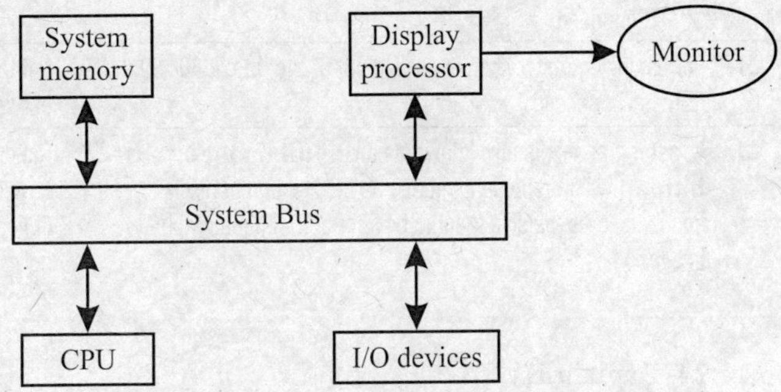

Figure 2.11 Architecture of a Random Display System

Graphics patterns are drawn on such system by directing the electron beam along the component lines of the picture. Lines are specified from the values of their coordinate endpoints which are then converted to x and y deflection voltages. This results in drawing of a scene by positioning the beam to one line at a time so as to fill in the line between specified endpoints.

22. What are the merits and demerits of random scan display system?

Ans. Random/vector scan display system is one of the types of computer graphics display which is based on the scan technology to generate graphics on the screen. It serves various advantages which are as follows:

- It has high resolution because it stores picture definition as line drawing commands.
- It requires less memory, as only display programs are needed to be stored.
- It produces smooth line drawings as the electron beam directly follows the line path.
- A line is generated randomly on the screen according to the input given by the user.

On the other hand, such systems have some disadvantages also. These are as follows:

- They are capable of displaying the pictures with only limited colors.
- Flickering can be seen as the complexity of picture increases.
- They are not capable of displaying realistic shaded scenes.

23. Distinguish between raster and random scan display systems.

Ans. Both raster and random display systems are based on CRT monitors where pictures displayed by them is said to be temporary. Several major differences can be discovered between them and are listed in Table 2.2.

Table 2.2 Differences Between Raster and Random Scan Display Systems.

Raster scan display system	Random scan display system
❑ The line segment is generated in a particular order, from left to right or top to bottom.	❑ The line segment can be generated randomly on the screen, according to the choices of input made by the user.
❑ Raster graphics are composed of array of pixels which together form an image.	❑ Random graphics are composed of paths or lines that are either straight or curved.
❑ These images are stored in varying formats such as in GIF or JPEG as an array of pixels of various colors.	❑ These paths or lines are in formats such as .EPS file or Adobe illustrator file.
❑ Image quality gets decreased while scaling its size, as each pixel also increases in size as the image is made larger.	❑ Images can be scaled to a larger size without losing their quality, as they are not made up of pixels.

Continued…

Table 2.2 (Continued)

❑ Refreshing on raster scan is carried out at the rate of 60–80 frames per second.	❑ Refreshing on random scan is carried out at 30–60 frames per second.
❑ A raster graphics is also known as a **digital image** or **bitmap** which represents image as a collection of pixels and is used as the sole graphic type for actual photographic images.	❑ Random graphics is also known as **geometric modelling** or **object oriented graphics** which makes use of geometrical primitives such as points, curves, lines, polygons and mathematical equations to represent images in computer graphics.

24. Explain DVST.

Ans. DVST was introduced at the end of 1960s to store the picture information inside the CRT instead of refreshing the screen. It served as an alternate solution to refresh display, which was very expensive because of the buffer memory and fast display process. The picture information is stored is in the form of charge distribution placed just behind the phosphor-coated screen. Its architecture is explained with the help of a diagram as shown in Figure 2.12. DVST makes use of two electron guns, namely, *primary gun* (also known as **writing gun**) and *flood gun*. **Primary gun** is used for storing picture pattern, whereas **flood gun** helps in maintaining the picture display. The beam is designed in such a way that it does not allow writing directly on the phosphor; instead a fine-mesh wire grid (called **storage grid**) coated with dielectric is mounted just behind the phosphor-coated screen. A pattern of positive charge is deposited on this grid which forms pattern of images. It is then transferred to the phosphor by a continuous flood of electrons emitted from the flood gun. However, DVST consists of one more grid, known as **collector**, which is mounted just behind the storage grid and is responsible for smoothening the electrons flood flowing from flood gun. These electrons then slowly pass through the collector and get attracted to the positively charged portions of storage grid and rest are repelled. The electrons which do not repelled by storage grid pass through it and strike the phosphor. A voltage is applied to thin aluminium coating between the tube face and the phosphor in order to control energy of electrons. This is done by maintaining the screen at high positive potential which in turn helps in displaying very complex pictures at high resolution without flicker.

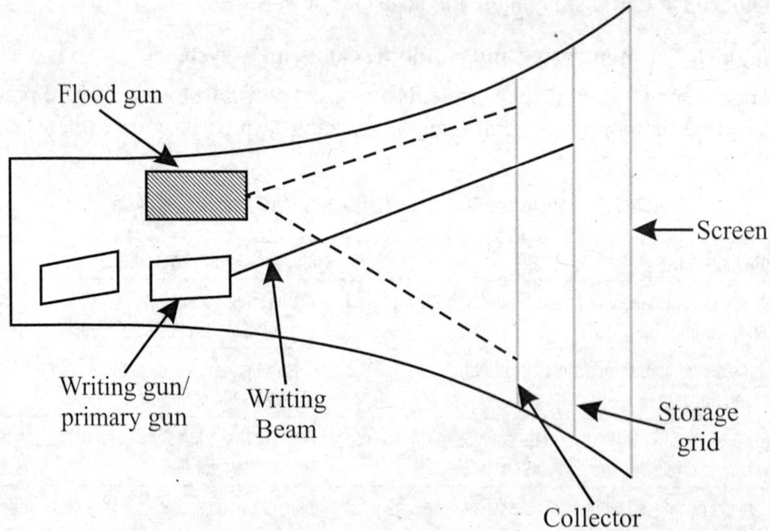

Figure 2.12 Architecture of DVST

25. Distinguish between DVST and refresh CRT.

Ans. DVST and CRT are the technologies which are used in video display devices in order to maintain picture information. However, there are some differences between these two technologies listed in Table 2.3.

Table 2.3 Differences between DVST and Refresh CRT

Basis of difference	DVST	Refresh CRT
❑ Storage tube	❑ It contains storage tube in order to retain the picture until it is erased.	❑ It does not have any storage tube.
❑ Performance	❑ Its performance is inferior (lesser) to refresh CRT.	❑ Its performance is superior to DVST.
❑ Refreshing	❑ Screen is not required to be refreshed.	❑ Screen is required to be refreshed at frequent intervals to maintain its visibility.
❑ Refresh buffer	❑ It does not have any refresh buffer, thus the entire screen must be erased to eliminate a picture section.	❑ It has refresh buffer, so there is no need to erase the entire screen for eliminating a screen section.
❑ Persistence	❑ It has extremely high persistence.	❑ It has low persistence as compared to DVST.
❑ Picture quality	❑ It creates bright pictures.	❑ It creates fine pictures.
❑ Contrast	❑ It has poor contrast.	❑ It has better contrast than DVST.

26. What is meant by flat-panel display?

Ans. The term **flat-panel display** refers to a class of video display devices which have reduced volume, weight, and power requirements compared to a CRT. The most important feature of these displays is that they are thinner than CRT devices, and can be easily hanged on walls or can be worn on our wrists. Uses of such displays are found in calculators, pocket video games, laptop computers, advertisement boards in elevators, etc. They can be divided into two categories which are as follows:

- **Emissive displays:** These are also known as **emitters** and convert electrical energy into light energy. Some examples of emissive displays are plasma panels, thin-film electroluminescent displays, and light-emitting diode (LED).
- **Non-emissive displays:** These are also known as **non-emitters.** They use optical effects to convert sunlight or light from other sources into graphics patterns. An example of non-emissive displays is LCD.

27. Write short notes on the following:

(a) Plasma panel

(b) LED

Ans. (a) Plasma panel (also known as **gas-discharge display**) is made up of two glass plates, where one of them consists of a set of vertical conducting ribbons, while other is built with a set of horizontal ribbons. Region between these glass plates is filled with a mixture of gases that usually includes neon. Firing voltages are applied to a pair of horizontal and vertical conductors which causes the gas at the intersection of these two conductors to breakdown into glowing plasma of electrons and ions. Here also, refresh buffer stores the picture information, whereas the firing voltages are applied to refresh the pixel position at the rate of 60 times per second. However, for producing brighter displays of images and providing faster applications of the firing voltages, alternating current methods can also be used. In this, separation between pixels is provided by the electric field of the conductors. Some of the advantages of plasma panel are as follows:

- It does not require any refreshing.
- It produces a very steady image, free from flickers.
- It has a flat screen and is less bulky than CRT.

On the other hand, it has some disadvantages also. These are as follows:

- It is costlier than CRT and has relatively poor resolution.
- It consumes a lot of power.
- It is strictly a monochromatic device, however, some systems are now been developed which are capable of displaying color and greyscale.

(b) An **LED display** is a flat-panel display which uses LEDs as video display. Here, a matrix of diodes is arranged to form the pixel position in the display, and picture information is stored in a refresh buffer. The information which is read from the refresh buffer is converted into voltage levels. These levels are then applied to the diodes for producing the light patterns in the display. LEDs serve several advantages over various other sources of light, such as longer life, smaller size, lower power consumption, improved robustness, etc. Some of its applications include lighting, advertising, automotive lighting, and traffic signals.

28. Write in detail about LCD.

Ans. LCD has made a big impact on computer market. LCD screens have been used since long on notebook computers, and also becoming popular as a desktop monitor. The term **liquid crystal** refers to the fact that molecules contained in these substances maintain their orientation as in a solid state, but also move around to different positions as in a liquid state. Manufacturers use this amazing ability of liquid crystals to display images. An LCD screen is a collection of multiple layers. A fluorescent light source, known as the **backlight**, makes up the rearmost layer. Light passes through the first of two polarizing filters. The polarized light then passes through a layer that contains thousands of liquid crystal blobs aligned in tiny containers called **cells**. These cells are aligned in rows across the screen; one or more cells make up one pixel. Electric leads around the edge of the LCD create an electric field that twists the crystal molecule, which lines the light up with the second polarizing filter and allows it to pass through.

However, color LCD is more complex. In a colored LCD panel, each pixel is made up of three liquid crystal cells. In front of each of these cells, there is a red, green, or blue filter. Light passing through the filtered cells creates the colors on the LCD. Nowadays, nearly every color LCD uses a thin-film transistor (TFT), also known as an **active matrix**, to activate each cell. TFT-based LCD creates sharp, bright images as compared to previous LCD technologies. The oldest of the matrix technologies, **passive matrix**, offers sharp text but leaves 'ghost images' on the screen when the display changes rapidly, making it less than optimal for moving video. LCDs can create sharper text than CRTs because they address each pixel individually.

29. What are the basic differences between LCD and CRT?

Ans. Although both the CRT and LCD monitors are most frequently types of displays in computers, they are apart in terms of what is important when making a purchase decision. The basic differences between the two are discussed as follows:

- **Size**: LCD is lightweight and compact, which saves desktop space as compared to a CRT.
- **Resolution**: LCD is designed to work in a single resolution while CRT is designed for many resolutions.
- **Pixel density**: Pixel density of LCD is generally not as tight as the dot pitch in CRT but for most applications, the density is acceptable.
- **Brightness**: The illuminated phosphor of a CRT is not nearly as bright as what the LCD can produce with its florescent backlight.
- **Power consumption**: LCD consumes significantly less power than CRT and has a low emission risk. Typically, an LCD consumes approximately half of the power of a typical CRT.
- **Flicker**: With CRT monitors, the goal is to get a faster refresh rate of at least 85 Hz, but LCD monitors are designed to run at a much slower refresh rate (usually about 60 Hz) and flicker is never an issue.
- **Pixel response time**: The time taken by a pixel to change its state is called **pixel response** time. CRT has extremely fast pixel response time but LCD can be quite slow. As a result, the user might see 'ghost images' when there is movement on the screen. The fastest LCD monitors today have a response time of 25 ms, which is still only about half the speed of a CRT monitor.
- **Viewing angle**: CRT can be viewed at almost any angle but LCD is best viewed 'head on'. Even when viewing a LCD head on, narrow viewing angles can appear to have inconsistent color and brightness.
- **Viewing area**: The viewing area of a CRT is usually less than its advertised area. Most 19-inch CRT monitors, for example, typically have about 18 inches of viewable area. However, the LCD monitors are measured exactly, that is, if a LCD monitor is advertised as 17.4 inch, it is the same.
- **Cost**: Prices for LCD screens are quite high but they are coming down. They are still much more costly than a CRT.

30. Write short notes on the following input devices.

(a) Joystick

(b) Image scanner

(c) Touch panel

(d) Light pen

(e) Voice system

(f) Data glove

Ans. (a) Joystick is a device that moves in all directions and controls the movement of the cursor. The basic design of a joystick consists of a stick that is attached to a plastic base with a flexible rubber sheath. This plastic base houses a circuit board that sits beneath the stick. The electronic circuitry measures the movement of the stick from its central position and sends the information for processing. Joystick also consists of buttons which can be programmed to indicate certain actions once a position on the screen has been selected using stick. It offers three types of control, namely, *digital, glide*, and *direct*. **Digital** control allows movement in a limited number of directions such as up, down, left, and right, whereas **glide** and **direct** control allow movements in all directions (360°). Direct control joysticks have the added ability to respond to the distance and speed with which the user moves the stick. A joystick is generally used to control the velocity of the screen cursor movement rather than its absolute position.

It is used for computer games. The other applications in which it is used are flight simulators, training simulators, CAD/CAM systems, and for controlling industrial robots.

(b) Image scanner (also known as **optical scanner**) is an input device that converts an image document into an electronic format by passing an optical scanning mechanism over it. The document can be graphs, color or black-and-white photos, drawings, etc., which can be stored as an electronic image. The electronic image can be edited, manipulated, combined, and printed by using the image editing software. One can also apply transformations to rotate, scale, or crop the image to a particular screen area. Most of the scanners come with a utility program that allows it to communicate with the computer and save the scanned image as a graphic file on the computer. Moreover, they can store images in both gray-scale and color mode.

(c) Touch panel (also known as **touch sensor)** is a clear glass panel with a touch responsive surface. It is placed over a display screen so that the responsive area of the panel covers the viewable area of the video screen. There are several different touch sensor technologies in the market today, each using a different method to detect touch input. These methods are *optical*, *acoustical*, and *electrical* methods. In **optical** method, the infra red beams interlace the surface of the screen and when a light beam is broken, that particular location is recorded. In **acoustical** method, the ultrasonic acoustic waves pass over the surface of the screen and when the wave signals are interrupted by some contact with the screen, the location is recorded. In **electrical** method, the panel has an electrical current going through it and touching the screen causes a voltage change, which is used to determine the location of the touch to the screen. It is normally used when information has to be accessed with minimum effort. However, it is not suitable for input of large amounts of data. Typically, it is used in information providing systems like the hospitals, airlines and railway reservation counters, amusement parks, and so on.

(d) Light pen (also known as a **mouse pen**) is a hand-held electro-optical pointing device which when touched to or aimed closely at a connected computer monitor, will allow the computer to determine where on that screen the pen is aimed. It facilitates drawing images and selects objects on the display screen by directly pointing to the objects. It is a pen like device, which is connected to the machine by a cable. It is named as light pen because its light-sensitive diode would sense the light coming from the screen. The light coming from the screen causes the photocell to respond by generating a pulse. This electric response is transmitted to the processor that identifies the position to which the light pen is pointing. With the movement of light pen over the screen, the lines or images are drawn. It gives user the full range of mouse capabilities without the use of a pad or any horizontal surface. Moreover, users can interact more easily with applications, in such modes as drag and drop, or highlighting. It is used directly on the monitor screen and it does not require any special hand/eye coordinating skills. Pushing the light pen tip against the screen activates a switch, which allows the user to make menu selections, draw, and perform other input functions. Light pens are perfect for applications where disk space is limited, in harsh workplace environments, and any situation where fast accurate input is desired. It is very useful to identify a specific location on the screen. However, it does not provide any information when held over a blank part of the screen. Light pen is economically priced and requires little or no maintenance.

(e) Voice system (also known as **speech recognizer**) is an input device used to accept voice commands. The user can simply instruct the computer with the help of a microphone (along with speech recognition software) what task to perform. It is the technology by which sounds, words, or phrases spoken by humans are converted into digital signals, and these signals are transformed into computer-generated text or commands. Most voice systems are speaker-dependent so they must be separately trained for each individual user. A predefined dictionary is set up for a particular user with his/her voice commands to be used into the system. The voice system 'learns' the voice of the user, who speaks isolated words repeatedly and establishes a frequency pattern for those words in the dictionary. Then, these voiced words are recognizable in the future. They allow the user to communicate with the computer directly without using a keyboard or a mouse. However, as compared to other input devices, the reliability of speech recogniser is less. Sometimes, it is unable to differentiate between two similar sounding words such as see and sea. It is also not suitable for noisy places.

(f) Data glove is another device which has the power of grasping a 'virtual' object. It is made up of series of sensors which helps to detect hand and finger motions. The input from a data glove can be used for positioning or manipulating objects in a virtual scene. Between transmitting and receiving antennas there exists an electromagnetic coupling which informs about the position and orientation of the hand. The antennas form a 3D Cartesian coordinate system as each of them is structured as a set of three mutually perpendicular coils. One can view a 2D projection of the scene on a video monitor, or a 3D projection with a headset.

31. Write in detail about digitizers.

Ans. Digitizer is an input device commonly used for painting, drawing, or interactively selecting coordinate positions (either 2D or 3D) on a flat surface object. In general, a digitizer scans over a drawing or an object and inputs a set of discrete coordinate positions which can be joined with straight-line segments to approximate the curve or surface shapes. A **graphics tablet** or **data tablet** is the most common type of digitizer used to input 2D coordinates with the help of stylus or hand cursor at selected position. A **stylus** is a pencil-shaped device pointing to a specific position on the tablet, whereas a hand cursor is a pointer containing cross hairs for observing positions. The size of tablets varies in accordance to their types, as for desktop models the size is 12 × 12 inches and for floor models the preferable size is 44 × 60 inches or larger. The procedure of selecting coordinate positions is very accurate in graphics tablets as it varies from 0.2 mm (approximately) on desktop models to 0.05 mm (approximately) on larger models. Most of the graphics tablets are made up of rectangular grid of wires embedded in their surface. Along with these wires, electromagnetic pulses are generated in consecutive order and an electric signal is stimulated in wire coil with an activated stylus or hand cursor to record the position on tablet. Depending on the technology, the position on the tablet is determined either by using signal strength, coded pulses, or phase shifts.

An acoustic (or sonic) tablet uses sound waves for detecting the stylus position. In such systems, stylus tip emits electrical spark with a sound that can be detected by using either strip microphones or point microphones. And, the stylus position is calculated with the help of time the sound is generated at different microphone positions. The microphones used in 2D acoustic tablets can be placed on any surface to form the tablet work area. This can be suitable for digitizing drawings in a book and many more applications. However, in 3D digitizers, sonic or electromagnetic transmissions are used to record positions. This method is very much similar to that used in data glove. In this method, a coupling between the transmitter and receiver is used to compute the position of a stylus as it moves over the object's surface.

32. Write in detail about hard copy technologies.

Ans. The physical form of output is known as **hard copy**. In general, it refers to the recorded information copied from a computer onto paper or some other durable surface such as microfilm. Hard copy output is permanent, highly portable, and a relatively stable form of output. Paper is one of the most widely used hard-copy output media. Printers and plotters are the most commonly used hard copy output devices. A **printer** is a device that prints information and data from the computer onto a paper, and its quality is determined by the clarity of a print it can produce, that is, its resolution. It is measured in dpi (dots per inch). The more dpi, the better will be the quality of image. Printers are divided into two basic categories, namely, *impact printers* and *non-impact printers*. **Impact printers** work by physically striking a head or needle against an ink ribbon to make a mark on the paper. This includes *dot matrix printers*, *daisy wheel printers*, and *drum printers*. In contrast, **non-impact printers** use techniques other than physically striking the page to transfer ink onto the page. This includes *ink-jet* and *laser printers.*

- **Dot matrix printer** prints one character at a time as pattern of dots. The print quality is determined by the number of pins (the mechanisms that print the dots), which can vary from 9 to 24. The more pins per inch, the higher the print resolution. Dot matrix printers are inexpensive and have low operating costs. These printers are able to use different types of fonts, different line densities, and different types of paper. However, they can print only in black and white, and produce low to medium quality printing as compared to other printers. The image printing ability is also very limited.
- **Daisy wheel printers** are commonly referred to as **letter quality printers** as the print quality is as good as that of a high-quality typewriter. The print head of this printer resembles a daisy flower, with the printing arms that appear like the petals of the flower. A raised character is placed on the tip of each of the daisy wheels 'petals'. Daisy wheel printers produce high-resolution output and are more reliable than dot matrix printers. However, they give only alphanumeric output. They cannot print graphics and cannot change fonts unless the print wheel is physically replaced.
- **Drum printer** is a line printer as it can print a line in a single operation. It uses special tractor-fed paper with pre-punched holes along each side. This arrangement allows a continuous high-speed printing. Though such printers are much faster than character printers, they tend to be quite loud, have limited multi-font capability, and often produce lower quality prints.
- **Ink-jet printer** places extremely small droplets of ink onto paper to create an image. Being a non-impact printer, it does not touch the paper while creating an image. Instead, it uses a series of nozzles to spray drops of ink directly onto the paper. Ink-jet printers are costlier than dot matrix printers but the quality is much better. These printers are able to print different shapes of characters, special characters, different sizes of print, and graphics such as charts and graphs.
- **Laser printer** provides the highest quality text and images for personal computers today. It is a very fast printer, which operates on the same principle as that of a photocopy machine. Most laser printers can print text and graphics with a very high quality resolution. These printers consist of a laser beam source, a photoconductive drum, and a toner. Laser printers are often faster than ink-jet printers but are more expensive to buy and maintain than the other printers.

Plotter is a pen-based output device that is attached to a computer for making vector graphics, that is, images created by a series of many straight lines. It is used to draw high-resolution charts, graphs, blueprints, maps, circuit diagrams, and other line-based diagrams. The lines drawn by these devices are continuous and very accurate. Plotters are classified as *pen plotters* and *electrostatic plotters*.

- **Pen plotter** creates plots by moving a pen or pencil under computer control over drafting paper. In these plotters, each pen can have ink of different color to produce multi-color designs. They are used to produce continuous output such as plotting earthquake activity or for long graphic output such as tall building structures.
- **Electrostatic plotter** uses electrostatic charges to create images made up of tiny dots on specially treated paper.

33. Write short note on various coordinate systems.

Ans: In computer graphics, one has to deal with different coordinate systems. To specify the coordinate values of a picture, different reference frames such as spherical and hyperbolic can be used. But, as general graphics packages are designed to be used with Cartesian coordinate specifications, the geometric descriptions if given in some other reference frame must be converted into Cartesian coordinates.

A 3D scene comprises various objects. To construct and display a 3D scene, we use various Cartesian reference frames. The shapes of individual objects in the scene are defined within a separate reference frame. These reference frames are known as **modeling coordinates** (also known as **local coordinates** or **master coordinates**). After specifying the individual object shapes, the next step is to construct the scene by placing objects in appropriate positions within a scene using another reference frame, known as **world coordinates**. For example, we have to construct (model) a robot, we can model the different parts such as face, arms, legs, body in a separate reference frame and these parts can be fitted together in world coordinates. Moreover, same components such as eyes need to be modelled only once and can be used twice. Modelling coordinates need not to be specified for the scenes that are less complicated. In such cases, modelling-transformation steps can be skipped.

The third step is to display the scene on one or more output devices. For this, the world-coordinate reference frame needs to be transformed into device coordinates or screen coordinates (in case of video monitor). This process is known as **viewing pipeline**. Based on the placement of camera, corresponding to the view we want the world coordinates to be converted to viewing coordinates. Since the output devices are two-dimensional in nature, we need to convert the object locations to 2D, storing the scene in normalized coordinates where each coordinate has value in the range from 0 to 1 or -1 to 1 based on the system. **Normalized coordinates** allow displaying the scene on any output device and hence, they are also known as **normalized device coordinates**. To accommodate differences in scales and aspect ratios, normalized coordinates are mapped into a square area of the output device so that proper proportions are maintained. Next, the parts of the picture that are beyond the bounds of view are eliminated, and finally, the picture is scan converted into refresh buffer of a raster system for display.

34. Consider three different raster systems with resolution of 640 × 480, 1280 × 1024, and 2560 × 2048. What size of frame buffer (in bytes) is needed for each of these systems to store 12 bits per pixel? How much storage is required for each system if 24 bits per pixel are to be stored?

Ans. Case 1: For 640 × 480

Total number of pixels required for 640 × 480 resolution

$$= 640 \times 480 \text{ pixels}$$

So, size of frame buffer required

$$= 640 \times 480 \text{ pixels}$$

Since, 1 pixel can store 12 bits.

Therefore, the size of frame buffer (in bits)

$$= 640 \times 480 \times 12 \text{ bit}$$

$$= \frac{640 \times 480 \times 12}{8} \text{ bytes (1 byte = 8 bit)}$$

$$= 460800 \text{ bytes}$$

$$= 450 \text{ KB (1024 bytes = 1 KB)}$$

For 1280 × 1024: Size of frame buffer (in bits)

$$= 1280 \times 1024 \times 12 \text{ bits}$$

$$= \frac{1280 \times 1024 \times 12}{8} \text{ bytes}$$

$$= 1920 \text{ KB}$$

For 2560 × 2048: Size of frame buffer

$$= \frac{2560 \times 2048 \times 12}{8} \text{ bytes}$$

$$= 7.5 \text{ MB}$$

Case 2: When one pixel can store 24 bits then frame buffer size will be twice.
For 640 × 480: Frame buffer size

$$= \frac{640 \times 480 \times 24}{8} \text{ bytes}$$

$$= 900 \text{ KB}$$

For 1280 × 1024: Frame buffer size

$$= 1920 \times 2 \text{ KB}$$

$$= 3840 \text{ KB}$$

$$= 3.75 \text{ MB}$$

For 2560 × 2048: Frame buffer size

$$= 7.5 \times 2 \text{ MB}$$

$$= 15 \text{ MB}$$

35. In a 600 × 400 pixel, how many kilobytes(KB) does a frame buffer need?

Ans. Given that resolution = 600 × 400
Assume 1 pixel can store n bit,
Then size of frame buffer

$$= \text{resolution} \times \text{bits per pixel}$$

$$= (600 \times 400) \times n \text{ bits}$$

$$= 24000\, n \text{ bits}$$

$$= \frac{24000\, n}{1024 \times 8} \text{ K bytes} \qquad (\because 1 \text{ KB} = 1024 \text{ b})$$

$$= 29.30\, n \text{ K bytes}$$

36. A laser printer is capable of printing two pages (size 9 × 11 inch) per second at resolution of 600 pixels per inch. How many bits per second does such device require?

Ans. Storage required per page (in pixel)

$$= 9 \times 11 \text{ inch/s}$$

$$= 9 \times 11 \times 600 \times 600 \text{ pixels/s} \qquad (\because 1 \text{ inch} = 600 \text{ pixels})$$

Since laser printer is capable of printing two pages per second.
Bits per second required by the printer

$$= 2 \times 9 \times 11 \times 600 \times 600 \text{ pixels/s}$$

$$= 7.128 \times 10^7 \text{pixels/s}$$

$$= 7.128 \times 10^7 n \text{ bits/s}$$

(Assume 1 pixel = n bits)

37. (a) Consider a non-interlaced raster monitor with a resolution of n × m, a refresh rate of r frames per second, a horizontal retrace time of t_h, and a vertical retrace time of t_v. What is the fraction of the total refresh time per frame spent in retrace of the electron beam?

(b) What is the fraction of the total refresh time per frame spent in retrace of the electron beam for a non-interlaced raster system with a resolution of 1280 by 1024, a refresh rate of 60 Hz, a horizontal retrace time of 5 µs. And a vertical retrace time of 500 µs?

Ans. (a) Since resolution is n × m
Therefore, raster system contains m scan lines, and system takes (m–1) horizontal retraces.
Total time taken for horizontal retrace

$$= (m - 1) \times \text{horizontal retrace time}$$

$$= (m - 1)\, t_h$$

If there are r frames, then time = $r.\,(m - 1)\, t_h$

Because there are r frames, then there will be (r–1) vertical retraces, vertical retrace time t_v.

Total time for vertical retrace = $(r - 1)\, t_v$

Total time for retrace = $r(m - 1)\, t_h + (r - 1)\, t_v$ (for r frames)

Total time taken in retrace for one frame = $\dfrac{r(m - 1)\, t_h + (r - 1)\, t_v}{r}$

Total refresh time for one frame = $\dfrac{1}{r}$

The fraction of the total refresh time per frame spent in retrace of the electron beam

$$= \frac{\dfrac{r(m - 1)\, t_h + (r - 1)\, t_v}{r}}{\dfrac{1}{r}}$$

$$= r(m - 1)\, t_h + (r - 1)\, t_v$$

(b) The fraction of the total refresh time per frame spent in retrace of the electron beam

$$= r(m-1)\,t_h + (r-1)\,t_v$$

Here, $n = 1280$, $m = 1024$, $r = 60$ Hz, $t_h = 5\mu s$, $t_v = 500\mu s$

$= 60(1024-1)5 + (60-1)500$

$= 0.3364s$

MULTIPLE CHOICE QUESTIONS

1. _______ refers to the number of times per second the pixels are recharged so that their glow remains bright.
   (a) Aspect ratio (b) Persistence
   (c) Refresh rate (d) Resolution
2. _________ is the time it takes the emitted light from the screen to decay to one-tenth of its original intensity.
   (a) Resolution (b) Refresh rate
   (c) Persistence (d) None of these
3. Which one of the following is a technique for generating colors on the screen?
   (a) Beam penetration (b) Shadow masking
   (c) Both (a) and (b) (d) None of these
4. NTSC stands for__________.
   (a) National television system committee (b) National television system communication
   (c) Northern television system committee (d) None of these
5. __________ contains the images created by the scan-conversion and raster operations.
   (a) CPU (b) Frame buffer
   (c) Video controller (d) Display processor
6. DPU stands for ___________.
   (a) Digital processing unit (b) Digital power unit
   (c) Display processing unit (d) None of these
7. Two electron guns used by DVST are ____________ and __________.
   (a) Primary gun and flood gun (b) Reading gun and writing gun
   (c) Primary gun and secondary gun (d) None of these
8. Plasma panel is also known as ________.
   (a) Flat-panel display (b) LED display
   (c) Gas-discharge display (d) Gas-charge display
9. LCD stands for ___________.
   (a) Liquid crystal diode (b) Liquid crystal display
   (c) Light cathode display (d) Light crystal diode
10. Which of the following is not an input device?
    (a) Light pen (b) Plotter
    (c) Data glove (d) Image scanner

Answers. 1. c 2. c 3. c 4. a 5. b 6. c 7. a 8. c 9. b 10. b

3

Output Primitives

1. What do you mean by graphics output primitives?

Ans. For creating pictures in graphics applications, we need a software package, which consists of a library of functions that we can directly use within a programming language. This package is known as **computer-graphics application programming interface (CG API)**. Since a graphics application consists of several component parts, the first thing we need to do is to describe the component parts of a scene. These components can be trees and terrain, atoms and molecules, or stars and galaxies, and so on. Then, for each type of scene, one needs to describe the structure of the individual objects with their coordinates within the scene. Thus, in a graphics package, the functions which are used to describe the various picture components are known as **graphics output primitives** or simply **primitives**. The output primitives describing the geometry of objects are known as **geometric primitives**. Some examples of geometric primitives are point positions, straight line segments, circles, and so on.

2. Give the procedure how line will be generated in analog devices (or vector-scan systems).

Ans. The procedure for displaying straight line in analog devices is based on the Cartesian slope-intercept equation. This equation is represented as follows:

$$y = mx + b \tag{1}$$

where m is the slope of the line; b is the y intercept; x is the horizontal distance from origin; and y is the vertical distance.

Now, we calculate the values of m and y intercept b as follows:

$$m = \frac{y_2 - y_1}{x_2 - x_1} = \frac{\Delta y}{\Delta x} \tag{2}$$

$$b = y_1 - m * x_1 \quad \text{or} \quad b = y_2 - m * x_2 \tag{3}$$

where (x_1, y_1) and (x_2, y_2) are the two endpoints of a line segment as shown in Figure 3.1.

If any x interval, Δx along a line is given, then one can calculate the corresponding y interval Δy from Equation (2) as follows:

$$\Delta y = m\Delta x \qquad (4)$$

Similarly, one can also obtain the x interval Δx corresponding to a specified Δy as follows:

$$\Delta x = \frac{\Delta y}{m} \qquad (5)$$

Thus, all these equations form the basis in analog devices for determining deflection voltages, where arbitrary small changes in deflection voltage are possible. There exist three cases:

- **$|m| < 1$:** In this case, Δx is set proportional to a small horizontal deflection voltage and the corresponding vertical deflection is set proportional to Δy [as calculated in Equation (4)].
- **$|m| > 1$:** In this case, Δy is set proportional to a small vertical deflection voltage and the corresponding horizontal deflection voltage is set proportional to Δx [as calculated in Equation (5)].
- **$|m| = 1$:** In this case, the horizontal and vertical deflection voltages are equal ($\Delta x = \Delta y$).

It is to be noted that in all the three cases, a smooth line with slope m is generated between the given endpoints.

However, in case of raster systems, a line is plotted with pixels. That is, step sizes in the horizontal and vertical directions are constrained by pixel separations and one needs to 'sample' a line at discrete positions (see Figure 3.2). This helps in determining the nearest pixel to the line at each sampled position. Such technique is implemented by the differential digital analyzer (DDA) algorithm and Bresenham's algorithm.

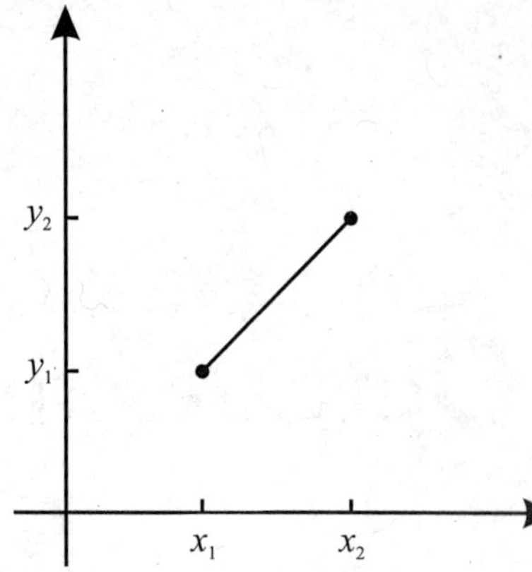

Figure 3.1 Line Path Between Endpoint Positions (x_1, y_1) and (x_2, y_2)

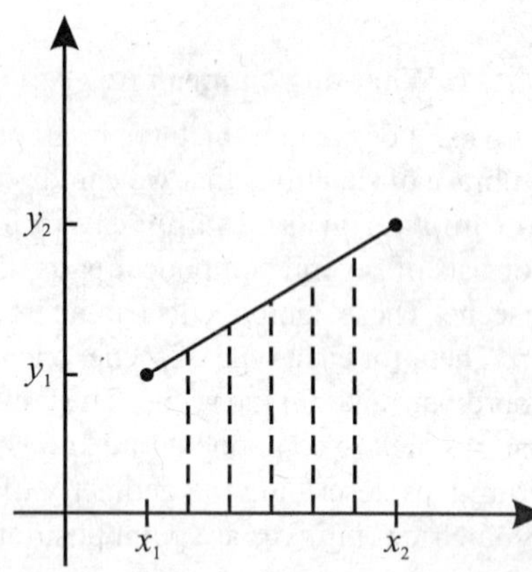

Figure 3.2 Straight Line Segment with Five Sampling Positions Along the *x*-Axis Between x_1 and x_2

3. Explain DDA line algorithm.

Ans. The **DDA** (digital differential analyzer) algorithm is an incremental scan-conversion line method. It is based on calculating either Δy or Δx, using the following equation:

$$\Delta y = m\Delta x$$

or

$$\Delta x = \frac{\Delta y}{m}$$

It traces out successive (x,y) values by simultaneously incrementing x and y by small steps proportional to the first derivative of x and y.

It works by first sampling a line at unit intervals in one coordinate, and then determining the corresponding integer values nearest to the line path for the other coordinate. Such an approach is characterized by performing calculations at each step using results from the preceding step. Suppose at step i we have calculated (x_i, y_i) to be a point on the line. Since the next point (x_{i+1}, y_{i+1}) should satisfy $\Delta y/\Delta x = m$, where $\Delta y = y_{i+1} - y_i$ and $\Delta x = x_{i+1} - x_i$, therefore, we have

$$y_{i+1} = y_i + m\Delta x \tag{1}$$

or

$$x_{i+1} = x_i + \frac{\Delta y}{m} \tag{2}$$

Now, Equations (1) and (2) are used in the DDA algorithm as follows:

- When $|m| \leq 1$, and line is processed from the left endpoint to the right endpoint, then we sample at unit x intervals ($\Delta x = 1$). Now, *y*-coordinate of each successive point on the line can be calculated as follows:

$$y_{i+1} = y_i + m \tag{3}$$

  The subscript i takes integer values starting from 0 for the first point and increases by 1 until the final endpoint is reached.

- When $|m| > 1$, and line is processed from the left endpoint to the right endpoint, then we sample at unit y intervals ($\Delta y = 1$). Now, the *x*-coordinate of each successive point on the line can be calculated as follows:

$$x_{i+1} = x_i + \frac{1}{m} \tag{4}$$

  However, if the processing is done from the right endpoint to the left endpoint, then $\Delta x = -1$ (for $m \leq 1$) and Equation (3) becomes

$$y_{i+1} = y_i - m \tag{5}$$

Similarly, $\Delta y = -1$, for ($m>1$) and equation becomes

$$x_{i+1} = x_i - \frac{1}{m} \tag{6}$$

4. Give the procedure for DDA algorithm.

Ans. The procedure for DDA algorithm is as follows:

```
procedure lineDDA(x0, y0, xend, yend : integer);
var
 dx, dy, steps, k : integer;
 xIncrement, yIncrement, x, y : real;
begin
 dx := xend - x0;
 dy := yend - y0;
 if abs(dx) > abs(dy), then steps := abs(dx)
 else steps := abs(dy);
 xIncrement := dx / steps;
 yIncrement := dy / steps;
 x := x0;
 y := y0;
 setPixel (round(x), round(y), 1);
 for k := 1 to steps do
    begin
          x := x + xIncrement;
          y := y + yIncrement;
```

```
            setPixel (round(x), round(y), 1)
        end
    end; (lineDDA)
```

The above procedure accepts the two integer endpoint pixel positions (x0, y0 and xend, yend) as an input. The horizontal and vertical differences between the endpoint positions are assigned to parameters dx and dy, respectively. The difference with the greater magnitude determines the value of parameter steps. Starting with pixel position (x0, y0), the offset needed at each step is determined so as to generate the next pixel position along the line path and, thus, process is repeated steps times. If the magnitude of dx is greater than the magnitude of dy and x0 is less than xend, then the values of the increments in the x and y directions are 1 and m, respectively. If the greater change is in the x-direction, but x0 is greater than xend, then the decrements -1 and -m are used to generate each new point on the line. Otherwise, there is a unit increment (or decrement) in the y-direction and an x increment (or decrement) of 1/m is used. It is assumed that points are to be plotted on a bi-level intensity system, such that there is a call to setPixel with an intensity value of 1.

5. Give advantages and disadvantages of DDA algorithm.

Ans. Some of the advantages of the DDA algorithm are as follows:

- This algorithm is a faster method for calculating pixel positions than the direct use of the line equation

$$y = mx + b$$

- It eliminates the floating-point multiplication which needs to be calculated in $y = mx + b$ equation. This is possible because DDA algorithm makes use of raster characteristics and appropriate increments are applied in the *x* or *y* directions to move from one pixel position to another along the line path.

Some of the disadvantages of the DDA algorithm are as follows:

- A floating-point addition is still needed to be done for determining each successive point.
- The cumulative error due to limited precision in the floating-point representation may cause calculated points to drift away from their true position for long line segments.
- The rounding off operations and floating-point arithmetic are time consuming.

6. Derive Bresenham's line-drawing algorithm.

Ans. It is a highly accurate and efficient incremental raster line-generating algorithm. It was developed by Bresenham and uses only incremental integer calculations for generating lines. Hence, named Bresenham's line-generating algorithm. In this algorithm, pixels along x and y directions are incremented by one unit depending upon the value of slope, m.

To understand the Bresenham's approach, first consider the scan-conversion process for lines with positive slope less than 1, that is, $0 < m < 1$. The pixel positions along a line path will be determined by sampling at unit x intervals. This means that if we start from the left endpoint (x_0, y_0) of a given line, then we step to each successive column (x position) and plot the pixel whose scan line y is closest to the line path. Due to the limit of m, the next pixel would be right to chosen pixel, that is, (x_0, y_0). The pixel at right constitutes a lower bound for the line whereas pixel at right and up constitutes an upper bound for the line. The line is best approximated by those pixels that fall the least distance from its true path between left endpoint and right endpoint.

As shown in Figure 3.3, assume that the coordinates of last chosen pixel is (x_i, y_i). The task is to choose the next one between the bottom pixel S and the top pixel T. If S is chosen, then $x_{i+1} = x_i+1$ and $y_{i+1} = y_i$. If T is chosen, then $x_{i+1} = S_i+1$ and $y_{i+1} = y_i+1$. Therefore, our choices are the

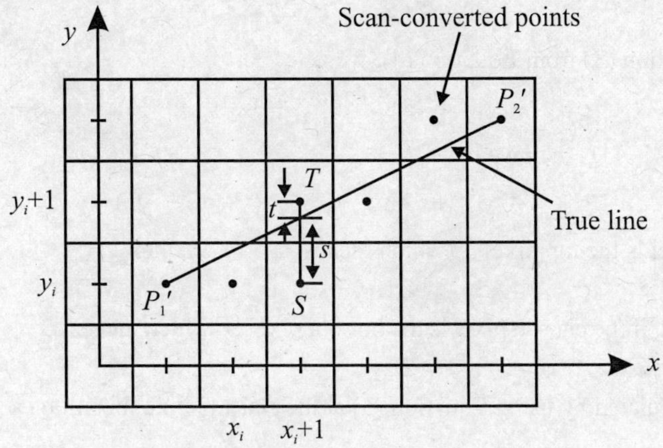

Figure 3.3 Scan Converting a Line

pixels at positions (x_i+1, y_i) and (x_i+1, y_i+1). At sampling position x_i+1, we assign vertical pixel separations from the line path as d_{lower} and d_{upper}. Then, the actual y-coordinate on the line at position $x = x_{i+1}$ is calculated as

$$y = mx_{i+1} + b = m(x_i + 1) + b \tag{1}$$

Now, the distance from S to the actual line in the y-direction is

$$d_{lower} = y - y_i = m(x_i + 1) + b - y_i$$

The distance from T to the actual line in the y-direction is

$$d_{upper} = (y_i + 1) - y = y_i + 1 - m(x_i + 1) - b$$

To determine which of the two pixels is closest to line path, consider the difference between the two distance values: $d_{lower} - d_{upper}$.

When $d_{lower} - d_{upper}$ is less than zero, then $d_{lower} < d_{upper}$ and the closest pixel is S. Conversely, when $d_{lower} - d_{upper}$ is greater than zero, then $d_{lower} > d_{upper}$ and the closest pixel is T. Moreover, T is also chosen when $d_{lower} - d_{upper}$ is equal to zero. This difference is given as follows:

$$\begin{aligned} d_{lower} - d_{upper} &= m(x_i + 1) + b - y_i - y_i - 1 + m(x_i + 1) + b \\ &= 2[m(x_i + 1)] - 2y_i + 2b - 1 \end{aligned} \tag{2}$$

To involve only integer calculations, we introduce a decision parameter, $d_i = \Delta x\ (d_{lower} - d_{upper})$, which is having the same sign as $(d_{lower} - d_{upper})$, since Δx is positive. Therefore, d_i can be calculated as follows:

$$\begin{aligned} d_i &= \Delta x[2m(x_i + 1) + 2b - 2y_i - 1] \\ &= 2m\Delta x * x_i + 2m\Delta x + 2b\Delta x - 2y_i\Delta x - \Delta x \\ &= 2\Delta y * x_i - 2\Delta x * y_i + 2\Delta y + \Delta x(2b-1) \\ &= 2\Delta y * x_i - 2\Delta x * y_i + C \end{aligned} \tag{3}$$

where $C = 2\Delta y + \Delta x(2b - 1)$ (using $m = \Delta y/\Delta x$) and is constant which is independent of the pixel position. C will be eliminated when recursive calculation is done for d_i.

Similarly, the decision parameter d_{i+1} for the next step can be written as follows:

$$d_{i+1} = 2\Delta y * x_{i+1} - 2\Delta x * y_{i+1} + C \quad (4)$$

Subtracting Equation (3) from Equation (4), we get

$$d_{i+1} - d_i = 2\Delta y(x_{i+1} - x_i) - 2\Delta x(y_{i+1} - y_i)$$

Since, $x_{i+1} = x_i + 1$, then we have,

$$d_{i+1} = d_i + 2\Delta y - 2\Delta x(y_{i+1} - y_i)$$

If the chosen pixel is the top pixel T (which means, $d_i \geq 0$), then $y_{i+1} = y_i + 1$.

Hence, $d_{i+1} = d_i + 2(\Delta y - \Delta x)$

On the other hand, if the chosen pixel is the bottom pixel S (which means, $d_i < 0$), then $y_{i+1} = y_i$.

Hence, $d_{i+1} = d_i + 2\Delta y$

Finally, d_0 is calculated by using Equation (3) at the starting pixel position (x_0, y_0) as follows:

$$d_0 = \Delta x\ [2m(x_0 + 1) + 2b - 2y_0 - 1]$$
$$= \Delta x\ [2(mx_0 + b - y_0) + 2m - 1]$$

Since, $mx_0 + b - y_0 = 0$ and $m = \Delta y/\Delta x$, therefore,

$$d_0 = 2\Delta y - \Delta x.$$

7. Give the Bresenham's line-drawing algorithm for a line with a positive slope less than 1.

Ans. The Bresenham's line-drawing algorithm for $|m| < 1$ is as follows:

1. Input the two line endpoints and store the left endpoint in (x_0, y_0).
2. Load (x_0, y_0) into the frame buffer; that is, plot the first point.
3. Calculate the values of Δx, Δy, $2\Delta y$, and $2\Delta y - 2\Delta x$, and obtain the starting value for the decision parameter as
   $$d_0 = 2\Delta y - \Delta x$$
4. At each x_i along the line, starting at $i = 0$, perform the following test:
   If $d_i < 0$, then the next point to plot is (x_i+1, y_i) and
   $$d_{i+1} = d_i + 2\Delta y$$
   Otherwise, the next point to plot is (x_i+1, y_i+1) and
   $$d_{i+1} = d_i + 2\Delta y - 2\Delta x$$
5. Repeat step 4 $\Delta x-1$ times.

8. Give the procedure for Bresenham's line-drawing algorithm.

Ans. The procedure for Bresenham's line-drawing algorithm for slopes in the range $0 < m < 1$ is as follows:

```
procedure lineBres (xa, ya, xb, yb : integer);
var
 dx, dy, x, y, xEnd, d : integer;
begin
 dx := abs(xa - xb);
 dy := abs(ya - yb);
 d := 2 * dy - dx;
{determine which point to use as start, which as end}
```

```
if xa > xb then
   begin
     x := xb;
     y := yb;
     xEnd := xa;
   end
else
   begin
     x := xa;
     y := ya;
     xEnd := xb;
     end;
setPixel (x, y, 1);
while x < xEnd do
   begin
     x := x + 1;
     if d < 0 then d := d + 2 * dy
     else
     begin
          y := y + 1;
          d := d + 2 * (dy-dx)
                end;
   setPixel (x, y, 1)
   end;
end; {end of procedure)
```

In the above procedure, endpoint pixel positions for the line are passed to the procedure, and pixels are plotted from the left endpoint to the right endpoint. The call to `setPixel` loads the intensity value 1 into the frame buffer at the specified `(x, y)` pixel position.

9. Give the advantages of Bresenham's line-drawing algorithm.

Ans. Some of the advantages of Bresenham's line-drawing algorithm are as follows:

- It is a faster and highly efficient incremental method for scan-converting lines than DDA algorithm.
- It uses only integer calculations such as addition/subtraction and bit shifting operations to give accurate results.
- The constants $2\Delta y$ and $2\Delta y-2\Delta x$ are computed only once for each line which is to be scan-converted.
- This algorithm can be adapted to display circles and other curves.

The main drawback of such algorithm is that it is meant for basic line drawing, that is, the line displayed will have have a jagged or stair-step appearance. To draw smooth lines, one has to look for a different algorithm.

10. Give the methods for generating a circle using parametric and non-parametric equation.

Ans. A **circle** is defined as the set of points that are all at a given distance r (called **radius**) from a centre position (x_c, y_c). As circle is most frequent component used in pictures and graphs, therefore, most graphic packages include a procedure for generating circles. There are two standard procedures which are used for generating a circle. These procedures are described as follows:

- **Using Pythagorean (non-parametric) theorem:** This theorem makes use of Cartesian coordinates in order to generate a circle. That is, the distance (r) from a centre position is expressed as follows:

$$(x - x_c)^2 + (y - y_c)^2 = r^2 \tag{1}$$

where x and y represent a point on the circle circumference. By making use of Equation (1), the position of points on a circle circumference can be calculated. This can be done by stepping along the x-axis in unit steps from $x_c - r$ to $x_c + r$ in order to calculate corresponding y values at each position as follows:

$$y = y_c \pm \sqrt{r^2 - (x - x_c)^2} \tag{2}$$

Similarly, corresponding x values at each position can be calculated by stepping along the y-axis as follows:

$$x = x_c \pm \sqrt{r^2 - (y - y_c)^2} \tag{3}$$

The main disadvantage of this method is that it involves significant computation at each step. That is, it involves multiplications and square-root calculations and hence, leads to more computation time. Second, the spacing between plotted pixel positions is not uniform. However, this problem can be overcome by interchanging x and y (stepping through y values and calculating x values) whenever the absolute value of the slope of the circle is greater than 1. This again increases the computation and processing time required by the algorithm.

- **Using parametric equations:** This procedure makes use of polar coordinates and helps in eliminating the unequal spacing problem of Pythagorean Theorem procedure. It calculates points along the circular boundary and expresses the circle equation in parametric polar form as follows:

$$x = x_c + r\cos\theta$$

$$y = y_c + r\sin\theta$$

where θ = angular displacement or step size that lies in the range $0 \leq \theta \leq 2\Pi$ and r = radius of the circle.

Using the above equations and a fixed angular step size (θ), a circle is generated with equally spaced points along the circumference. But, these equations still involve multiplications and trigonometric calculations. Hence, the circle could be efficiently generated if it involves only simple integer operations, as done in the Bresenham's line algorithm.

11. Discuss and explain Bresenham's algorithm for circle generation.

Ans. Bresenham's circle algorithm is one of the efficient algorithms to generate a circle as it does not involve square-root and trigonometric calculations. This algorithm works in the following manner.

This algorithm takes into account the symmetry of circles, thus reducing the computation. As we know, the shape of the circle is similar in each quadrant. That is, if we know the curve positions in the first quadrant, then by considering the symmetry of two circle sections with respect to y-axis, we can determine the circle section in the second quadrant of the xy-plane. Similarly, by considering symmetry about the x-axis, we can obtain the circle sections in the third and fourth quadrants from the circle sections of the first and second quadrants. In addition to this symmetry, circles also show symmetry even within each quadrant. That is, the circle sections in adjacent octants within one quadrant are symmetric with respect to the 45° line dividing the two octants (see Figure 3.4).

The algorithm first computes the coordinates (x, y) for the first quadrant sector by varying x = 0 to x = R/2 using the following equations:

$$y = y_c \pm \sqrt{r^2 - (x - x_c)^2}$$

$$x = x_c \pm \sqrt{r^2 - (y - y_c)^2}$$

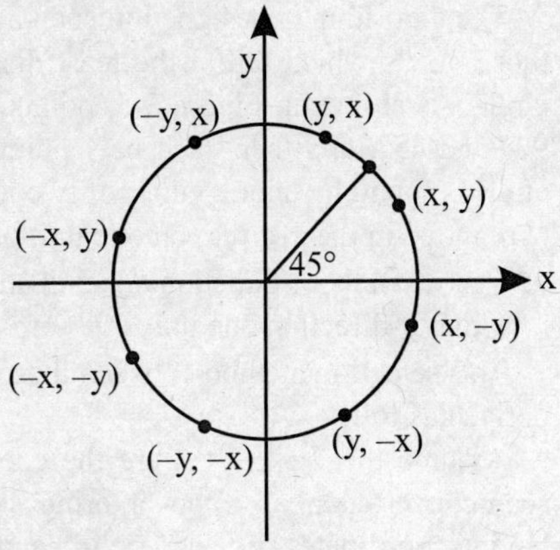

Figure 3.4 Symmetric Circle Plotting

The algorithm then uses the symmetry of the circle to obtain the pixels corresponding to other sectors.

If the eight-way symmetry of a circle is used to generate a circle, then points will only have to be generated through a 45° angle. And, if points are generated from 90° to 45°, then moves will be made only in the +x and −y directions (see Figure 3.5).

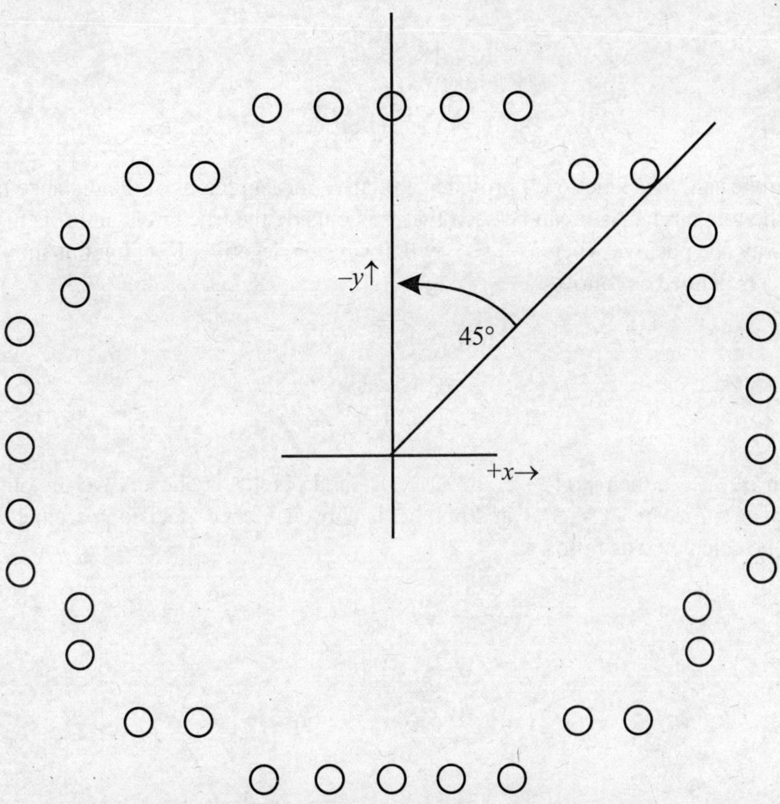

Figure 3.5 Circle Scan-converted with Bresenham's Algorithm

The algorithm is designed in such a way that it chooses those pixels which fall at the least distance from the true circle. As shown in Figure 3.5, points are generated from 90° and 45°, and then each new point closest to the true circle is found by taking either of two actions:

- move in the x-direction one unit or,
- move in the x-direction one unit and move in the negative y-direction one unit.

This selection method between these two choices can be derived as follows:

Assume that (x_i, y_i) are the coordinates of the last scan-converted pixel upon entering step i with pixel T having coordinates $(x_i + 1, y_i)$ and pixel S having coordinates $(x_i + 1, y_i - 1)$ [see Figure 3.6].

Let D(T) be the distance from the origin to pixel T squared minus the distance to the true circle squared, and D(S) be the distance from the origin to pixel S squared minus the distance to the true circle squared. That is,

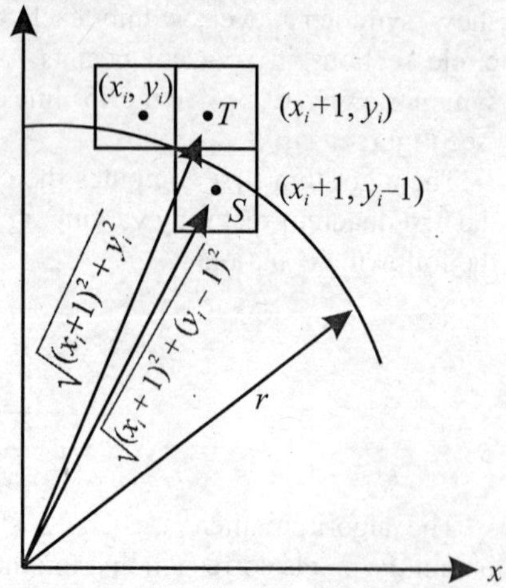

Figure 3.6 Choosing Pixels in Bresenham's Circle Algorithm

$$D(T) = (x_i + 1)^2 + y_i^2 - r^2$$

$$D(S) = (x_i + 1)^2 + (y_i - 1)^2 - r^2$$

Thus, it can be said that function D provides a relative measurement of the distance from the centre of a pixel to the true circle. As it can be seen that T is outside the true circle and S is inside, therefore, D(T) will always be positive whereas D(S) will always be negative. Keeping this in mind, a decision parameter (d_i) is defined as follows:

$$d_i = D(T) + D(S)$$

$$d_i = 2(x_i + 1)^2 + y_i^2 + (y_i - 1)^2 - 2r^2 \qquad (1)$$

Now, when $d_i < 0$, then $|D(T)| < |D(S)|$ and pixel T is chosen. On the other hand, when $d_i \geq 0$, then $|D(T)| < |D(S)|$ and pixel S is chosen. Hence, decision parameter, d_{i+1}, for the next step can be calculated as follows:

$$d_{i+1} = 2(x_{i+1} + 1)^2 + y_{i+1}^2 + (y_{i+1} - 1)^2 - 2r^2$$

Thus,

$$d_{i+1} - d_i = 2(x_{i+1} + 1)^2 + y_{i+1}^2 + (y_{i+1} - 1)^2 - 2(x_i + 1)^2 - y_i^2 - (y_i - 1)^2 \qquad (2)$$

Since, $x_{i+1} = x_i + 1$, solving Equation (2):

$$\begin{aligned} d_{i+1} - d_i &= 2(x_i + 2)^2 + y^2_{i+1} + y^2_{i+1} + 1 - 2y_{i+1} - 2(x_i + 1)^2 - y_i^2 - (y_i - 1)^2 \\ &= 2\left[x_1^2 + 4 + 4x_i\right] + 2y^2_{i+1} + 1 - 2y_{i+1} - 2x^2_i - 2 - 4x_i - y^2_i - (y_i - 1)^2 \\ &= 4x_i + 7 + 2y^2_{i+1} - 2y_{i+1} - y_i^2 - y_i^2 - 1 + 2y_i \\ &= 4x_i + 2\left(y^2_{i+1} - y_i^2\right) - 2(y_{i+1} - y_i) + 6 \end{aligned}$$

$$d_{i+1} = d_i + 4x_i + 2(y^2_{i+1} - y^2_i) - 2(y_{i+1} - y_i) + 6 \quad (3)$$

If T is the chosen pixel, then $y_{i+1} = y_i$ and Equation (3) becomes

$$d_{i+1} = d_i + 4x_i + 6$$

On the other hand, if S is the chosen pixel, then $y_{i+1} = y_i - 1$ and Equation (3) becomes

$$d_{i+1} = d_i + 4(x_i - y_i) + 10$$

Finally, we calculate d_0 by using Equation (1) by setting (0, r) as the starting pixel coordinates.

$$d_0 = 2(0 + 1)^2 + r^2 + (r - 1)^2 - 2r^2 = 3 - 2r$$

12. Write a C program for Bresenham's circle algorithm.

Ans.

```
#include<graphics.h>
#include<iostream.h>
#include<conio.h>
#define r 100 //representing radius
void main()
{
 int gdriver = DETECT, gmode;
 initgraph(&gdriver, &gmode, "C:\\TC\\BGI");
 int x = 1, y = r, d = 3 - 2 * r;
 int x_center = 180, y_center = 150;
 while(x <= y)
 {
    putpixel (x_center + x, y_center + y, RED);
    putpixel (x_center + x, y_center - y, RED);
    putpixel (x_center - x, y_center + y, RED);
    putpixel (x_center - x, y_center - y, RED);

    putpixel (x_center + y, y_center + x, RED);
    putpixel (x_center + y, y_center - x, RED);
    putpixel (x_center - y, y_center + x, RED);
    putpixel (x_center - y, y_center - x, RED);
```

```
if (d < 0)
 d = d + 4 * x + 6;
else
{
 d = d + 4 * (x - y) + 10;
 y--;
}
x++;
 }
 getch();
 closegraph();
 }
```

13. Derive midpoint circle algorithm.

Ans. This algorithm is an incremental circle algorithm similar to Bresenham's approach. It basically tests for the spatial relationship between an arbitrary point (x, y) and a circle of radius r centered at the origin by using the following function:

$$f_{circle}(x, y) = x^2 + y^2 - r^2 \begin{cases} < 0, \text{ if } (x, y) \text{ is inside the circle boundary} \\ = 0, \text{ if } (x, y) \text{ is on the circle boundary} \\ > 0, \text{ if } (x, y) \text{ is outside the circle boundary} \end{cases}$$

Figure 3.7 shows the midpoint between the two candidate pixels at the sampling position $x_i + 1$. Assuming we have just plotted the pixel at (x_i, y_i), we next need to determine whether the pixel T at position $(x_i + 1, y_i)$ or the pixel S at position $(x_i + 1, y_i - 1)$ is closer to the circle. Now, consider the coordinates of the point halfway between pixel T and pixel S as $\left(x_i + 1, y_i - \frac{1}{2}\right)$. This is called the **midpoint** and can be used to define a decision parameter as follows:

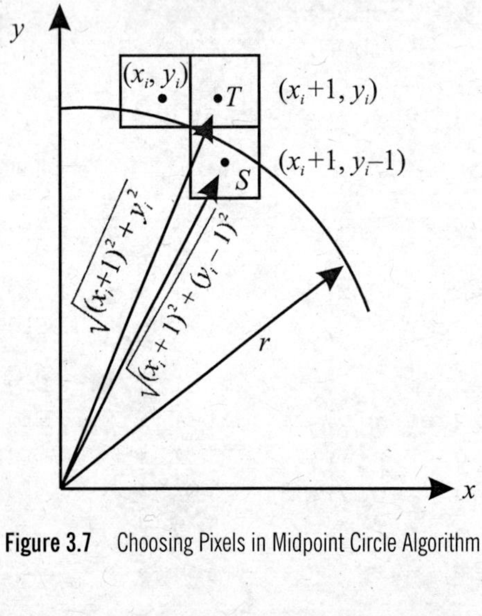

Figure 3.7 Choosing Pixels in Midpoint Circle Algorithm

$$d_i = f_{circle}\left(x_i + 1, y_i - \frac{1}{2}\right) = (x_i + 1)^2 + \left(y_i - \frac{1}{2}\right)^2 - r^2 \quad (1)$$

If d_i is negative ($d_i < 0$), then the midpoint is inside the circle, and pixel T on the scan line y_i is closer to the circle boundary and is chosen. On the other hand, if d_i is positive (or equal to zero), then the midpoint is outside the circle (or on the circle), and pixel S on scan line $y_i - 1$ is chosen. Similarly, the decision parameter for the next step is given as follows:

$$d_{i+1} = f_{circle}\left(x_{i+1} + 1, y_{i+1} - \frac{1}{2}\right) = (x_{i+1} + 1)^2 + \left(y_{i+1} - \frac{1}{2}\right)^2 - r^2 \quad (2)$$

Since, $x_{i+1} = x_i + 1$, hence,

$$d_{i+1} = [(x_i + 1) + 1]^2 + \left(y_{i+1} - \frac{1}{2}\right)^2 - r^2$$

Subtracting Equation (1) from Equation (2), we get:

$$d_{i+1} - d_i = (x_{i+1} + 1)^2 - (x_i + 1)^2 + \left(y_{i+1} - \frac{1}{2}\right)^2 - \left(y_i - \frac{1}{2}\right)^2$$

$$d_{i+1} - d_i = [(x_i + 1) + 1]^2 - (x_i + 1)^2 + \left(y_{i+1} - \frac{1}{2}\right)^2 - \left(y_i - \frac{1}{2}\right)^2$$

$$d_{i+1} - d_i = [x_i + 2]^2 - (x_i + 1)^2 + \left(y_{i+1} - \frac{1}{2}\right)^2 - \left(y_i - \frac{1}{2}\right)^2$$

Hence, we get:

$$d_{i+1} - d_i = 2(x_i + 1) + 1 + (y_{i+1}^2 - y_i^2) - (y_{i+1} - y_i)$$

$$d_{i+1} = d_i + 2(x_i + 1) + 1 + (y_{i+1}^2 - y_i^2) - (y_{i+1} - y_i)$$

where y_{i+1} is either y_i or $y_i - 1$.

If pixel T is chosen (which means, $d_i < 0$), then $y_{i+1} = y_i$. On the other hand, if pixel S is chosen (which means, $d_i \geq 0$), then $y_{i+1} = y_i - 1$. Thus,

$$d_{i+1} = \begin{cases} d_i + 2(x_i + 1) + 1 & \text{if } d_i < 0 \\ d_i + 2(x_i + 1) + 1 - 2(y_i - 1) & \text{if } d_i \geq 0 \end{cases}$$

If we continue to simplify the above equations, then we get

$$d_{i+1} = \begin{cases} d_i + 2x_i + 3 & \text{if } d_i < 0 \\ d_i + 2(x_i - y_i) + 5 & \text{if } d_i \geq 0 \end{cases}$$

In terms of (x_{i+1}, y_{i+1}),

$$d_{i+1} = \begin{cases} d_i + 2x_{i+1} + 1 & \text{if } d_i < 0 \\ d_i + 2(x_{i+1} - y_{i+1}) + 1 & \text{if } d_i \geq 0 \end{cases}$$

Finally, the initial value for the decision parameter using the original definition of d_i and $(0, r)$ is computed as follows:

$$d_0 = f_{circle}\left(1, r - \frac{1}{2}\right) = 1 + \left(r - \frac{1}{2}\right)^2 - r^2 = \frac{5}{4} - r \quad (3)$$

In the Equation (3), if we specify the radius r as an integer, then $d_0 = 1 - r$. The error of being 1/4 less than the precise value does not prevent d_0 from getting the appropriate sign. It does not affect the rest of the scan-conversion process as the decision variable is only updated with integer increments in subsequent steps.

14. Give the midpoint circle algorithm.

Ans. The midpoint circle algorithm is given as follows:

1. Input radius r and centre of the circle (x_c, y_c), and obtain the first point on the circumference of a circle centered on the origin as (0, r).
2. Calculate the initial value of the decision parameter as

$$d_0 = \frac{5}{4} - r$$

3. At each x_i position, starting at i = 0, perform the following test: If $d_i<0$, the next point along the circle centered at (0, 0) will be (x_{i+1}, y_i) and

$$d_{i+1} = d_i + 2x_{i+1} + 1$$

   Else, the next point along the circle will be (x_i+1, y_i-1) and

$$d_{i+1} = d_i + 2x_{i+1} + 1 - 2y_{i+1}$$

   where, $x_{i+1} = x_i+1$ and $y_{i+1} = y_i-1$.
4. Plot all the symmetrical points in other seven octants.
5. Move each calculated pixel position (x, y) onto the circular path centered at (x_c, y_c) by adding x_c and y_c to the calculated x and y. That is,

$$x = x + x_c, \quad y = y + y_c$$

6. Repeat steps 3 through 5 until $x \geq y$.

15. Define an ellipse. Discuss its two properties.

or

Give the two methods of mathematically defining an ellipse.

Ans. An **ellipse** is defined as the set of points such that the sum of the distances from two fixed positions (foci) is the same for all points. If d_1 and d_2 are the distances to the two foci from any point P = (x, y) on the ellipse, then the general equation of an ellipse is given as follows:

$$d_1 + d_2 = \text{constant} \tag{1}$$

The distances d_1 and d_2 can be expressed in the terms of the focal coordinates $F_1 = (x_1, y_1)$ and $F_2 = (x_2, y_2)$, thus we have

$$\sqrt{(x - x_1)^2 + (y - y_1)^2} + \sqrt{(x - x_2)^2 + (y - y_2)^2} = \text{constant} \tag{2}$$

The general ellipse equation can be rewritten by squaring Equation (2), then keeping apart the remaining radical, and then squaring again as follows:

$$Ax^2 + By^2 + Cxy + Dx + Ey + F = 0 \tag{3}$$

where A, B, C, D, E, and F are the coefficients (evaluated in terms of the focal coordinates) and are the dimensions of the major and minor axes of the ellipse. **Major axis** is the straight line segment which extends from one side of the ellipse to the other through foci whereas **minor axis** bisects the major axis at the ellipse centre between the two foci. That is, it is the shorter dimension of the ellipse.

If we know the values of two foci and a point on the ellipse boundary, then we can evaluate the constant in Equation (2). Then, the values for the coefficients in Equation (3) can be computed. These values can then be used for generating pixels along the elliptical path. However, these computations involve a lot of time. Thus, to save such effort, minor and major axes are oriented to align with x and y axes. Then, an ellipse in standard position (shown in Figure 3.8) can be defined in terms of the ellipse centre coordinates and parameters r_x (or semimajor axis) and r_y (or semiminor axis) by an expression as follows:

$$\left(\frac{x - x_c}{r_x}\right)^2 + \left(\frac{y - y_c}{r_y}\right)^2 = 1 \tag{4}$$

This method is known as the **polynomial method** of defining at ellipse.

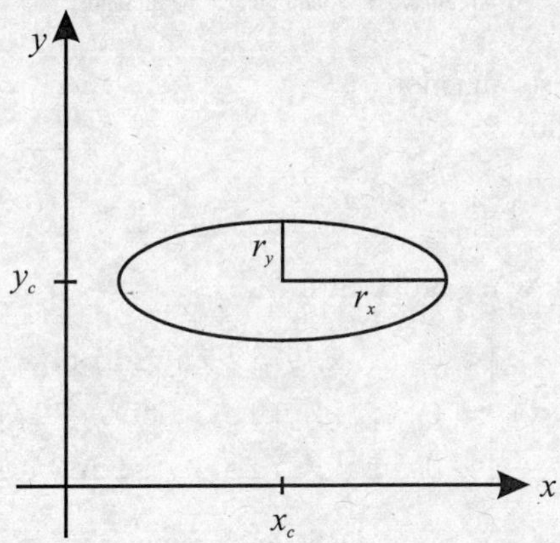

Figure 3.8 Ellipse Centered at (x_c, y_c) with Semimajor Axis r_x and Semiminor Axis r_y

Moreover, by making use of polar coordinates (r and θ) one can also describe the ellipse in standard position (major axis parallel to x-axis and minor axis parallel to y-axis) as follows:

$$x = x_c + r_x \cos \theta$$
$$y = y_c + r_y \sin \theta$$

This method is known as the **trigonometric method** of defining an ellipse.

16. Explain the midpoint ellipse algorithm.

Ans. The midpoint ellipse algorithm is an incremental algorithm for scan-converting an ellipse, which is centered at the origin in the standard position (that is, the major and minor axes are parallel to the x and y axes, respectively). Like circle algorithm, it also considers the symmetry of an ellipse to reduce computations. The main difference between the symmetry of a circle and an ellipse is that an ellipse shows four-way symmetry. That is, an ellipse is symmetric between quadrants only and not between the two octants of a quadrant. Thus, we must calculate the pixel positions along the elliptical arc throughout one quadrant. We can then use the four-way symmetry property to obtain curve positions in the remaining three quadrants (see Figure 3.9).

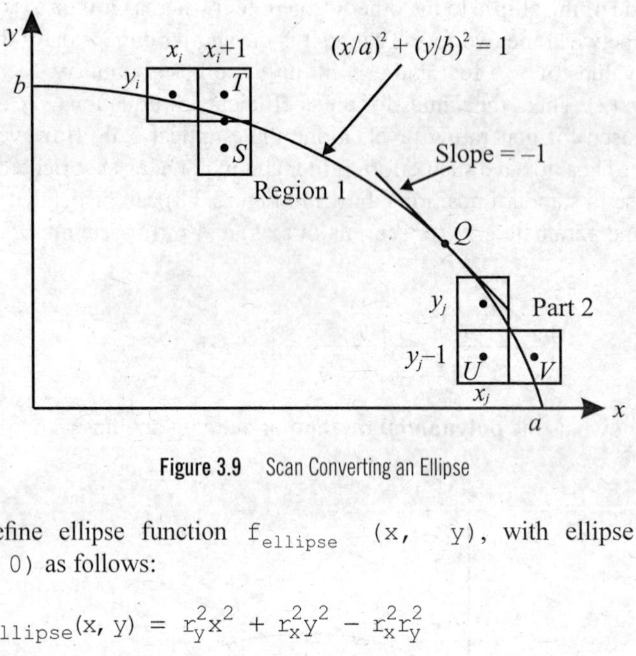

Figure 3.9 Scan Converting an Ellipse

We will first define ellipse function $f_{ellipse}(x, y)$, with ellipse centre coordinates $(x_c, y_c) = (0, 0)$ as follows:

$$f_{ellipse}(x, y) = r_y^2x^2 + r_x^2y^2 - r_x^2r_y^2$$

This ellipse function has following properties:

$$f_{ellipse}(x, y) \begin{cases} < 0, \text{ if } (x, y) \text{ is inside the ellipse boundary} \\ = 0, \text{ if } (x, y) \text{ is on the ellipse boundary} \\ > 0, \text{ if } (x, y) \text{ is outside the ellipse boundary} \end{cases}$$

Thus, $f_{ellipse}(x, y)$ serves as the decision parameter in this algorithm. Now, we divide the elliptical curve into two parts from $(0, r_y)$ to $(r_x, 0)$ at point Q, where the slope of the curve is –1.

At each sampling position, we select the next pixel along the ellipse path according to the sign of ellipse function calculated at the midpoint between the two candidate pixels. That is, at each step we need to check the value of slope of the curve. As we know, the slope of the curve defined by $f(x, y) = 0$ is

$$\frac{dy}{dx} = -\frac{fx}{fy},$$

where fx and fy are partial derivatives of $f(x, y)$ with respect to x and y, respectively.

Now, $fx = 2r_y^2x$, $fy = 2r_x^2y$.

Therefore, slope will be defined as follows:

$$\frac{dy}{dx} = -\frac{2r_y^2x}{2r_x^2y}$$

At the boundary, between the region 1 and region 2, $\frac{dy}{dx} = -1$, thus $2r_y^2x = 2r_x^2y$

Therefore, we move out of region 1, whenever $2r_y^2x \geq 2r_x^2y$.

Starting from $(0, r_y)$, suppose that the coordinates of the last scan-converted pixel upon entering step i is (x_i, y_i). Then, either $T(x_i+1, y_i)$ or $S(x_i+1, y_i-1)$ will be selected as the next pixel. This is done by evaluating the decision parameter, d_i at the midpoint of the vertical line connecting T and S as follows:

$$d_i = f_{ellipse}\left(x_i + 1, y_i - \frac{1}{2}\right) = r_y^2(x_i + 1)^2 + r_x^2\left(y_i - \frac{1}{2}\right)^2 - r_x^2r_y^2 \qquad (1)$$

If $d_i < 0$, then the midpoint is inside the curve, and pixel T is chosen. Otherwise, the midpoint is outside or on the curve, and pixel S is chosen. In a similar manner, the decision parameter for the next step could be written as:

$$d_{i+1} = f_{ellipse}\left(x_{i+1} + 1, y_{i+1} - \frac{1}{2}\right) = r_y^2(x_{i+1} + 1)^2 + r_x^2\left(y_{i+1} - \frac{1}{2}\right)^2 - r_x^2r_y^2$$

Since, $x_{i+1} = x_i+1$, we have

$$d_{i+1} = r_y^2\left[(x_i + 1) + 1\right]^2 + r_x^2\left(y_{i+1} - \frac{1}{2}\right)^2 - r_x^2r_y^2 \qquad (2)$$

Now, subtracting Equation (1) from Equation (2), we have,

$$d_{i+1} - d_i = 2r_y^2(x_i + 1) + r_y^2 + r_x^2\left[\left(y_{i+1} - \frac{1}{2}\right)^2 - \left(y_i - \frac{1}{2}\right)^2\right]$$

$$\Rightarrow d_{i+1} = d_i + 2r_y^2(x_i + 1) + r_y^2 + r_x^2\left[\left(y_{i+1} - \frac{1}{2}\right)^2 - \left(y_i - \frac{1}{2}\right)^2\right]$$

If pixel T is chosen (which means, $d_i < 0$), then $y_{i+1} = y_i$. On the other hand, if pixel S is chosen (which means, $d_i > 0$), then $y_{i+1} = y_i - 1$. Thus, we can express $d_i = 1$ in terms of d_i and (x_{i+1}, y_{i+1}) as follows:

$$d_{i+1} = \begin{cases} d_i + 2r_y^2 x_{i+1} + r_y^2 & \text{if } d_i < 0 \\ d_i + 2r_y^2 x_{i+1} + r_y^2 - 2r_x^2 y_{i+1} & \text{if } d_i \geq 0 \end{cases}$$

In region 1, the initial value for the above recursive expression can be obtained by evaluating the original definition of d_i at the start position $(x_0, y_0) = (0, r_y)$ as follows:

$$d_0 = r_y^2 + r_x^2\left(r_y - \frac{1}{2}\right)^2 - r_x^2 r_y^2 = r_y^2 - r_x^2 r_y + \frac{1}{4} r_x^2$$

Now, we derive a similar formula for region 2 of the curve. Suppose pixel (x_j, y_j) has just been scan converted upon entering step j, then the next pixel which would be selected is either $U(x_j, y_j - 1)$ or $V(x_j + 1, y_j - 1)$. For this part, the midpoint of the horizontal line connecting U and V is used to define the decision parameter (q_j) as follows:

$$q_j = f_{ellipse}\left(x_j + \frac{1}{2}, y_j - 1\right) = r_y^2\left(x_j + \frac{1}{2}\right)^2 + r_x^2\left(y_j - 1\right)^2 - r_x^2 r_y^2 \qquad (3)$$

If $q_j < 0$, then the midpoint is inside the curve and V is chosen. Otherwise, it is outside or on the curve and U is chosen. Now, evaluating the ellipse function at the next sampling step $y_{j+1} = y_j - 1$ as follows:

$$q_{j+1} = f_{ellipse}\left(x_{j+1} + \frac{1}{2}, y_{j+1} - 1\right) = r_y^2\left(x_{j+1} + \frac{1}{2}\right)^2 + r_x^2\left[\left(y_j - 1\right) - 1\right]^2 - r_x^2 r_y^2 \qquad (4)$$

Now, subtracting Equation (3) from Equation (4), we have,

$$q_{j+1} - q_j = -2r_x^2\left(y_j - 1\right) + r_x^2 + r_y^2\left[\left(x_{j+1} + \frac{1}{2}\right)^2 - \left(x_j + \frac{1}{2}\right)^2\right]$$

$$\Rightarrow q_{j+1} = q_j - 2r_x^2\left(y_i - 1\right) + r_x^2 + r_y^2\left[\left(x_{j+1} + \frac{1}{2}\right)^2 - \left(x_j + \frac{1}{2}\right)^2\right]$$

If V is the chosen pixel (which means, $q_j < 0$), then $x_{j+1} = x_j + 1$. On the other hand, if pixel U is chosen (which means, $q_j \geq 0$), then $x_{j+1} = x_j$. Thus, we can express q_{j+1} in terms of q_j and (x_{j+1}, y_{j+1}) as follows:

$$q_{j+1} = \begin{cases} q_j + 2r_y^2 x_{j+1} - 2r_x^2 y_{j+i} + r_x^2 & \text{if } q_j < 0 \\ q_j - 2r_x^2 y_{j+1} + r_x^2 & \text{if } q_j \geq 0 \end{cases}$$

After entering region 2, the start position (x_0, y_0) is taken as the last position selected in region 1 and the initial decision parameter q_0 in region 2 is computed as follows:

$$q_0 = f_{ellipse}\left(x_0 + \frac{1}{2}, y_0 - 1\right) = r_y^2\left(x_0 + \frac{1}{2}\right)^2 + r_x^2(y_0 - 1)^2 - r_x^2 r_y^2$$

17. Give the midpoint ellipse algorithm.

Ans. The midpoint ellipse algorithm is as follows:

1. Input r_x, r_y, and ellipse centre (x_c, y_c), and obtain the first point on an ellipse centered at the origin as

$$(x_o, y_0) = (0, r_y)$$

2. Calculate the initial value of the decision parameter in region 1 as

$$d_0 = r_y^2 - r_x^2 r_y + \frac{1}{4} r_x^2$$

$$d_i = r_y^2(x_i + 1)^2 + r_x^2\left(y_i - \frac{1}{2}\right)^2 - r_x^2 r_y^2$$

3. At each x_i position in region 1, starting at i = 0, perform the following test:

   If $d_i<0$, the next point along the ellipse centered on (0,0) is (x_i+1, y_i) and

$$d_{i+1} = d_i + 2r_y^2 x_{i+1} + r_y^2$$

   Otherwise, the next point along the ellipse is (x_i+1, y_i-1) and

$$d_{i+1} = d_i + 2r_y^2 x_{i+1} - 2r_x^2 y_{i+1} + r_y^2$$

   with

$$2r_y^2 x_{i+1} = 2r_y^2 x_i + 2r_y^2, \quad 2r_x^2 y_{i+1} = 2r_x^2 y_i - 2r_x^2$$

4. Calculate the initial value of the decision parameter in region 2 using the last point (x_0, y_0) calculated in region 1 as

$$q_j = r_y^2\left(x_0 + \frac{1}{2}\right)^2 + r_x^2(y_0 - 1)^2 - r_x^2 r_y^2$$

5. At each y_j position in region 2, starting at j = 0, perform the following test:

   If $q_j > 0$, the next point along the ellipse centered on (0, 0) is (x_j, y_j-1) and

$$q_{j+1} = q_j - 2r_x^2 y_{j+1} + r_x^2$$

   Otherwise,. the next point along the circle is (x_j+1, y_j-1) and

$$q_{j+1} = q_j + 2r_y^2 x_{j+1} - 2r_x^2 y_{j+1} + r_x^2$$

   using the same incremental calculations for x and y as in region 1.
6. Determine symmetry points in the other three quadrants.
7. Move each calculated pixel position (x, y) onto the elliptical path centered on (x_c, y_c) and plot the coordinate values:

$$x = x + x_c, \qquad y = y + y_c$$

8. Repeat the steps for region 1 until $2r_y^2 x \geq 2r_x^2 y$.

18. What is polygon fill? Name the various fill algorithms.

Ans. Polygon fill is the process of filling all the pixels inside the polygon with a desired color. There are basically three fill algorithms:

- Scan-line fill algorithm
- Boundary fill algorithm
- Flood fill algorithm

The scan-line fill algorithm is basically used in general graphics packages so as to fill polygons, circles, ellipses, and other simple curves. However, the other two algorithms are useful with more complex boundaries and in interactive painting systems.

19. Explain scan-line polygon fill algorithm.

Ans. The scan-line polygon fill is one of the approaches used for filling areas on raster systems. It basically handles polygon regions that are geometrically defined by the coordinates of their vertices (along with the edges that connect the vertices). For example in Figure 3.10, a polygon region is represented by a sequence of vertices $V_1, V_2, V_3, \ldots, V_9$ connected by edges $E_1, E_2, E_3, \ldots, E_9$. This algorithm is much more efficient as it makes use of the information regarding edges which are available during scan conversion in order to facilitate the filling of interior pixels.

The algorithm begins with the first scan line the polygon occupies and proceeds line by line towards the last scan line. For example, in Figure 3.10 scan line y_3 intersects edges E_2, E_3, E_4, and E_5 at points a, b, c, and d, respectively. These intersection points are sorted left to right, or according to the x-coordinates. These points are then grouped into pairs such as (a,b) and (c,d). The frame-buffer positions between each pair are set to the specified fill color.

While working with scan-line algorithm, few cases must be considered.

- Horizontal edges are ignored as the pixels belonging to them are filled automatically during the scan conversion. For example, in our case, the edge E_9 is drawn when the corresponding scan line is processed.

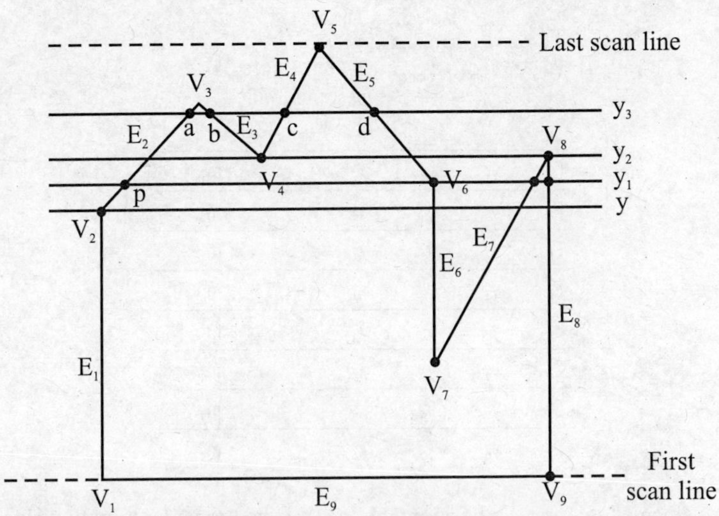

Figure 3.10 Scan Converting a Polygon Region

- If the vertex is a local minimum or maximum, then it does not require any special treatment.
- If a scan line passes through a vertex, which is common to two edges, and the edges are on the same side of the scan line, then the shared vertex needs to be counted as two intersection points. For example, in our case, the scan line y_2 is passing through the vertex V_4, which is shared by two edges E_3 and E_4, and both these edges are lying on the same side of the vertex. Therefore, vertex V_4 is counted twice as the intersection point for the scan line y_2. Similarly, the last scan line is passing through the vertex V_5, which is shared by two edges E_4 and E_5, and both these edges are lying on the same side of the vertex. Therefore, vertex V_5 is counted twice as the intersection point for the last scan line.
- If a scan line passes through a vertex, which is common to two edges, and the edges are on the opposite side of the scan line, then the shared vertex needs to be counted as a single intersection point. For example, in our case, the scan line y is passing through the vertex V_2, which is shared by two edges E_1 and E_2, and both these edges are lying on the opposite side of the vertex. Therefore, V_2 is counted only once as the intersection point for the scan line y. Similarly, the scan line y_1 is passing through the vertex V_6, which is shared by two edges E_5 and E_6, and both these edges are lying on the opposite side of the vertex. Therefore, V_6 is counted only once as the intersection point for the scan line y_1.

For efficient implementation of the scan-line algorithm, a data structure known as **edge list** is created (see Table 3.1). The list consists of only non-horizontal edges, which occupy one row (or record) each and the information stored in row includes:

- y-coordinate of the two endpoints of the edge, that is, y_{min}(smaller value) and y_{max}(larger value);
- x-coordinate of the endpoint, whose *y*-coordinate is y_{min}.
- inverse of the slope of the edge m.

It is to be noted that in edge list, rows are sorted according to y_{min}.

Table 3.1 An Edge List

Edge	y_{min}	y_{max}	x-coordinate of vertex with $y = y_{min}$	1/m
E_1	y_1	$y_2 - 1$	x_1	m_1
E_2	y_2	y_3	x_2	m_2
E_3	y_4	y_3	x_4	m_3
E_4	y_4	y_5	x_4	m_4
E_5	y_6	y_5	x_6	m_5
E_6	y_7	$y_6 - 1$	x_7	m_6
E_7	y_7	y_8	x_7	m_7
E_8	y_9	y_8	x_9	m_8

In our example, since edge E_9 is the horizontal edge, it is not considered in the edges list. The edges in the edge list become active when the *y*-coordinate of the current scan line matches their y_{min} value. On the other hand, an edge is deactivated from the edge list, when the scan line *y*-coordinate matches with its y_{max} value. It is to be noted that only active edges are involved in the calculation of intersection points and the first intersection point between an active edge and a scan line is always the lower endpoint of the edge, whose coordinates are already stored in the edge's record. For example, when the algorithm begins at the first scan line, the edge E_1 becomes active and intersects the scan line at (x_1, y_1). Additional intersection points between an edge and successive scan lines can be calculated incrementally. For instance, if an edge intersects the current scan line at (x, y), then it will intersect the next scan line at $(x + 1/m, y + 1)$. In our example, as edge E_2 intersects scan line y_1 at point p, the next intersection point on the next scan line y_2 is calculated by $\Delta x = 1/m_2$ with Δy equals to 1. This new calculated x value is then kept in x field of the edge's record.

Note that in Table 3.1, the y_{max} value for edges E_1 and E_6 is computed by subtracting one from the y_{max} value of the lower edge. This is done for those vertices where two monotonically increasing or decreasing edges meet. This implies that the lower edge is deactivated one line before the scan line that intersects the vertex. For example, the y_{max} value of edge E_1 is y_2, however, because of the above-mentioned reason it is set as $y_2 - 1$.

20. Explain inside-outside tests.

Ans. Graphics packages are often needed to identify the interior regions of an object. This task is not difficult for standard polygon shapes such as triangles, rectangles, pentagons, and octagons. This is because the component edges of these polygons are joined only at the vertices, thus identification of interior regions becomes easy. The problem arises when objects are formed from any sequence of vertices, which include those sequences also that are able to produce intersecting edges as well (see Figure 3.11).

The reason of concern behind such objects or shapes is that one cannot clearly identify which regions should be designated as interior and which one as exterior. To solve this, graphics packages makes use of the either of the following two rules:

- **Odd-even rule (also known as odd-parity rule or even-odd rule):** In this rule, we first conceptually draw a line from any position P to a distance point Q outside the coordinate extents of the

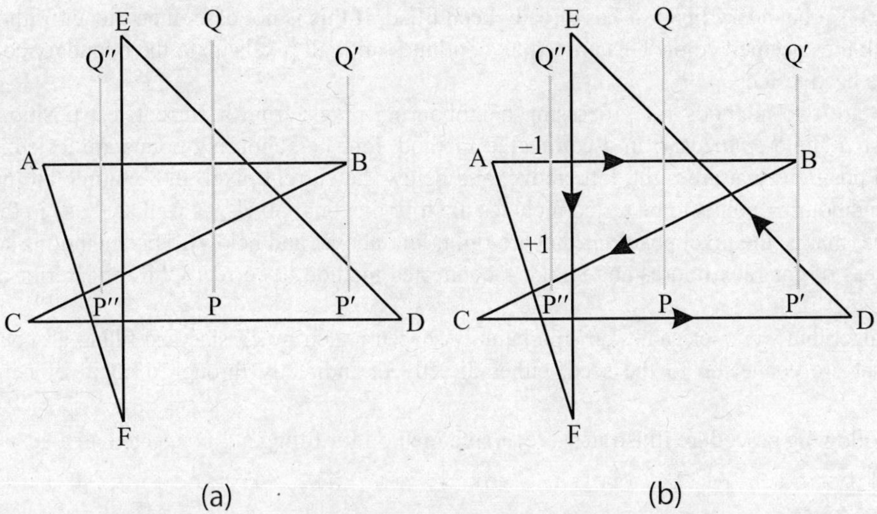

Figure 3.11 Identifying Interior and Exterior Regions for a Self-Intersecting Polygon

polygon. Now, we count the number of line segments intersecting this line. If the number of intersections is odd, then `P` is an interior point, otherwise it is considered as an exterior point. In case the line is intersecting at the vertex of the polygon, then we count the number of intersections as an even number if these two points lie on the same side of the intersecting line, otherwise we count it as single intersection point. Figure 3.11a shows the illustration of this rule. In this figure, the points `P` and `P'` are interior points of the polygon, whereas `P''` is exterior to the polygon.

- **Non-zero winding number rule:** In this rule, each side of the polygon is initialized to a number 0 (called as **winding number**). Then, like odd-even rule, a line is drawn from any position `P` to a distant point outside the object. Now, we count the number of times the polygon edges wind around a particular point in the counterclockwise direction. That is, every time a polygon edge is intersected by this line from right to left, we add 1 to the winding number; else we subtract 1 from it whenever edge is intersected from left to right. The total count of this winding number (called as **net winding number**) is then calculated so as to determine whether P lies outside or inside the region. If the net winding number comes out to be non-zero, then it lies inside the region otherwise outside. Figure 3.11b shows the illustration of this rule.

Note that both these rules may give different results when applied on the same complicated objects. However, for standard polygon shapes, both these rules show the same results.

21. Write a short note on boundary-fill algorithm.

Ans. Boundary fill algorithm is another approach used for area filling that starts from a given interior point and paint outwards from this point until the specified boundary condition (or color) is encountered. This algorithm is particularly useful in interactive painting packages, where the interior points are easily selected. An artist or designer by using any interactive device first sketch a figure outline, select a fill color from color menu and selects an interior point. The system then fills the figure interior with the specified color. In case the artist wants to display a solid color region (without border), he/she can choose the same color as the fill color and the boundary color.

It is a recursive algorithm that starts from an interior point (`x, y`), or a starting pixel (known as **seed**), a fill color, and a boundary color. The algorithm then checks to determine whether the neighbouring pixel of (x, y) is a boundary pixel or has already been filled. If this is not case, then the algorithm fills this pixel with the specified color. This procedure continues until all pixels up to the boundary color for the area have been tested.

There are two methods for processing neighbouring pixels from a current test position, namely, *4-connected* and *8-connected*. In **4-connected** method, four neighbouring points are tested. These are the pixel positions that are right, left, above, and below the current pixel. In **8-connected** method, the set of neighbouring points to be tested includes the four diagonal pixels, as well as those in the cardinal directions (that is, the pixel positions that are right, left, above, and below). This method is suitable for filling areas of complex figures and unlike 4-connected method, it correctly fill the interior of the area defined.

This algorithm works elegantly on an arbitrarily shaped region by chasing and filling all non-boundary pixels that are connected to the seed, either directly or indirectly through a chain of neighbouring relations.

The following procedure illustrates a recursive method for filling a 4-connected area.

```
void boundaryFill4 (int x, int y, int fill, int boundary)
{
  int current;
  current = getPixel (x, y);
  if ((current != boundary)&&(current != fill))
  {
     setColor (fill);
     setPixel (x, y);
     boundaryFill4 (x + 1, y, fill, boundary);
     boundaryFill4 (x - 1, y, fill, boundary);
     boundaryFill4 (x, y + 1, fill, boundary);
     boundaryFill4 (x, y - 1, fill, boundary);
  }
}
```

22. Give some of the disadvantages of the boundary-fill algorithm.

Ans. Some of the disadvantages of the boundary-fill algorithm are as follows:

- It can take time and memory to execute due to the potentially high number of recursive calls, especially when the size of the region is relatively large.
- It may not fill regions correctly if some interior pixels are already displayed in the fill color. The reason for this is that the algorithm checks next pixels both for the boundary color and for fill color. When a pixel is encountered with the fill color, it could cause the termination of a recursive branch, leaving other interior pixels unfilled.
- It requires significant stacking of neighbouring points.

23. Write a recursive pseudo code procedure to implement the boundary-fill algorithm in its basic form, using the 8-connected definition for region pixels.

Ans. The procedure for boundary-fill algorithm using 8-connected definition is as follows:

```
void boundaryFill8 (int x, int y, int fill, int boundary)
{
  int current = getPixel (x, y);
```

```
if ((current != boundary)&&(current != fill))
{
    setColor (fill);
    setPixel (x, y);
    boundaryFill8 (x + 1, y, fill, boundary);
    boundaryFill8 (x - 1, y, fill, boundary);
    boundaryFill8 (x, y + 1, fill, boundary);
    boundaryFill8 (x, y - 1, fill, boundary);
    boundaryFill8 (x + 1, y + 1, fill, boundary);
    boundaryFill8 (x + 1, y - 1, fill, boundary);
    boundaryFill8 (x - 1, y + 1, fill, boundary);
    boundaryFill8 (x - 1, y - 1, fill, boundary);
}
}
```

24. Write a short note on the flood-fill algorithm and give the procedure also.

Ans. It is sometimes required that we want to fill in (or recolor) an area which is not defined within a single color boundary. That is, an area is bordered by serveral different color regions. In such cases, we do not search for boundary color value, rather we paint areas by replacing a specified interior color with the desired fill color. Such approach to fill an area is called as a **flood-fill algorithm**. Suppose, we want to color the entire area whose original color is interior color, and we need to replace it with desired fill color. Like boundary-fill algorithm, this algorithm also begins with a starting pixel (`x, y`) inside the region. It then reassigns all pixel values that are currently set to a given interior color with a desired fill color. It also checks whether the area which we want to paint has more than one interior color. If this is the case, then it reassigns pixel values so that all interior points have the same color. After this, we step through pixel positions until all interior points have been repainted. This can be done by either using a 4-connected or 8-connected approach.

Thus, this algorithm shares great similarities in its operating principle with the boundary-fill algorithm. It is particularly useful when the region to be filled has no uniformly colored boundary. On the other hand, a region that has a well-defined boundary would be better handled by the boundary-fill method.

The procedure for flood-fill algorithm for filling 4-connected region is as follows:

```
void floodFill4 (int x, int y, int fillColor, int oldColor)
{
 if (getPixel(x, y) == oldColor)
 {
    setColor (fillColor);
    setPixel(x, y);
    floodFill4 (x + 1, y, fillColor, oldColor);
    floodFill4 (x - 1, y, fillColor, oldColor);
    floodFill4 (x, y + 1, fillColor, oldColor);
    floodFill4 (x, y - 1, fillColor, oldColor);
 }
}
```

25. Write a recursive pseudo code procedure to implement the flood-fill algorithm in its basic form, using the 8-connected definition for region pixels.

Ans. The procedure for flood-fill algorithm using 8-connected definition is as follows:

```
void floodFill8 (int x, int y, int fillColor, int oldColor)
{
 if (getPixel(x, y) == oldColor)
 {
    setColor (fillColor);
    setPixel(x, y);
    floodFill8 (x + 1, y, fillColor, oldColor);
    floodFill8 (x - 1, y, fillColor, oldColor);
    floodFill8 (x, y + 1, fillColor, oldColor);
    floodFill8 (x, y - 1, fillColor, oldColor);
    floodFill8 (x + 1, y + 1, fillColor, oldColor);
    floodFill8 (x + 1, y - 1, fillColor, oldColor);
    floodFill8 (x - 1, y + 1, fillColor, oldColor);
    floodFill8 (x - 1, y - 1, fillColor, oldColor);
 }
}
```

26. What is typeface? Give its categorization.

Ans. Letters, numbers, digits, and other special characters are the building blocks of the textual contents of an image. They are helpful in labeling and dimensioning any drawing and design. They can be presented in a variety of styles and sizes. The overall design and style for a set (or family) of characters is known as **typeface** or **font**. Nowadays, hundreds of fonts are available for computer applications such as Times New Roman, Arial, Courier New, and so on. The fonts could be of any regional language, for example, Korean, Japanese, English, Hindi, and in addition, they can also be formatted as bold, italic, or underlined. Initially, font and typeface were different terms, that is, font was referred to as a set of cast metal characters in a particular size and format. For example, 10-point Courier Italic or 12-point Palatino Bold, and so on. Since, now printing is no longer done with cast metal forms, both terms are used interchangeably.

The fonts can be categorized into two groups, namely, *serif* and *sans serif*. The **serif** type has small lines or accents at the ends of the main character strokes. This type of font is more readable when applied to longer blocks of text. Some of the examples of serif font are Courier New, Times New Roman, and Book Antiqua. On the other hand, **sans serif** type does not contain accents. The individual characters in this type of font are easier to recognize, hence, are said to be more legible. Such font is considered good for labelling and short headings. Some of the examples of sans serif font are Arial, Calibri, Comic Sans MS, Tahoma, and Verdana.

27. Discuss some methods that are used for representing characters in a particular typeface.

or

How are computer fonts stored?

Ans. Some methods used for representing character shapes in a particular typeface are as follows:

- **Bitmap font** (also known as **raster font**): In this type of representation, rectangular grid patterns are used for representing the characters or letters in a particular typeface. The grid over which the character pen is passed is turned ON representing a digital 1 bit. These bits designate which pixel positions are to be displayed on the monitor. That is, each 1 bit causes the corresponding bit on the screen to glow with the required color value. The remaining bits are turned OFF, representing digital bit 0. The main advantage of this representation is that it is simplest to define and display. This is because characters are already stored in scan converted form thus, enabling character grid to map only to a frame-buffer position. The disadvantage of this representation is that fonts require more space as each variation (size and format) is stored in a font cache. Also, the size of a bitmap font is dependent on image resolution. More the resolution of font, more its size and, hence more space it need in font cache. However, one can generate different sizes and other variations (such as bold and italic) from one set, but the result is not of desired quality.
- **Outline font** (also known as **vector font**): In this type of representation, graphical primitives such as straight lines, arcs, and curve segments are used for defining the outline of each character shapes. To display the character shapes, the interior of the character outline must be filled using the scan-line fill approach. These fonts require less storage as each variation in fonts does not require distinct font cache. Moreover, one can produce boldface, italic, or different sizes by manipulating the curve definitions for the character outlines. In addition, it is easier to clip such fonts, as character can be considered as a general polygon. However, disadvantage of this representation is that outline definition of each character is less compact and takes more time for processing as each font must be scan converted into the frame buffer.

28. What are the adverse side effects of scan conversion?

Ans. The various forms of distortion are seen when scan conversion operation is performed. These distortions are collectively known as **aliasing effects**. Some of these effects are as follows:

- **Aliasing:** The term *aliasing* refers to the plotting of a point in a location other than its true location in order to fit the point into the raster. For example, let the true location of the point is given by the following equation

`y = mx + b`, where `b = 1`, `m = 0.5`, `x = 3`.

Solving for y, the true point comes out to be (3, 2.5). Since, the raster does not contain fractional locations, so the point is plotted at the alias location (3, 3) (see Figure 3.12).

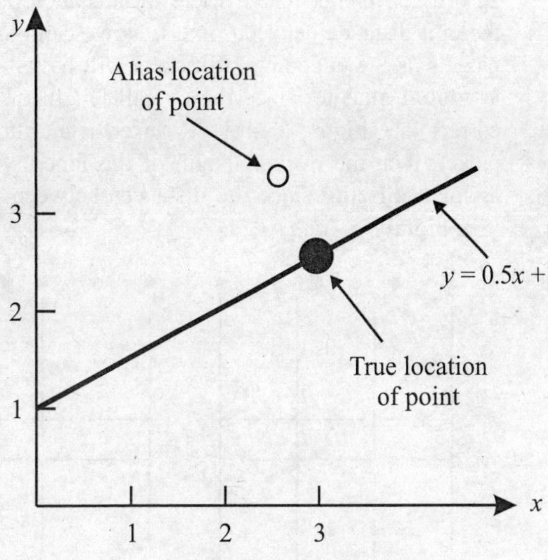

Figure 3.12 Aliasing Effect

- **Staircase:** When primitives such as a line or a circle are scan converted, jagged appearance is observed. Moreover, the stair steps or jaggies could also be seen along the border of a filled region.

- **Unequal brightness:** This effect of scan conversion shows the unequal brightness of lines at different orientation. A slanted line appears dimmer than a horizontal or vertical line, although all are presented at the same intensity level. This problem occurs as the human perception on light depends on both the density and the intensity of a light source. As shown in Figure 3.13, the pixels on the horizontal line are placed one unit apart, while the pixels on the diagonal line are approximately 1.614 units apart. Thus, this difference in density produces the perceived difference in brightness.

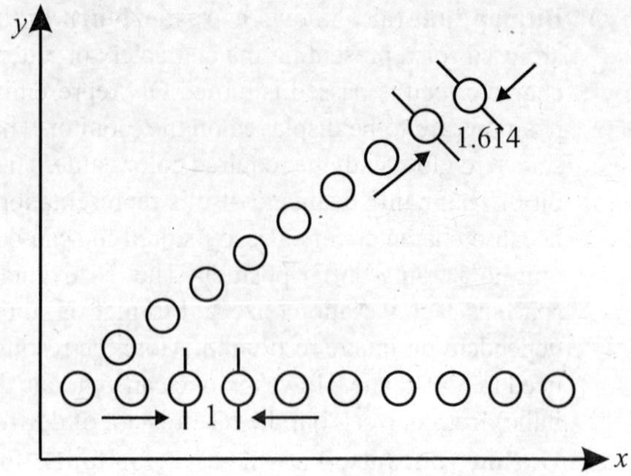

Figure 3.13 Unequal Intensity Effect

- **Overstrike:** This occurs when the same pixel is written more than once. Though, in most of the applications, it has little effect on the output of a raster computer graphics system but consequence of it is that the speed of output is slightly degraded as much time is spent in scan converting the same point two or more times. Moreover, in case of photographic medium when output is sent to slide, the overstrike amounts to double or triple exposures on the same portion of film. As a result, the pixel appears with greater intensity on the slide.
- **The picket fence problem:** This problem occurs when a user attempts to scan convert an object that is not aligned with, or does not fit into, the pixel grid properly. Figure 3.14a shows an original picket fence where the distance between two adjacent pickets is not a multiple of the unit distance between pixels. Now scan converting it will lead to uneven distances between pickets as the endpoints of pickets will have to be snapped to pixel coordinates. This is known as **global aliasing** since the overall length of the picket fence comes out to be approximately correct [see Figure 3.14b]. However, if an attempt is made to maintain equal spacing between picket, then the overall length of the fence will be distorted to a great extent. This is known as **local aliasing** since the distances between pickets are kept close to their original distances [See Figure 3.14c].

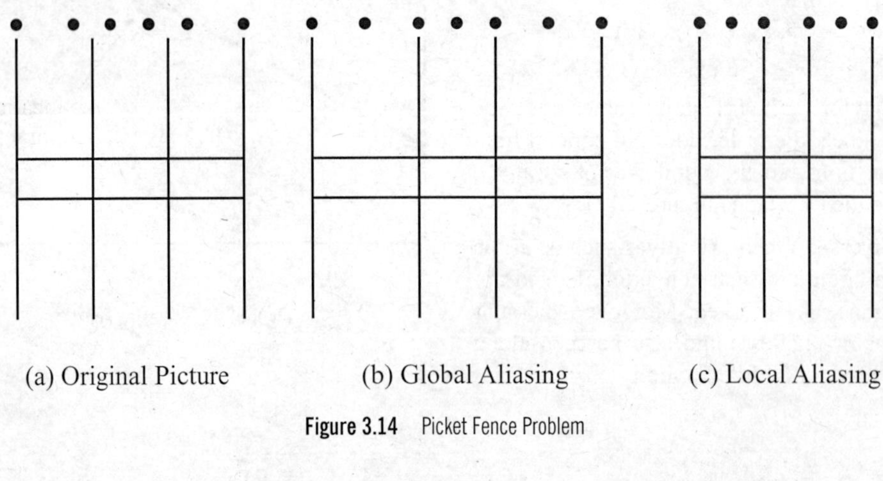

(a) Original Picture (b) Global Aliasing (c) Local Aliasing

Figure 3.14 Picket Fence Problem

29. Write a short note on antialiasing.

Ans. Antialiasing is a technique used for reducing the aliasing effects and helps in improving the appearance of displayed raster lines or images without increasing their resolution. Some of the techniques of antialiasing are as follows:

- **Pre-filtering:** It is one of the general-purpose antialiasing techniques. This technique works on the true signal in the continuous space to derive proper values for individual pixels (filtering before sampling).

  Antialiasing by computing overlap areas is known as **area sampling**. The area sampling is a pre-filtering technique as the intensity of the pixel as a whole is determined without calculating the sub-pixel intensities. In this technique, the pixel intensity is determined by calculating the areas of overlap of each pixel with the objects to be displayed. A pixel grid pattern is superimposed onto the continuous object definition. The pixel overlapped areas are obtained by determining where object boundaries intersect pixel boundaries and a percentage of overlap by the object is calculated. This percentage determines the proportion of the overall intensity value of the corresponding pixel. Higher the percentage of overlap, greater is the influence of an object on the pixel's overall intensity value.

  Figure 3.15 illustrates the method for estimating pixel overlap areas. In this, the pixel with screen grid coordinates (10, 20) is about 80% covered by the line area, hence its intensity is set as 80% of the maximum intensity. Similarly, the pixel at (10, 22) would be set to an intensity of about 20% of the maximum intensity.

  The total number of sub-pixels within the line boundaries is approximately equal to the overlap area and this estimation could be further improved by using finer sub-pixel grids. In case of color displays, the area of pixel overlap with different color regions is calculated and the final pixel color is taken as the average color of the various overlap areas.

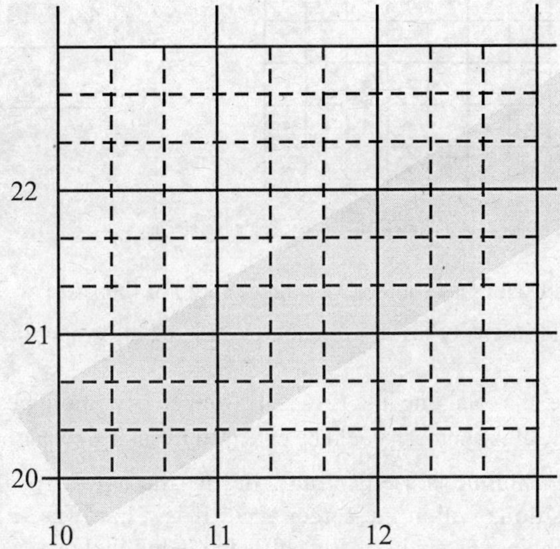

Figure 3.15 Area Sampling

- **Post-filtering:** It is another general-purpose antialiasing technique. This technique takes discrete samples of the continuous signal and uses the samples to compute pixel values (sampling before filtering). The technique of sampling object characteristics at a high resolution and displaying the results at a lower resolution is known as **super sampling**. Super sampling is a post-filtering technique as it first computes intensities at sub-pixel grid positions, and then combines the results for obtaining the pixel intensities. Using the super sampling technique, one can obtain the intensity information from multiple points that contribute to the overall intensity of a pixel. In this technique, each pixel is subdivided into sub-pixels and the position of each sub-pixel is checked in relation to the object to be scan-converted. In this approach, the object's contribution to a pixel's overall intensity value is proportional to the number of sub-pixels that are inside the area occupied by the object. The super sampling technique can be viewed as an approximation to the area sampling technique as only a finite number of values in each pixel area are used for approximating the accurate analytical result. Figure 3.16 explains the example for super sampling technique. In this example, a white object is bounded by two slanted lines on a black background. Each pixel is subdivided into nine (3 × 3) sub-pixels and then the scene is mapped to the pixel values. In this, the pixel at the upper right corner is assigned 7/9 as seven out of nine sub-pixels are inside the object area. For red (1, 0, 0) and background light yellow (0.5, 0.5, 0), the computed pixel value is $\left(1 \times \frac{7}{9} + 0.5 \times \frac{2}{9}, 0.5 \times \frac{2}{9}, 0\right)$, that is, $\left(\frac{8}{9}, \frac{1}{9}, 0\right)$.

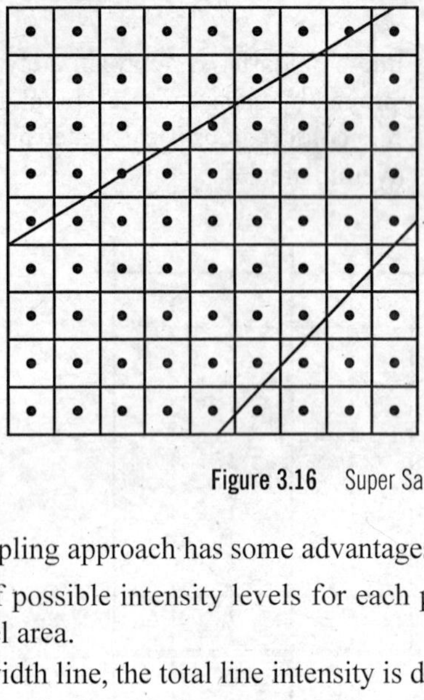

0	2/9	7/9
6/9	1	8/9
1	8/9	1/9

Figure 3.16 Super Sampling Technique

The super sampling approach has some advantages. Some of them are as follows:

- The number of possible intensity levels for each pixel is equal to the total number of sub-pixels within the pixel area.
- With a finite-width line, the total line intensity is distributed over more pixels.
- In case of a color display, this approach could be extended by taking background colors into account.

- **Pixel phasing:** This technique is used for antialiasing the objects of raster systems that can address sub-pixel positions within the screen grid. It is a hardware-based antialiasing technique in which the graphics system basically shifts the individual pixels from their normal positions in the pixel grid by a fraction of the unit distance between pixels. The fraction is typically 1/4, 1/2, or 3/4 of the pixel diameter. This technique is very effective as it smoothens onto the stair-steps without reducing the sharpness of the edges. This technique is applied by micropositioning the electron beam to more nearly approximate positions in relation to object geometry.

30. Implement the DDA algorithm to draw a line from (0, 0) to (6, 6).

Ans. Compute initial values:

```
(x0, y0) = (0, 0)
(xend, yend) = (6, 6)
dx = xend - x0 = 6 − 0 = 6
dy = yend - y0 = 6 − 0 = 6
steps = 6
xIncrement = dx/steps = 6/6 = 1
yIncrement = dy/steps = 6/6 = 1
```

The following table indicates the values computed by the algorithm.

S. No	*x*	*y*
1	0	0
2	1	1
3	2	2
4	3	3
5	4	4
6	5	5
7	6	6

The pixels positions along this line path are shown in Figure 3.17.

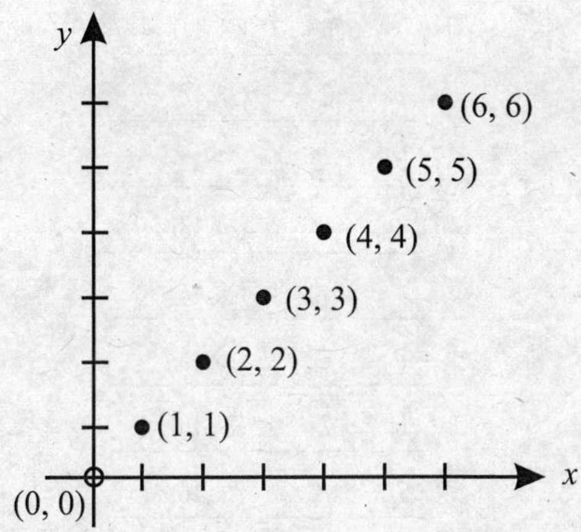

Figure 3.17 Pixels Positions along the Line Path Using DDA Algorithm

31. Solve using Bresenham's line-drawing algorithm (20, 10) to (30, 18).

Ans. Here, $(x_1, y_1) = (20, 10)$ and $(x_2, y_2) = (30, 18)$

$$\Delta x = x_2 - x_1 = 30 - 20 = 10$$

$$\Delta y = y_2 - y_1 = 18 - 10 = 8$$

$$2\Delta y = 16$$

$$d_0 = 2\Delta y - \Delta x = 16 - 10 = 6$$

$$2\Delta y - 2\Delta x = 16 - 20 = -4$$

Plot the initial point $(x_1, y_1) = (20, 10)$, and determine the successive pixel positions along the line path from the decision parameter as follows:

For $i = 0, d_0 = 2\Delta y - \Delta x = 16 - 10 = 6$

Here, $d_0 > 0$, as per the Bresenham's line-drawing algorithm, coordinates of next pixel positions (x_{i+1}, y_{i+1}) becomes (x_i+1, y_i+1), that is (21, 11)

And, $d_1 = d_0 + 2\Delta y - 2\Delta x = 6 - 4 = 2$

For $i = 1, d_1 = 2$.

Since, $d_1 > 0$, hence coordinates of next pixel positions becomes (22, 12)
And, $d_2 = d_1 + 2\Delta y - 2\Delta x = 2 - 4 = -2$

For $i = 2, d_2 = -2$.

Since, $d_2 < 0$, the coordinates of next pixel positions becomes (x_i+1, y_i), that is (23, 12)
And, $d_3 = d_2 + 2\Delta y = -2 + 16 = 14$

Similarly, all the values for the entire successive pixel positions are shown in the table as follows:

i	d_i	(x_{i+1}, y_{i+1})
0	6	(21, 11)
1	2	(22, 12)
2	-2	(23, 12)
3	14	(24, 13)
4	10	(25, 14)
5	6	(26, 15)
6	2	(27, 16)
7	-2	(28, 16)
8	14	(29, 17)
9	10	(30, 18)

The plot of the pixels generated along this line path is shown in Figure 3.18.

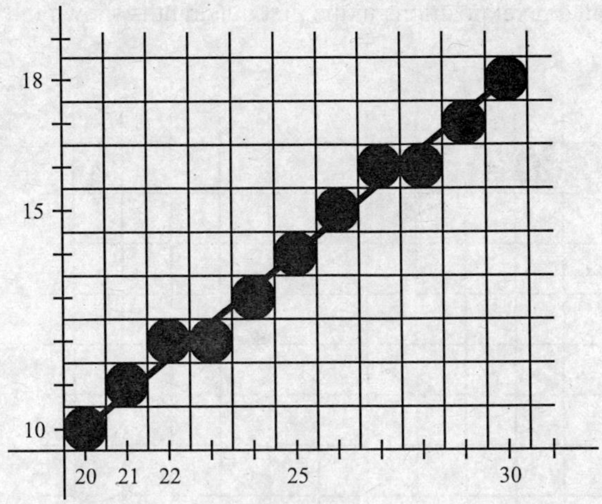

Figure 3.18 Pixel Positions along the Line Path between Endpoints (20, 10) and (30, 18), Plotted with Bresenham's Line Algorithm

32. Demonstrate the midpoint circle algorithm by determining positions along the circle octant in the first quadrant for a given radius, r = 10.

Ans. Given radius of the circle, r = 10

For the circle centered on the coordinate origin, the initial point is $(x_0, y_0) = (0, r) = (0, 10)$.

The initial value of the decision parameter, $d_0 = 1 - r = 1 - 10 = -9$ (As the radius is specified as an integer).

For $i = 0$, $d_0 = -9$, as per the midpoint circle algorithm $d_0 < 0$, the next point along the circle centered on (0, 0) is $(x_i + 1, y_i)$, that is $(x_1, y_1) = (x_0 + 1, y_0) = (1, 10)$ and $d_1 = d_0 + 2x_1 + 1 = -9 + 2 + 1 = -6$

For $i = 1$, $d_1 = -6$, $d_1 < 0$, the next point along the circle centered on (0, 0) is $(x_i + 1, y_i)$, that is $(x_2, y_2) = (x_1 + 1, y_1) = (2, 10)$ and $d_2 = d_1 + 2x2 + 1 = -6 + 4 + 1 = -1$

For $i = 2$, $d_2 = -1$, $d_2 < 0$, the next point along the circle centered on (0, 0) is $(x_i + 1, y_i)$, that is $(x_3, y_3) = (x_2 + 1, y_2) = (3, 10)$ and $d_3 = d_2 + 2x3 + 1 = -1 + 6 + 1 = 6$

For $i = 3$, $d_3 = 6$, $d_3 > 0$, the next point along the circle centered on (0, 0) is $(x_i + 1, y_i - 1)$, that is $(x_4, y_4) = (x_3 + 1, y_3 - 1) = (4, 9)$ and $d_4 = d_3 + 2x_4 + 1 - 2y_4 = 6 + 8 + 1 - 18 = -3$

Similarly, all the successive decision parameter values and the positions along the circle path are calculated using the midpoint algorithm in the table given as follows:

i	d_i	(x_{i+1}, y_{i+1})
0	-9	(1, 10)
1	-6	(2, 10)
2	-1	(3, 10)
3	6	(4, 9)
4	-3	(5, 9)
5	8	(6, 8)
6	5	(7, 7)

The plot of the generated pixel positions in the first quadrant is shown in Figure 3.19.

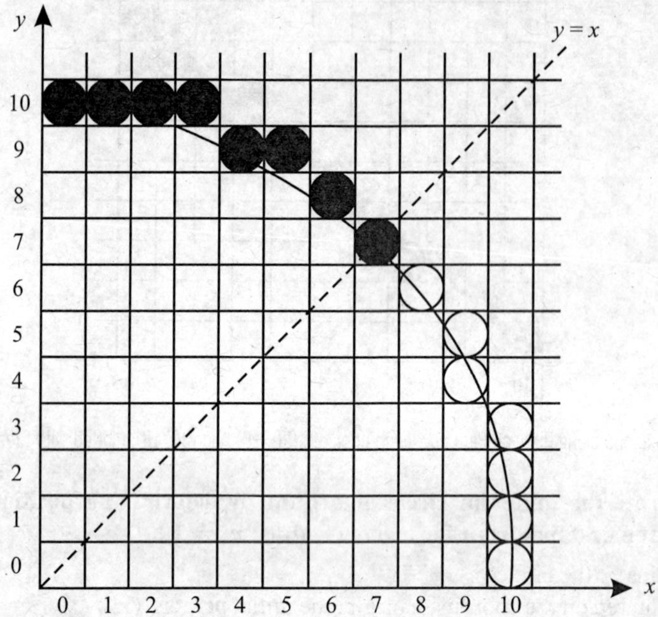

Figure 3.19 Selected Pixel Positions (Solid Circles) along a Circle Path with Radius, $r = 10$ Centered on the Origin, Using the Midpoint Circle Algorithm. Open Circles Show the Symmetry Positions in the First Quadrant.

33. Show graphically that an ellipse has four-way symmetry by plotting four points on the ellipse:

$x = a \cos \theta + h$

$y = b \sin \theta + h$

where $a = 2, b = 1, h = 0, k = 0$

$\theta = \Pi/4, 3\Pi/4, 5\Pi/4, 7\Pi/4$

Ans. Solving for $\theta = \Pi/4$:

```
x = 2 cos (Π/4) + 0 = 1.414
y = 1 sin (Π/4) + 0 = 0.7071
```

Solving for $\theta = 3\Pi/4$:

```
x = 2 cos (3Π/4) + 0 = -1.414
y = 1 sin (3Π/4) + 0 = 0.7071
```

Solving for $\theta = 5\Pi/4$:

```
x = 2 cos (5Π/4) + 0 = -1.414
y = 1 sin (5Π/4) + 0 = -0.7071
```

Solving for $\theta = 7\Pi/4$:

```
x = 2 cos (7Π/4) + 0 = 1.414
y = 1 sin (7Π/4) + 0 = -0.7071
```

The graphical representation of an ellipse is shown in Figure 3.20.

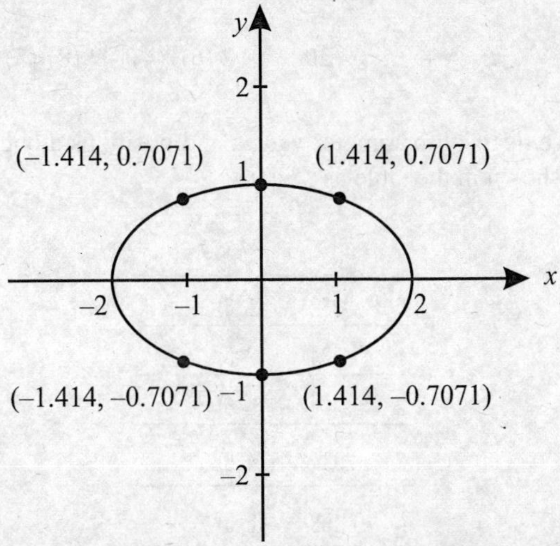

Figure 3.20 Graphical Representation of an Ellipse

34. Using midpoint ellipse algorithm, solve for $r_x = 8$ and $r_y = 6$.

Ans. Given $r_x = 8$
and $r_y = 6$
The ellipse centre is (x_c, y_c).

For region 1:

The first point on an ellipse centered on the origin $(x_0, y_0) = (0, r_y) = (0, 6)$
The initial value of the decision parameter is as:

$$d_0 = r_y^2 - r_x^2 r_y + \frac{1}{4} r_x^2 = (6)^2 - (8)^2(6) + \tfrac{1}{4}(8)^2 = 36 - 384 + 16 = -332$$

For $i = 0$, $d_0 = -332 < 0$, then by the midpoint ellipse algorithm, the next point along the ellipse centered on (0, 0) is $(x_i + 1, y_i)$, that is, $(x_1, y_1) = (x_0 + 1, y_0) = (1, 6)$ and

$$d_1 = d_0 + 2r_y^2 x_1 + r_y^2 = -332 + 2(6)^2(1) + (6)^2 = -332 + 72 + 36 = -224.$$

For $i = 1$, $d_1 = -224 < 0$, the next point along the ellipse centered on (0, 0) is $(x_i + 1, y_i)$, that is, $(x_2, y_2) = (x_1 + 1, y_1) = (2, 6)$ and

$$d_2 = d_1 + 2r_y^2 x_2 + r_y^2 = -224 + 2(6)^2(2) + (6)^2 = -224 + 144 + 36 = -44.$$

For $i = 2$, $d_2 = -44 < 0$, the next point along the ellipse centered on (0, 0) is $(x_i + 1, y_k)$, that is, $(x_3, y_3) = (x_2 + 1, y_2) = (3, 6)$ and

$$d_3 = d_2 + 2r_y^2 x_3 + r_y^2 = -44 + 2(6)^2(3) + (6)^2 = -44 + 216 + 36 = 208.$$

For $i = 3, d_3 = 208 > 0$, the next point along the ellipse centered on (0, 0) is $(x_i + 1, y_i - 1)$, that is, $(x_4, y_4) = (x_3 + 1, y_3 - 1) = (4, 5)$ and

$d_4 = d_3 + 2r_y^2 x_4 - 2r_x^2 y_4 + r_y^2 = 208 + 2(6)^2(4) - 2(8)^2(5) + (6)^2 = 208 + 288 - 640 + 36 = -108$.

Similarly, the successive decision parameter values and positions along the ellipse path are calculated using this algorithm shown in the table as follows:

i	d_i	(x_{i+1}, y_{i+1})
0	–332	(1, 6)
1	–224	(2, 6)
2	–44	(3, 6)
3	208	(4, 5)
4	–108	(5, 5)
5	288	(6, 4)
6	244	(7, 3)

For region 2:

The initial point is $(x_0, y_0) = (7, 3)$.

The initial value of the decision parameter is

$$d_0 = r_y^2\left(x_0 + \frac{1}{2}\right)^2 + r_x^2(y_0 - 1)^2 - r_x^2 r_y^2$$

$$= (6)^2(7 + 1/2)^2 + (8)^2(3 - 1)^2 - (8)^2(6)^2$$

$$= 36(15/2)^2 + 64(4) - (64)(36)$$

$$= 36(225/4) + 256 - 2304$$

$$= 2025 + 256 - 2304 = -23$$

For $i = 0, d_0 = -23 < 0$, then by the midpoint ellipse algorithm, the next point along the ellipse centered on (0, 0) is $(x_i + 1, y_i - 1)$, that is, $(x_1, y_1) = (x_0 + 1, y_0 - 1) = (8, 2)$ and $d_1 = d_0 + 2r_y^2 x_1 - 2r_x^2 y_1 + r_x^2 = 361$.

For $i = 1, d_1 = 361 > 0$, then by the midpoint ellipse algorithm, the next point along the ellipse centered on (0, 0) is $(x_i, y_i - 1)$, that is, $(x_2, y_2) = (x_1, y_1 - 1) = (8, 1)$

and $d_2 = d_1 - 2r_x^2 y_2 + r_x^2 = 297$

For $i = 2, d_2 = 269 > 0$, then by the midpoint ellipse algorithm, the next point along the ellipse centered on (0, 0) is $(x_i, y_i - 1)$, that is, $(x_3, y_3) = (x_2, y_2 - 1) = (8, 0)$

and $d_3 = d_2 - 2r_x^2 y_3 + r_x^2 = 361$

Similarly, the successive decision parameter values and positions along the ellipse path are calculated using this algorithm shown in the table as follows:

i	d_i	(x_{i+1}, y_{i+1})
0	−23	(8, 2)
1	361	(8, 1)
2	297	(8, 0)

A plot of the selected positions around the ellipse boundary within the first quadrant is shown in Figure 3.21.

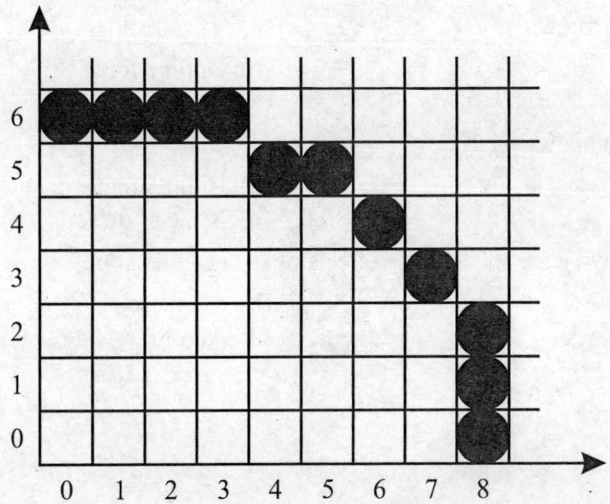

Figure 3.21 Positions along an Elliptical Path Centered on the Origin with $r_x = 8$ and $r_y = 6$, using the Midpoint Algorithm to Calculate Pixel Positions in the First Quadrant

MULTIPLE CHOICE QUESTIONS

1. DDA stands for:
   (a) Digital differential analyzer
   (b) Differential digital analyzer
   (c) Digital differential analysis
   (d) Differential digital analysis
2. Which of the following algorithms can be used for circle generation?
   (a) Bresenham's algorithm
   (b) Midpoint algorithm
   (c) Both (a) and (b)
   (d) None of these
3. The scan line polygon fill algorithm uses ___________.
   (a) Edge list/table
   (b) Vertex table
   (c) Polygon table
   (d) Active edge table

4. Inside-outside test uses _______________.

   (a) Odd-even rule
   (b) Non-zero winding number rule
   (c) Both (a) and (b)
   (d) None of these

5. Odd-even rule is also known as _____________.

   (a) Odd parity rule
   (b) Even-odd rule
   (c) Both (a) and (b)
   (d) Parity rule

6. The boundary-fill algorithm uses _____________.

   (a) 4-connected
   (b) 8-connected
   (c) Both (a) and (b)
   (d) None of these

7. Fonts can be categorized as _______________.

   (a) Serif
   (b) Sans serif
   (c) Both (a) and (b)
   (d) None of these

8. Bitmap font is also known as ___________.

   (a) Raster font
   (b) Outline font
   (c) Vector font
   (d) None of these

9. Outline font is also known as ___________.

   (a) Vector font
   (b) Bitmap font
   (c) Raster font
   (d) None of these

10. Which of the following are the adverse effects of scan conversion?

   (a) Aliasing
   (b) Staircase
   (c) Unequal brightness
   (d) All of these

Answer. 1. a 2. c 3. a 4. c 5. c 6. c 7. c 8. a 9. a 10. d

4

Attributes of Output Primitives

1. What are attribute parameters? What are the different ways of incorporating attribute options into a graphics package?

Ans. Any parameter that influences the way a primitive is to be displayed is referred to as an **attribute parameter**. There are various attributes that control the basic display properties of graphics primitives such as color, size and style. For example, a line can be represented in different ways such as solid or dashed, red or pink and thin or thick. Also, text can appear reading from left to right, slanted diagonally across the screen or in vertical columns. Similarly, characters can be appeared in different fonts, sizes and colors.

There are two ways of incorporating attribute options into a graphics package—one is to extend the parameter list associated with each primitive function in order to include the appropriate attribute values, and other is to maintain a system list of current attribute values, and then include separate functions in the graphics package for setting the current values in the attribute list. Some graphics packages use a combination of both the methods.

2. Define the terms state system and state variables.

Ans. A graphics system maintaining a list of current values of attributes and other parameters is known as **state system** or **state machine**. The **state variables** (also known as **state parameters**) refer to the attributes of output primitives and some other parameters such as the current frame-buffer position. Assigning a value to one or more state parameters implies that we are putting the system into a particular state. The system remains in that state only until we change the value of a state parameter.

3. Describe various line attributes.

Ans. A **line** is the basic element for art and designing. It is a one-dimensional element measured only in length. A line with endpoints is referred to as a line segment. Various graphics packages (such as MS Paint, CorelDraw, etc.) provide a line tool to draw straight line segments of different width and style. In addition, they also provide some pen or brush options to draw line segments with other effects. Thus, the basic properties associated with a line segment are its width, style and color.

Line width

Implementation of line width options is based on the capabilities of the output device. A video monitor, for example, displays a thick line as adjacent parallel lines, whereas, a pen plotter uses different pen options to draw lines of varied thickness. In raster implementations, a line segment of standard thickness is drawn by placing a single pixel at each sample position. A thick line can be drawn by plotting additional pixels along adjacent parallel line paths (also known as **pixel span**). The number of pixels to be placed is set to equal to the integer value of the line width.

Though thick lines can be generated quickly using horizontal or vertical pixel spans, the displayed width of a line vary according to the slope of the line. A 45° line will be displayed thinner by a factor of $1 / \sqrt{2}$ as compared to a horizontal or vertical line with same-length pixel spans. Another problem with the pixel span method is that it generates line segments whose ends are either horizontal or vertical irrespective of its slope. For thicker lines, this effect becomes more visible. To reduce this effect, we add line caps to the ends of the line. Line cap attribute controls how the ends of line segments are displayed when printed. There are three types of line caps used in graphic applications, as shown in Figure 4.1.

- **Butt caps:** With butt caps, the line segments are terminated with square ends perpendicular to the line path. If a line with slope m is drawn, the square ends of the thick line will have the slope -1/m.
- **Round caps:** With round caps, the line segments are terminated with filled semicircles centered at the middle of the thick line and having a diameter equal to the line thickness.
- **Projecting square caps:** These are similar to the butt caps with the only difference that the caps are extended beyond the line end points for a distance equal to one-half of the line width.

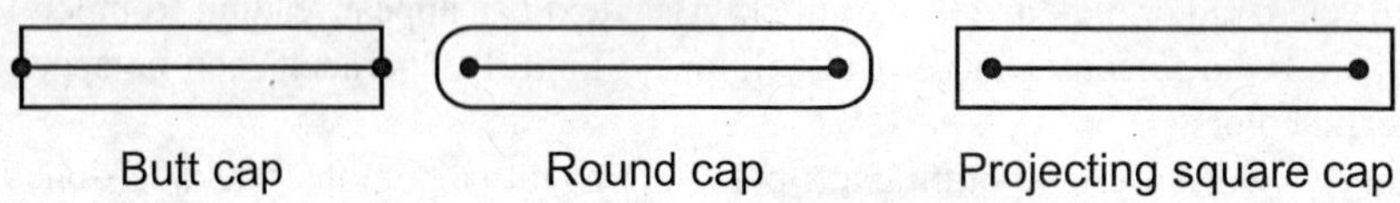

Figure 4.1 Thick Lines drawn with Butt Cap, Round Cap and Projecting Square Cap

Line style

Different types of lines used in graphics applications are solid lines, dashed lines and dotted lines (see Figure 4.2). A solid line can be plotted by setting its length and the distance it covers along the line path. A dashed line can be plotted by including an interdash spacing in a line that must be equal to the length of the solid line segments (or dashes). Users are permitted to set the length of the dashes and interdash spacing. A dotted line can be generated by including very short length dashes with the spacing equal to or greater than the dash size.

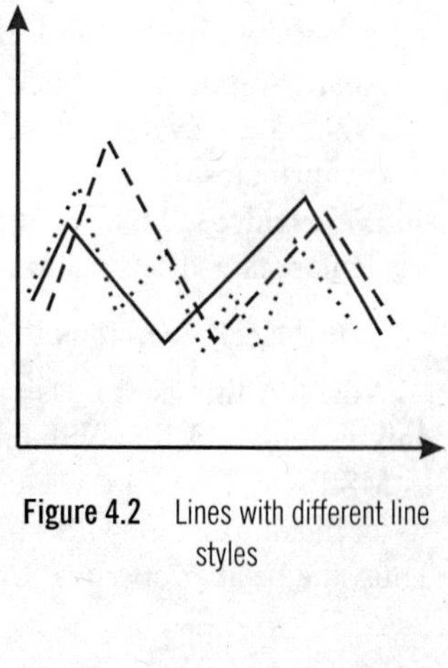

Figure 4.2 Lines with different line styles

In raster-line algorithms, line type attributes are displayed by generating pixel spans. Number of pixels in a span and the interspan spacing are defined in a pixel mask. **Pixel mask** is a string of digits (0s and 1s) according to which the pixels are plotted on the specified position along the line path. For example, 11100 represent a dashed line with a dash length of three pixels and an interdash spacing of two pixels.

Thick line joins

In general, connecting thick line segments with each other is not an easy task. On joining two thick line segments, an angle is generated at the segment endpoints where the two lines join, that is, at the joining point (see Figure 4.3).

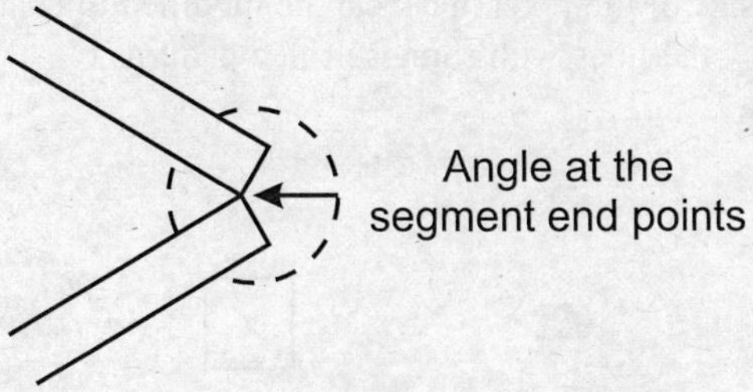

Figure 4.3 Angle at the joining point

This discreteness occurs due to the thickness of line segments. To remove this, some additional processing is required at the segment endpoints. We need to add an extra portion to the joint that will make the connection smooth. Figure 4.4 illustrates three methods for smoothly joining the two thick line segments.

- ❑ **Miter join:** It is formed by extending the exterior boundaries of the thick line segments up to their intersection point where these two line segments meet. This join forms a corner. Figure 4.4(a) depicts the construction of miter join.
- ❑ **Round join:** In this, the exterior boundaries are connected with a circular arc whose diameter is equal to the thickness of the lines. Figure 4.4(b) depicts the construction of round join.
- ❑ **Bevel joint:** In this, butt caps are used for drawing the line segments and the small triangular gap created at the join is filled with the color of the two line segments. Figure 4.4(c) depicts the construction of bevel join.

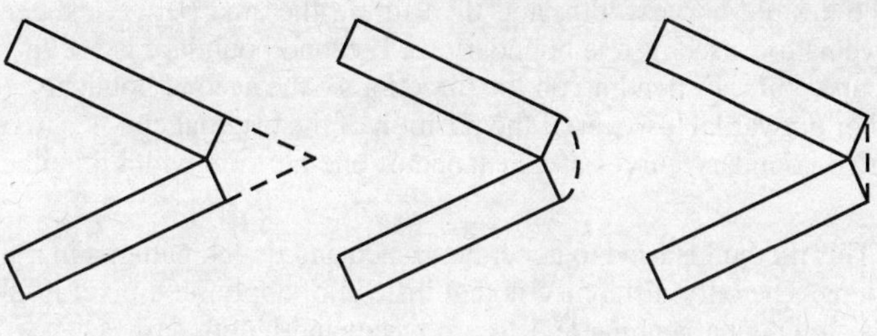

Figure 4.4 Line joins

Line color

Graphic applications offer a wide range of colors for drawing purposes. Line color attribute controls the color intensity of a line segment. System provides a list of attribute values in which the current color index is included. This color value is first set into the frame buffer and a line is displayed in the current color. The number of color choices depends on the number of bits available per pixel in the frame buffer.

4. Discuss the use of pen and brush options available in graphics applications.

Ans. In many graphics applications, lines are generated with pen or brushes selections. These pens or brushes can be of different shapes, sizes and patterns. These shapes are stored in a pixel mask through which the array of given pixel positions can be described along the line path. Figure 4.5 depicts some pen or brush shapes. The size of the pixel mask can be modified to change the line width, if required. It is also possible to display the lines with some selected patterns by superimposing the pattern values onto the pen or brush mask.

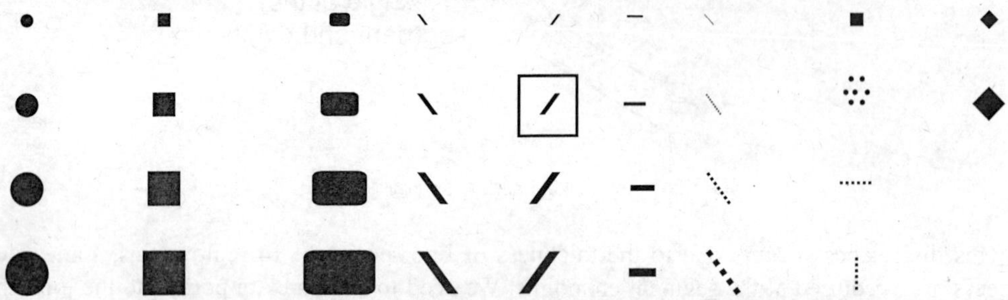

Figure 4.5 Pen and Brush shapes for line display

5. Discuss the various ways of generating curves with different width and style.

Ans. Like straight line segments, curves can also be drawn with different widths, styles and colors. Methods used for curve-drawing algorithm is similar to those for line-drawing algorithms. The various methods used to generate curves are discussed as follows:

- **Pixel span:** Curves of different widths can be generated using the method of horizontal or vertical pixel spans. In this method, if magnitude of the curve slope is >1, then vertical spans are plotted whereas if magnitude of the curve slope is <1, then horizontal spans are plotted.
- **Parallel curves method:** In this method, two parallel curves are plotted whose separation distance is equal to the desired curve width, and then filling the area between them. To perform this, the specified curve path is used as one boundary, and second boundary is set up either inside or outside the original curve path. Depending on the direction of the second boundary, original path is shifted either inward or outward. However, if the position of the original curve is to be maintained, then we can plot the two boundary curves at a distance of one-half the width on either side of the specified curve path.
- **Pixel mask:** This method is used to generate dashed and dotted patterns in a similar way as done for line-type options. The only difference is that instead of applying a pixel mask with constant spans, we plot pixels along equal angular arcs to produce equal-length dashes.
- **Pen or brush options**: Curves of varied thickness and styles can also be generated using different pen or brush options as in line-segment generation. If a rectangular pen is used for generating curves, the curve displayed will be thicker where the magnitude of the curve slope is 1. To draw a curve of uniform thickness, we can use a circular pen shape. The curves can also be displayed with selected patterns by superimposing the pattern values onto the pen or brush mask.

6. Explain color and grayscale levels.

Ans. Depending on the capabilities and design objectives of a system, several color and intensity level options are made available to users. For example, random-scan monitors offer only few colors choices whereas general purpose raster systems offer large range of colors depending on the amount of storage provided per pixel in the frame buffer. The colors are represented by color codes which are positive integers ranging from 0 to 255. These color codes are treated in different ways for different situations. For CRT monitors, they are transformed into intensity level settings for the electron beams, and for color plotters, these codes help in controlling ink-jet deposits or pen selections. There are two ways of storing color information in the frame buffer, as discussed below.

- **Directly in the frame buffer:** In this scheme, the color codes are stored directly in the frame buffer. Whenever a particular color code is specified in an application program, its equivalent binary code is stored in the frame buffer. With 3 bits storage per pixel, a total of 8 (2^3) color values are available (see Table 4.1). Each bit position controls the intensity level (on or off) of the corresponding electron gun in an RGB monitor. The leftmost bit controls the red gun, the middle bit controls the green gun, and the rightmost bit controls the blue gun. With 6 bits per pixel, a total of 64 (2^6) color codes are available. High quality raster graphics systems having 24 bits per pixel frame buffer provide around 17 billion color choices for each pixel. This frame buffer in such systems requires 3 MB of storage space. Thus, more the number of color choices, the larger will be size of the frame buffer.

Table 4.1 The eight color code for 3-bit per pixel frame buffer

COLOR CODE	STORED COLOR VALUES IN FRAME BUFFER			DISPLAYED COLOR
	RED	GREEN	BLUE	
0	0	0	0	Black
1	0	0	1	Blue
2	0	1	0	Green
3	0	1	1	Cyan
4	1	0	0	Red
5	1	0	1	Magenta
6	1	1	0	Yellow
7	1	1	1	White

- **Color lookup table:** In this approach, a separate table (known as color look table) is used to store color codes and the pixel values are used as an index into this table. This approach provides a better way of providing extended color capabilities to a user without having large frame buffers. The frame buffer now stores the pixel values, which are used as indices into the color table. Figure 4.6 shows an example color table, which can store 64 entries, and each entry in the table uses 12 bits to specify an RGB component. The first 4 bits represent red component, middle 4 bits represent green component and last 4 bits represent blue component. The value 40 stored at pixel position (x, y) references the location in this table containing the value 356, which further references its binary equivalent. Each 4-bit segment controls the intensity level of one of the three electron guns in an RGB monitor. Though color table reduces the frame buffer storage requirements, it reduces the number of colors that can be displayed simultaneously as compared to a full-color system.

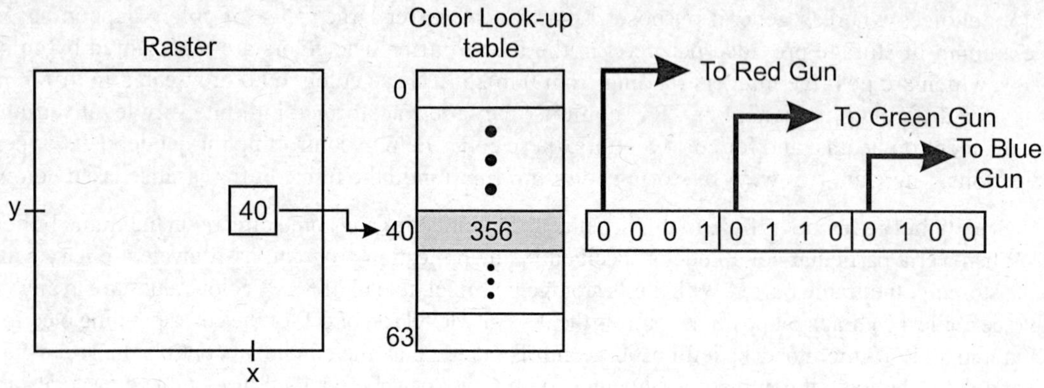

Figure 4.6 A color lookup table

Grayscale

For the monochrome monitors, the color functions are used to set the shades of gray or grayscale (white → light gray → dark gray → black) for displaying primitives within an application program. Greyscale levels are specified in the range from 0 to 1. These levels are transformed into the appropriate binary codes for storage in the raster. Table 4.2 lists the intensity codes for a four-level greyscale system where these intensity values are stored in the frame buffer.

Alternatively, such intensity values can be stored as voltage values that will generate grayscale level on the output device (monitor). For this, each intensity code needs to be converted directly into its corresponding voltage values.

Table 4.2 Intensity codes for a four-level greyscale system

INTENSITY CODES	STORED INTENSITY VALUES IN THE FRAME BUFFER (Binary Code)		DISPLAYED GRAY SCALE
0.0	0	(00)	Black
0.33	1	(01)	Dark Gray
0.67	2	(10)	Light Gray
1.0	3	(11)	White

7. Explain the area-fill attributes.

Ans. Area-fill attributes are applied to the closed output primitives such as polygons, circles, ellipses, etc. There exist several options for filling the area such as solid color, patterned fill or various brush styles, colors and transparency parameters. The choices for area-filling depend on the capabilities of the available package. Thus, the area-fill attributes include *fill style* and *fill color*. Other fill options could be the style, width and color of the outline of the filled region. The values for these attributes can be set independent of the fill style or fill color. That is, the outline of the closed region can be set to any thickness, color or style (dotted, dashed or solid) irrespective of how the interior area of the region is filled.

Fill style

There are three basic fill styles, namely, hollow with a color border, filled with a solid color and filled with a specified pattern. The hollow areas are displayed using only the boundary outline—the interior color is set equal to the background color. The solid fill fills the area with a single color including the boundary line of the closed region. A patterned fill fills the area with a specified pattern. A fill pattern can be defined in rectangular color arrays that list different colors for different positions in the array. The process of filling an area with a rectangular pattern is known as **tiling**, and the rectangular fill patterns are known as **tiling patterns**. Figure 4.7 illustrates different fill styles.

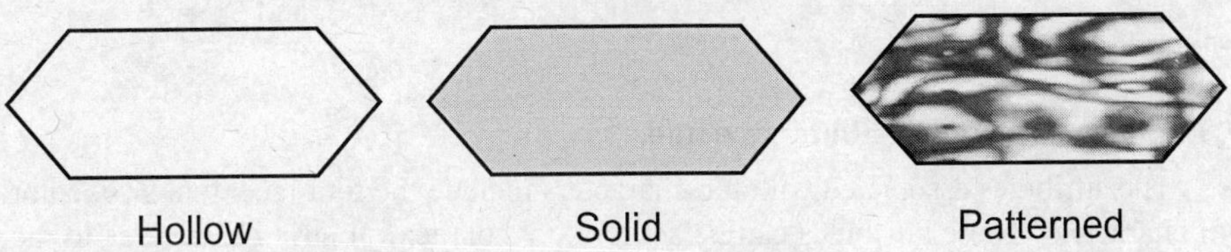

Figure 4.7 Fill styles

In addition, some predefined fill patterns are also available in a system. These are known as **hatch fill patterns**. A hatch is used to fill an area with selected hatching patterns such as parallel or crosses lines as shown in Figure 4.8.

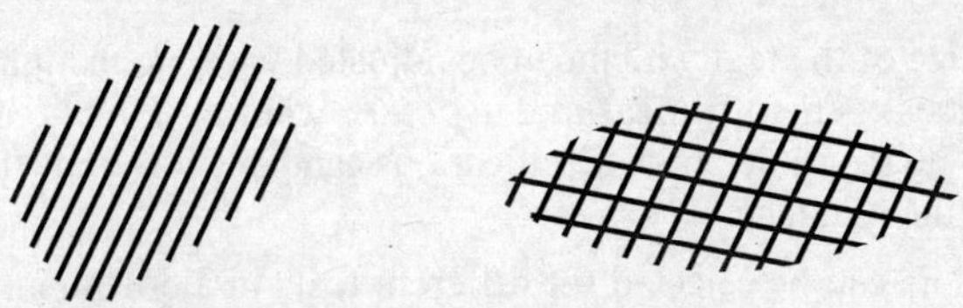

Figure 4.8 Areas filled with hatch patterns

Fill color

Fill color determines the color used to fill a region with a solid color. In most of graphics packages, the default fill color is black.

8. Explain soft fill procedures.

Ans. Soft fill (also known as **tint fill**) is a filling method in which the foreground color (fill color) is mixed with the background colors to soften the fill colors at the object boundaries that have been blurred. This algorithm also allows you to repaint the color area that was originally filled with a semi-transparent brush. The new color after repainting will be the mixture of the brush color and the background colors behind the area. Soft-fill procedures provide a new color for an area that has the same variations as the original fill color.

The linear soft-fill procedure is an example of soft-fill algorithm which repaints an area that was originally painted by combining a foreground color F with a single background color B, where F≠B. It is based on the assumption that the original fill was a linear combination of foreground and background colors. We can then determine this same linear relationship from the frame buffer settings and use it to paint the region in a new color. The new RGB color N of each pixel within the region to be refilled is some linear combination of F and B, as follows:

$$N = tF + (1-t)B$$

where

t = transparency factor ranging from 0 to 1. For $t < 0.5$, the background color contributes more to the interior color of the region as compared to the foreground color.

N, F and B hold values for each RGB component of the colors. That is,

$$N = (N_R, N_G, N_B), \quad F = (F_R, F_G, F_B), \quad B = (B_R, B_G, B_B)$$

We can now calculate the value of t using one of the RGB color component as follows:

$$t = \frac{N_i - B_i}{F_i - B_i}, \quad i = R, G, \text{ or } B, \text{ and } F_i \neq B_i$$

9. Explain character attributes in detail.

Ans. The attributes associated with the characters include the font face, font size, color and orientation of characters. These attributes can be set to the whole text or string as well as to the individual characters defined as marker symbols. There are many text options available in graphic applications, which are discussed as follows:

- **Font:** The font (also known as **typeface**) is a set of characters with a particular design style such as Courier New, Helvetica, Times New Roman, and so on. Text can also be displayed with various underline styles (dashed, double or thick), in italics, in boldface, as subscript or superscript, or with shadow.
- **Font size:** It is the size of the text which can be adjusted without changing the width to height ratio of characters. Text size is generally measured in *points*, where 1 point is equal to 0.013837 inch. Note that different fonts with the same point specifications can have different character sizes depending on shape and design of the typeface.
- **Color:** Different colors can be selected for different texts in a document or even for different characters of a single string.
- **Character height:** It is defined as the distance between the baseline and capline of the characters. Some characters like f or j (known as **kerned** characters) extend beyond the character-body limits, whereas some other characters like g, y, p, q, j extend below the baseline.
- **Character width:** It is the attribute used to scale the body width of the characters. This attribute does not affect the character height attribute.
- **Character spacing:** Character spacing is defined as the space between the characters in a string or a text. If character height or width is increased or decreased then the character spacing and its width and height will be adjusted to maintain the height and width ratio of the given text. The negative value for character spacing results into overlapped characters, whereas a positive value inserts space to spread the characters.
- **Orientation:** Orienting the text rotates the displayed text at some angle. By default, the text is appeared horizontally. We can set the orientation such that it is displayed vertically (top-to-bottom) or in slating direction.
- **Alignment:** This attribute specifies the position of text with respect to the start coordinates. It controls both the horizontal as well as vertical alignments.

10. What is a marker symbol and where it is used?

Ans. Sometimes, it is important to highlight a single character in the entire string or text. This single character is referred to as a **marker symbol.** It can be displayed different colors and in different sizes.

Marker symbols are used to draw point features and point graphics. They can be used in conjunction with other symbols for decorating line attributes, creating fill patterns and creating text backgrounds. They can also be used as cartographic elements in maps and charts for showing important places such as capitals, airports, hospitals, forests areas, etc. The attributes associated with marker symbols are color, size and style.

- ❑ **Marker color:** It determines the color of the marker. In most graphics applications, the default color is black.
- ❑ **Marker size:** It determines the size of the marker. In most graphics applications, the default size is 1.0, which corresponds to 8 pixels. That is, a square marker symbol with size 1 will be drawn with a side equal to 8 pixels on the screen.
- ❑ **Marker style:** It determines the shape of the marker symbol. It could be a dot (.), a circle (O), a plus (+), an asterisk (*), a triangle (Δ), a square (□), a star (★), etc. The *.jpeg*, *.png* or *.bmp* images can also be used as marker symbols. Each graphics application provides a built-in library of graphics symbol, which can be directly used in a drawing.

11. Discuss about inquiry functions.

Ans. Inquiry functions return information about the current status or settings for the attributes and other parameters, such as workstation types and status. The user can also copy the current values into some specified parameters so that the values can be saved for later reuse. These values can also be used to check the current state of the system in case an error occurs.

MULTIPLE CHOICE QUESTIONS

1. Which of these is not an attribute of a line?

   (a) Line width (b) Line color
   (c) Line depth (d) Line style

2. Which of these joins is formed by extending the exterior boundaries of the thick line segments up to their intersection point where these two line segments meet?

   (a) Round join (b) Miter join
   (c) Butt join (d) Corner join

3. Which of these color codes (RGB value) displays yellow color?

   (a) 110 (b) 101
   (c) 000 (d) 111

4. If a system provides 6 bits storage per pixel, how many color codes are available?

   (a) 12 (b) 64
   (c) 8 (d) 32

5. Which of these is not an area-fill attribute?

   (a) Fill style (b) Fill color
   (c) Both (a) and (b) (d) None of these

6. ______________ is a filling method in which the foreground color (fill color) is mixed with the background colors.

   (a) Soft fill (b) Tiling
   (c) Color mixing (d) Color combining

7. A single character which can be displayed in different colors and sizes to highlight it in the entire string is known as ______________.
   (a) Graphic symbol
   (b) Highlighted text
   (c) Marker symbol
   (d) Emphasized text
8. Which is of these is/are the attribute of marker symbol?
   (a) Marker style
   (b) Marker color
   (c) Marker size
   (d) All of these

Answers. 1. c 2. b 3. a 4. b 5. c 6. a 7. c 8. d

5

Two-dimensional Transformations and Viewing

1. What do you mean by geometric transformation? How points can be represented in the coordinate system?

Ans. The process of changing the coordinate descriptions of objects such as its size, orientation, shape, or position by making use of mathematical operations such as matrix algebra is known as **geometric transformation**. This results in a more realistic and pictorial representation of objects on the screen, and thus resembles the appearance of objects as seen in the real world. Moreover, these transformed objects can be effectively used in a variety of applications such as animations and CAD. Some of the basic transformations that can be applied on the objects include *translation*, *rotation*, and *scaling*. These transformations are basic in the sense that they are included in almost every graphics package and are used for repositioning and resizing of 2D objects. However, some packages also provide two additional transformations, namely, *reflection* and *shear* to facilitate complicated transmutation.

In the coordinate system, the coordinates (also called **points**) are stored in a computer in the form of series. Such series of points is represented by a matrix which defines their respective position. Hence, they are also known as **position vectors**. These points in turn help us to generate lines, curves or pictures of different sizes and lengths. The matrix can be represented in either of the following forms:

- **Row-wise representation:** In this form, the matrix consists of one row and 2 to 3 columns depending on the dimensions. For example, a point (x,y) using this technique is represented as follows:

$$[x\ y]_{1\times 2} \rightarrow \text{in 2D}$$

where 1 × 2 indicates that there are 1 row and 2 columns.

Similarly, a point (x, y, z) is represented as follows:

$$[x \ y \ z]_{1\times3} \rightarrow \text{in 3D}$$

- **Column-wise representation:** In this form, the matrix contains one column and 2 to 3 rows. For example, a point (x,y) using this technique is represented as follows:

$$\begin{bmatrix} x \\ y \end{bmatrix}_{2\times1} \rightarrow \text{in 2D}$$

where 2 × 1 indicates that there are 2 rows and 1 column.
Similarly, a point (x, y, z) is represented as follows:

$$\begin{bmatrix} x \\ y \\ z \end{bmatrix}_{3\times1} \rightarrow \text{in 3D}$$

2. Explain 2D translation with the help of an example.

Ans. Translation is one of the basic transformations which is applied to the 2D objects to change their position along a straight-line path from one coordinate location to the other. The object can be a point, a straight-line segment, a polygon, or any curved one such as circle, ellipse, etc. Note that transformations on the objects are done by considering their respective coordinate position (x, y). Translation is said to be a rigid-body transformation as it moves an object without changing its shape. That is, every point on the proposed object is translated by the same amount when translation is done. For example, to move or translate the point (x, y) to a new location (x', y'), we add translation distances, t_x and t_y, to its original coordinate positions (see Figure 5.1). The translation distance pair (t_x, t_y) is known as a **translation vector** or **shift vector**. The addition of distances is done in the following manner:

$$x' = x + t_x, \ y' = y + t_y \qquad (1)$$

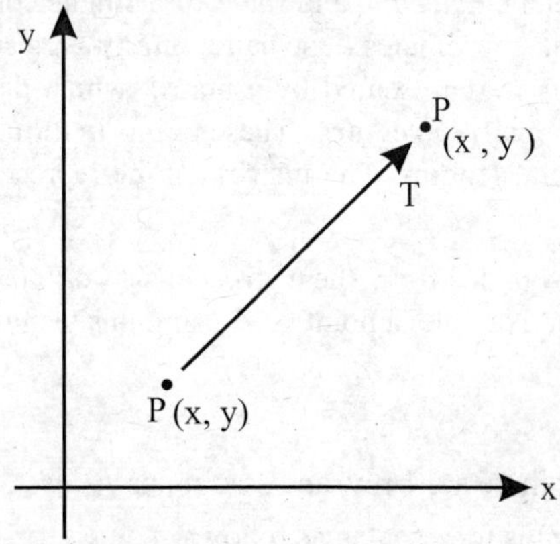

Figure 5.1 Translating a Point from Position P to P'

Note that Equation (1) can also be written in either row-vector form or column-vector form in order to represent a translation vector in a much simpler form. In general, the convention of column-vector representation is followed as it is a standard mathematical notation for a point and various graphics packages such as GKS and PHIGS follow such form of representation. In column-vector representation, original and translated coordinate positions and translation vector are represented as:

$$P = \begin{bmatrix} x \\ y \end{bmatrix}, P' = \begin{bmatrix} x' \\ y' \end{bmatrix}, T = \begin{bmatrix} t_x \\ t_y \end{bmatrix} \qquad (2)$$

In the case of row-vector, they are represented as:

$$P = [x\ y], P' = [x'\ y'], T = [t_x\ t_y] \qquad (3)$$

Thus, from Equations (2) and (3), we can say:

$$P' = P + T \qquad (4)$$

We can use similar methods to translate polygons and curved objects. To translate a polygon, we apply Equation (4) on each of its vertices. Figure 5.2 illustrates such transformation where a polygon is moved from position A to another position B with the translation vector (5.50, 4.50). Similarly, to change the position of a circle or ellipse, the centre coordinates are translated and the object is redrawn in the new location.

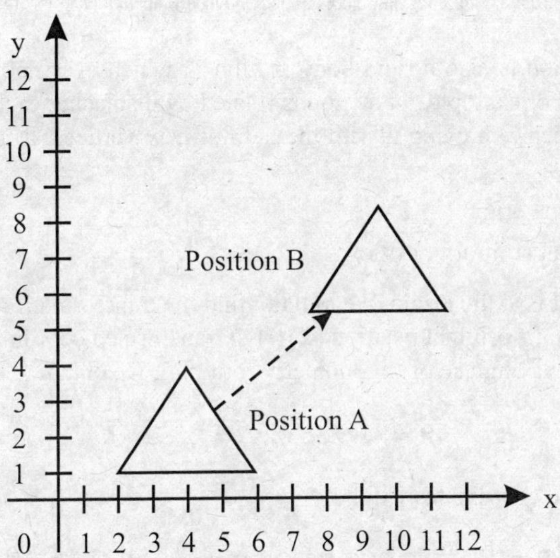

Figure 5.2 Translating an Object from Position A to B

3. Explain in detail 2D rotation with the help of an example.

or

Obtain a transformation matrix for rotating an object about a specified pivot point.

Ans. Rotation is a basic transformation which is applied to the objects (such as a point, straight-line segment, etc.) to change their position along a circular path in the xy plane. To perform rotation on objects, one needs to specify a **rotation angle** (θ) and the **rotation point** (also known as **pivot point**) as (x_r, y_r). Depending on the value of rotation angle an object can be rotated in anticlockwise or clockwise direction. If θ has a positive value, then the object will be rotated in anticlockwise direction about the pivot point (x_r, y_r), whereas for negative values, the object will be rotated in clockwise direction (as shown in Figure 5.3). Pivot point indicates the point about which the object needs to be rotated. One can also describe this translation as a rotation about a rotation axis which is perpendicular to the xy plane.

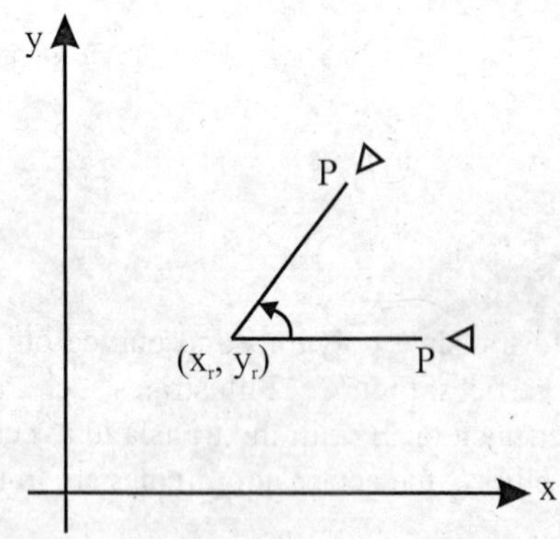

Figure 5.3 Rotating an Object through an Angle θ about a Pivot Point (x_r, y_r)

Like translation, rotation is also a rigid-body motion in which every point on an object is rotated through the same angle. For example, a polygon is rotated by displacing each vertex through the specified rotation angle and then redrawing it with the help of new vertices. Rotation can be implemented when:

(a) the pivot point is at the origin.

(b) the pivot point is at an arbitrary position.

(a) When the pivot point is at the origin, we initially find the transformation Equations of a point which is rotated from its original position (x, y) to transformed coordinate (x′, y′) (see Figure 5.4). Therefore, by making use of trigonometry formulas, we obtain x and y as follows:

$$x = r\cos\phi,\ y = r\sin\phi \tag{1}$$

Similarly, the transformed coordinates will be:

$$\begin{aligned} x' &= r\cos(\phi+\theta) = r\cos\phi\cos\theta - r\sin\phi\sin\theta \\ y' &= r\sin(\phi+\theta) = r\cos\phi\sin\theta + r\sin\phi\cos\theta \end{aligned} \tag{2}$$

where r denotes the constant distance of the point from the origin, θ denotes the rotation angle, and ϕ denotes the original angular position of the point from the x-axis.

By substituting the values in Equation (1) in Equation (2), we get the transformation Equations for rotating a point (x, y) through an angle about the origin:

$$\begin{aligned} x' &= x\cos\theta - y\sin\theta \\ y' &= x\sin\theta + y\cos\theta \end{aligned} \tag{3}$$

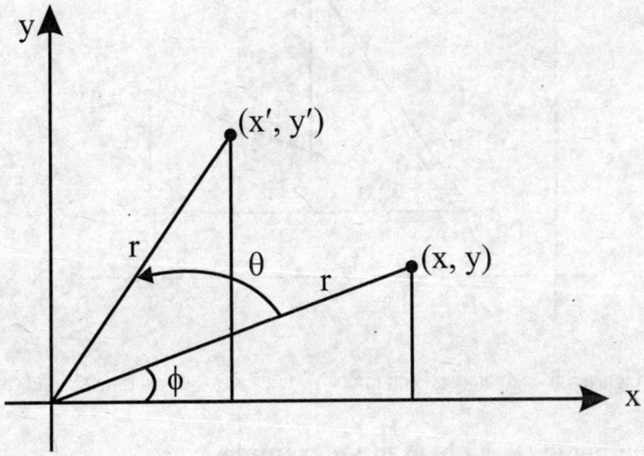

Figure 5.4 Rotating a Point through an Angle θ about the Origin

Like translation, we also express Equation (3) in the column-vector matrix form as follows:

$$P' = R \cdot P \tag{4}$$

where R is the rotation matrix and is represented as follows:

$$R = \begin{bmatrix} \cos\theta & -\sin\theta \\ \sin\theta & \cos\theta \end{bmatrix} \tag{5}$$

In the case of row-vector representation, the rotation Equation is obtained by transposing the matrix product of Equation (4). That is,

$$\begin{aligned} P'^T &= (R \cdot P)^T \\ &= P^T \cdot R^T \end{aligned}$$

where $P^T = [x\ y]$ and R^T is obtained by simply interchanging rows and columns of matrix R as given in Equation(5).

(b) When the pivot point is at an arbitrary position, say (x_r, y_r), we need to determine the transformation Equations for rotation of a point about this specified position (see Figure 5.5). This can be done by generalizing Equation (3) and including additive terms and multiplicative factors on the coordinate values, as follows:

$$x' = x_r + (x - x_r)\cos\theta - (y - y_r)\sin\theta$$
$$y' = y_r + (x - x_r)\sin\theta + (y - y_r)\cos\theta$$

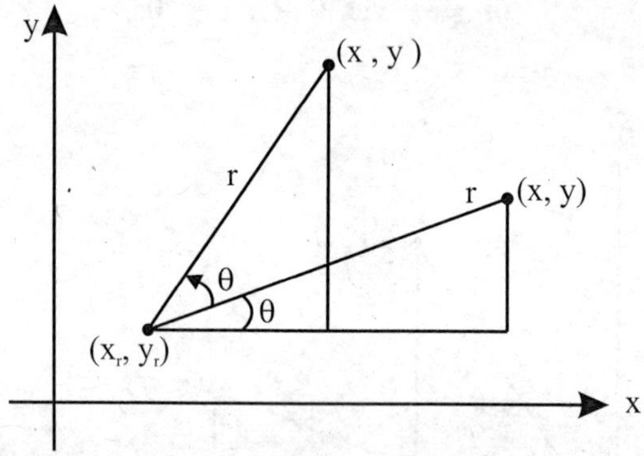

Figure 5.5 Rotating a Point through an Angle θ about Rotation Point (x_r, y_r)

4. Illustrate 2D scaling with the help of an example.

Ans. Scaling is a basic transformation that changes or alters the size of an object. If scaling is performed on polygons, the coordinate values (x, y) of each vertex are multiplied by **scaling factors** s_x and s_y to produce the transformed coordinates (x', y') as follows:

$$x' = x \cdot s_x, \qquad y' = y \cdot s_y \tag{1}$$

As the symbol suggests, s_x scales an object in the x-direction while s_y scales an object in the y-direction. We can assign any positive numerical value to the scaling factors s_x and s_y, which in turn scales an object accordingly. Values less than 1 reduce the object size, and values greater than 1 enlarge the object size, while value 1 given to both s_x and s_y leave the object size unchanged.

Equation (1) can also be written in the following column-vector matrix form:

That is,

$$P' = S \cdot P,$$
$$\begin{bmatrix} x' \\ y' \end{bmatrix} = \begin{bmatrix} s_x & 0 \\ 0 & s_y \end{bmatrix} \cdot \begin{bmatrix} x \\ y \end{bmatrix} \tag{2}$$

Here, S is a 2×2 **scaling matrix**.

If equal values are assigned to both s_x and s_y, then a **uniform scaling** is produced, which maintains relative object proportions. In case unequal values are assigned to s_x and s_y, then **differential scaling** is produced. Such scaling has a great deal of use in design applications where initially pictures are built using a few basic shapes which are later adjusted using scaling and positioning transformations. For example, in Figure 5.6 a square is changed to a rectangle with scaling factors $s_x=2$ and $s_y=1$.

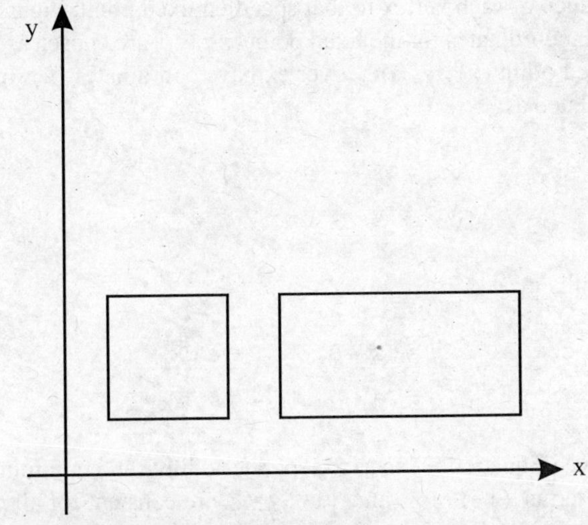

Figure 5.6 Differential Scaling with $s_x = 2$ and $s_y = 1$

Note that scaling not only changes the size of the object, but also repositions it from the origin. For example, in Figure 5.7, when value 2 is assigned to both s_x and s_y, both the size and the distance of the square from the origin are increased by a factor of 2. If the values of scaling factors are less than 1, the objects will move closer to the origin; whereas values greater than 1 will move the objects farther from the origin.

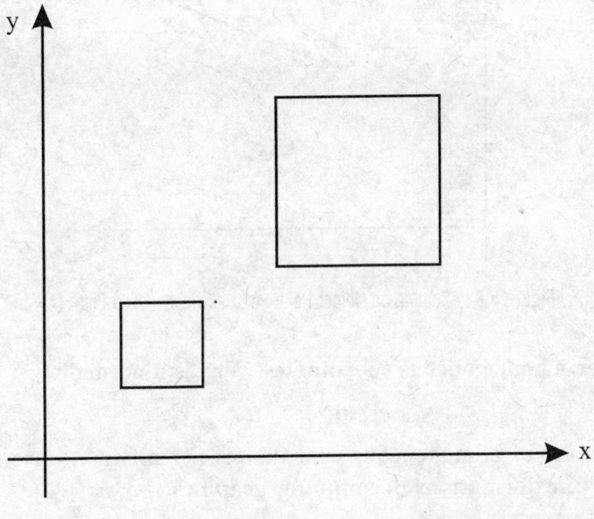

Figure 5.7 Object Scaled with $s_x = s_y = 2$ is Increased in Size and Moved Farther from the Coordinate Origin

If you do not want to reposition the object, then you can choose a fixed point (x_f, y_f) that will remain unchanged even after the scaling transformation. The fixed point could be chosen as one of the vertices or centroid of an object, or any other position. Now, the object is scaled relative to the fixed point by scaling the distance of each vertex to that specified fixed point. Figure 5.8 illustrates the scaling of a polygon in which coordinates for the fixed point (x_f, y_f) are chosen as an arbitrary point. Now, with reference to the fixed point (x_f, y_f), let a vertex have coordinates (x, y), then its scaled coordinates (x', y') are calculated as:

$$\begin{aligned} x' &= x_f + (x - x_f)\, s_x \\ y' &= y_f + (y - y_f)\, s_y \end{aligned} \tag{3}$$

Solving Equation (3) results in:

$$\begin{aligned} x' &= x \cdot s_x + (1 - s_x)x_f \\ y' &= y \cdot s_y + (1 - s_y)y_f \end{aligned}$$

Note that we have solved Equation (3) so as to separate additive and multiplicative terms. The reason for doing this is that the terms $(1-S_x)\, x_f$ and $(1-S_y)\, y_f$ are constant for all points in the object, and hence reducing the calculation tasks to a large extent.

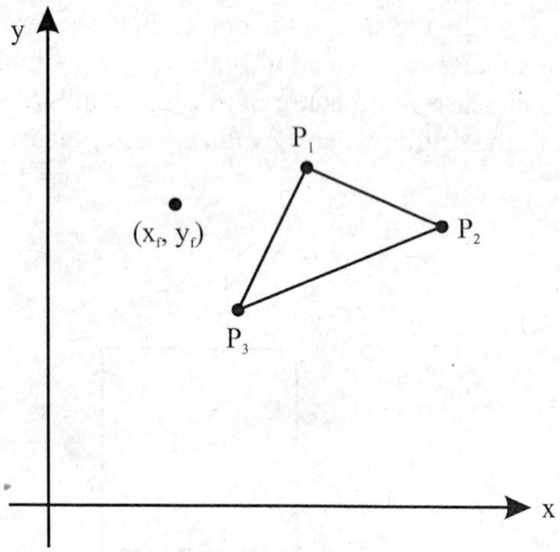

Figure 5.8 Scaling an Object Relative to a Chosen Fixed Point (x_f, y_f)

5. Explain the term homogeneous coordinates. Why is it needed?

or

Discuss how the use of homogeneous coordinates permits us to use efficient computing of geometrical transformations in computer graphics.

Ans. In general, most of the graphics applications, such as design and picture construction applications, involve sequence of geometric transformations. For example, an animation sequence may consist of scaling followed by rotation and then translation. One way to produce such a sequence is to use the general matrix form for each of the basic transformations, which is as follows:

$$P' = M_1 \cdot P + M_2 \tag{1}$$

where P and P′ are represented as column vectors, M_1 is a 2×2 matrix containing multiplicative factors, and M_2 is a two-element column matrix containing translation terms. However, this approach requires a lot of computation time as the transformed coordinates must be calculated one step at a time. That is, first the scaled coordinates need to be calculated, which are then rotated, and finally the rotated coordinates are translated.

To reduce the computation time, we can use a more efficient approach in which the transformations are combined in such a way that the final coordinate positions are obtained directly from the initial coordinates, without requiring to calculate the intermediate coordinate values. For this, Equation (1) is reformulated so as to eliminate the matrix addition associated with the translation terms in M_2. The basic idea behind this approach is to combine the multiplicative and translation terms into a single matrix by expanding all 2×2 matrices into 3×3 matrices including the matrices for coordinate positions. This allows us to express all transformation Equations in terms of matrix multiplications. For this, we represent each Cartesian coordinate position (x, y) with the **homogeneous-coordinate** triple (x_h, y_h, h), where

$$x_h = x.h, \qquad y_h = y.h$$

Here, h is known as the **homogeneous parameter**. It can be set to any nonzero value, which results in an infinite number of equivalent homogeneous representations. However, for simplicity we set h = 1. Thus, the homogeneous-coordinate triple now becomes $(x_h, y_h, 1)$. Higher values of h can be set in matrix formulations of 3D viewing transformations.

6. Give the homogeneous coordinates for translation, rotation, and scaling.

Ans. In homogeneous coordinate's representation, transformation operations are represented as 3×3 matrices, while its original and transformed coordinates are represented as 1×3 matrices. Thus, **translation** transformation can be expressed in the form of matrix multiplication as follows:

$$\begin{bmatrix} x' \\ y' \\ 1 \end{bmatrix} = \begin{bmatrix} 1 & 0 & t_x \\ 0 & 1 & t_y \\ 0 & 0 & 1 \end{bmatrix} \cdot \begin{bmatrix} x \\ y \\ 1 \end{bmatrix}$$

which can be abbreviated as:

$$P' = T(t_x, t_y) \cdot P$$

where $T(t_x, t_y)$ is a 3×3 translation matrix with t_x and t_y as the translation parameters. To obtain the inverse of the translation matrix, parameters t_x and t_y are replaced by $-t_x$ and $-t_y$ respectively.

In a similar way, **rotation** about the coordinate origin can be expressed in the form of matrix multiplication as follows:

$$\begin{bmatrix} x' \\ y' \\ 1 \end{bmatrix} = \begin{bmatrix} \cos\theta & -\sin\theta & 0 \\ \sin\theta & \cos\theta & 0 \\ 0 & 0 & 1 \end{bmatrix} \cdot \begin{bmatrix} x \\ y \\ 1 \end{bmatrix}$$

which can be abbreviated as :

$$P' = R(\theta) \cdot P$$

where $R(\theta)$ is a 3×3 rotation matrix with θ as the rotation parameter; and to obtain its inverse, parameter θ is replaced by $-\theta$.

Scaling about the coordinate origin can be expressed in the form of matrix multiplication as follows:

$$\begin{bmatrix} x' \\ y' \\ 1 \end{bmatrix} = \begin{bmatrix} s_x & 0 & 0 \\ 0 & s_y & 0 \\ 0 & 0 & 1 \end{bmatrix} \cdot \begin{bmatrix} x \\ y \\ 1 \end{bmatrix}$$

which can be abbreviated as:

$$P' = S(s_x, s_y) \cdot P$$

where $S(s_x, s_y)$ is a 3×3 scaling matrix with s_x and s_y as the scaling parameters; and its inverse is obtained by replacing s_x and s_y with their multiplicative inverses $1/s_x$ and $1/s_y$ respectively.

7. What is composite transformation matrix? Explain it with suitable equations for translation, scaling and rotation.

Ans. A matrix which is obtained by multiplying the matrices of any two individual transformations is known as a **composite transformation matrix** and the process is known as **composition** or **concatenation of matrices.** Composite transformations for translation, rotation and scaling are calculated as follows:

- **Translation:** If any two successive translation vectors, say, (t_{x1}, t_{y1}) and (t_{x2}, t_{y2}) are applied to a coordinate position P, the resulting or final transformed location (P')is calculated as:

$$\begin{aligned} P' &= T(t_{x2}, t_{y2}) \cdot \{T(t_{x1}, t_{y1}) \cdot P\} \\ &= \{T(t_{x2}, t_{y2}) \cdot T(t_{x1}, t_{y1})\} \cdot P \end{aligned}$$

where P and P' are homogeneous-coordinate column vectors.

Thus, the composite transformation matrix for such translation sequence is:

$$\begin{bmatrix} 1 & 0 & t_{x2} \\ 0 & 1 & t_{y2} \\ 0 & 0 & 1 \end{bmatrix} \cdot \begin{bmatrix} 1 & 0 & t_{x1} \\ 0 & 1 & t_{y1} \\ 0 & 0 & 1 \end{bmatrix} = \begin{bmatrix} 1 & 0 & t_{x1} + t_{x2} \\ 0 & 1 & t_{y1} + t_{y2} \\ 0 & 0 & 1 \end{bmatrix}$$

which can be abbreviated as:

$$T(t_{x2}, t_{y2}) \cdot T(t_{x1}, t_{y1}) = T(t_{x1} + t_{x2}, t_{y1} + t_{y2}) \qquad (1)$$

It is clear from Equation (1) that two successive translations are additive in nature. Thus, the final translated coordinates can be calculated with the composite translated matrix. That is,

$$P' = T(t_{x1} + t_{x2}, t_{y1} + t_{y2}) . P$$

- **Rotation:** If two successive rotations are applied to a point P, the resulting transformed position P′ is calculated as:

$$\begin{aligned} P' &= R(\theta_2) \cdot \{R(\theta_1) \cdot P\} \\ &= \{R(\theta_2) \cdot R(\theta_1)\} \cdot P \end{aligned}$$

By multiplying the two rotation matrices, we can easily verify that the two successive rotations are additive in nature. That is,

$$R(\theta_2) \cdot R(\theta_1) = R(\theta_1 + \theta_2)$$

Thus, the final rotated coordinates can be calculated with the composite rotation matrix as follows:

$$P' = R(\theta_1 + \theta_2) \cdot P \qquad (2)$$

- **Scaling:** If two successive scaling vectors, say, (s_{x1}, s_{y1}) and (s_{x2}, s_{y2}) are applied to a point P, the resulting transformed position P′ is calculated as:

$$\begin{aligned} P' &= S(s_{x1}, s_{y1}) . \{S(s_{x2}, s_{y2})\} .P) \\ &= \{S(s_{x1}, s_{y1}) . S(s_{x2}, s_{y2})\} .P \end{aligned}$$

The composite scaling matrix for two successive scaling operations is obtained as follows:

$$\begin{bmatrix} s_{x2} & 0 & 0 \\ 0 & s_{y2} & 0 \\ 0 & 0 & 1 \end{bmatrix} \begin{bmatrix} s_{x1} & 0 & 0 \\ 0 & s_{y1} & 0 \\ 0 & 0 & 1 \end{bmatrix} = \begin{bmatrix} s_{x1} \cdot s_{x2} & 0 & 0 \\ 0 & s_{y1} \cdot s_{y2} & 0 \\ 0 & 0 & 1 \end{bmatrix}$$

which can be abbreviated as:

$$S(s_{x2}, s_{y2}) \cdot S(s_{x1} \cdot s_{y1}) = S(s_{x1} \cdot s_{x2}, s_{y1} \cdot s_{y2}) \qquad (3)$$

It is clear from Equation (3) that successive scaling operations are multiplicative in nature.

To understand the concept of composite translation, rotation and scaling transformations, consider an object on which these transformations are to be applied. Suppose we want to move the object by two points from the current position twice in succession, then the final displacement of the object would be four points (2+2) from the original position. That is, the two successive translations are added. Similarly, if we want to rotate the object 45° in clockwise direction twice in succession, then the final rotation would be 90° from the original position. Thus, in this case also, the successive rotations are added.

Now, suppose we want to triple the size of the object twice in succession, the final size would be nine times (3*3) that of the original. It indicates that the successive scaling operations are multiplicative in nature.

8. If a graphics package provides only a rotate function with respect to the coordinate origin, is it possible to rotate an object with respect to any other pivot point? If yes, write the steps to perform this rotation.

Ans. If a graphics package provides only a rotate function with respect to the coordinate origin, then also we can rotate an object with respect to any other pivot point, say, (x_r, y_r). This can be achieved by performing the sequence of 'translate–rotate–inverse translate' operations as follows (see Figure 5.9):

1. **Translate:** In this operation, translation of an object is performed in such a way that the pivot-point-position is moved to the origin. (see Figure 5.9b).
2. **Rotate:** In this operation, the object is rotated about the coordinate origin as shown in Figure 5.9 (c).
3. **Inverse translate:** In this operation, the object is translated in such a manner that the pivot point will return to its original position (see Figure 5.9d).

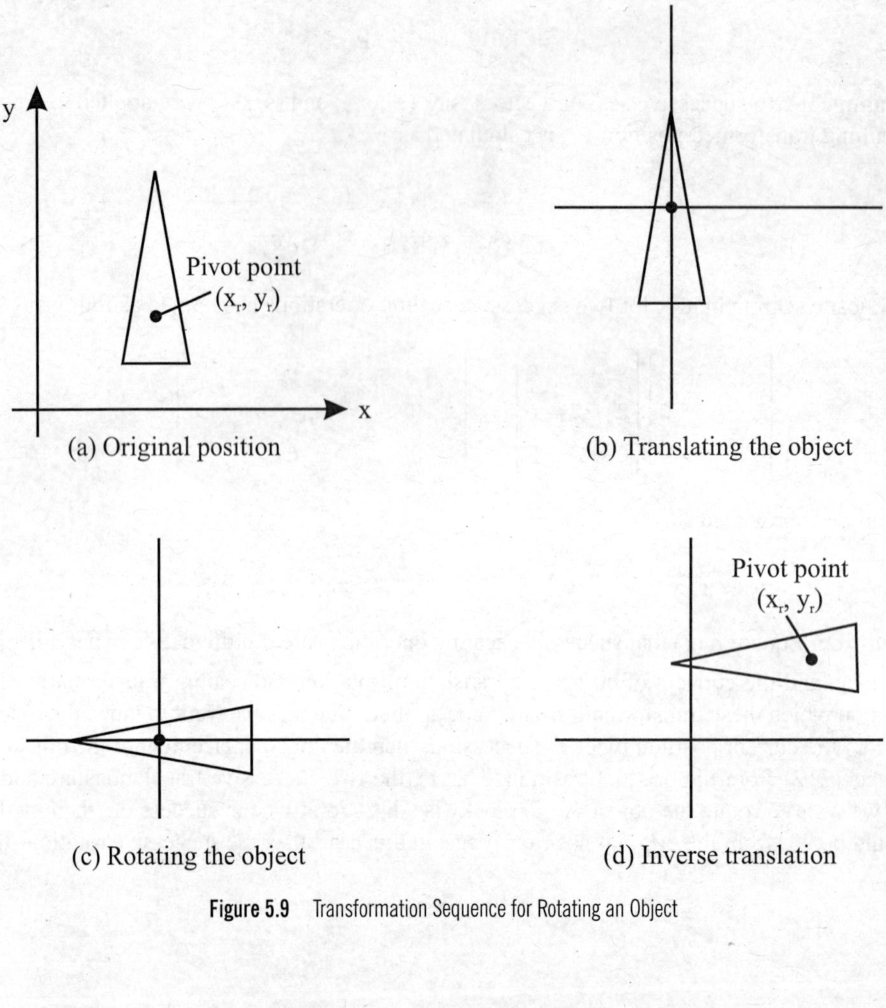

Figure 5.9 Transformation Sequence for Rotating an Object

The composite transformation matrix for such sequence of operations is obtained by concatenating the three transformation operation matrices as follows:

$$\begin{bmatrix} 1 & 0 & x_r \\ 0 & 1 & y_r \\ 0 & 0 & 1 \end{bmatrix} \cdot \begin{bmatrix} \cos\theta & -\sin\theta & 0 \\ \sin\theta & \cos\theta & 0 \\ 0 & 0 & 1 \end{bmatrix} \cdot \begin{bmatrix} 1 & 0 & -x_r \\ 0 & 1 & -y_r \\ 0 & 0 & 1 \end{bmatrix}$$

This will result in the following matrix:

$$\begin{bmatrix} \cos\theta & -\sin\theta & x_r(1-\cos\theta) + y_r \sin\theta \\ \sin\theta & \cos\theta & y_r(1-\cos\theta) - x_r \sin\theta \\ 0 & 0 & 1 \end{bmatrix}$$

which can be abbreviated as follows:

$$T(x_r, y_r) \cdot R(\theta) \cdot T(-x_r, -y_r) = R(x_r, y_r, \theta)$$

where

$$T(-x_r, -y_r) = T^{-1}(x_r, y_r)$$

9. If a graphics package provides a function that can scale an object with respect to the coordinate origin, how can we scale an object with respect to any other fixed point?

Ans. If a graphics package provides a function that can scale an object with respect to the coordinate origin, then also we can scale an object with respect to any other fixed point, say, (x_f, y_f). This can be achieved by performing the sequence of 'translate–scale–inverse translate' operations as follows (see Figure 5.10):

1. **Translate:** In this operation, the object is translated in order to make the fixed point coincide with the coordinate origin as shown in Figure 5.10b.
2. **Scale:** In this operation, the object is scaled with respect to the coordinate origin as shown in Figure 5.10c.
3. **Inverse translate:** In this operation, the inverse translation of step 1 is performed so that the object returns to its original position as shown in Figure 5.10d.

The composite transformation matrix for such sequence of operations is obtained by concatenating the three transformation matrices as follows:

$$\begin{bmatrix} 1 & 0 & x_f \\ 0 & 1 & y_f \\ 0 & 0 & 1 \end{bmatrix} \cdot \begin{bmatrix} s_x & 0 & 0 \\ 0 & s_y & 0 \\ 0 & 0 & 1 \end{bmatrix} \cdot \begin{bmatrix} 1 & 0 & -x_f \\ 0 & 1 & -y_f \\ 0 & 0 & 1 \end{bmatrix} = \begin{bmatrix} s_x & 0 & x_f(1-s_x) \\ 0 & s_y & y_f(1-s_y) \\ 0 & 0 & 1 \end{bmatrix}$$

which can be abbreviated as:

$$T(x_f, y_f) \cdot S(s_x, s_y) \cdot T(-x_f, -y_f) = S(x_f, y_f, s_x, s_y)$$

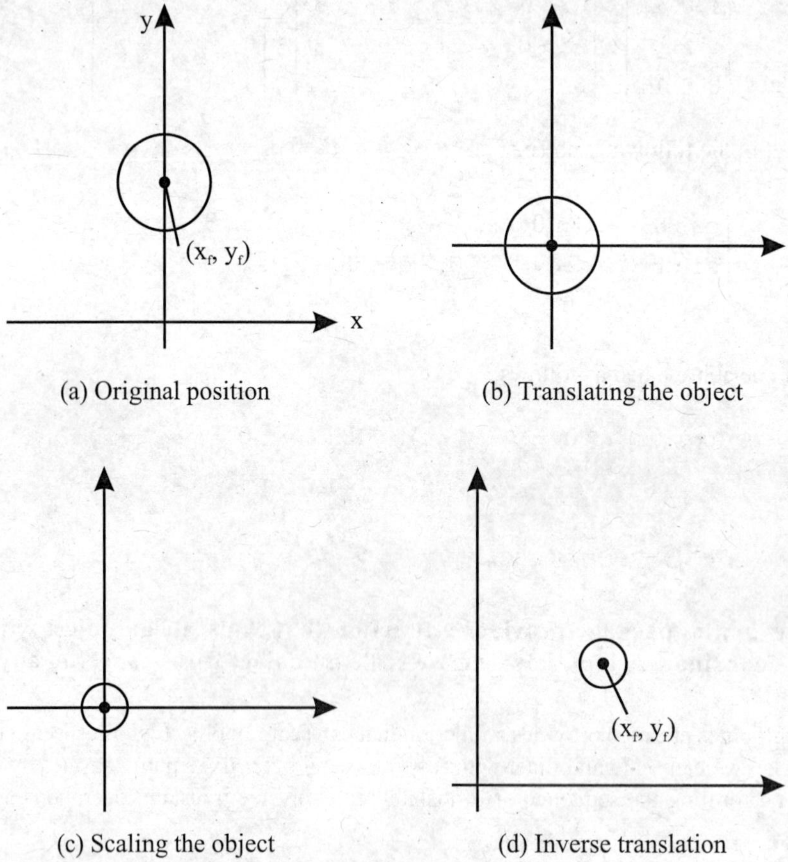

Figure 5.10 Transformation Sequence for Scaling an Object

Note that the systems which provide scale function for the coordinates of the fixed point generate such transformation automatically.

10. Explain reflection and shearing about x-axis and y-axis. Represent these transformations with the help of matrices and diagrams.

Ans. Besides the basic transformations, there are two more additional transformations, namely, *reflection* and *shear*, which are included in some graphics packages. These two transformations are discussed as follows:

Reflection

This transformation produces a mirror image of a 2D object. That is, an object is rotated by 180° with respect to the axis of reflection which can be either in the xy plane or perpendicular to the xy plane so as to generate the mirror image of an object. When the reflection axis is in the xy plane, the rotation path about this axis will be in a plane perpendicular to the xy plane. On the other hand, when the reflection axis is perpendicular to the xy plane, the rotation path will lie in the xy plane. Some of the reflection transformations in different situations are explained as follows:

Case 1: Reflecting an object about the x-axis, that is, about the line y=0.
In this case, the values of x coordinates remain the same, only the y values get flipped (see Figure 5.11). The transformation matrix for such case is as follows:

$$\begin{bmatrix} 1 & 0 & 0 \\ 0 & -1 & 0 \\ 0 & 0 & 1 \end{bmatrix}$$

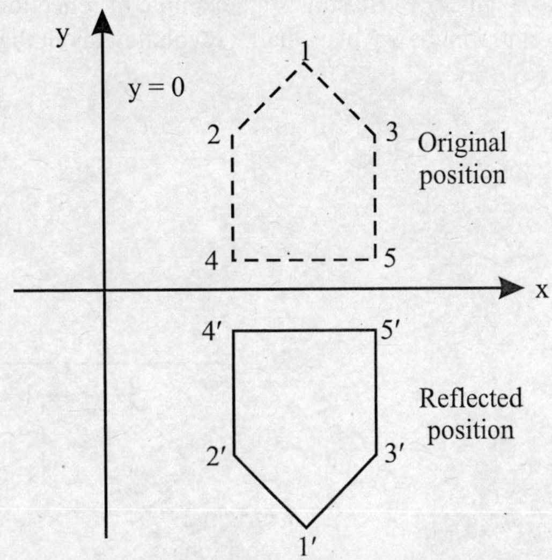

Figure 5.11 Reflecting an Object about the x -axis

Case 2: Reflecting an object about the y-axis, that is, about the line x=0.
In this case, the values of y coordinates remain the same, only the x values get flipped (see Figure 5.12). The transformation matrix for such case is as follows:

$$\begin{bmatrix} -1 & 0 & 0 \\ 0 & 1 & 0 \\ 0 & 0 & 1 \end{bmatrix}$$

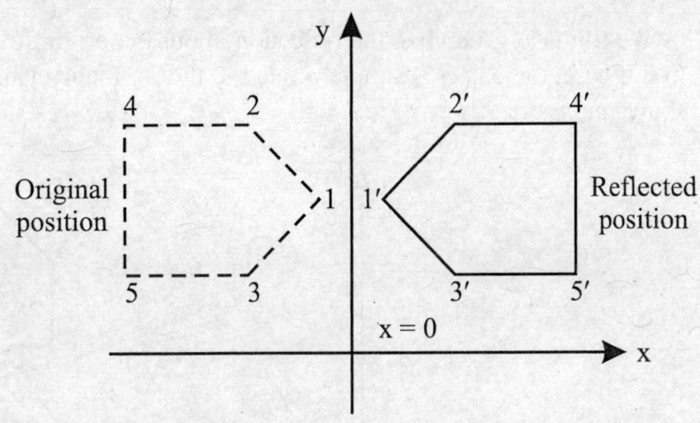

Figure 5.12 Reflecting an Object about the Origin the y -axis

Case 3: Reflecting an object relative to an axis that is perpendicular to the xy plane.
In this case both the x and y coordinates are flipped. Such kind of reflection is implemented with respect to the coordinate origin whose transformation matrix (R(θ), where θ=180°) is represented as follows:

$$\begin{bmatrix} -1 & 0 & 0 \\ 0 & -1 & 0 \\ 0 & 0 & 1 \end{bmatrix}$$

Figure 5.13 illustrates an example of reflection about the origin. In this figure, the object is simply rotated in the xy plane half a revolution about the origin.

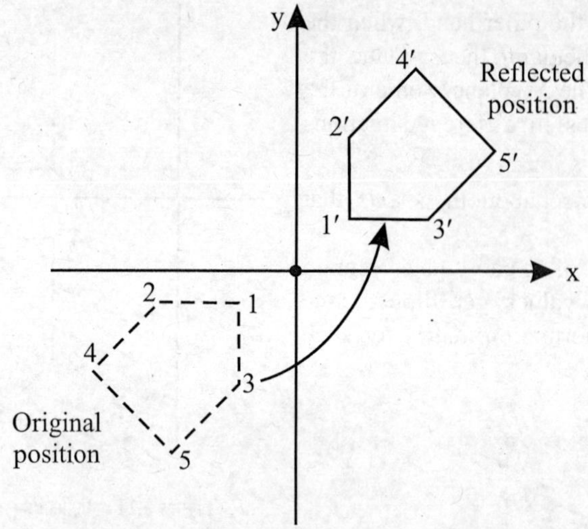

Figure 5.13 Reflecting an Object about the Origin

We can also generalize the reflection about the origin to any reflection point P_{ref} in the xy plane. In this case, the object is simply rotated in the xy plane using the reflection point as the pivot point as shown in Figure 5.14.

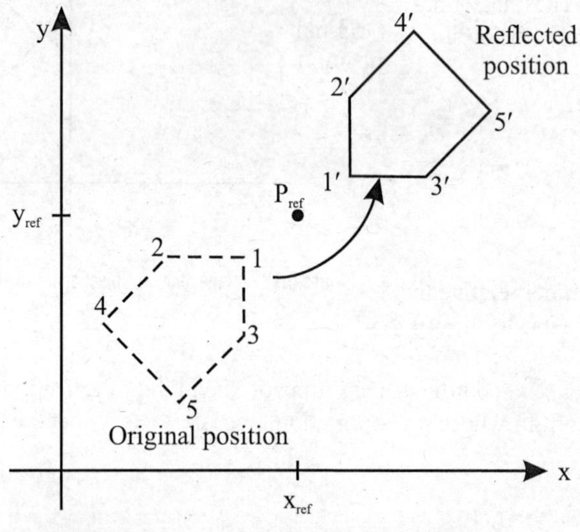

Figure 5.14 Reflecting an Object about a Point P_{ref}

Case 4: Reflecting an object about the diagonal line y=x (see Figure 5.15).
Such a reflection can be produced by performing a sequence of transformations.

One possible sequence is illustrated in Figure 5.16. First, the line y=x is rotated clockwise by 45° onto the x-axis. Then, reflection about the x-axis is performed and finally, anticlockwise rotation by 45° is performed so that the line y=x back to its original position. The transformation matrix representation for such case of reflection is as follows:

$$\begin{bmatrix} 0 & 1 & 0 \\ 1 & 0 & 0 \\ 0 & 0 & 1 \end{bmatrix}$$

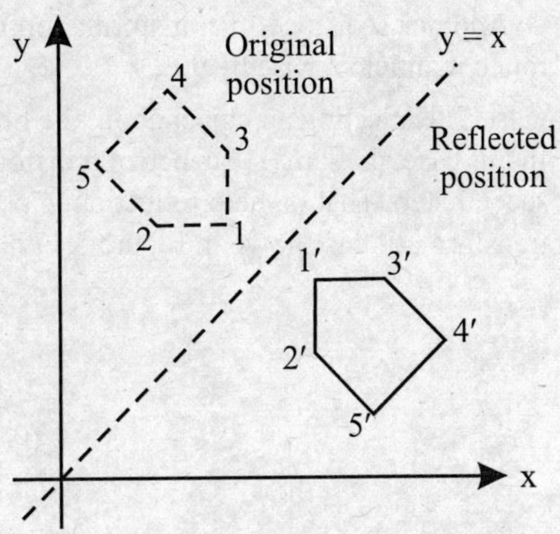

Figure 5.15 Reflecting an Object about the line y=x

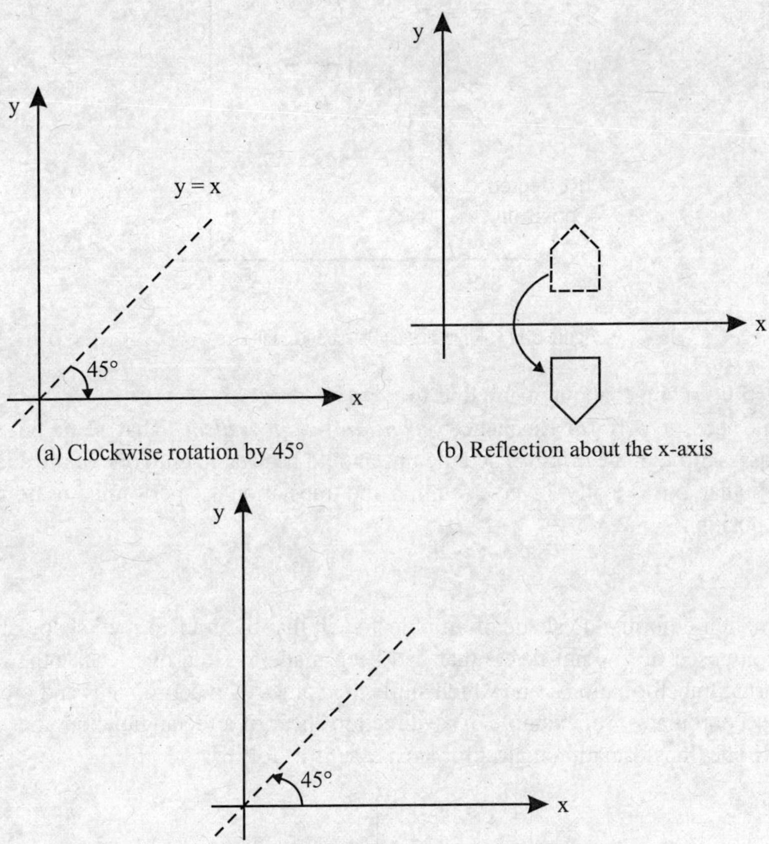

(a) Clockwise rotation by 45°

(b) Reflection about the x-axis

(c) Counterclockwise rotation by 45°

Figure 5.16 Sequence of Transformation to Achieve Reflection about the Line y=x

Another sequence of transformation could be to first reflect the object about the x-axis and then rotate it anticlockwise by 90°.

Case 5: Reflecting an object about the line y=−x.
In this case, the same sequence of transformations is performed as in case 4 except for implementing the second step. That is, here reflection is performed about the y-axis instead of the x-axis. The resulting transformation is shown in Figure 5.17 and the transformation matrix is represented as follows:

$$\begin{bmatrix} 0 & -1 & 0 \\ -1 & 0 & 0 \\ 0 & 0 & 1 \end{bmatrix}$$

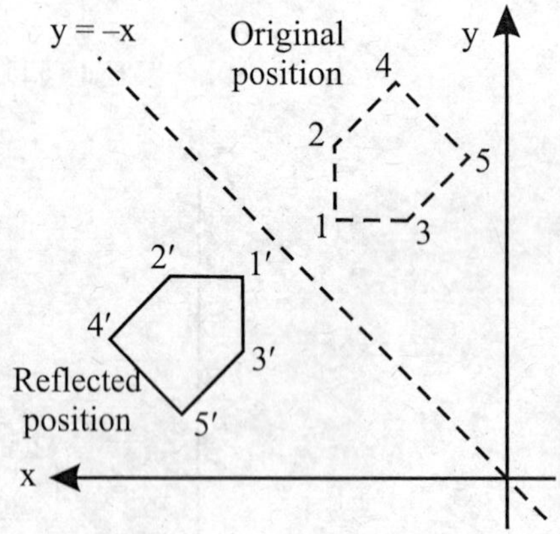

Figure 5.17 Reflecting an Object about the Line y = - x

Case 6: Reflecting an object about at any line y=mx+b in the xy plane.
In this case, one needs to perform a sequence: *'translate–rotate–reflect'*. That is, the line is first translated so that it passes through the origin. Then the line should be rotated onto one of the axes and reflected about that particular axis. Finally, inverse rotation and translation are performed to bring the line back to its original position.

Shear

This transformation deforms the shape of an object such that the transformed shape appears as if the object were composed of internal layers that had been made to slide over each other. There are two common shearing transformations: one which shifts the values of x coordinates and other which shifts the values of y coordinates. An example of x−direction shear of a rectangle about the x-axis is shown in Figure 5.18. The transformation matrix for such case is as follows:

$$\begin{bmatrix} 1 & sh_x & 0 \\ 0 & 1 & 0 \\ 0 & 0 & 1 \end{bmatrix}$$

where sh_x is the shear parameter which can be assigned any real number.

Thus, the matrix obtained in Equation (1) transforms the original coordinate positions x and y into x' and y' as follows:

$$x' = x + sh_x.y, \qquad y'=y \qquad (2)$$

Equation (2) indicates that a coordinate position x is shifted in horizontal direction by the quantity proportional to its perpendicular distance (y value) from the x-axis, whereas y position remains unchanged. Assigning positive values to sh_x shifts the coordinate positions to the right, whereas negative values shift the coordinate positions to the left. For example, in Figure 5.18, applying shear transformation on a rectangle with positive value of sh_x transforms it into a parallelogram.

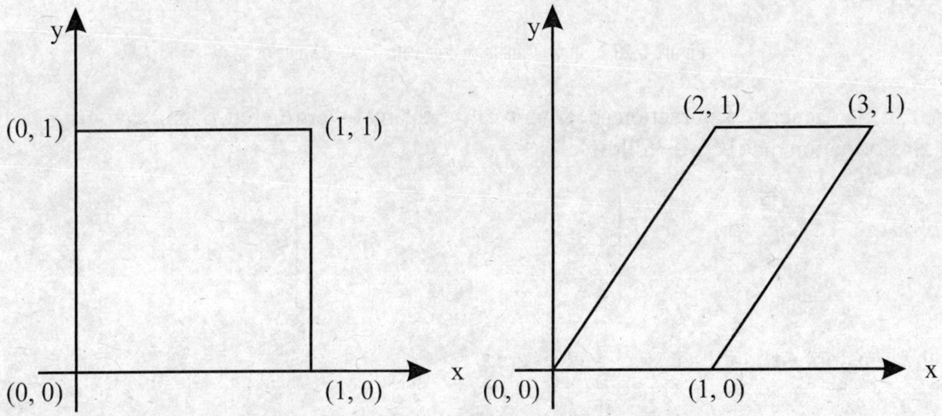

Figure 5.18 Shear Transformation with Positive Value of sh_x

An example of a y-direction shear for a rectangle about the y-axis is shown in Figure 5.19 whose transformation matrix is as follows:

$$\begin{bmatrix} 1 & 0 & 0 \\ sh_y & 1 & 0 \\ 0 & 0 & 1 \end{bmatrix}$$

where

sh_y is the shear parameter which can be assigned any real value. Here, the transformed coordinate positions x' and y' are:

$$x' = x$$
$$y' = y + sh_y \cdot x$$

In this case, the positive values of sh_y shift the coordinate positions in upward direction, whereas negative values shift the coordinate positions in downward direction.

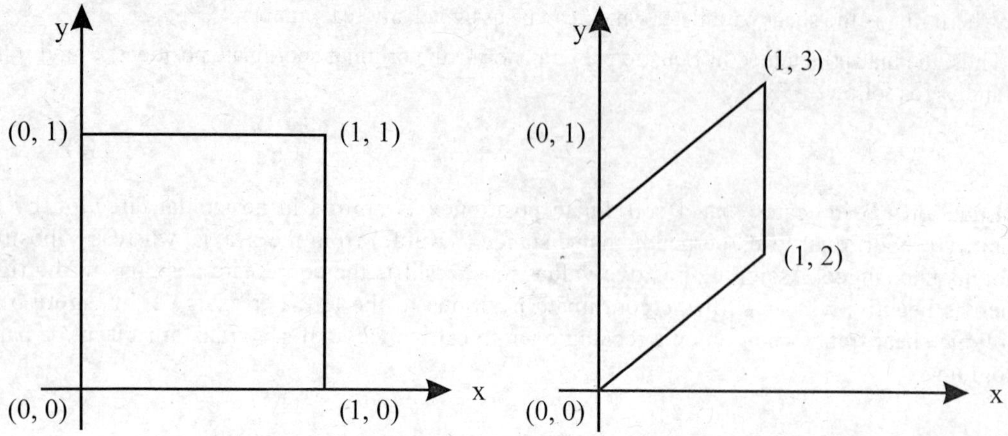

Figure 5.19 Shear Transformation with Positive Value of sh_y

One can also generate x-direction shearing relative to any other reference line, say, $y=y_{ref}$. In such case, transformation matrix is as follows:

$$\begin{bmatrix} 1 & sh_x & -sh_x.y_{ref} \\ 0 & 1 & 0 \\ 0 & 0 & 1 \end{bmatrix}$$

Now, the transformed coordinates x' and y' are:

$$x' = x + sh_x(y - y_{ref})$$
$$y' = y$$

In a similar way, one can also generate y−direction shearing relative to any other reference line, say, $x=x_{ref}$. In such case, the transformation matrix is as follows:

$$\begin{bmatrix} 1 & 0 & 0 \\ sh_y & 1 & -sh_y.x_{ref} \\ 0 & 0 & 1 \end{bmatrix}$$

Thus, the transformed coordinates x' and y' are:

$$x' = x$$
$$y' = y + sh_y(x - x_{ref})$$

11. How transformation between two Cartesian frames or systems can be done?

Ans. During various stages of scene processing, it is required to transform coordinate positions from one reference frame to another. For example, while displaying a scene on an output device it is required to transform object descriptions from world coordinates to device coordinates. Such transformations are performed by the viewing routines available in computer graphics applications. Similarly, for modelling and design applications, the local Cartesian references of individual objects must be transformed into positions and orientations within the overall scene coordinate system. To understand the transformations involved in converting from one 2D Cartesian frame to another, consider a Cartesian system x′y′ shown in Figure 5.20.

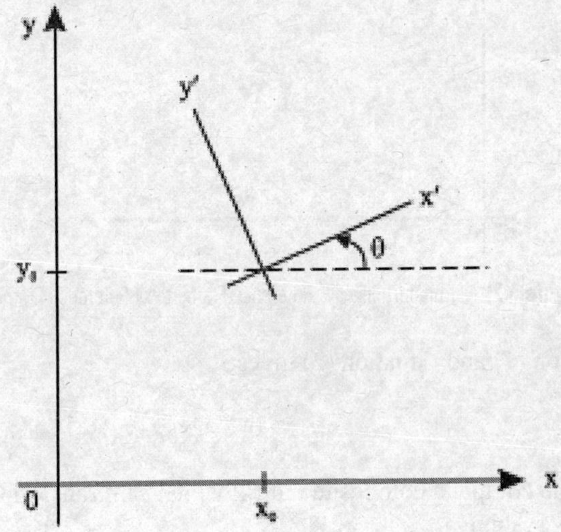

Figure 5.20 Cartesian x′y′ System Positioned at (x_0, y_0) with Respect to the xy System

This system is specified with coordinate origin (x_0, y_0) and orientation angle θ with reference to a Cartesian xy reference frame. Now, to convert object descriptions from xy coordinates to x′y′ coordinates, we need to perform a set of transformations that places the x′y′ axes over the xy axes. For this, the following steps need to be performed:

1. The origin (x_0, y_0) of the x′y′ system is translated so that it is moved to the origin (0,0) of the xy system (as shown in Figure 5.21). The translation matrix in this case is expressed as follows:

$$T(-x_0, -y_0) = \begin{bmatrix} 1 & 0 & -x_0 \\ 0 & 1 & -y_0 \\ 0 & 0 & 1 \end{bmatrix} \tag{1}$$

2. The x′-axis is rotated onto the x-axis. For example, in Figure 5.21, to get the axes of the two systems into coincidence, we perform the rotation in clockwise direction. The rotation matrix is expressed as follows:

$$R(-\theta) = \begin{bmatrix} \cos\theta & \sin\theta & 0 \\ -\sin\theta & \cos\theta & 0 \\ 0 & 0 & 1 \end{bmatrix} \tag{2}$$

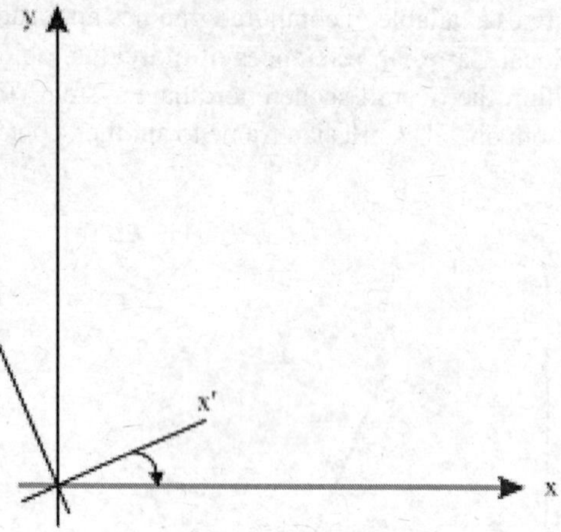

Figure 5.21 Transforming x'y' Reference Frame to xy Reference Frame

Now concatenating Equation (1) and Equation (2) gives:

$$M_{xy,x'y'} = R(-\theta)\,T(-x_0, -y_0) \tag{3}$$

Equation (3) gives us the complete composite matrix which can transform object descriptions from the xy system to the x′y′ system.

12. Write a short note on 2D affine transformations.

Ans. When transformed coordinate positions, x' and y', are represented in the following form, then such transformation is referred to as a **2D affine transformation**.

$$x' = a_{xx}x + a_{xy}y + b_x \tag{1}$$

$$y' = a_{yx}x + a_{yy}y + b_y \tag{2}$$

where x and y are the original coordinate positions of a system, x' and y' are the transformed coordinates—represented as the linear function of the original coordinates x and y, and a_{ij} and b_k are the constants determined by the type of transformation.

Affine transformations possess two important properties that parallel lines are transformed into parallel lines and finite points are mapped to finite points. All the five types of transformations, namely, translation, rotation, scaling, reflection, and shear are examples of affine transformations. Any affine transformation can be expressed as some composition of these five transformations. For example, the conversion of coordinate descriptions for a scene from one reference frame to another is a combination of translation and rotation. Hence, it is also an affine transformation. Note that when affine transformation involves only translation, rotation, and reflection, the line lengths and angles between any two lines are preserved even after transformation.

13. Describe raster methods for transforming the objects.

Ans. The capability of raster systems to store the pixel information in the form of pixel patterns in the frame buffer gives an alternative method for performing certain 2D transformations of objects. The basic transformations such as translation, rotation and scaling can be performed quickly and easily by manipulating an array of pixel values with the help of a few arithmetic operations. For example, the object translation can be performed rapidly by simply moving the rectangular arrays of stored pixel values from one location to another within the frame buffer. The raster functions that manipulate the rectangular array of pixel values are called **raster operations**. The operation of moving a block of pixels from one location to another is called a **block transfer** of pixel values. On bit-level systems, this operation is referred to as **bitBlt** or **bit-block transfer**, whereas on multi-level systems implementation of the same operation is referred to as **pixblt**.

The implementation of this method avoids the long procedure of calculating transformed coordinates and also applying scan conversion routines to each point of an object so that it can be displayed at a new position. However, a few arithmetic operations are needed to make the pixel transformation more efficiently. The three most common raster functions which are provided in graphics packages are as follows:

- **copy:** moves a block of pixels from one raster position to another.
- **read:** saves a block of pixels into an intended or designated array.
- **write:** transfers a block of pixels to a desired position in the frame buffer.

Whenever a block of pixel values is moved to a new location in the frame buffer, the simplest operation is to replace the old values with the new values. However, one can also use the Boolean operations AND, OR and Exclusive OR (XOR) and binary arithmetic operations to combine the pixel values. For example, with XOR operation, two successive copies of a block to the same raster area restore the original values. This technique helps in moving an object across a scene without destroying the background.

14. Discuss how raster systems perform the three basic transformations.

Ans. The raster systems perform the three basic transformations as follows:

Raster Translation

This is accomplished by copying a block of pixels onto the new location within the frame buffer. This is done by first reading the pixel intensities from the specified raster rectangular area into an array, and then copying that array back into the raster at a new location. Figure 5.22 illustrates such transformation in which coordinate positions P_{min} and P_{max} are the limits of the rectangular block to which it can be moved, and P_{drp} is the destination reference position.

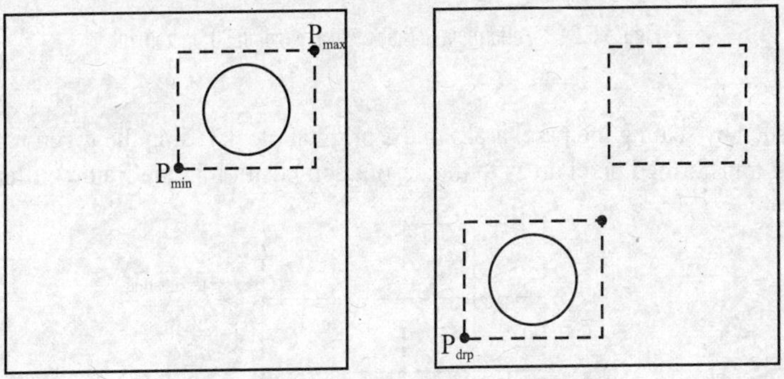

Figure 5.22 Raster Translation

Raster Rotation

The rotations in multiples of 90° can be easily performed with block transfers. For example, if we need to rotate an object by 90° counterclockwise, it can be accomplished by first reversing the pixel values in each row of the array, and then interchanging the rows and columns. Similarly, to obtain 180° rotation, we first reverse the order of the elements in each row of the array, and then we reverse the order of the rows. Figure 5.23 shows 90° and 180° rotations.

$$\begin{bmatrix} 1 & 2 & 3 \\ 4 & 5 & 6 \\ 7 & 8 & 9 \\ 10 & 11 & 12 \end{bmatrix} \qquad \begin{bmatrix} 3 & 6 & 9 & 12 \\ 2 & 5 & 8 & 11 \\ 1 & 4 & 7 & 10 \end{bmatrix} \qquad \begin{bmatrix} 12 & 11 & 10 \\ 9 & 8 & 7 \\ 6 & 5 & 4 \\ 3 & 2 & 1 \end{bmatrix}$$

(a) Original array orientation (b) Array orientation after 90° rotation (c) Array orientation after 180° rotation

Figure 5.23 Rotating an Array of Pixel Values in 90^{0} Increments

However, for performing rotations that are not in multiples of 90°, more computations are required. For this, the following steps need to be performed.

1. Each destination pixel area is mapped onto the rotated array.
2. The amount of overlap with the rotated pixel areas is calculated.
3. Intensity for the destination pixel is then computed by taking the average of intensities for the overlapped source pixels, weighted by their percentage of area overlap (see Figure 5.24).

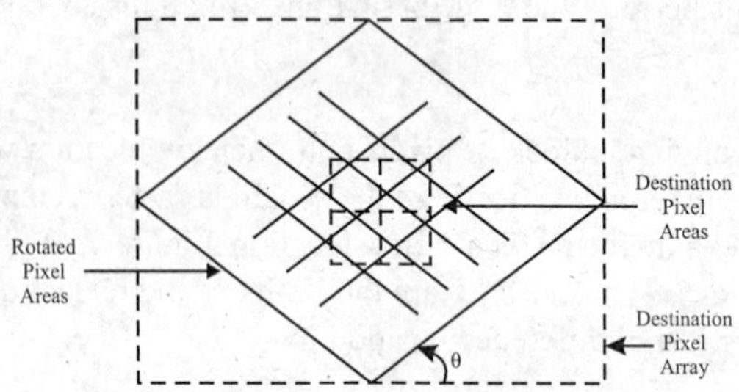

Figure 5.24 Performing Rotation which is not in 90^{0} Increments

Raster Scaling

This is accomplished by scaling the pixel areas in the original block (using the given values for s_x and s_y) and then mapping transformed pixel areas to the destination position in the frame buffer (see Figure 5.25).

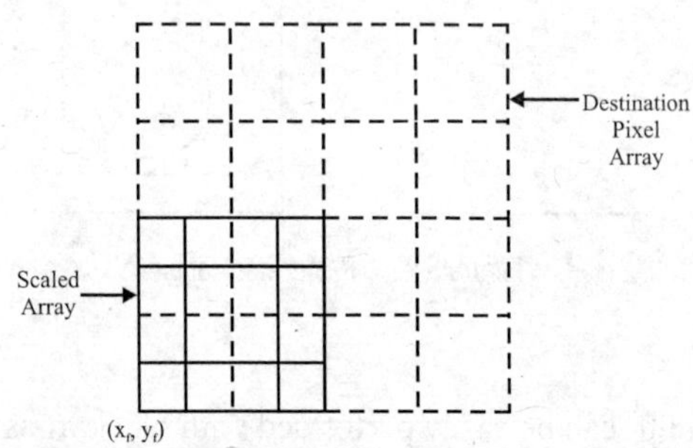

Figure 5.25 Raster Scaling

Finally, intensity of each destination pixel is assigned according to its area of overlap with the scaled pixel areas.

15. Explain the 2D viewing transformation pipeline.

Ans. The **2D viewing transformation** is the process of mapping a selected portion of a world-coordinate scene to device coordinates for displaying the views of a picture in an output device. The portion of a world-coordinate scene that has been selected for display is referred to as a **window**. The area on a display device to which a window is mapped is called a **viewport**. In simple words, a window defines what is to be viewed while a viewport defines the location where it is to be displayed. Hence, such type of mapping is sometimes also known as the **window-to-viewport transformation** or the **windowing transformation**. In general, windows and viewports are rectangular in shape with rectangle edges parallel to the coordinate axes. However, other shapes such as circles or any polygon shape can also be used as windows or viewports but these shapes take longer to process. Figure 5.26 demonstrates the viewing transformation in which a portion of a picture (within a rectangular window) is mapped onto an intended rectangular viewport.

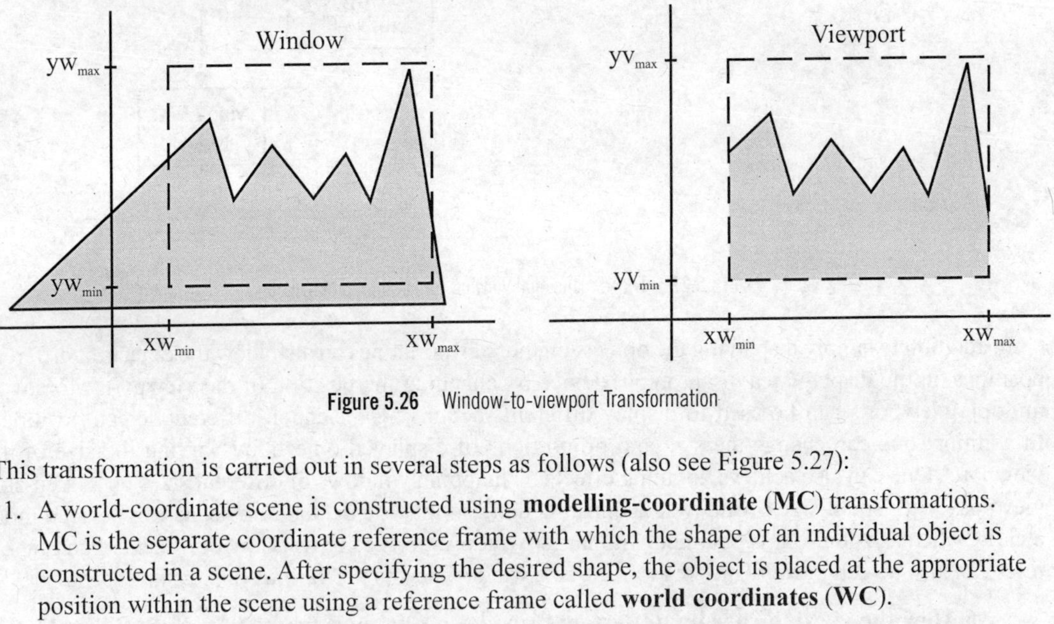

Figure 5.26 Window-to-viewport Transformation

This transformation is carried out in several steps as follows (also see Figure 5.27):

1. A world-coordinate scene is constructed using **modelling-coordinate** (**MC**) transformations. MC is the separate coordinate reference frame with which the shape of an individual object is constructed in a scene. After specifying the desired shape, the object is placed at the appropriate position within the scene using a reference frame called **world coordinates** (**WC**).
2. Now, a 2D **viewing-coordinate system** is set up in the world-coordinate plane and a window is defined in the viewing-coordinate system so as to obtain an arbitrary orientation for rectangular windows. After establishing the viewing reference frame, the descriptions in world coordinates are transformed into **viewing coordinates** (**VC**).
3. A viewport is then defined in normalized coordinates (that is, in the range from 0 to 1), and the VC description of the scene is mapped to **normalized viewing coordinates** (**NVC**). The normalized coordinates provide a means for making the viewing and other transformations independent of the requirements of any output device.
4. The contents of the normalized viewport are finally mapped to **device coordinates** (**DC**) after clipping (eliminating) the portions of picture that lie outside the viewport.

This whole procedure is known as the **2D viewing transformation pipeline**.

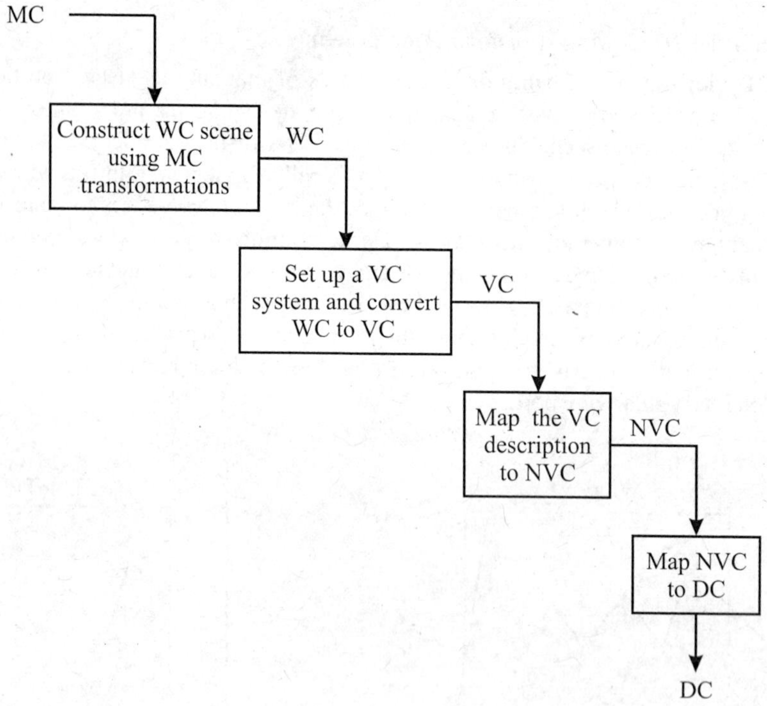

Figure 5.27 Two-dimensional Viewing Transformation Pipeline

In addition to simply displaying the objects on the viewport, one can also view the objects at different positions on the display area of an output device by changing the position of the viewport. Moreover, multiple viewports can be used to display different sections of a scene at different screen positions. In addition, one can change the size and proportions of displayed objects by varying the size of the viewports. One can also achieve zooming effects by mapping windows of different sizes on a fixed-size viewport. With small-sized windows, zoom-in is done so that the details of a scene can be seen more clearly, whereas zoom-out is obtained with larger windows to obtain overview of a scene. Panning effects can also be achieved by moving a fixed-size window across the various objects in a scene.

16. How the viewing-coordinate system provides a reference frame to specify the world-coordinate window?

Ans. For specifying the world-coordinate window, initially a viewing-coordinate origin is selected at some world position, say, at $P_0=(x_0, y_0)$. Then, we obtain the matrix for converting world-coordinate positions to viewing coordinates in the following two steps:

1. The viewing origin is translated into the world origin, and
2. The viewing-coordinate reference frame is rotated so that it gets aligned with world-coordinate reference frame (see Figure 5.28). Such 2D composite transformation is described as follows:

$$M_{WC,VC} = R.T$$

where T is the translation matrix that takes the viewing origin point P_0 to the world origin and R is the rotation matrix which aligns the two reference frames.

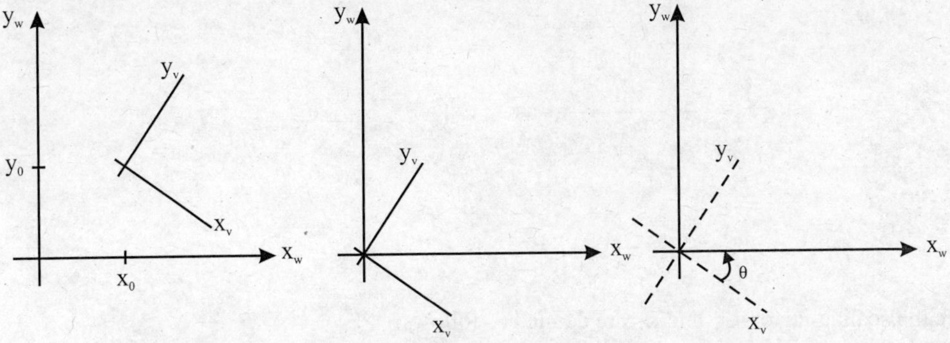

Figure 5.28 Moving the Viewing-coordinate Reference Frame into Coincidence with the World Frame

17. Derive the window-to-viewport coordinate transformation and elaborate.

or

Derive the formulas required for transforming a point (xw,yw) in a window to point (xv,yv) in viewport.

Ans. The main objective of window-to-viewport transformation is to convert the world-coordinate point which is positioned at (xw, yw) in a designated window into its corresponding viewport coordinates (xv, yv). This conversion is done in such a way that the relative placements of objects in both reference frames remain same (see Figure 5.29). Thus, maintaining such conversion requires:

$$\frac{xv - xv_{min}}{xv_{max} - xv_{min}} = \frac{xw - xw_{min}}{xw_{max} - xw_{min}} \quad \text{and}$$

$$\frac{yv - yv_{min}}{yv_{max} - yv_{min}} = \frac{yw - yw_{min}}{yw_{max} - yw_{min}} \qquad (1)$$

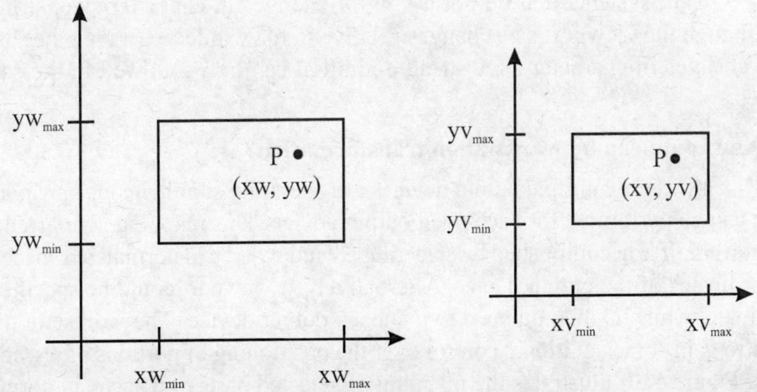

Figure 5.29 Maintaining the Relative Positions of a Point P in the Two Areas

To obtain viewport position (xv, yv), we solve Equation (1) as follows:

$$xv - xv_{min} = \frac{xw - xw_{min}}{xw_{max} - xw_{min}} \times (xv_{max} - xv_{min})$$

$$= xv_{min} + \frac{xw - xw_{min}}{xw_{max} - xw_{min}} \times (xv_{max} - xv_{min})$$

$$\Rightarrow \quad \begin{aligned} xv &= xv_{min} + (xw - xw_{min})s_x \\ yv &= yv_{min} + (yw - yw_{min})s_y \end{aligned} \qquad (2)$$

where the scaling factors s_x and s_y are defined as follows:

$$s_x = \frac{xv_{max} - xv_{min}}{xw_{max} - xw_{min}}$$

$$s_y = \frac{yv_{max} - yv_{min}}{yw_{max} - yw_{min}}$$

An alternate method to obtain the result as that of Equation (2) is to perform the following sequence of transformations:

1. **Scaling:** Scale the window area to the size of the viewport using a fixed-point position of (xw_{min}, yw_{min}).
2. **Translation:** Translate the scaled window area of step 1 to the position of the viewport.

Note that if the scaling factors (s_x and s_y) are equal, then the objects will be stretched or contracted equally in both directions (horizontally and vertically). However, if the scaling factors have different values, the relative proportions of objects are not maintained. That is, the objects will be stretched or contracted either horizontally or vertically when displayed on the output device. Furthermore, handling of character strings when they are mapped to a viewport depends on the system on which they are being displayed. In systems that do not allow for changes in character size, string size remains constant even though the viewport size changes relative to the window. On the other hand, in systems that allow for changes in character size, string definition can be windowed in the same way as the other primitives.

18. What do you mean by workstation transformation?

Ans. In a system, where multiple output devices are operating simultaneously, window-to-viewport transformation can be performed for each open output device. This mapping is referred to as **workstation transformation**. It is accomplished by selecting a window area in normalized space and a viewport area in the coordinates of the output device. Alternatively, a viewport could be specified within a normalized coordinate, which is then mapped to a chosen output device. The workstation transformation allows the user to gain some additional control over the positioning of portions of a scene on individual output devices. Figure 5.30 illustrates the mapping of selected parts of a scene in normalized space to various output devices.

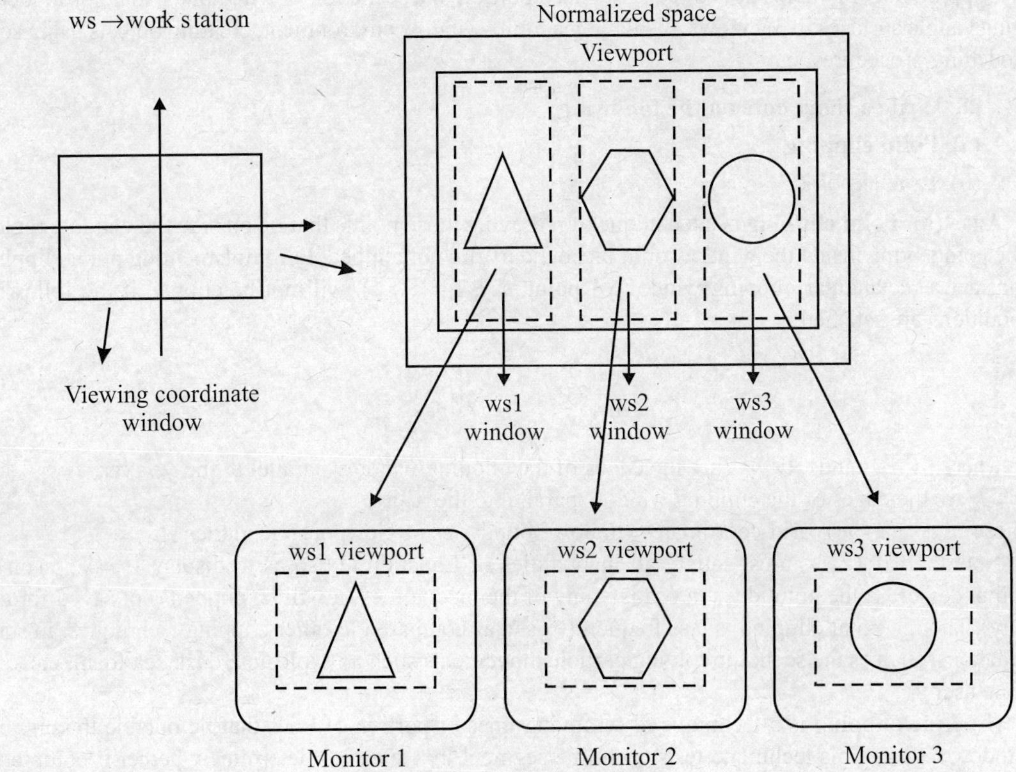

Figure 5.30 Workstation Transformation

19. What is clipping? Discuss its two types.

Ans. Clipping is a technique of identifying (or extracting) those parts of a scene that are either inside or outside of a specified region of space. An algorithm that performs the clipping operation is known as a **clipping algorithm**. The region against which the objects are to be clipped is known as a **clipping window** or **clipping region**. Depending on the application, the clipping region can be a rectangle, general polygon, or even can have curved boundaries. Let us consider a rectangular clipping region. For the viewing transformation, we are interested in displaying only those parts of a scene which are lying inside the window area. Thus, any portion lying outside the window area must be discarded. There are two ways of performing clipping:

- **World-coordinate clipping:** In this technique, the clipping algorithm is applied to the world coordinates so that only the parts lying inside the window are mapped to the device coordinates. This clipping saves a lot of processing time as parts outside the window are not considered at all.
- **Viewport clipping:** In this technique, the complete world-coordinate scene is first mapped to device coordinates, and then clipped against the viewport boundaries. The main advantage of this technique is that it allows concatenation of viewing and geometric transformation matrices, which reduces calculations. However, it requires more processing time as the transformation to device coordinate needs to be performed even for those objects which are lying outside the window area.

Clipping not only helps in extracting selected portion of a scene for viewing, but also helps in identifying visible surfaces in 3D views, displaying a multi-window environment, creating objects using solid modelling procedures, etc.

20. Write a short note on the following:

(a) Point clipping

(b) Line clipping

Ans. (a) Point clipping is a technique of removing those points that lie outside the window region. The points lying inside the window or at its boundary are not clipped. For implementing point clipping, consider a rectangular clipping window. A point, say, $P=(x, y)$ will not be clipped if the following conditions are satisfied:

$$\begin{aligned} xw_{min} &\le x \le xw_{max} \\ yw_{min} &\le y \le yw_{max} \end{aligned} \quad (1)$$

where xw_{min} and xw_{max} are the edges of the clipping window parallel to the y-axis; yw_{min} and yw_{max} are the edges of the clipping window parallel to the x-axis.
These edges can be world-coordinates window boundaries or viewport boundaries.

Note that $P(x, y)$ must satisfy all inequalities of Equation (1) so as to display $P=(x, y)$ on an output device. If the point does not satisfy any of the inequalities, it will be clipped (not saved for display). Though point clipping is less frequently used as compared to other clipping techniques, in some situations, such as the scenes involving particle movements such as explosion, dust, sea foam, etc., it is quite useful.

(b) Line clipping is a technique of removing lines or portion of lines that lie outside the clipping window region. This technique tests each line segment in a scene to determine whether it completely lies inside the clipping window, or outside the clipping window, or intersects one or more clipping boundaries. The line segments are processed by applying the inside–outside tests. The line segments with both end points inside the clipping window are saved for display. The line segments with both end points outside the clipping window are clipped. For all those lines which intersect one or more clipping boundaries, some more calculations need to be performed. In Figure 5.31, since the line segment P_3P_4 lies completely inside the clipping boundaries, it is saved for display; whereas the line segment P_1P_2 lies completely outside the clipping boundaries, hence, it is discarded. However, the line segment P_5P_6 intersects the left clipping boundary, and some more calculations are to be performed. To reduce such intersection calculations, we can apply more efficient clipping algorithms.

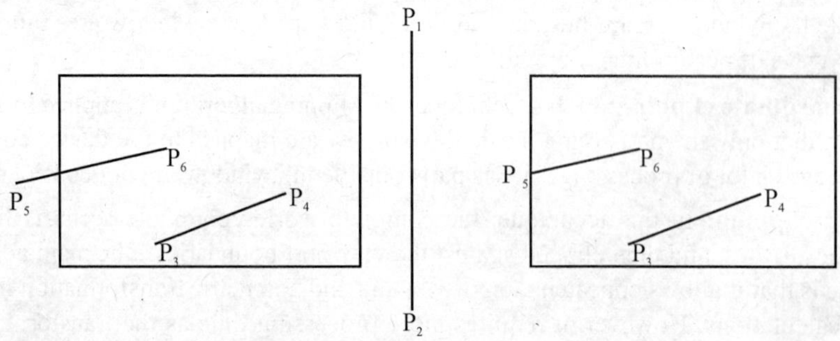

Figure 5.31 Line Clipping

For any line segment whose one or both endpoints lie outside the clipping windows, we can use the following parametric representation:

$$x = x_1 + u(x_2 - x_1)$$
$$y = y_1 + u(y_2 - y_1), 0 \le u \le 1$$

where (x_1, y_1) and (x_2, y_2) are the end points of a line segment and u is the parameter ranging from 0 to 1.

From this representation, we could find the value of parameter u, which further helps us in determining the intersections with the clipping boundaries. If the value of u does not lie between 0 and 1, the line does not enter the interior of the window at that boundary and thus can be discarded. Otherwise, the line segment intersects the clipping area. This procedure is iteratively applied to each clipping boundary edge in order to determine which part of the line segment is to be displayed. However, such tests require a good deal of computation and are slower as well. Thus, faster approaches to clipping have been developed, namely, *Cohen–Sutherland algorithm*, *midpoint subdivision algorithm* and *Liang–Barsky algorithm*.

21. Explain Cohen–Sutherland line-clipping algorithm with the help of an example.

Ans. It is one of the oldest and popular algorithms used for clipping line segments. The basic idea behind this algorithm is to perform some initial tests on line segments in order to reduce the number of intersections to be calculated and to speed up the processing of line segments. The algorithm determines whether a line segment lies completely inside the clipping window, or completely outside the clipping window, or intersects the clipping window. Depending on its positions with reference to the clipping window, a line falls in one of the following three defined clipping categories:

- **Visible:** In this, both the line endpoints lie inside the clipping window. For example, in Figure 5.32, lines PQ and ST are visible lines.
- **Not visible:** In this, both the line endpoints lie outside the clipping window. For example, in Figure 5.32, line WX is not visible.
- **Clipping candidate:** In this, the line endpoints neither lie inside nor outside the clipping window completely. That is, the line intersects one or more clipping boundaries. For example, in Figure 5.32, lines UV and YZ are clipping candidates.

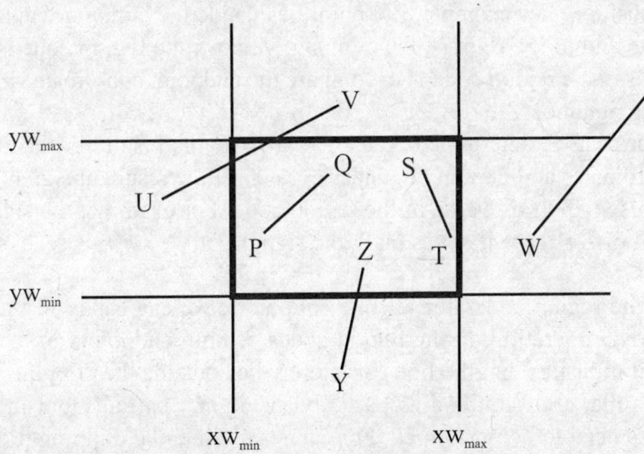

Figure 5.32 Visible, not Visible and Clipping Candidate Lines

To find the category of each line in an efficient manner, the following procedure is employed:

A four digit binary code (called **region code**) is assigned to each endpoint of a line according to the location of the particular point with respect to the boundaries of the clipping window (see Figure 5.33). Each bit of the region code indicates one of the four relative coordinate positions of the point with reference to the clipping window. These relative positions are left (L), right (R), below (B) and above (A). We can arrange these positions in any order in the region code. One possible order could be ABRL. That is,

- the rightmost bit, that is, bit 1 indicates left,
- bit 2 indicates right,
- bit 3 indicates below,
- bit 4 indicates above.

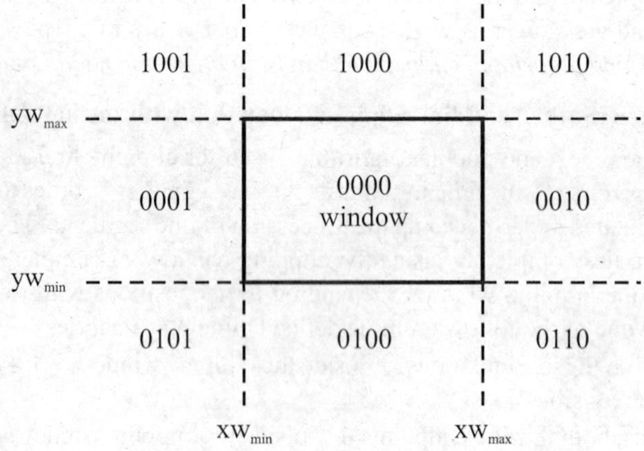

Figure 5.33 Region Codes

Starting from the left most bit, each bit of the code is either set to 1 or 0. The value 1 indicates that the point is in that relative position with reference to the clipping window; and 0 indicates that it is not lying in that relative position. For example, if a point lies inside the clipping window, the region code is 0000. If it lies above and to the right of the clipping window, the region code is 1010. One way to determine the bit values in the region code is to compare the endpoint coordinate values (x, y) with the clip boundaries. For the rightmost bit, if $x<xw_{min}$, the value is set to 1; otherwise, it is set to 0. Similarly, the other three bit values can be determined. The alternative method is to first calculate the differences between endpoint coordinates and clipping boundaries, and set the resultant sign bit of each difference calculation as the corresponding bit value in the region code. For example, the sign bit of $x-xw_{min}$ is set as bit 1, the sign bit of $xw_{max}-x$ is set as bit 2, the sign bit of $y-yw_{min}$ is set as bit 3, the sign bit of $yw_{max}-y$ is set as bit 4.

After establishing the region codes for all line endpoints, we can easily test a line for total clipping by performing AND operation on the region codes of both endpoints of the line. If any of the bits in the result is 1, it indicates that the line completely lies outside the clipping window, and hence is discarded. For lines that are identified as partially inside and partially outside the clipping window, certain other tests need to be performed. For each such line, the clipping process is initiated by comparing an outside endpoint with a clipping boundary so as to determine how much of the line can be clipped. We then check the remaining part of the line against the other clipping boundaries. This process is repeated until either the line is completely discarded or a section is found inside the clipping window.

To understand the Cohen–Sutherland algorithm, consider a set of lines shown in Figure 5.34. Starting with the line P_1P_2, we first check the point P_1 to determine whether it lies left, right, above or below with respect to the clipping window. We found that P_1 lies below the clipping window. Now, we will find the intersection point of P_1 with the bottom boundary. This intersection point is P_1'. Therefore, we discard the section P_1 to P_1'. This reduces the line segment from P_1' to P_2. The same task is performed for the endpoint P_2. We found the first intersection point P_2', but it is to the right of the clipping window, and hence discarded. Now, we calculate the second intersection point P_2'. Since, it lies on the clipping boundary, it is saved. Now, no more endpoints of this line are left for processing, the line from P_1' to P_2'' is saved as it is completely lying inside the clipping window. The same process is repeated for the next line P_3P_4.

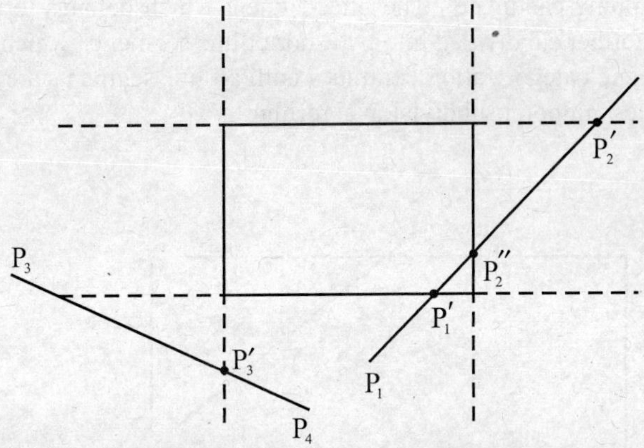

Figure 5.34 Illustrating Cohen–Sutherland Algorithm

Generally, an intersection point is calculated using the slope-intercept form of the line Equation. For a line having endpoint coordinates as (x_1, y_1) and (x_2, y_2), the y coordinate of the intersection point with a vertical boundary line is obtained as follows:

$$y = y_1 + m(x - x_1)$$

where m is the slope of the line which is $\dfrac{(y_2 - y_1)}{(x_2 - x_1)}$ and x is either xw_{min} or xw_{max}.

In a similar way, the x coordinate of the intersection point with a horizontal boundary line is calculated as follows:

$$x = x_1 + \frac{y - y_1}{m}$$

where y is either yw_{min} or yw_{max}.

22. Describe the midpoint subdivision algorithm.

Ans. As Cohen–Sutherland line-clipping algorithm consumes a lot of time in calculating the coordinates of the intersection point, an alternate and efficient method to process a line intersecting one or more clipping boundaries is the **midpoint subdivision algorithm**. This algorithm is based on binary search. It divides a line which is a clipping candidate from its midpoint into two shorter line segments. The midpoint coordinates (x_m, y_m) of such a line are calculated as follows:

$$x_m = \frac{x_1 + x_2}{2}$$

$$y_m = \frac{y_1 + y_2}{2}$$

where (x_1, y_1) and (x_2, y_2) are the endpoints of the line.

The region codes of the two shorter line segments are tested to determine their clipping categories (visible, invisible, or clipping candidate). The line segment which belongs to the clipping candidate category (category 3) is further subdivided into two shorter line segments, which are again categorized. This process of division and categorization continues until all line segments are either visible or invisible. Figure 5.35 illustrates midpoint subdivision algorithm.

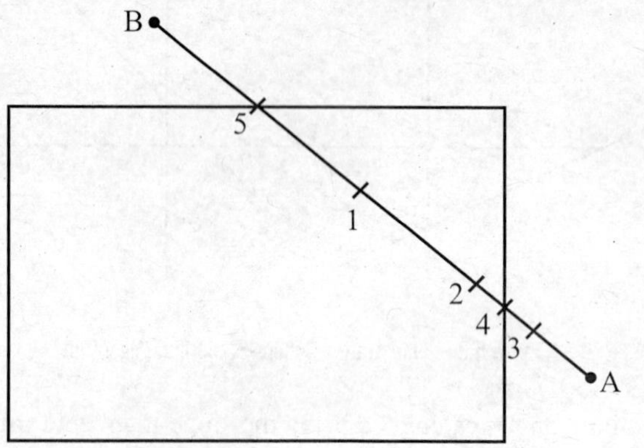

Figure 5.35 Illustrating Midpoint Subdivision Algorithm

23. Explain Liang–Barsky algorithm.

Ans. Liang–Barsky algorithm is one of the fastest line-clipping algorithms which is based on parametric Equation of a line segment. Such Equations can be represented as follows:

$$x = x_1 + \Delta x \,.\, u$$

$$y = y_1 + \Delta y \,.\, u$$

where $\Delta x = x_2 - x_1$, $\Delta y = y_2 - y_1$ and u is the parameter ranging from 0 to 1.

This approach saves a point, say $P(x, y)$, for a display if the following inequalities are satisfied:

$$xw_{min} \leq x_1 + \Delta x \,.\, u \leq xw_{max}$$

$$yw_{min} \leq y_1 + \Delta y \,.\, u \leq yw_{max}$$

These four inequalities can be rewritten as:

$$u\,p_1 \le q_1,\ u\,p_2 \le q_2,\ u\,p_3 \le q_3,\ u\,p_4 \le q_4$$

Or can be summed as $u\,P_i \le q_i$, $i=1,2,3,4$,
where

$$p_1 = -\Delta x,\quad q_1 = x_1 - xw_{min} \text{ (left)}$$
$$p_2 = \Delta x,\quad q_2 = xw_{max} - x_1 \text{ (right)}$$
$$p_3 = -\Delta y,\quad q_3 = y_1 - yw_{min} \text{ (bottom)}$$
$$p_4 = \Delta y,\quad q_4 = yw_{max} - y_1 \text{ (top)}$$

Now depending on the values of p_i and q_i, for $i=1$ to 4, we have following facts:

- If $p_i = 0$, the line is parallel to the corresponding clipping boundary. For instance, if $p_1=0$, it implies that the line is parallel to the left edge of the clipping boundary. However, for same value of i, if $q_i<0$, then the line is completely outside the boundary and can be rejected. Otherwise, the line is inside the clipping boundary and must be considered.
- If $p_i<0$, then the infinite extension of the line proceeds from outside to inside of the corresponding boundary line.
- If $p_i>0$, then the infinite extension of the line proceeds from inside to outside of the corresponding boundary line.
- If $p_i \neq 0$, then the value of u corresponding to the intersection point is qi/pi.

The main objective of Liang–Barsky algorithm is to find those lines or portion of lines that are visible within the window region (see Figure 5.36). To fulfil this objective, we calculate two parameters, namely, u_1 and u_2 for each line. These parameters define the part of line which lies within the clipping window. The value of u_1 is calculated when $p<0$, whereas the value of u_2 is calculated when $p>0$. The algorithm is implemented in the following manner:

1. For any value of i, if $p_i=0$ and $q_i<0$, the line is rejected and the process is terminated. Otherwise, step 2 is executed.
2. For all i such that $p_i<0$, we calculate $r_i=q_i/p_i$. Then, we take the value of u_1 as the largest of the set containing 0 and the calculated r values.
3. For all i such that $p_i>0$, we calculate $r_i=q_i/p_i$. Then, we take the value of u_1 as the smallest of the set containing 1 and the calculated r values.
4. If $u_1>u_2$, then the line is rejected because it lies completely outside the window region. Otherwise, u_1 and u_2 are used to calculate the endpoints of the clipped line.

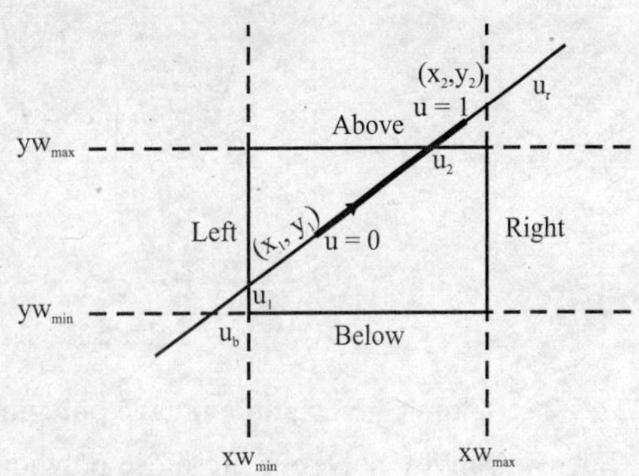

Figure 5.36 Illustrating Liang–barsky Algorithm

24. Among Cohen–Sutherland clipping algorithm and Liang–Barsky algorithm, which one is more efficient? Why?

Ans. Liang–Barsky algorithm is more efficient than Cohen–Sutherland clipping algorithm because of reduced intersection calculations. In Liang–Barsky algorithm, each update of parameters u_1 and u_2

requires only one division. In addition, window intersections of the line are computed only for once when computing the final values of u_1 and u_2. On the other hand, in Cohen–Sutherland clipping algorithm, repetitive intersection calculations are required along a line path, even if the line completely lies outside the window. Moreover, each intersection calculation requires both a division and a multiplication.

25. What do you mean by polygon clipping?

Ans. Polygon clipping is a technique of removing the portions of a polygon not lying inside the clipping window. Though polygon clipping can be performed with the help of line-clipping algorithms, with line-clipping algorithms polygon boundary is displayed as a series of disconnected line segments, depending on the orientation of the polygon with respect to the clipping window (see Figure 5.37).

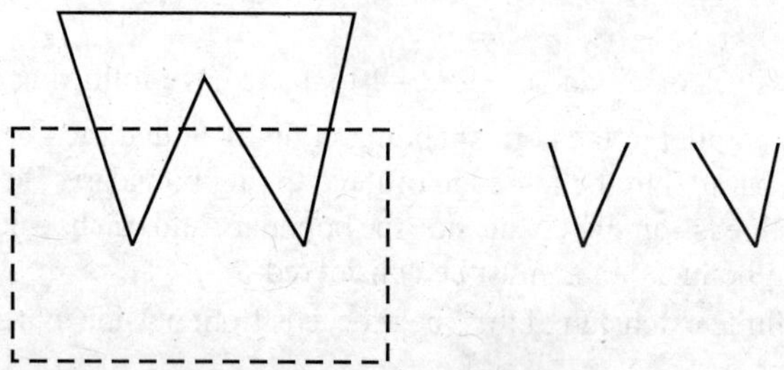

Figure 5.37 Performing Polygon Clipping using Line-clipping Algorithm

However, our objective is to generate a bounded area after clipping. Thus, we need an algorithm that generates one or more closed areas after clipping that can be then scan converted for the appropriate area fill. Thus, the output generated after performing the polygon-clipping algorithm is a series of vertices defining the boundaries of the clipped polygon (see Figure 5.38).

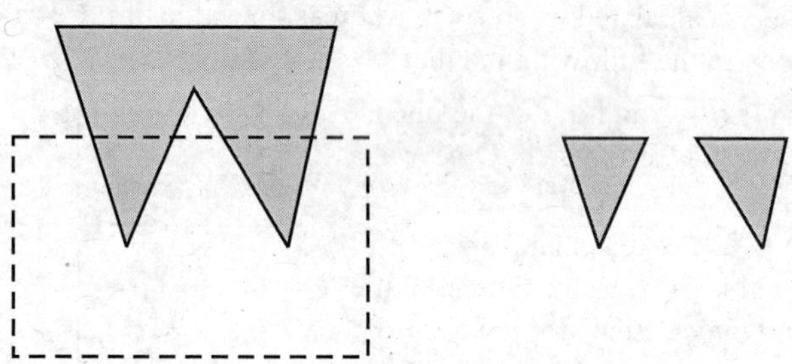

Figure 5.38 Displaying Correctly Clipped Polygon

26. Define convex and concave polygon.

Ans. Convex polygons are those polygons whose all interior angles measure less than 180°. The vertices of such polygons always point outwards, that is, away from the interior of the shape (see Figure 5.39a). Moreover, all the diagonals of convex polygon lie entirely inside it, and the polygon is divided exactly into two parts if any line is drawn through it.

Concave polygons (also known as **non-convex polygons**) are those polygons whose atleast one interior angle measures greater than 180°. The vertices of such polygons always point inwards, that is, towards the interior of the shape (see Figure 5.39b). Unlike convex polygon, some of the diagonals lie outside the concave polygon, and depending on the line drawn, the polygon is divided into more than two parts.

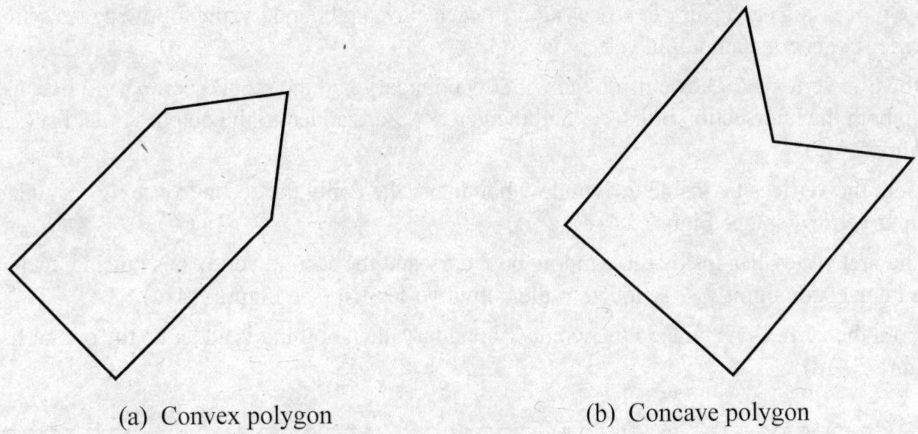

Figure 5.39 Convex and Concave Polygons

27. Explain the Sutherland–Hodgeman polygon-clipping algorithm.

Ans. Sutherland–Hodgeman algorithm is generally used for clipping convex polygons. This method is implemented by processing all polygon vertices against each window boundary in turn. Taking the initial set of vertices into account, the algorithm starts clipping the polygon against the left clipping boundary to generate a new sequence of vertices of polygon. This set of vertices is then successively passed to the right clipping boundary, then to the bottom clipping boundary, and finally to the top clipping boundary. At each step, a new set of vertices is produced which is passed to the next clipping boundary. Figure 5.40 illustrates the process of polygon clipping against successive window boundaries.

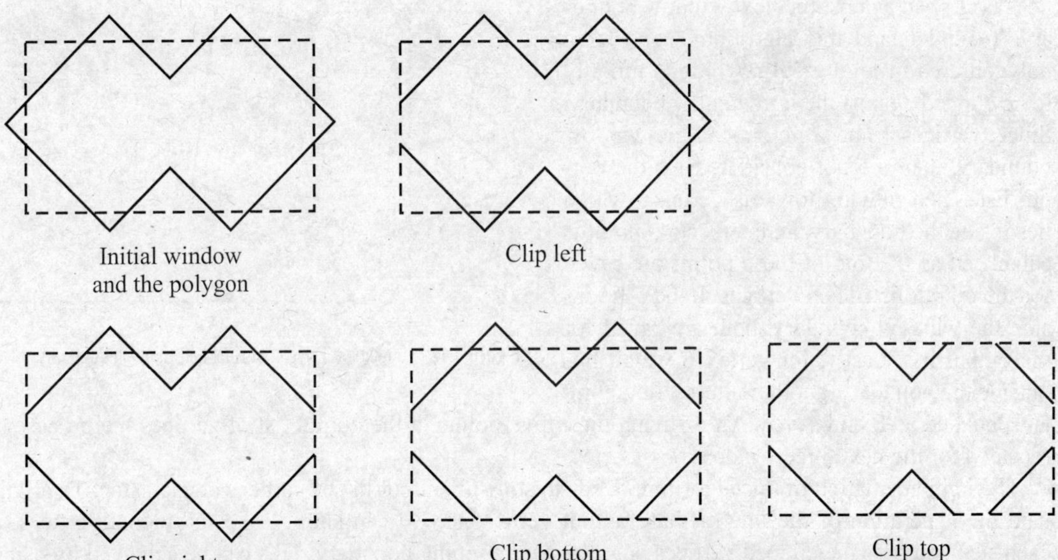

Figure 5.40 Clipping a Polygon against Successive Window Boundaries

While processing each pair of vertices against each clipping boundary, the following tests are carried out in order to generate an output vertex list:

1. If the first vertex (V_1) lies outside the window boundary and the second vertex (V_2) lies inside, then both the intersection point V_1' and the vertex V_2 are added to the output vertex list (see Figure 5.41a).
2. If both the vertices lie inside the window boundary, then only the second vertex V_2 is added to the output vertex list (see Figure 5.41b).
3. If the first vertex lies inside the window boundary and the second vertex lies outside, then only the intersection point V_1' is added to the output vertex list (see Figure 5.41c).
4. If both the vertices lie outside the window boundary, then nothing is added to the output list (see Figure 5.41d).

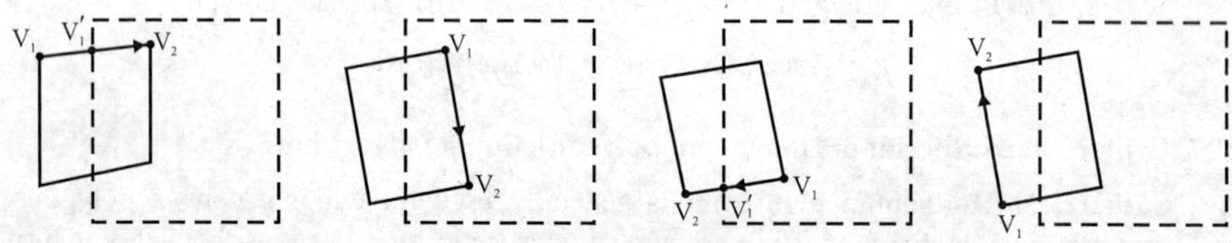

(a) Vertex 1 lies outside (b) Both vertices lie inside (c) Vertex 2 lies outside (d) Both vertices lie outside

Figure 5.41 Successive Processing of a Pair of Polygon Vertices against Left Clipping Boundary

After processing all the polygon vertices for the left window boundary, the output list of vertices is clipped against the next window boundary. To understand this algorithm, consider a polygon area in Figure 5.42, which is initially to be clipped against the left window boundary. Since, vertices 1 and 2 lie outside the window boundary, they are not considered for the output list. Then moving towards vertex 3 which lies inside the boundary, an intersection point is calculated as a. Both of these points are saved for the output list. Then vertices 4 and 5 lie inside the window boundary, both are saved for the output list. Lastly, for vertex 6 which lies outside the boundary, another intersection point is calculated as b and saved. After saving these five points in the output list of vertices the process is repeated for the next three window boundaries.

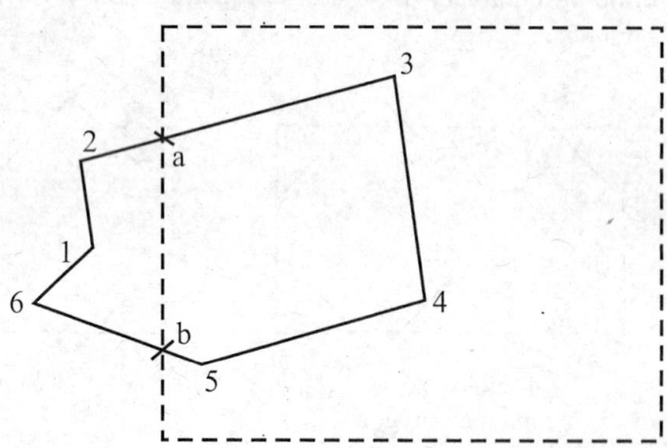

Figure 5.42 Clipping a Polygon against Left Clipping Boundary

The implementation of this algorithm needs to store an output list of vertices at each step. To eliminate the generation of the intermediate output vertex list, we can simply clip individual vertices at each step and pass the clipped vertices onto the next clipping boundary. This can be achieved by using parallel processors, or a single processor coupled with a pipeline of clipping routine. In this approach, an input vertex or a calculated intersection point is added in the output list only if it is inside the window or on one of clipping boundary; otherwise, it is not considered further in the pipeline.

28. Write a short note on curve clipping.

Ans: Curve clipping is a bit complex as compared to polygon clipping because curve-clipping procedures involve nonlinear equations. Like polygon clipping, the bounding rectangle of a circle or any other curved object is used to first test the overlap with the rectangular clip window. There exist three cases as follows:

- Case 1: If the bounding rectangle for the object is completely inside the clip window, the object is saved for display [see Figure 5.43(a)].
- Case 2: If the bounding rectangle for the object is completely outside the clip window, the object is discarded [see Figure 5.43(b)].
- Case 3: If the two regions overlap, more computations need to be performed to determine the clipping intersection points. Figure 5.43(c) shows circle clipping against a rectangular window.

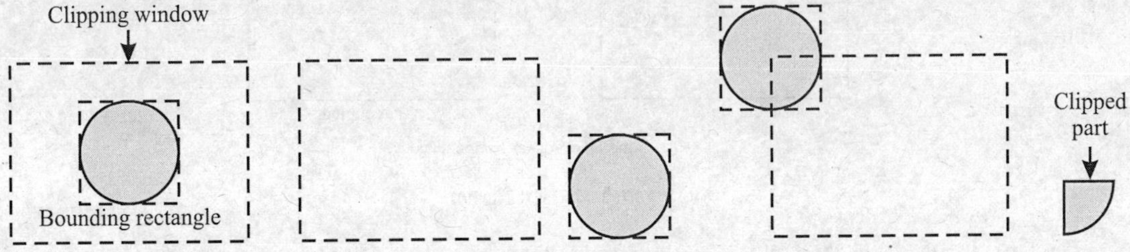

Figure 5.43 Curve clipping

29. Write a short note on text clipping.

Ans. Text clipping refers to the process of either removing the entire string if it does not lie completely inside the clipping window or removing that character from the string which overlaps with a window boundary. There are three ways of text clipping, which are as follows:

- **All-or-none string clipping:** In this approach, if the string completely lies inside the clipping window, it is displayed; otherwise, it is discarded. It is the simplest and fastest text clipping technique. To implement this technique, a bounding rectangle is taken around the string. The boundary positions of the rectangle are then compared to the boundaries of the window. The string is discarded if it overlaps the window or lies completely outside the window (see Figure 5.44a).
- **All-or-none character clipping:** In this technique, only those characters are considered which completely lie inside the window. To implement this technique, the boundary limits of individual characters are compared to the boundaries of the window. Any character that overlaps the window or lies outside the window is discarded (see Figure 5.44b).
- **Clipping character components:** In this approach, components of individual characters are considered for clipping. To implement this technique, the characters are treated like lines. We discard only that part of the character which overlaps a window boundary (see Figure 5.44c).

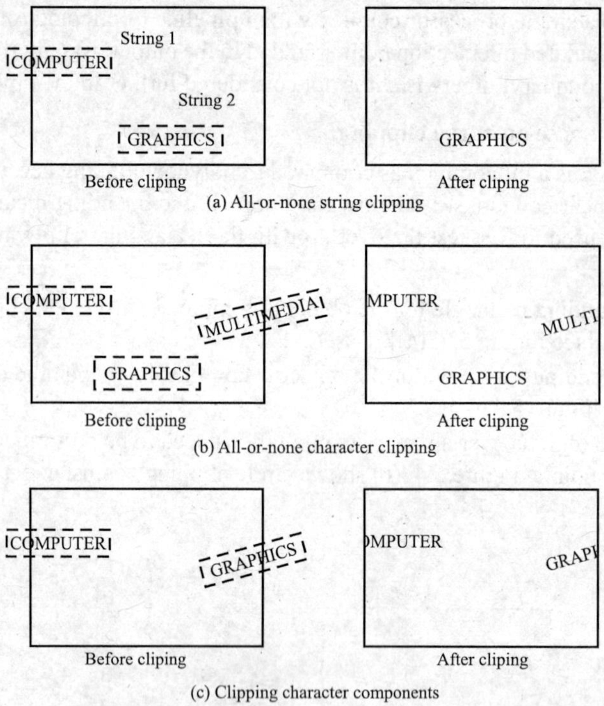

Figure 5.44 Text Clipping

30. Prove that two 2D rotations about the origin commute, that is, $R_1R_2 = R_2R_1$.

Ans. Let R_1 be the rotation by an angle θ about origin counterclockwise and R_2 be the rotation following R_1 in the same direction by an angle ϕ. Thus,

$$R_1 = \begin{bmatrix} \cos\theta & -\sin\theta \\ \sin\theta & \cos\theta \end{bmatrix}$$

$$R_2 = \begin{bmatrix} \cos\phi & -\sin\phi \\ \sin\phi & \cos\phi \end{bmatrix}$$

$$R_1R_2 = \begin{bmatrix} \cos\theta\cos\phi - \sin\theta\sin\phi & -\cos\theta\sin\phi - \sin\theta\cos\phi \\ \sin\theta\cos\phi + \cos\theta\sin\phi & -\sin\theta\sin\phi + \cos\theta\cos\phi \end{bmatrix}$$

Since

$$\cos(\theta + \phi) = \cos\theta\cos\phi - \sin\theta\sin\phi$$
$$\sin(\theta + \phi) = \sin\theta\cos\phi + \cos\theta\sin\phi$$

Thus,

$$R_1R_2 = \begin{bmatrix} \cos(\theta + \phi) & -\sin(\theta + \phi) \\ \sin(\theta + \phi) & \cos(\theta + \phi) \end{bmatrix} \quad (1)$$

Now,

$$R_2R_1 = \begin{bmatrix} \cos\phi\cos\theta - \sin\phi\sin\theta & -\cos\phi\sin\theta - \sin\phi\cos\theta \\ \sin\phi\cos\theta + \cos\phi\sin\theta & -\sin\phi\sin\theta + \cos\phi\cos\theta \end{bmatrix}$$

$$= \begin{bmatrix} \cos(\theta + \phi) & -\sin(\theta + \phi) \\ \sin(\theta + \phi) & \cos(\theta + \phi) \end{bmatrix} \quad (2)$$

Thus, from Equations (1) and (2),

$$R_1R_2 = R_2R_1$$

31. Prove that two scaling transformations commute, that is, $S_1 S_2 = S_2 S_1$.

Ans. Let S_1 be scaled by a factor u about the origin and S_2 be scaled by a factor v after S_1. Then, we have

$$S_1 = \begin{bmatrix} u & 0 & 0 \\ 0 & u & 0 \\ 0 & 0 & 1 \end{bmatrix}$$

$$S_2 = \begin{bmatrix} v & 0 & 0 \\ 0 & v & 0 \\ 0 & 0 & 1 \end{bmatrix}$$

Therefore,

$$S_1S_2 = \begin{bmatrix} uv & 0 & 0 \\ 0 & uv & 0 \\ 0 & 0 & 1 \end{bmatrix}$$

It can also be written as

$$= \begin{bmatrix} vu & 0 & 0 \\ 0 & vu & 0 \\ 0 & 0 & 1 \end{bmatrix}$$

Now,

$$S_2S_1 = \begin{bmatrix} vu & 0 & 0 \\ 0 & vu & 0 \\ 0 & 0 & 1 \end{bmatrix}$$

Thus,

$$S_1S_2 = S_2S_1$$

32. Perform a 45° rotation of triangle A (0,0), B (1,1) and C (5,2).
(a) about the origin
(b) about the point (–1, –1)

Ans. (a) Rotation about origin

Matrix for the triangle is

$$\Delta = \begin{bmatrix} 0 & 1 & 5 \\ 0 & 1 & 2 \\ 1 & 1 & 1 \end{bmatrix}$$

Matrix for rotation

$$R_{45^\circ} = \begin{bmatrix} \cos 45^\circ & -\sin 45^\circ & 0 \\ \sin 45^\circ & \cos 45^\circ & 0 \\ 0 & 0 & 1 \end{bmatrix}$$

$$= \begin{bmatrix} \frac{1}{\sqrt{2}} & -\frac{1}{\sqrt{2}} & 0 \\ \frac{1}{\sqrt{2}} & \frac{1}{\sqrt{2}} & 0 \\ 0 & 0 & 1 \end{bmatrix}$$

The rotated coordinates of the triangle are calculated as follows:

$$\Delta' = R_{45^\circ} \cdot \Delta$$

$$= \begin{bmatrix} \frac{1}{\sqrt{2}} & -\frac{1}{\sqrt{2}} & 0 \\ \frac{1}{\sqrt{2}} & \frac{1}{\sqrt{2}} & 0 \\ 0 & 0 & 1 \end{bmatrix} \begin{bmatrix} 0 & 1 & 5 \\ 0 & 1 & 2 \\ 1 & 1 & 1 \end{bmatrix}$$

$$= \begin{bmatrix} 0 & 0 & \frac{3}{\sqrt{2}} \\ 0 & \sqrt{2} & \frac{7}{\sqrt{2}} \\ 1 & 1 & 1 \end{bmatrix}$$

Therefore,

$A'(0, 0)$, $B'(0, \sqrt{2})$ and $C'\left(\frac{3}{\sqrt{2}}, \frac{7}{\sqrt{2}}\right)$

(b) Rotation about a point (–1, –1)

As we know rotation about a specific point is carried out by performing the sequence of 'translate–rotate–inverse translate' operations. The composite matrix for such sequence of operations is obtained as follows:

$$\begin{bmatrix} 1 & 0 & x_r \\ 0 & 1 & y_r \\ 0 & 0 & 1 \end{bmatrix} \cdot \begin{bmatrix} \cos\theta & -\sin\theta & 0 \\ \sin\theta & \cos\theta & 0 \\ 0 & 0 & 1 \end{bmatrix} \cdot \begin{bmatrix} 1 & 0 & -x_r \\ 0 & 1 & -y_r \\ 0 & 0 & 1 \end{bmatrix}$$

where (x_r, y_r) is the specified point about which the object is to be rotated.
Therefore, substituting (–1, –1) for (x_r, y_r) and 45° for θ, we get:

$$R_{45^{\circ}, p} = \begin{bmatrix} 1 & 0 & -1 \\ 0 & 1 & -1 \\ 0 & 0 & 1 \end{bmatrix} \begin{bmatrix} \frac{1}{\sqrt{2}} & -\frac{1}{\sqrt{2}} & 0 \\ \frac{1}{\sqrt{2}} & \frac{1}{\sqrt{2}} & 0 \\ 0 & 0 & 1 \end{bmatrix} \begin{bmatrix} 1 & 0 & 1 \\ 0 & 1 & 1 \\ 0 & 0 & 1 \end{bmatrix}$$

$$= \begin{bmatrix} \frac{1}{\sqrt{2}} & -\frac{1}{\sqrt{2}} & -1 \\ \frac{1}{\sqrt{2}} & \frac{1}{\sqrt{2}} & -1 \\ 0 & 0 & 1 \end{bmatrix} \begin{bmatrix} 1 & 0 & 1 \\ 0 & 1 & 1 \\ 0 & 0 & 1 \end{bmatrix}$$

$$= \begin{bmatrix} \frac{1}{\sqrt{2}} & -\frac{1}{\sqrt{2}} & -1 \\ \frac{1}{\sqrt{2}} & \frac{1}{\sqrt{2}} & (\sqrt{2}-1) \\ 0 & 0 & 1 \end{bmatrix}$$

Therefore, the rotated coordinates of the triangle are calculated as follows:

$$\Delta' = R_{45^{\circ}, p} \cdot \Delta$$

$$= \begin{bmatrix} \frac{1}{\sqrt{2}} & -\frac{1}{\sqrt{2}} & -1 \\ \frac{1}{\sqrt{2}} & \frac{1}{\sqrt{2}} & (\sqrt{2}-1) \\ 0 & 0 & 1 \end{bmatrix} \begin{bmatrix} 0 & 1 & 5 \\ 0 & 1 & 2 \\ 1 & 1 & 1 \end{bmatrix}$$

$$= \begin{bmatrix} -1 & -1 & (\frac{3}{\sqrt{2}}-1) \\ (\sqrt{2}-1) & (2\sqrt{2}-1) & (\frac{9}{\sqrt{2}}-1) \\ 1 & 1 & 1 \end{bmatrix}$$

Therefore, A' $\left(-1, \sqrt{2} - 1\right)$, B' $(-1, 2\sqrt{2} - 1)$ and C' $\left(\frac{3}{\sqrt{2}} - 1, \frac{9}{\sqrt{2}} - 1\right)$

33. Show that the composition of two rotations is additive by concatenating the matrix representations for R(θ_1) and R(θ_2) to obtain R(θ_1) . R(θ_2) = R(θ_1+θ_2).

Ans. Using the value of R_1R_2 as calculated in Q30, that is,

$$R_1R_2 = \begin{bmatrix} \cos(\theta + \phi) & -\sin(\theta + \phi) \\ \sin(\theta + \phi) & \cos(\theta + \phi) \end{bmatrix}$$

and putting $\theta = \theta_1, \phi = \theta_2, R_1 = R(\theta_1)$ and $R_2 = R(\theta_2)$, we get:

$$R(\theta_1) \cdot R(\theta_2) = \begin{bmatrix} \cos(\theta_1 + \theta_2) & -\sin(\theta_1 + \theta_2) \\ \sin(\theta_1 + \theta_2) & \cos(\theta_1 + \theta_2) \end{bmatrix}$$

$$R(\theta_1) \cdot R(\theta_2) = R(\theta_1 + \theta_2)$$

Hence proved.

34. Construct a triangle ABC whose coordinates are A (4, 1), B (5, 2) and C (4, 3).

(a) Reflect the given triangle about the x-axis

(b) Reflect the give triangle about the y-axis

(c) Reflect the given triangle about an axis perpendicular to x y plane passing through the origin

(d) Reflect the given triangle about x = y-axis

In each case find the coordinates of the reflected triangle.

Ans. Let us construct a triangle with the coordinates A (4, 1), B (5, 2) and C (4, 3) as shown in Figure 5.45.

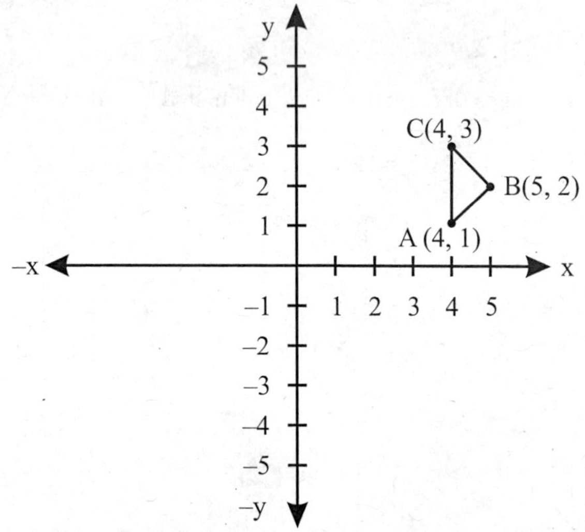

Figure 5.45 Triangle with Coordinates A (4, 1), B (5, 2) and C (4, 3)

(a) Reflection of the given triangle about x-axis is shown in Figure 5.46a.
The coordinates of the reflected triangle are A (4, –1), B (5, –2) and C (4, –3)

(b) Reflection of the given triangle about y-axis is shown in Figure 5.46b.
The coordinates of the reflected triangle are A (–4, 1), B (–5, 2) and C (–4, 3)

(c) Reflection of the given triangle about an axis perpendicular to x y plane passing through the origin is shown in Figure 5.46c.
The coordinates of the reflected triangle are A (–4, –1), B (–5, –2) and C (–4, –3)

(d) Reflection of the given triangle about x = y-axis is shown in Figure 5.46d.
The coordinates of the reflected triangle are A (1, 4), B (2, 5) and C (3, 4)

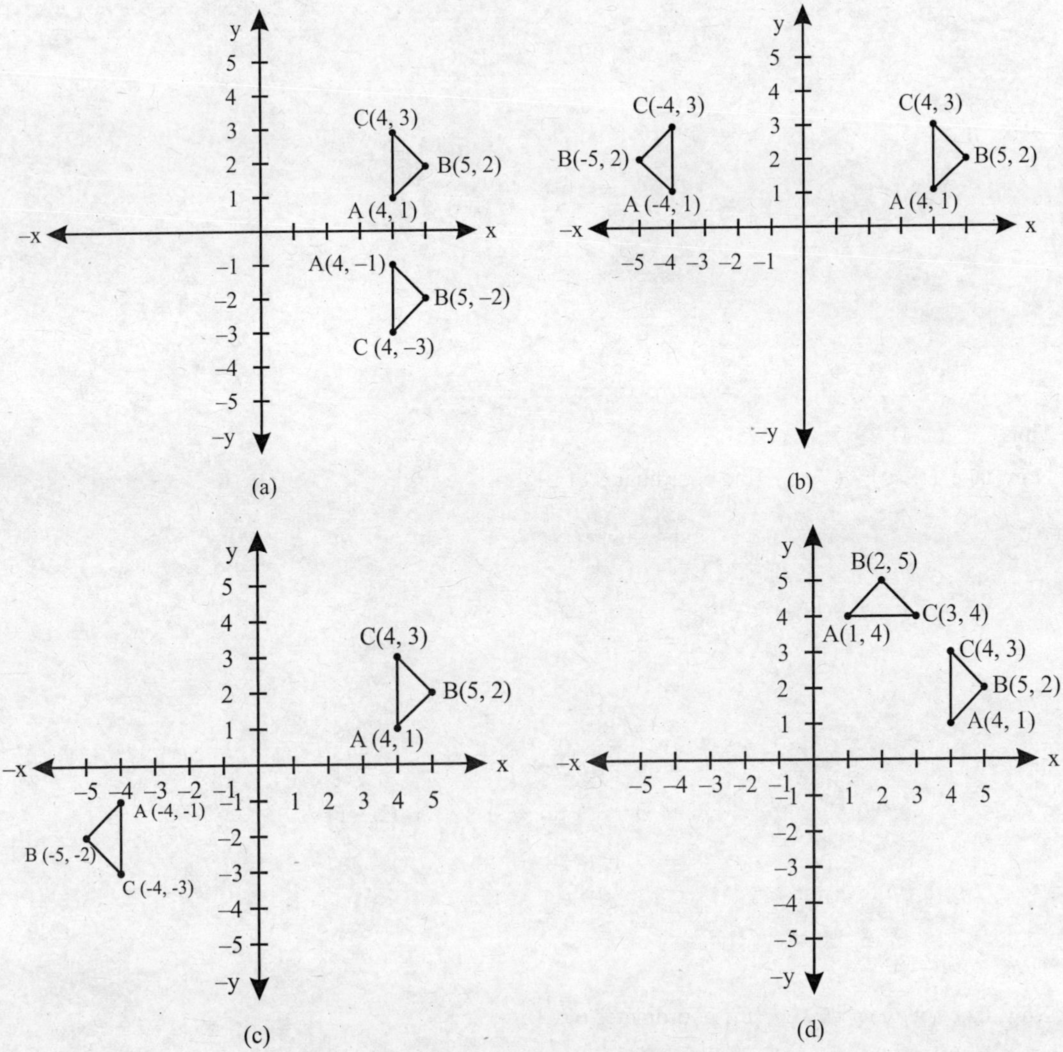

Figure 5.46 Reflecting a given Griangle about Different Axes

35. Perform a 45° rotation of object A (2,1), B (5,1), C (5,6) in clockwise direction about an arbitrary point and give the coordinates of the transformed objects.

Ans. To perform a 45° rotation of the object, we do

$$x' = x_r + (x - x_r)\cos\theta - (y - y_r)\sin\theta$$
$$y' = y_r + (x - x_r)\sin\theta + (y - y_r)\cos\theta$$

Let us choose $(x_r, y_r) = (3, 3)$ and $(x, y) = (2, 1)$ [the coordinates of A]

$$x' = 3 + (2 - 3)\,{}^{1}\!/\!_{\sqrt{2}} - (1 - 3)\,{}^{1}\!/\!_{\sqrt{2}}$$
$$= 3 + {}^{1}\!/\!_{\sqrt{2}}$$
$$= 3 + 0.707$$
$$= 3.707$$
$$= 4 \text{ (approx.)}$$

$$y' = 3 + (2 - 3)\,{}^{1}\!/\!_{\sqrt{2}} + (1 - 3)\,{}^{1}\!/\!_{\sqrt{2}}$$
$$= 3 - {}^{3}\!/\!_{\sqrt{2}}$$
$$= 3 - 2.121$$
$$= 0.87$$
$$= 1 \text{ (approx.)}$$

Thus, A' (4, 1).

Now, take $(x, y) = (5, 1)$ [the coordinates of B]

$$x' = 3 + (5 - 3)\,{}^{1}\!/\!_{\sqrt{2}} - (1 - 3)\,{}^{1}\!/\!_{\sqrt{2}}$$
$$= 3 + {}^{2}\!/\!_{\sqrt{2}} + {}^{2}\!/\!_{\sqrt{2}}$$
$$= 3 + {}^{4}\!/\!_{\sqrt{2}}$$
$$= 3 + 2.828$$
$$= 5.828$$
$$= 6 \text{ (approx.)}$$
$$y' = 3 + (5 - 3)\,{}^{1}\!/\!_{\sqrt{2}} + (1 - 3)\,{}^{1}\!/\!_{\sqrt{2}}$$
$$= 3 + {}^{2}\!/\!_{\sqrt{2}} - {}^{2}\!/\!_{\sqrt{2}}$$
$$= 3$$

Thus, B' (5, 3)

Now, take $(x, y) = (5, 6)$ [the coordinates of C]

$$x' = 3 + (5-3)\,{}^{1}/_{\sqrt{2}} - (6-3)\,{}^{1}/_{\sqrt{2}}$$
$$= 3 + {}^{2}/_{\sqrt{2}} - {}^{3}/_{\sqrt{2}}$$
$$= 3 - {}^{1}/_{\sqrt{2}}$$
$$= 3 - 0.707$$
$$= 2.293$$
$$= 2\text{ (approx.)}$$
$$y' = 3 + (5-3)\,{}^{1}/_{\sqrt{2}} + (6-3)\,{}^{1}/_{\sqrt{2}}$$
$$= 3 + {}^{2}/_{\sqrt{2}} + {}^{3}/_{\sqrt{2}}$$
$$= 3 + {}^{5}/_{\sqrt{2}}$$
$$= 3 + 3.535$$
$$= 6.535$$
$$= 7\text{ (approx.)}$$

Thus, C′ (2,7)

Therefore, the rotated coordinates are A' (4, 1), B' (6, 3), C' (2, 7)

36. Prove that simultaneous shearing in both directions (x & y directions) is not equal to the composition if pure shear along the x-axis followed by pure shear along the y-axis.

Ans. We know that simultaneous shearing

$$S_h = \begin{bmatrix} 1 & a \\ b & 1 \end{bmatrix}$$

Shearing in the x-direction

$$S_{hx} = \begin{bmatrix} 1 & a \\ 0 & 1 \end{bmatrix}$$

Shearing in the y-direction

$$S_{hy} = \begin{bmatrix} 1 & 0 \\ b & 1 \end{bmatrix}$$

Therefore, shearing in the x-direction followed by the y-direction,

$$= \begin{bmatrix} 1 & a \\ 0 & 1 \end{bmatrix}\begin{bmatrix} 1 & 0 \\ b & 1 \end{bmatrix}$$
$$= \begin{bmatrix} 1 + ab & a \\ b & 1 \end{bmatrix} \neq S_h$$

Hence proved.

37. Find the normalization transformation N which uses the rectangle A (1,1), B (5,3), C (4,5) and D (0,3) as a window and the normalized device screen as a viewport where x extent is from 0 to 1 and y extent is from 0 to 1.

Ans. Let us construct the rectangle with the coordinates A (1,1), B (5,3), C (4,5), and D (0,3) as shown in Figure 5.47.

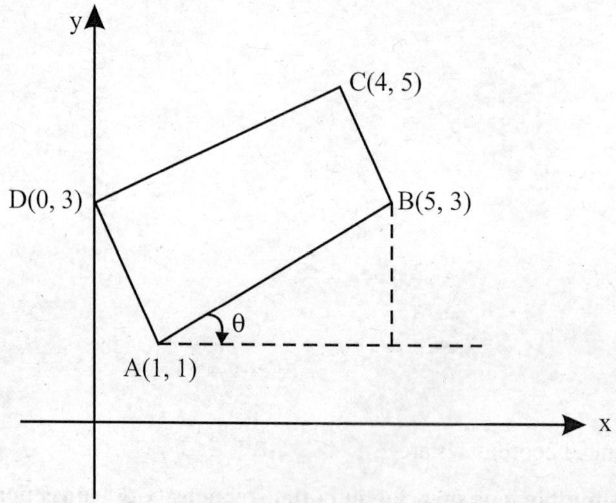

Figure 5.47 Rectangle with Coordinates A (1,1), B(5,3), C(4,5), and D(0,3)

Now, rotate the rectangle clockwise by θ (that is, align with the x-axis) about point A. Therefore,

$$\theta = \tan^{-1}\left(\frac{3-1}{5-1}\right) = \tan^{-1}\left(\frac{1}{2}\right)$$

So, $\sin\theta = \frac{1}{\sqrt{5}}$, $\cos\theta = \frac{2}{\sqrt{5}} = \cos(-\theta)$, and $\sin(-\theta) = -\frac{1}{\sqrt{5}}$

The rotation matrix about A (1,1) is given by the following matrix:

$$R_{-\theta,A} = \begin{bmatrix} \frac{2}{\sqrt{5}} & \frac{1}{\sqrt{5}} & \left(1-\frac{3}{\sqrt{5}}\right) \\ -\frac{1}{\sqrt{5}} & \frac{2}{\sqrt{5}} & \left(1-\frac{1}{\sqrt{5}}\right) \\ 0 & 0 & 1 \end{bmatrix}$$

The x extent of the rotated window is the length of AB $= \sqrt{2^2 + 4^2} = 2\sqrt{5}$

And the y extent is the length of AD $= \sqrt{1^2 + 2^2} = \sqrt{5}$

Since x and y extent of the normalized device screen are 1, then

$$\frac{xv_{max} - xv_{min}}{xw_{max} - xw_{min}} = \frac{1-0}{2\sqrt{5}-0} = \frac{1}{2\sqrt{5}}$$

$$\frac{yv_{max} - yv_{min}}{yw_{max} - yw_{min}} = \frac{1-0}{\sqrt{5}-0} = \frac{1}{\sqrt{5}}$$

Therefore,

$$N = T_V S_{s_x,s_y} \cdot T_{-V} = \begin{bmatrix} \frac{1}{2\sqrt{5}} & 0 & -\frac{1}{2\sqrt{5}} \\ 0 & \frac{1}{\sqrt{5}} & -\frac{1}{\sqrt{5}} \\ 0 & 0 & 1 \end{bmatrix}$$

The normalized transformation is

$$N_R = N \cdot R_{-\theta,A}$$

$$= \begin{bmatrix} \frac{1}{2\sqrt{5}} & 0 & -\frac{1}{2\sqrt{5}} \\ 0 & \frac{1}{\sqrt{5}} & -\frac{1}{\sqrt{5}} \\ 0 & 0 & 1 \end{bmatrix} \begin{bmatrix} \frac{2}{\sqrt{5}} & \frac{1}{\sqrt{5}} & \left(1-\frac{3}{\sqrt{5}}\right) \\ -\frac{1}{\sqrt{5}} & \frac{2}{\sqrt{5}} & \left(1-\frac{1}{\sqrt{5}}\right) \\ 0 & 0 & 1 \end{bmatrix}$$

$$N_R = \begin{bmatrix} \frac{1}{5} & \frac{1}{10} & -\frac{3}{10} \\ -\frac{1}{5} & \frac{2}{5} & -\frac{1}{5} \\ 0 & 0 & 1 \end{bmatrix}$$

38. Using the Cohen–Sutherland line-clipping algorithm find the visible portion of the line P (40,80), Q (120,30) inside the window, the window is defined as ABCD: A (20,20), B (60,20), C (60,40) and D (20,40).

Ans. All the four bits of region code can be calculated as:

$$\text{Bit 1} = \text{sign}(y - y_{max}) = \text{sign}(y - 40)$$

$$\text{Bit2} = \text{sign}(y_{min} - y) = \text{sign}(20 - y)$$

$$\text{Bit3} = \text{sign}(x - x_{max}) = \text{sign}(x - 60)$$

$$\text{Bit4} = \text{sign}(x_{min} - x) = \text{sign}(20 - x)$$

$$\text{sign}(a) = \begin{cases} 1, & \text{if positive} \\ 0, & \text{otherwise} \end{cases}$$

Region codes for the point P(40, 80) → 1000 and Q(120, 30) → 0010

Therefore, (1000) AND (0010) = 0000 which is zero.

Equation of PQ ⇒ $5x + 8y = 840$

Solving this Equation with all four Equations of window boundary,

$$x = 20 \Rightarrow y = 92.5$$
$$x = 60 \Rightarrow y = 67.5$$
$$y = 20 \Rightarrow x = 136$$
$$y = 40 \Rightarrow x = 104$$

Since both the values of y are greater than y_{max} and both the values of x are also greater than x_{max}, the line segment PQ completely lies outside the window.

39. Using the Sutherland–Hodgeman algorithm, clip the following polygon against the rectangle given in Figure 5.48.

Ans. Clipping of polygon EFGHE against rectangle ABCD is described by the following steps: Clip the polygon against the line AB

Equation of line AB ⇒ $y = 25$

Equation of line EF ⇒ $y - 50 = -1(x - 0)$

$$x + y = 50$$

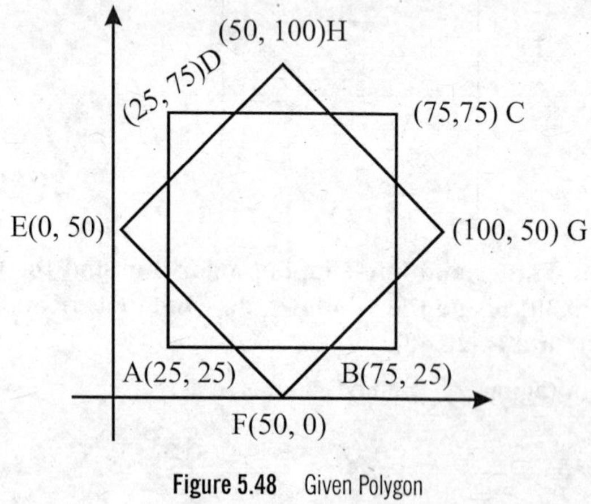

Figure 5.48 Given Polygon

Equation of the line FG ⇒ $x - y = 50$.

Finding intersection of the line segment AB with the line segment EF and FG, we get vertices P_1 and P_2.

$$P_1 = (25, 25)$$
$$P_2 = (75, 25) = P_3$$
$$P_4 = (75, 75) = P_5$$
$$P_6 = (25, 75) = P_7$$
$$P_8 = P_1 = (25, 25)$$

It is very clear from the intersection points of the polygon and the rectangle that the polygon is totally outside clipping boundaries, that is, not a single vertex is inside the clipping window. Therefore, output will be zero.

MULTIPLE CHOICE QUESTIONS

1. Translation, rotation, and scaling are the basic _______.
   (a) Coordinates (b) Position vectors
   (c) Transformations (d) Representations
2. _________ enables the user to represent all geometric transformation Equations as matrix multiplications.
   (a) Homogeneous coordinates (b) Rotation
   (c) Scaling (d) None of these
3. By performing the sequence of ______________ scaling about any selected fixed point is generated.
   (a) Translate–scale–inverse translate (b) Translate–inverse scale–translate
   (c) Scale–rotate–translate (d) Any of these
4. _________ is the movement of pixels from one location to another.
   (a) Block manipulation (b) Block transfer
   (c) Pixel transfer (d) None of these
5. NVC stands for __________.
   (a) Normalized viewing coordinates (b) Normalized viewing clipping
   (c) Normalized video controller (d) None of these
6. MC stands for ___________.
   (a) Modelling coordinates (b) Measuring coordinates
   (c) Measuring clipper (d) None of these
7. WC stands for __________.
   (a) Window clipper (b) Window coordinates
   (c) World coordinates (d) None of these
8. Clipping window is also known as ________.
   (a) Coordinate clipper (b) Clipping coordinates
   (c) Clipping ratio (d) Clipping region

9. __________ is based on parametric Equations of a line segment.
   (a) Midpoint subdivision algorithm
   (b) Liang–Barsky algorithm
   (c) Cohen–Sutherland algorithm
   (d) All of these
10. _________ the process of removing the portion of a polygon which does not lie within the clipping window.
   (a) Polygon removal
   (b) Polygon cutting
   (c) Polygon clipping
   (d) None of these

Answers 1.(c) 2.(a) 3.(a) 4.(b) 5.(a) 6.(a) 7.(c) 8.(d) 9.(b) 10.(c)

6

Three-dimensional Transformations and Viewing

1. Explain the following terms:

(a) 3D translation

(b) 3D rotation and

(c) 3D scaling

Ans. (a) Like 2D translation, 3D translation is also performed by moving an object from its original position by a given distance and direction. However, in 3D one needs to consider the z-coordinate also in addition to x and y coordinates. If we need to translate a given surface in 3D, then each of its vertices should be transformed so that the surface can be generated in the new or translated position. For example, a point P on a cubic surface is translated from its original position P(x, y, z) to a new position P'(x', y', z') by the following translation matrix expression (also see Figure 6.1):

$$\begin{bmatrix} x' \\ y' \\ z' \\ 1 \end{bmatrix} = \begin{bmatrix} 1 & 0 & 0 & t_x \\ 0 & 1 & 0 & t_y \\ 0 & 0 & 1 & t_z \\ 0 & 0 & 0 & 1 \end{bmatrix} \cdot \begin{bmatrix} x \\ y \\ z \\ 1 \end{bmatrix} \qquad (1)$$

where t_x, t_y, and t_z are the parameters that specify the translation distances for the coordinate directions x, y, and z, respectively. Note that these parameters can be assigned any real values. The matrix representation expressed in Equation (1) is equivalent to:

$$P' = T \cdot P$$

where T is the translation operator, which is a 4 × 4 matrix, and

$$x' = x + t_x$$
$$y' = y + t_y$$
$$z' = z + t_z$$

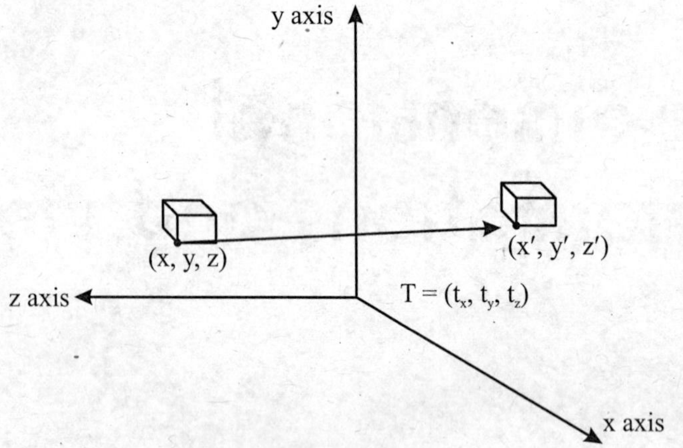

Figure 6.1 Translating an Object with Translation Vector $T=(T_x, T_y, T_z)$

In order to perform translation in the opposite direction, one needs to find the inverse of the translation matrix. This is done by replacing the translation distances, namely, t_x, t_y, and t_z by $-t_x$, $-t_y$, and $-t_z$, respectively. Then the desired matrix will be expressed as follows:

$$T^{-1} = \begin{bmatrix} 1 & 0 & 0 & -t_x \\ 0 & 1 & 0 & -t_y \\ 0 & 0 & 1 & -t_z \\ 0 & 0 & 0 & 1 \end{bmatrix}$$

(b) Performing rotation transformation in 3D is much more complex as compared to that of rotation transformation in 2D. This is because 3D rotation transformation can be specified around any line in space whereas in 2D, rotation is always specified in the xy plane. Thus, one can say that 3D rotation requires an axis of rotation (about which an object is to be rotated) rather than the center of rotation in addition to the prescription of an angle of rotation θ (the amount of angular rotation). Note that the positive rotation angles produce anti-clockwise rotations about a coordinate axis, while negative rotation angles produce clockwise rotations.

The rotation of a 3D object about the x-axis (see Figure 6.2) can be expressed by the following transformation equations:

$$\begin{aligned} x' &= x \\ y' &= y\cos\theta - z\sin\theta \\ z' &= y\sin\theta + z\cos\theta \end{aligned} \qquad (2)$$

where θ specifies the rotation angle.

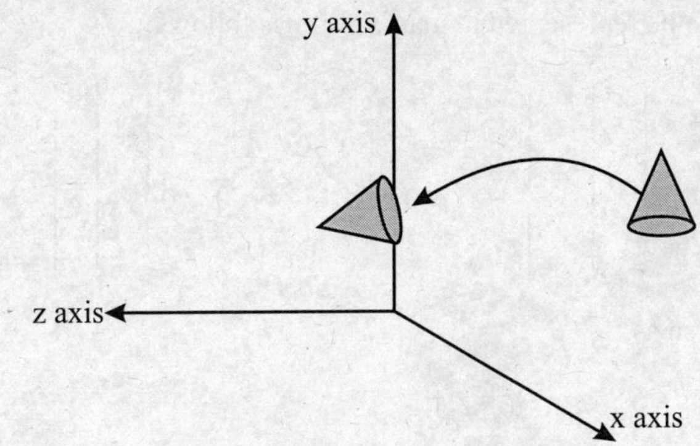

Figure 6.2 Rotating an Object about the x-axis

Equation (2) can now be represented in matrix form (or homogeneous coordinate form) as follows:

$$\begin{bmatrix} x' \\ y' \\ z' \\ 1 \end{bmatrix} = \begin{bmatrix} 1 & 0 & 0 & 0 \\ 0 & \cos\theta & -\sin\theta & 0 \\ 0 & \sin\theta & \cos\theta & 0 \\ 0 & 0 & 0 & 1 \end{bmatrix} \cdot \begin{bmatrix} x \\ y \\ z \\ 1 \end{bmatrix}$$

which can then be rewritten as:

$$P' = R_x(\theta) \,.\, P$$

where $R_x(\theta)$ specifies the rotation angle about the x-axis.

In a similar way, the rotation of a 3D object about the y-axis (see Figure 6.3) can be expressed as follows:

$$\begin{aligned} x' &= z\sin\theta + x\cos\theta \\ y' &= y \\ z' &= z\cos\theta - x\sin\theta \end{aligned} \qquad (3)$$

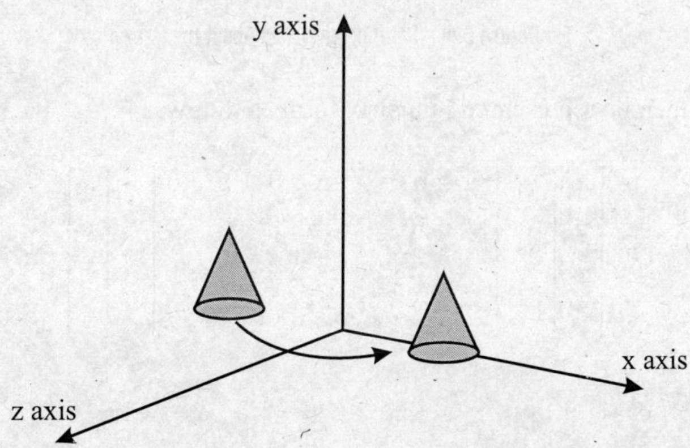

Figure 6.3 Rotating an Object about the y-axis

Equation (3) can then be represented in matrix form as follows:

$$\begin{bmatrix} x' \\ y' \\ z' \\ 1 \end{bmatrix} = \begin{bmatrix} \cos\theta & 0 & \sin\theta & 0 \\ 0 & 1 & 0 & 0 \\ -\sin\theta & 0 & \cos\theta & 0 \\ 0 & 0 & 0 & 1 \end{bmatrix} \cdot \begin{bmatrix} x \\ y \\ z \\ 1 \end{bmatrix} \tag{4}$$

which can be rewritten as:

$$P' = R_y(\theta) \, . \, P$$

For rotation about the z-axis (see Figure 6.4), the transformation equations are:

$$\begin{aligned} x' &= x\cos\theta - y\sin\theta \\ y' &= x\sin\theta + y\cos\theta \\ z' &= z \end{aligned} \tag{5}$$

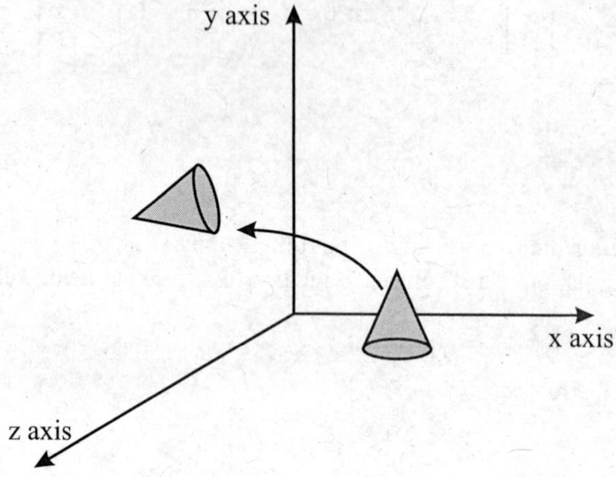

Figure 6.4 Rotating an Object about the z-axis

Equation (5) can then be represented in matrix form as follows:

$$\begin{bmatrix} x' \\ y' \\ z' \\ 1 \end{bmatrix} = \begin{bmatrix} \cos\theta & -\sin\theta & 0 & 0 \\ \sin\theta & \cos\theta & 0 & 0 \\ 0 & 0 & 1 & 0 \\ 0 & 0 & 0 & 1 \end{bmatrix} \cdot \begin{bmatrix} x \\ y \\ z \\ 1 \end{bmatrix} \tag{6}$$

which can be rewritten as:

$$P' = R_z(\theta) \, . \, P$$

One can also obtain the inverse of the rotation matrix (R^{-1}) for any axis by negating the rotation angle θ. This will generate rotation in the clockwise direction. However, if we interchange the rows and columns of a rotation matrix, then also one can obtain an R^{-1} matrix (that is, $R^T = R^{-1}$).

(c) Like 2D scaling, in 3D scaling also, the size of an object is changed by compressing or expanding its dimensions, and then repositioning an object with respect to the coordinate origin. For example, the point P will be scaled from its original position P(x,y,z) to a new position P'(x',y',z') relative to the coordinate origin from the following scaling matrix expression:

$$\begin{bmatrix} x' \\ y' \\ z' \\ 1 \end{bmatrix} = \begin{bmatrix} s_x & 0 & 0 & 0 \\ 0 & s_y & 0 & 0 \\ 0 & 0 & s_z & 0 \\ 0 & 0 & 0 & 1 \end{bmatrix} \cdot \begin{bmatrix} x \\ y \\ z \\ 1 \end{bmatrix} \tag{7}$$

where s_x, s_y, and s_z are the scaling parameters which can take any positive values.

$$x' = x \cdot s_x$$
$$y' = y \cdot s_y$$
$$z' = z \cdot s_z$$

Thus, Equation (7) can also be rewritten as follows:

$$P' = S \cdot P$$

Figure 6.5 illustrates the scaling transformation of a 3D object. In this figure, we have set the scaling parameters $s_x=s_y=s_z=3$, which increases both the size and the distance of the object by a factor of 3.

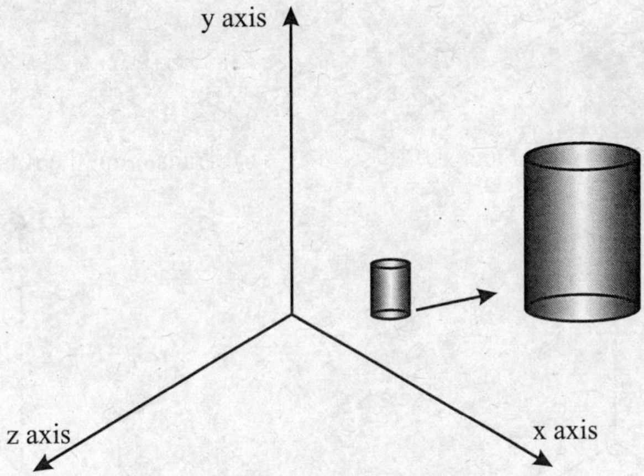

Figure 6.5 Scaling an Object by a Factor of 3

To obtain an opposite scaling transformation, one needs to calculate the inverse of the scaling matrix. This is done by replacing the scaling parameters s_x, s_y, and s_z by their respective reciprocals. That is, by $\frac{1}{s_x}$, $\frac{1}{s_y}$ and $\frac{1}{s_z}$, respectively.

2. Give the steps required for rotating an object:
(a) about an axis parallel to one of the coordinate axis
(b) about an axis not parallel to any of the coordinate axis.

Ans. (a) To rotate an object about an axis which is parallel to one of the coordinate axes (see Figure 6.6(a), following steps need to be performed:

1. **Translate:** The object is translated in such a manner that the rotation axis coincides with the parallel coordinate axis (see Figure 6.6b).
2. **Rotate:** The object is then rotated by the specified angle about that axis (see Figure 6.6c).
3. **Translate:** The object is finally translated so that the rotation axis is moved back to its original position (see Figure 6.6d).

Any coordinate position P on the rotated object when transformed to position P' will be mathematically expressed as follows:

$$P' = T^{-1} \cdot R_x(\theta) \cdot T \cdot P$$

where $R(\theta) = T^{-1} \cdot R_x(\theta) \cdot T$ is the composite transformation.

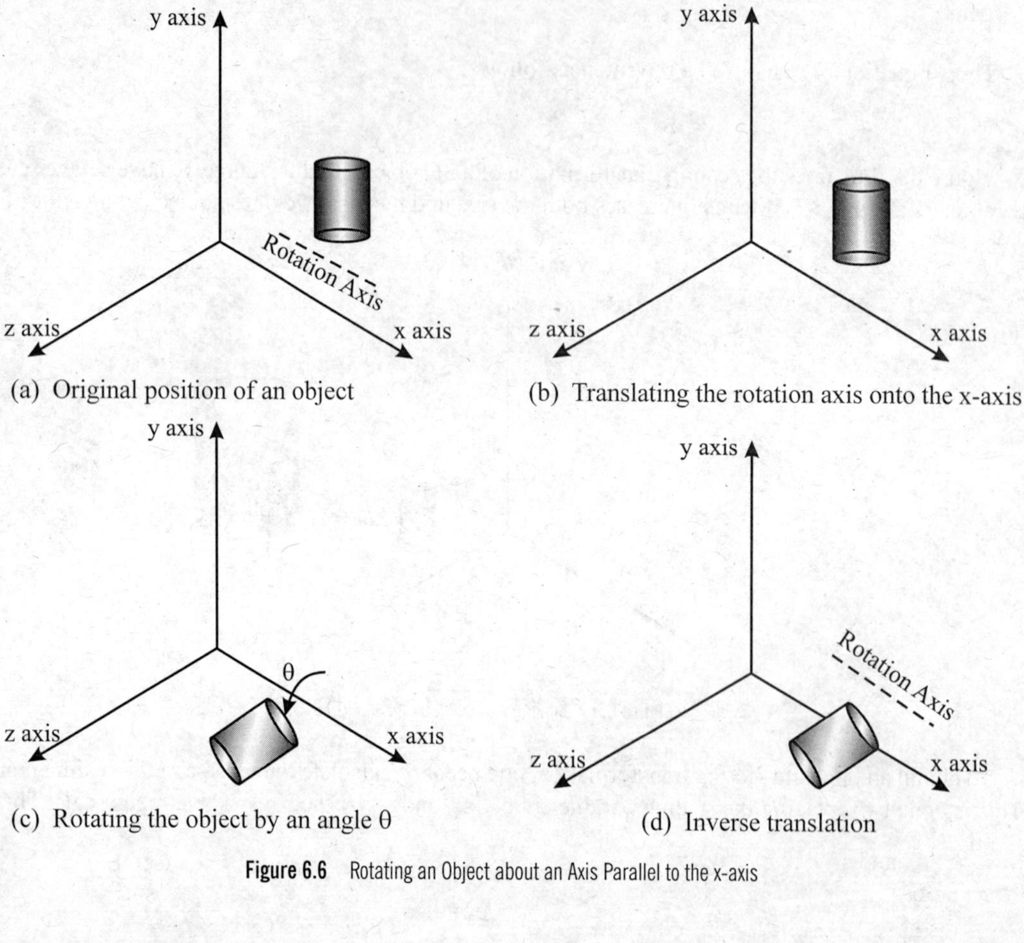

Figure 6.6 Rotating an Object about an Axis Parallel to the x-axis

(b) To rotate a 3D object about an arbitrary axis that is not parallel to any of the coordinate axes, the following steps need to be performed:

1. **Translate:** The object is translated in such a manner that the rotation axis passes through the coordinate origin.
2. **Rotate:** The object is then rotated such that its axis of rotation coincides with any of the coordinate axes.
3. **Rotate:** The object is again rotated by the specified angle about that coordinate axis from where the axis of rotation has passed.
4. **Inverse rotation:** This is done to bring back the rotation axis to its original orientation.
5. **Inverse translation:** This is applied to bring back the rotation axis to its original position.

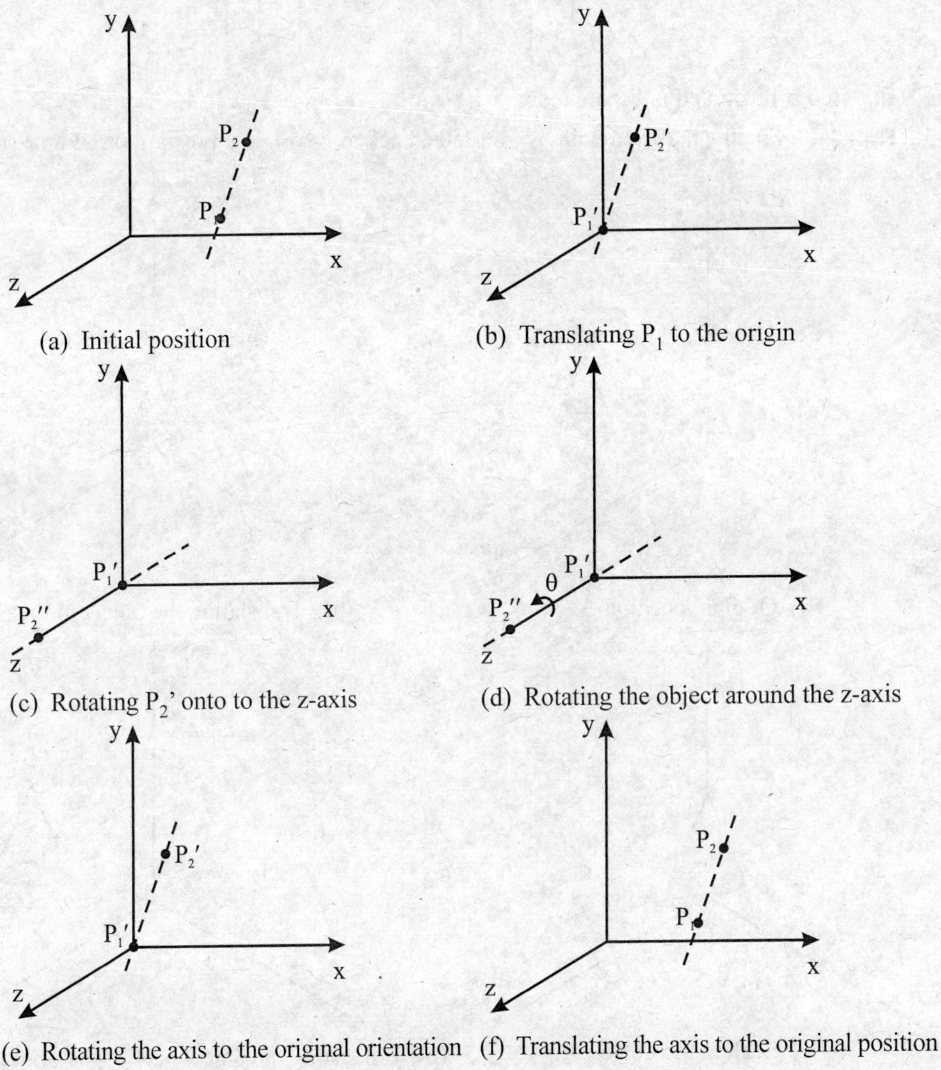

Figure 6.7 Rotating an Object about an Arbitrary Axis

3. Give the steps required for performing scaling with respect to any selected fixed position.

Ans. Let the object be placed at the x-axis, which is to be scaled with respect to a selected fixed point (x_f, y_f, z_f) (see Figure 6.8a). The steps required for performing such a transformation are as follows:

1. **Translate:** The selected fixed point (x_f, y_f, z_f) is translated in such a manner that it coincides with the origin (see Figure 6.8b).
2. **Scale:** Now, scale the object with respect to the origin by using the following equation:

$$\begin{bmatrix} x' \\ y' \\ z' \\ 1 \end{bmatrix} = \begin{bmatrix} s_x & 0 & 0 & 0 \\ 0 & s_y & 0 & 0 \\ 0 & 0 & s_z & 0 \\ 0 & 0 & 0 & 1 \end{bmatrix} \cdot \begin{bmatrix} x \\ y \\ z \\ 1 \end{bmatrix}$$

   This step is illustrated in Figure 6.8c.
3. **Translate:** Finally, the fixed point is translated back to its original position (see Figure 6.8d).

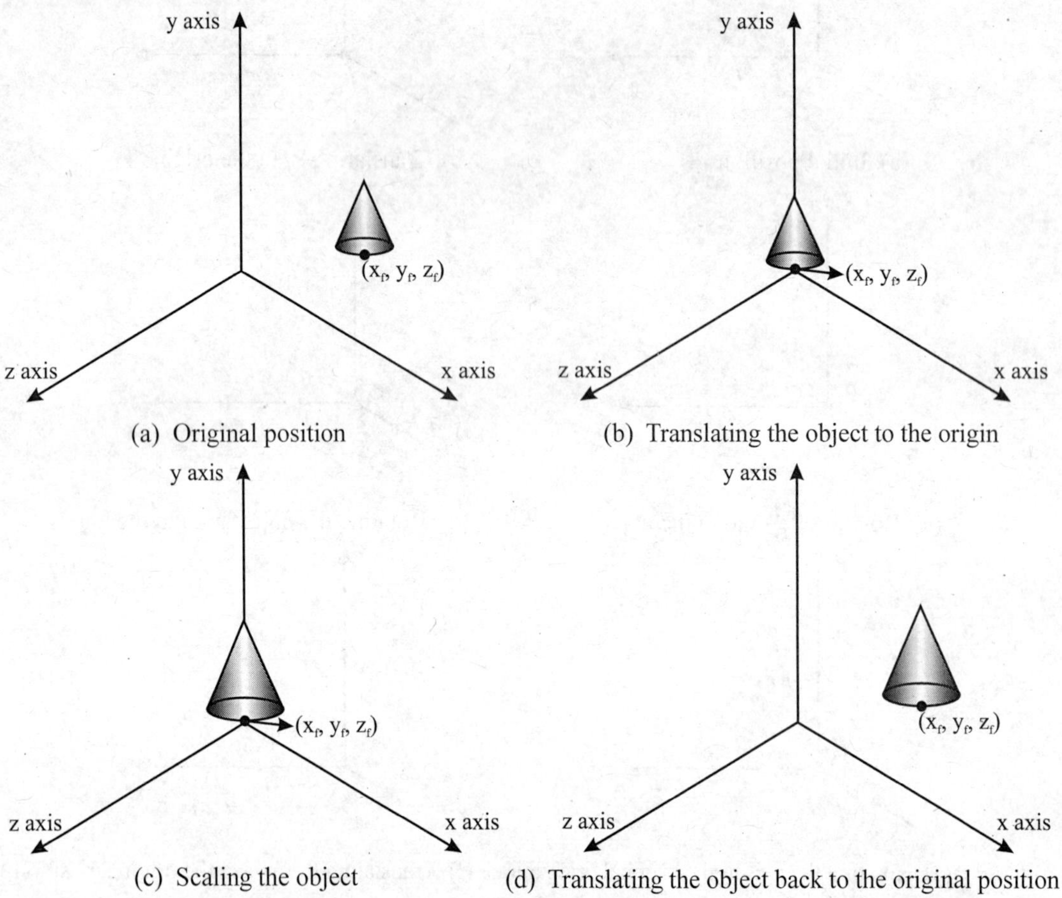

Figure 6.8 Scaling an Object with Respect to a Specified Fixed Point

One can express the above three steps as the concatenation of translate–scale–inverse translate matrix as follows:

$$T(x_f, y_f, z_f) \cdot S(s_x, s_y, s_z) \cdot T(-x_f, -y_f, -z_f) = \begin{bmatrix} s_x & 0 & 0 & (1 - s_x)x_f \\ 0 & s_y & 0 & (1 - s_y)y_f \\ 0 & 0 & s_z & (1 - s_z)z_f \\ 0 & 0 & 0 & 1 \end{bmatrix}$$

4. Derive the quaternion rotation matrix for rotation about an arbitrary axis in the 3D domain.

or

Explain how quaternions are used in rotation in a 3D space.

Ans. The use of quaternion representation for the rotation transformation is a more efficient method for obtaining rotation about a specified axis. A quaternion (q) can be thought of as an ordered pair consisting of a **scalar part** s and a **vector part** v. Thus, q can be defined as:

$$q = (s, v) \tag{1}$$

To perform rotation about any arbitrary axis, we will set s and v to the following values:

$$s = \cos\frac{\theta}{2}, \qquad v = u \sin\frac{\theta}{2} \tag{2}$$

where u is the unit vector along the selected rotation axis, and θ is the specified rotation angle about that arbitrary axis.

The quaternion can also be thought of as a high-order complex number with a real part (scalar part) and three complex parts (the elements of vector V).

Now, any point position, say P, which is to be rotated by this quaternion, can be represented by the following quaternion notation:

$$P = (0, p)$$

where p is the vector part of P having coordinates (x, y, z).

Rotating P will result in its new position, that is, P'. This rotation is carried out with the following quaternion operation:

$$P' = qPq^{-1} \tag{3}$$

where q^{-1} is the inverse of Equation (1) and is expressed as $(s, -v)$. Note that its scalar and vector parts have the same value as given in Equation (2). After such rotation, the new quaternion is produced which is as follows:

$$P' = (0, p')$$

Such quaternion scalar part is equal to 0 and the vector part is calculated as follows:

$$p' = s^2p + v\,(p \cdot v) + 2s\,(v \times p) + v \times (v \times p) \tag{4}$$

where s and v have the same values as given in Equation (2).

To obtain the rotation matrix, we assume the components of vector part (v) of q as (a,b,c) and define a 3×3 matrix as follows:

$$M_R(\theta) = \begin{bmatrix} 1-2b^2-2c^2 & 2ab-2sc & 2ac+2sb \\ 2ab+2sc & 1-2a^2-2c^2 & 2bc-2sa \\ 2ac-2sb & 2bc+2sa & 1-2a^2-2b^2 \end{bmatrix}$$

In addition, we need to include the translations that move the rotation axis to the coordinate axis and back to its original position in order to obtain the complete general rotation equation as follows:

$$R(\theta) = T^{-1} \cdot M_R \cdot T$$

For example, to perform a rotation about the z-axis, we can set the unit quaternion parameters as

$$s = \cos\frac{\theta}{2}, \qquad v = (0, 0, 1)\sin\frac{\theta}{2}$$

where a=0, b=0, and $c = \sin\frac{\theta}{2}$

Substituting these values into the matrix and using the following trigonometric identities

$$\cos^2\frac{\theta}{2} - \sin^2\frac{\theta}{2} = 1 - 2\sin^2\frac{\theta}{2} = \cos\theta$$

$$2\cos\frac{\theta}{2}\sin\frac{\theta}{2} = \sin\theta$$

we obtain the 3x3 version of the z-axis rotation matrix $R_z(\theta)$.

5. Give some advantages of quaternions.

Ans. Quaternions offer the following advantages:

- They are useful in generating 3D fractals and in various computer graphics procedures such as in the calculation of a 3D rotation matrix.
- It is simpler to write quaternion procedures for transformation sequences and require less storage space.
- They are very useful in animations which require complicated motion sequences and motion interpolations between two specified positions of an object.

6. Explain reflection with respect to any plane in 3D transformations.

Ans. Reflection (also known as **mirror reflection**) is one of the transformations which can be useful in various 3D graphics applications. A 3D reflection can be performed in one of the following ways:

- with respect to a selected reflection axis,
- with respect to a selected reflection plane.

If reflection is performed with respect to a selected reflection axis, then the object is rotated by 180º about that axis. On the other hand, if it is performed with respect to a selected reflection plane, then also the object is rotated by 180º, but now the rotation is performed in 4D space. In case the reflection plane is a coordinate plane (that is, either xy, xz or yz), then the transformation can be thought of as a conversion between a right-handed viewing system (RHVS) and a left-handed viewing system (LHVS), and vice versa. For example, when reflection is applied relative to the xy plane, only the sign of the z-coordinate is reversed while x and y-coordinate values remain unchanged. For such a plane, the transformation matrix is as follows:

$$RF_z = \begin{bmatrix} 1 & 0 & 0 & 0 \\ 0 & 1 & 0 & 0 \\ 0 & 0 & -1 & 0 \\ 0 & 0 & 0 & 1 \end{bmatrix} \tag{1}$$

Figure 6.9 illustrates the reflection transformation with respect to the xy plane.

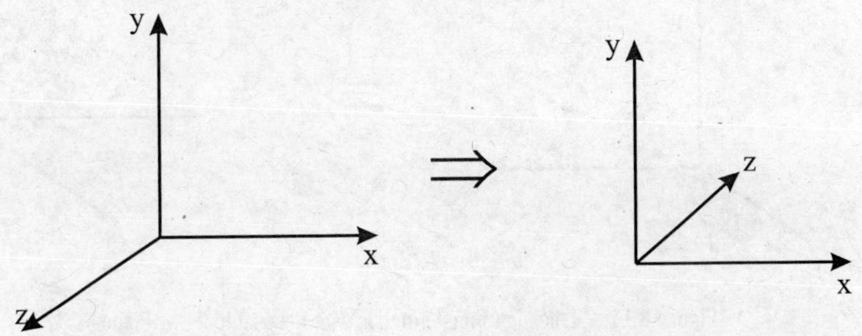

Figure 6.9 Reflection Transformation with Respect to the xy Plane

Similarly, the transformation matrix representation for the reflection of points with respect to the xz plane (in which only the sign of the y-coordinate value is changed) is given as follows:

$$RF_y = \begin{bmatrix} 1 & 0 & 0 & 0 \\ 0 & -1 & 0 & 0 \\ 0 & 0 & 1 & 0 \\ 0 & 0 & 0 & 1 \end{bmatrix} \tag{2}$$

Figure 6.10 illustrates the reflection transformation with respect to the xz plane.

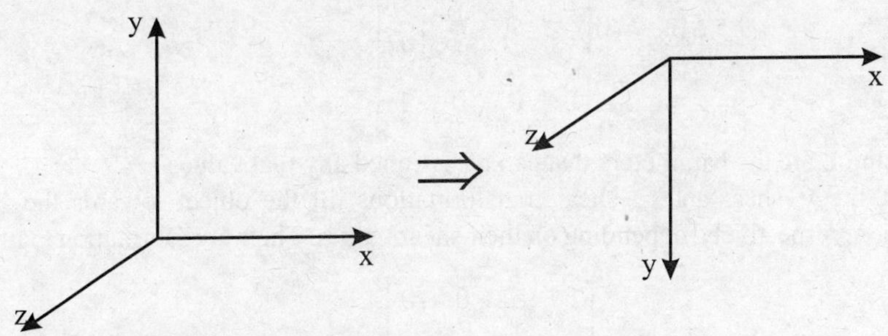

Figure 6.10 Reflection Transformation with Respect to the xz Plane

In a similar manner, the transformation matrix representation for the reflection of points with respect to the yz plane (in which only the sign of the x-coordinate value is changed) is given as follows:

$$RF_x = \begin{bmatrix} -1 & 0 & 0 & 0 \\ 0 & 1 & 0 & 0 \\ 0 & 0 & 1 & 0 \\ 0 & 0 & 0 & 1 \end{bmatrix} \quad (3)$$

Figure 6.11 illustrates the reflection transformation with respect to the yz plane.

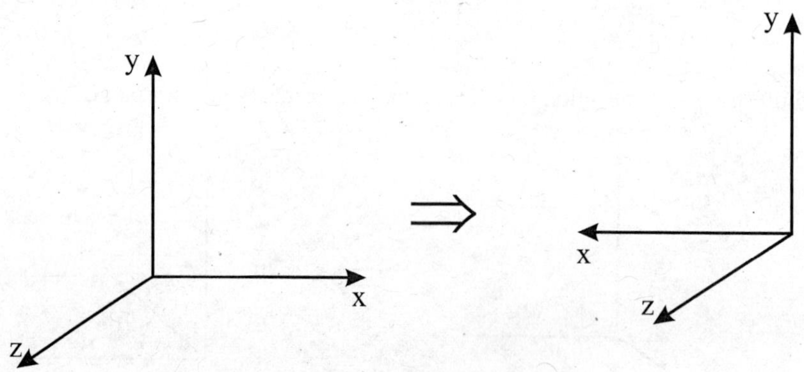

Figure 6.11 Reflection Transformation with Respect to the yz Plane

7. Explain the shearing transformations in 3D.

Ans. A 3D shearing transformation is similar to that of 2D shearing transformation except that in 3D one can also generate shears along the z-axis. Like 2D shearing, 3D shearing is used to produce distortions in the shapes of 3D objects. When shearing is done relative to the x-axis, the y-coordinate and z-coordinate remain unchanged while x-coordinate values get changed. This results in tilting of the object towards the x-direction (either to the left or to the right, depending on the x-shear value). A 3D shearing with respect to the x-axis is represented by the following transformation matrix:

$$SH_x = \begin{bmatrix} 1 & 0 & 0 & 0 \\ a & 1 & 0 & 0 \\ b & 0 & 1 & 0 \\ 0 & 0 & 0 & 1 \end{bmatrix}$$

where a and b are the parameters that can be assigned any real values.

Similarly, the y-shear and z-shear transformations tilt the object towards the y-direction and z-direction, respectively, depending on their shear values. Their transformation matrix is as follows:

$$SH_y = \begin{bmatrix} 1 & a & 0 & 0 \\ 0 & 1 & 0 & 0 \\ 0 & b & 1 & 0 \\ 0 & 0 & 0 & 1 \end{bmatrix}$$

$$SH_z = \begin{bmatrix} 1 & 0 & a & 0 \\ 0 & 1 & b & 0 \\ 0 & 0 & 1 & 0 \\ 0 & 0 & 0 & 1 \end{bmatrix}$$

Shearing transformations are very useful for modifying the shapes of objects and are also used in obtaining the general projection transformations.

8. Draw 3D transformation pipeline from modeling coordinates to final device coordinates.

Ans. Figure 6.12 illustrates the steps required for modeling and converting the world coordinate description of a view to the final device coordinates.

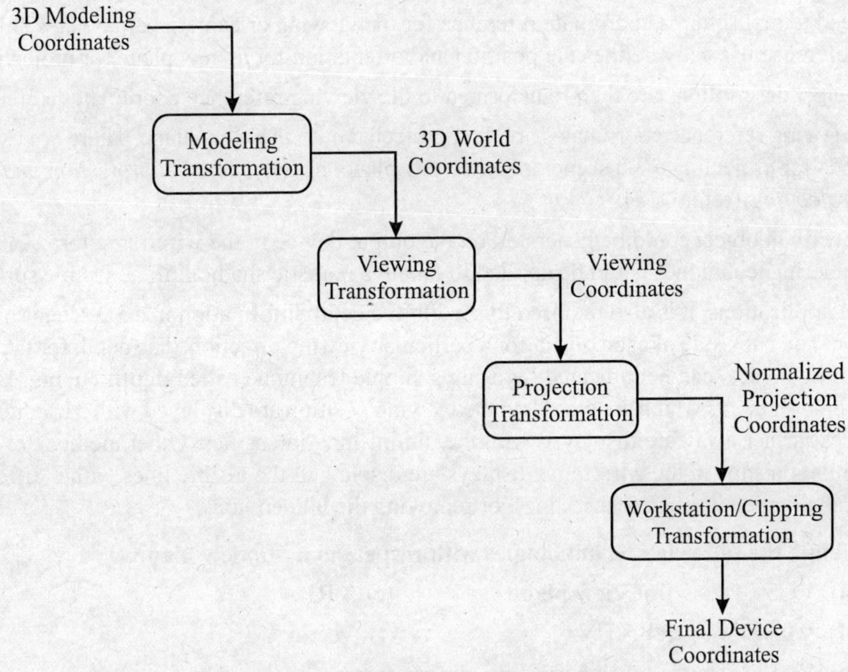

Figure 6.12 A General 3D Transformation Pipeline

First, 3D scenes are modeled using modeling transformation to generate world coordinates. After modeling a view or scene, the world coordinates are converted to the viewing coordinates by applying viewing transformation. The viewing-coordinate system helps in specifying the viewing position of observer as well as the position of the projection plane. Then, the projection operations are applied on the viewing coordinates to convert the viewing-coordinate description of the view to the coordinate positions on the projection plane. This will result in normalized projection coordinates which will then be mapped to the output device using workstation transformation. In the workstation/clipping transformation, the objects that are lying outside the specified viewing limits are clipped and are not considered in further processing. The remaining objects (or unclipped ones) are processed using visible-surface identification and surface-rendering procedures in order to display them within the device viewport.

9. What is a three-dimensional viewing process? Compare it with the 2D viewing process.

Ans. The process of generating a view of a three-dimensional scene is similar to the process of taking a photograph with a camera. To take a photograph, we first need to set the position of the camera at a particular point in the space. Then we need to set the orientation of the camera at a specified angle. Now, when we click the camera button, the scene is cropped to the size of the window or aperture of the camera. These ideas are incorporated into 3D graphics packages so as to generate views of a 3D scene.

The process of viewing a 2D scene is much simpler than the 3D viewing process. In 2D viewing, we simply specify a window in the 2D world and a viewport on the 2D view surface. Then coordinates of the object are clipped against the window so as to transform them into the viewport for display. On the other hand, the 3D viewing process is inherently complex because of the added dimension (z-axis) and the fact that the display devices are only two-dimensional. Thus, to obtain the view of a 3D world-coordinate scene, a series of steps needs to be performed, which are as follows:

1. We need to first set up a coordinate reference for the viewing or camera parameters. This coordinate reference basically defines the position and orientation for a view plane (or projection plane).
2. The object descriptions are then transformed to the viewing reference coordinates (refer Q11).
3. The viewing reference coordinates are then projected onto the view plane. There are two different methods for projecting a 3D scene onto the view plane, namely, *parallel projection and perspective projections* (refer Q12).

The view of an object could be generated on the output device in the wireframe form, or lighting or surface-rendering techniques could be applied to obtain a realistic shading of the visible surfaces.

In some applications, it is also required to specify the depth information in a 3D scene so as to identify the front and back side of each object for a particular viewing direction. The depth for the wireframe displays of the objects can be indicated by using a simple technique called **depth cueing**. In this technique, the line segments which are closest to the viewing position are displayed with a brighter intensity, and the lines farther away are displayed with the diminishing intensities. Other methods of specifying the depth relationships in the wireframe displays are displaying the visible lines with a different color, displaying the hidden lines as dashed lines, or removing the hidden lines.

10. Define the following terminologies with respect to a 3D view plane:

(a) VCS **(b) View plane** **(c) VRP**

(d) VPNV **(e) VUV** **(f) Vector U**

Ans. (a) VCS: It stands for **viewing-coordinate system**. We need to first establish this system to specify any view plane which helps in choosing a particular view of a scene. This system is also known as **view reference coordinate system**.

(b) View plane: It is that plane which is perpendicular to the viewing axis (z_v). Such a plane is set up after establishment of VCS. The view plane is also known as **projection plane**.

(c) VRP: It stands for **view reference point**. This point is the origin of our viewing-coordinate system. It can be chosen near or on the surface of some object in a scene. Alternatively, we can choose a point at the center of an object, or at the center of a group of objects, or somewhere out in front of the scene. In the former case, the point can be thought of as the position where we might want to aim a camera to take a picture of the object. In the later case, we could think this point as the camera position.

(d) VPNV: It stands for **view-plane normal vector**, symbolized by N. This vector helps in establishing the positive direction for the z_v-axis and orientation of the view plane.

(e) VUV: It stands for **view-up vector**, symbolized by V. This vector helps in establishing the positive direction for the y_v-axis. VUV can also be defined as a world-coordinate vector, or in some graphics packages, it is specified with a twist angle (θ_t) about the z_v-axis. Note that for a general orientation of normal vector N, the direction of V is precisely perpendicular to N. However, we can choose V to be in any convenient direction which is not parallel to N.

(f) Vector U: This vector helps in establishing the direction for the x_v-axis and is perpendicular to both N and V. This vector is computed by using the vectors V and N. After having direction for all U, V and N vectors, the viewing system is then referred to as the **uvn system** (see Figure 6.13).

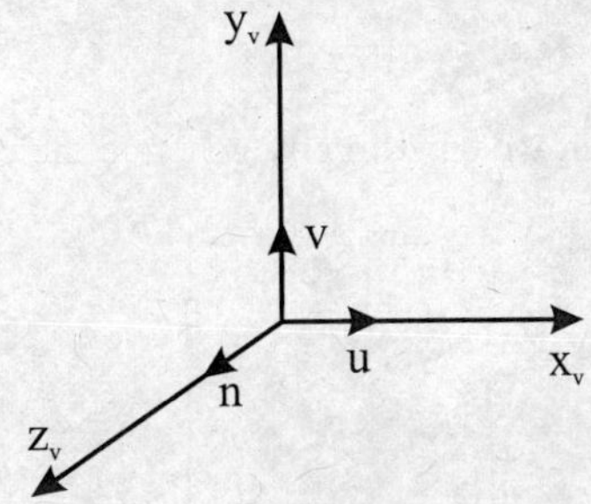

Figure 6.13 Right-handed uvn System

11. How objects are transformed from world coordinates to viewing coordinates in 3D?

Ans. In 3D viewing pipeline, after constructing a scene or before projecting object descriptions (or world coordinates) of that scene to the view plane, the object descriptions must be transformed into viewing-coordinates. This operation is equivalent to superimposing the viewing reference frame onto the world reference frame using the basic geometric translation–rotation transformations as follows:

1. **Translate:** In this operation, the view reference point is translated in such a manner that it coincides with the origin of the world-coordinate system (see Figure 6.14b). If the view reference point, P, is positioned at world position (x_0, y_0, z_0), then such point is translated to the origin with the help of the following transformation matrix:

$$T = \begin{bmatrix} 1 & 0 & 0 & -x_0 \\ 0 & 1 & 0 & -y_0 \\ 0 & 0 & 1 & -z_0 \\ 0 & 0 & 0 & 1 \end{bmatrix}$$

2. **Rotate:** In this operation, rotations are applied so as to align the view axes x_v, y_v, and z_v with the world axes x_w, y_w, and z_w, respectively. However, depending on the chosen direction of N, mostly which is not aligned with any world-coordinate axis, we need to perform rotation up to three times by following the transformation sequence $R_z \cdot R_y \cdot R_x$. That is,

   (1) first the rotation is made around the x_w-axis in order to bring z_v into the $x_w z_w$ plane;

   (2) then rotation is made around the y_w-axis to align the z_w and z_v axes;

   (3) finally, the rotation is made about the z_w-axis to align the y_w and y_v axes.

However, in case the view reference system is left-handed, then in addition to rotations, reflection of any one of the viewing axis (say, the z_v-axis) is also required.

Another way to generate a rotation–transformation matrix is to calculate unit n, v, u vectors when N and V vectors are specified. This can be done as follows:

$$n = \frac{N}{|N|} = (n_x, n_y, n_z)$$

$$u = \frac{V \times N}{|V \times N|} = (u_x, u_y, u_z)$$

$$v = n \times u = (v_x, v_y, v_z)$$

By using the values of n, u and v, we can directly generate the composite rotation matrix. That is,

$$R = \begin{bmatrix} u_x & u_y & u_z & 0 \\ v_x & v_y & v_z & 0 \\ n_x & n_y & n_z & 0 \\ 0 & 0 & 0 & 1 \end{bmatrix} \quad (1)$$

This matrix transforms u, v and n onto the world axis x_w, y_w and z_w, respectively.

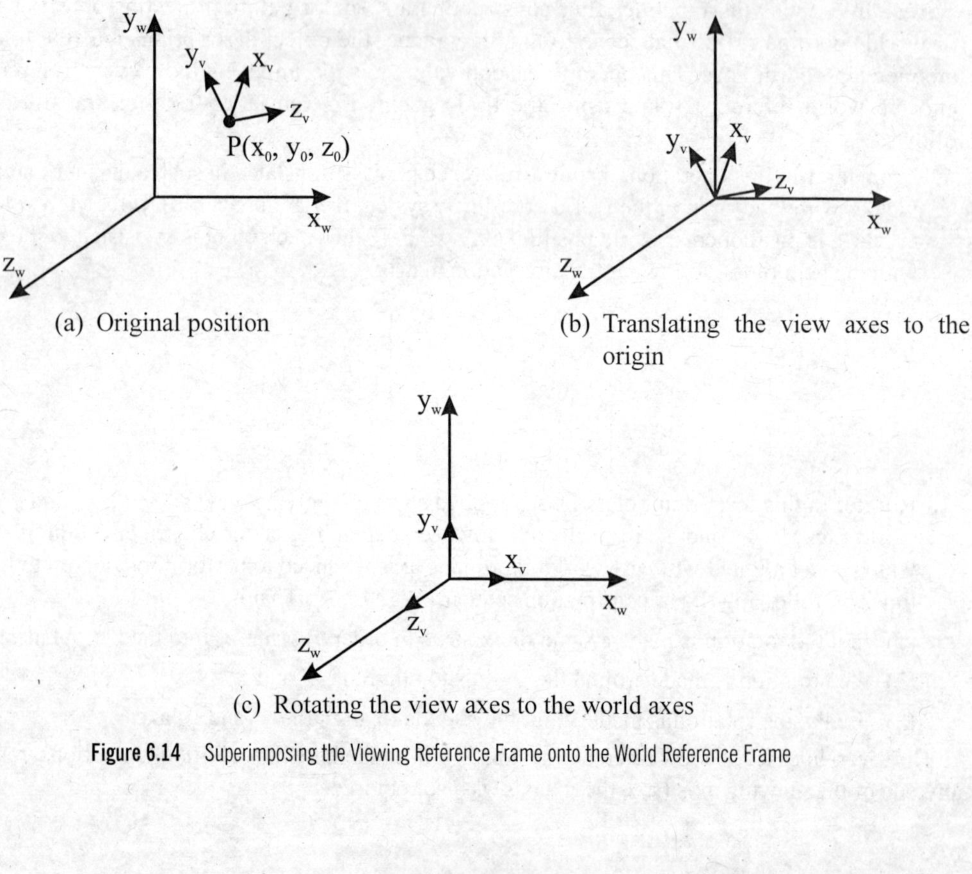

Figure 6.14 Superimposing the Viewing Reference Frame onto the World Reference Frame

The main advantage of this method is that it automatically adjusts the direction vector `V` so that `V` becomes perpendicular to `N`. Moreover, the matrix obtained in Equation (1) automatically performs the reflection whenever a left-handed viewing system is encountered for transformation.

Thus, the entire world-to-viewing coordinate transformation matrix can be obtained as follows:

$$M_{WC,VC} = R \cdot T$$

which is then applied to transfer the coordinate descriptions of the objects in a scene to the viewing reference frame.

12. Define the term projection.

Ans. The term **projection** is defined as the representation (or mapping) of a given point `P` having coordinates `(a,b,c)` onto its image as `P′ (a′,b′,c′)` in the view plane (or projection plane), which constitutes the display surface (see Figure 6.15). Such mapping can be ascertained by a straight projection line known as **projector** that emanates through point `P` and intersects the view plane at point `P′`. Such type of projections are also known as **planar geometric projections** as the projections are done onto a plane surface rather than some curved surface, and straight line projectors are used rather than curved projectors.

The most important feature of performing projection is that it preserves lines. That is, the line joining the projections of the endpoints of the original line is the same as the projection of the line itself. Thus, only the line endpoints need actually to be projected rather than projecting the line itself. Note that the result of such projection depends on the spatial relationship among the projectors and the spatial relationship between the projectors and the view plane. The concept of projection has been basically introduced to solve the problems of mismatch between 3D objects and 2D output devices.

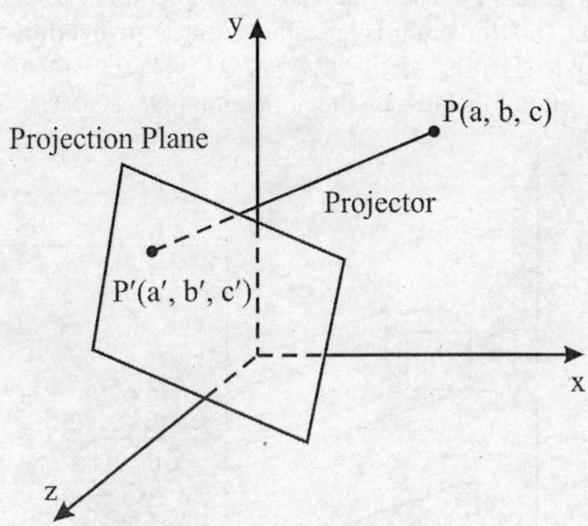

Figure 6.15 Projection of a Point P on the Projection Plane

13. Give the classification of planar geometric projection.

Ans. Planar geometric projection is basically divided into two classes, namely, *parallel* and *perspective* projections. In a **parallel projection**, object positions are transformed to the view plane along parallel lines whereas in a **perspective projection**, object positions are transformed to the view plane along that line which converges to another point known as **center of projection** (also known as **projection**

reference point). Both these projections are further classified into various types of projections as shown in Figure 6.16.

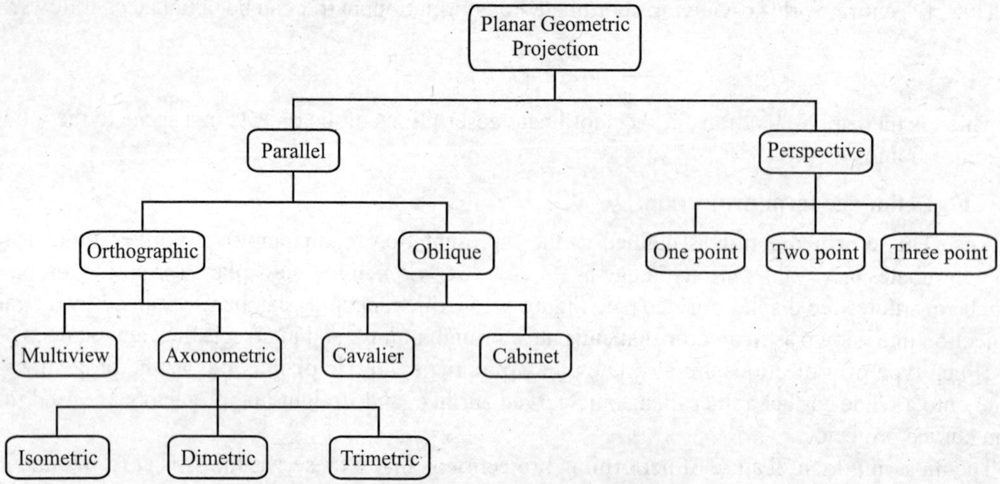

Figure 6.16 Classification of Planar Geometric Projections

14. Write a short note on parallel projection.

Ans. In parallel projection, coordinate positions are transformed to the view plane along parallel lines. All the projectors are parallel to each other and the direction of each projection is the prescribed direction for all projectors. This direction is specified using a **projection vector (V)**. It is computed by subtracting the two points. That is, `(x,y,z,1)-(x',y',z',1) =(a,b,c,0)`. Figure 6.17 illustrates the parallel projection of a cube on the projection plane.

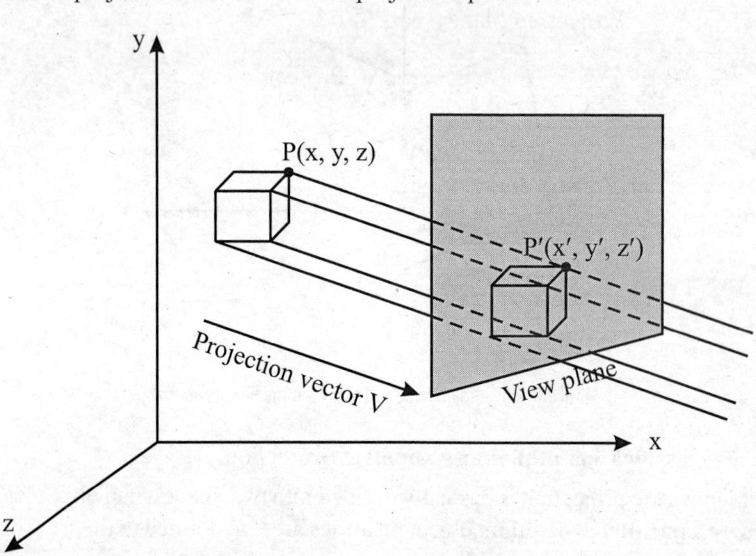

Figure 6.17 Parallel Projection of a Cube

The most important feature of parallel projection is that it preserves relative proportions of objects (that is, their shape and scale), and thus, is used by drafters for producing scale drawings of 3D objects. Moreover, such projections help to obtain the accurate views of the sides of various objects. They are also useful for engineers to create architectural drawings, blueprints or schematics of objects by maintaining their relative proportions. However, parallel projection lacks in providing a realistic representation of the appearance of a 3D object.

15. Explain the various types of parallel projection.

Ans. The parallel projection is further divided into two types, namely, *orthographic projection* and *oblique projection*. Both these projections are discussed as follows:

Orthographic Parallel Projection

When the projection vector (V) is perpendicular to the view plane, the projection is said to be **orthographic parallel projection** (see Figure 6.18).

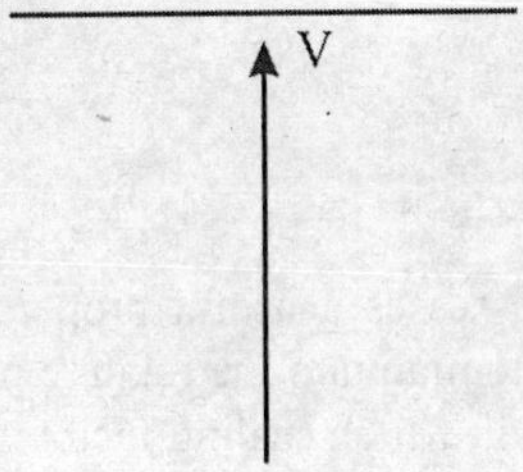

Figure 6.18 Orthographic Parallel Projection

Such projections are often used to produce the top, front, rear and side views of an object (as shown in Figure 6.19). Orthographic projections are useful in the area of engineering and architectural drawings to depict the machine parts and assemblies, and buildings because the lengths and angles can be accurately and easily measured from such drawings. However, it is very difficult to infer the 3D nature of the projected object even if all the views are studied simultaneously.

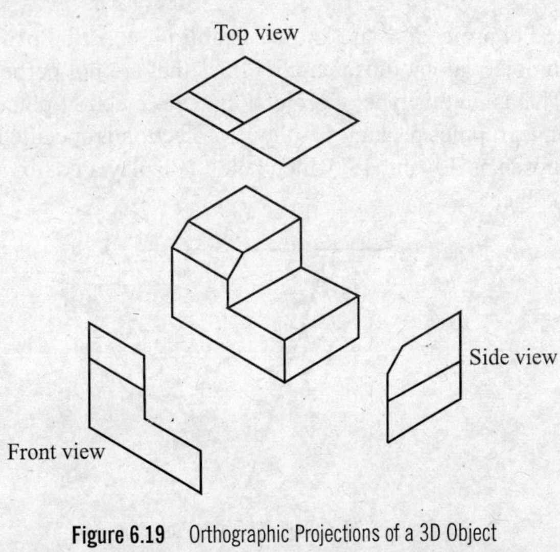

Figure 6.19 Orthographic Projections of a 3D Object

Orthographic parallel projection is further divided into the following types:

- **Multiview projection:** In this type of projection, the direction of projection is parallel to any of the principal axes (that is, either x, y or z). This results in the front, rear, top, and side views of an object. The front, side, and rear orthographic projections of an object are called **elevations**, and the top orthographic projection is known as a **plan view**.
- **Axonometric projection:** In this type of projection, the direction of projection is not parallel to any of the principal axes. These projections are capable of displaying more than one face of an object at the same time. In this type of projection, parallelism of lines is preserved but angles are not. This type of projection is further subdivided into three types as follows:
    - **Isometric projection:** It is the most commonly used axonometric projection in which the direction of projection makes equal angles with each of the three principal axes. In other words, the projection plane is aligned in such a manner that it intersects each principal axis at the same distance from the origin. If the projection-plane normal is (d_x, d_y, d_z), then for isometric projection one must havé:

    $$|d_x| = |d_y| = |d_z|$$

    or

    $$\pm d_x = \pm d_y = \pm d_z$$

    The isometric projection possesses a useful property that all the three coordinate axes are equally foreshortened so as to maintain the relative proportions. This is not the case in a general axonometric projection, in which scaling factors may be different for the three coordinate axes. Hence, it is named iso (for equal) metric (for measurement). Moreover, the coordinate axes project in such a way that they make equal angles with one another.
    - **Dimetric projection:** In this type of projection, as the name suggests, the direction of projection makes equal angles with exactly any of the two principal axes.
    - **Trimetric projection:** In this type of projection, the direction of projection makes unequal angles with all the three principal axes.

Oblique Parallel Projection

The non-orthographic parallel projections are known as **oblique parallel projections**. It is obtained by projecting positions of an object along those parallel lines that are not perpendicular to the projection plane (see Figure 6.20). That is, in this type of projection, the projection-plane normal and the direction of projection differ. In some graphics packages, oblique projection is specified with two angles ϕ and α. Mostly, values of ϕ are chosen as 30° and 45° which help to display a combined view of the front, side, and top (or bottom) of an object.

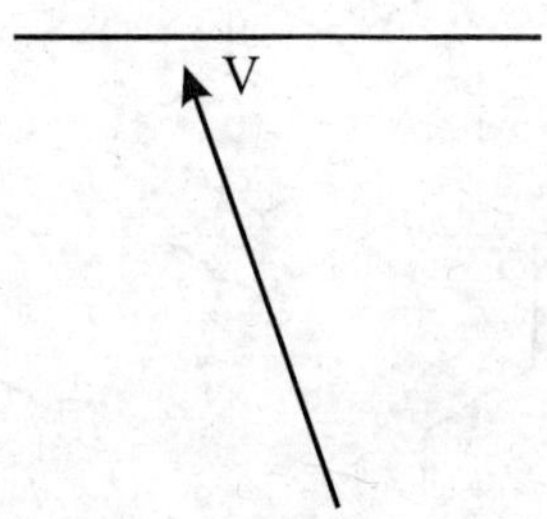

Figure 6.20 Oblique Parallel Projection

The oblique projection is further subdivided into two types, which are as follows:

- **Cavalier projection:** In this type of projection, the direction of projection makes a 45° angle with the projection plane. That is, α=45°. As a result, all lines perpendicular to the projection plane are projected with no change in length. That is, there is no foreshortening of lengths. Figure 6.21 shows examples of cavalier projections of a unit cube with ϕ=30° and ϕ=45°.

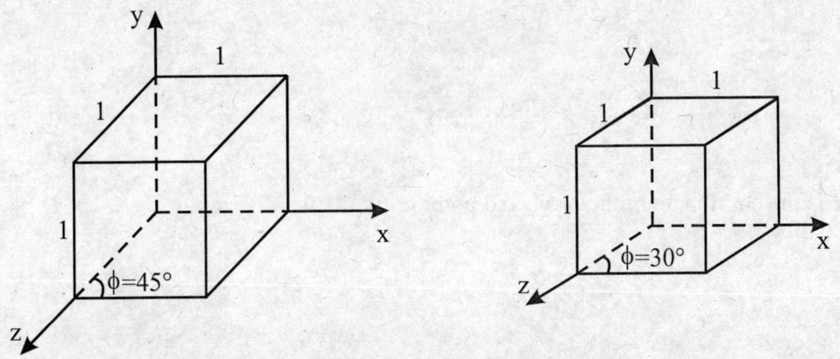

Figure 6.21 Cavalier Projection

- **Cabinet projection:** In this type of projection, the direction of projection makes a 63.4° angle (approx.) with the projection plane. That is, α=63.4°. As a result, all lines perpendicular to the projection plane are projected at one-half their length. That is, the lengths are foreshortened by exactly one-half of their actual lines. Figure 6.22 shows examples of cabinet projections of a unit cube with ϕ=30° and ϕ=45°.

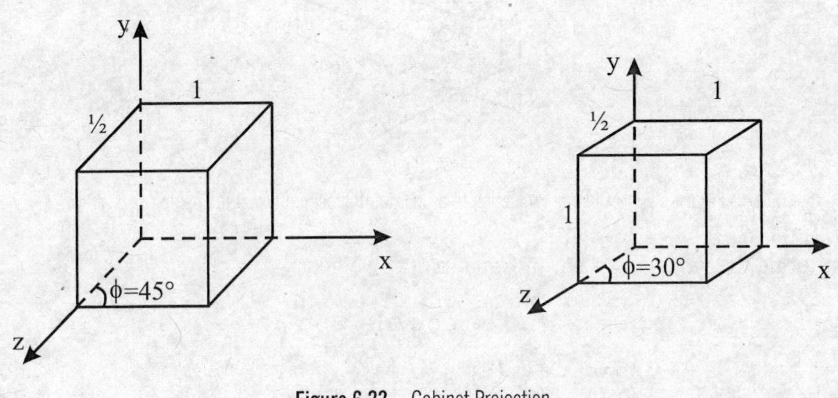

Figure 6.22 Cabinet Projection

16. How can we mathematically express the projection coordinates for any parallel projection?

Ans. Let us assume that the point P(x, y, z) is to be projected to position (x_p, y_p) on the view plane. Moreover, assume that orthographic projection coordinates on the plane are (x, y) (see Figure 6.23). It can be observed that the oblique projection line from (x, y, z) to (x_p, y_p) makes an angle α with the line on the projection plane joining (x_p, y_p) and (x, y). This line of length (L) makes an angle ϕ with the horizontal direction in the projection plane. Thus, the projection coordinates (x_p, y_p) can be expressed in terms of x, y, L and ϕ as follows:

$$x_p = x + L\cos\phi$$
$$y_p = y + L\sin\phi \qquad (1)$$

Applying trigonometric function on triangle ABC, we found that:

$$\tan\alpha = \frac{z}{L}$$

$$\Rightarrow \quad L = \frac{z}{\tan\alpha} = zL_1$$

where z is the coordinate of the projected point p and L_1 is:

$$L_1 = \frac{1}{\tan\alpha} \text{ or } \tan\alpha^{-1}$$

Note that for z=1, $L_1 = L$.

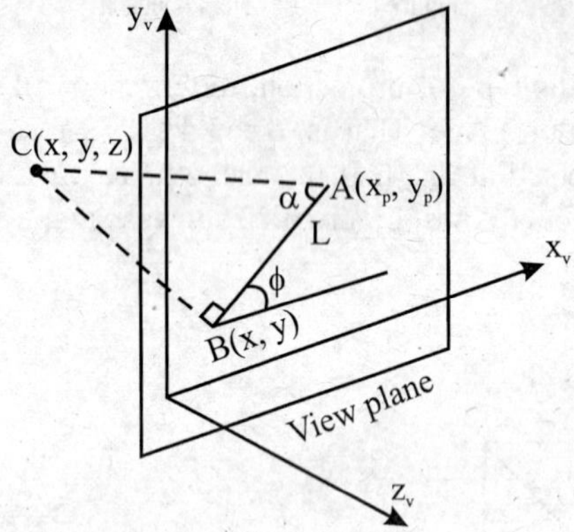

Figure 6.23 Oblique Projection of a Coordinate Position (x,y,z) to Position (x_p,y_p)

By substituting the value of $L=ZL_1$ in Equation (1) we get:

$$x_p = x + z(L_1\cos\phi) \qquad (2)$$
$$y_p = y + z(L_1\sin\phi)$$

Hence, to produce any parallel projection onto the $x_v y_v$ plane, we can write the general form of transformation matrix as follows:

$$M_{parallel} = \begin{bmatrix} 1 & 0 & L_1\cos\phi & 0 \\ 0 & 1 & L_1\sin\phi & 0 \\ 0 & 0 & 0 & 0 \\ 0 & 0 & 0 & 1 \end{bmatrix}$$

By substituting $L_1 = 0$ (which occurs at a projection angle $\alpha=90^\circ$) in Equation (1), we obtain the following projection coordinates:

$$x_p = x$$
$$y_p = y$$

These are the transformation equations for an orthographic parallel projection (see Figure 6.24). However, for nonzero values of L_1, we obtain the oblique parallel projections.

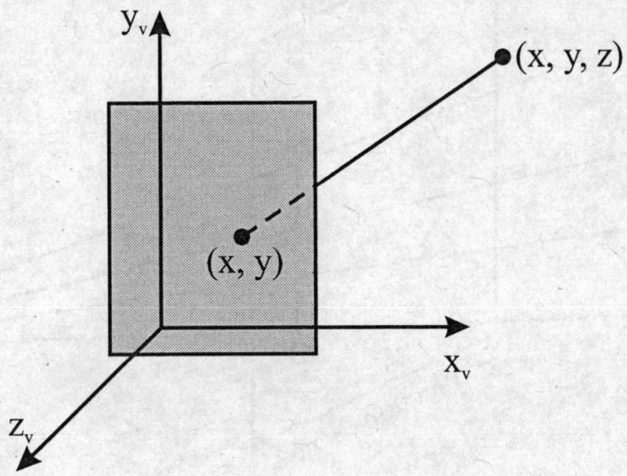

Figure 6.24 Orthographic Projection of a Point onto a Viewing Plane

17. Write a short note on perspective projection.

Ans. In perspective projection, coordinate positions are transformed to the view plane along the lines which converge to a point known as **center of projection** (also known as **projection reference point**). Thus, while defining a perspective projection, we explicitly specify its center of projection. Since the center of projection is a point, it is defined in the form of homogeneous coordinates (x, y, z, 1). Figure 6.25 illustrates the perspective projection of a cube on the projection plane.

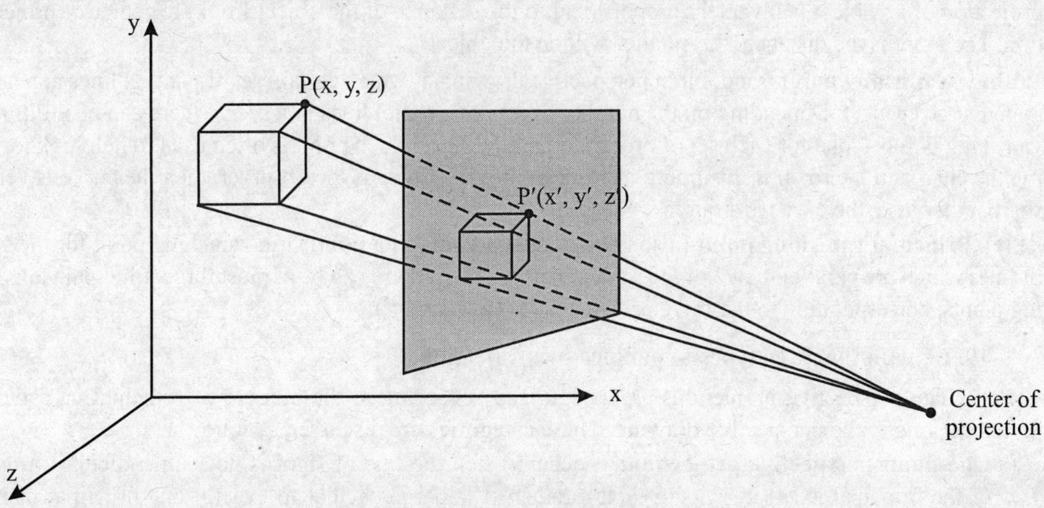

Figure 6.25 Perspective Projection of a Cube

The main advantage of perspective projection is that it gives us a realistic representation of the appearance of a 3D object. However, it does not preserve relative proportions of objects. In addition, projections of distant objects are smaller than the projections of objects of the same size that are closer to the projection plane. For example, in Figure 6.26, the projection of line AB (distant from the view plane) is smaller than the projection of line CD (closer to the view plane).

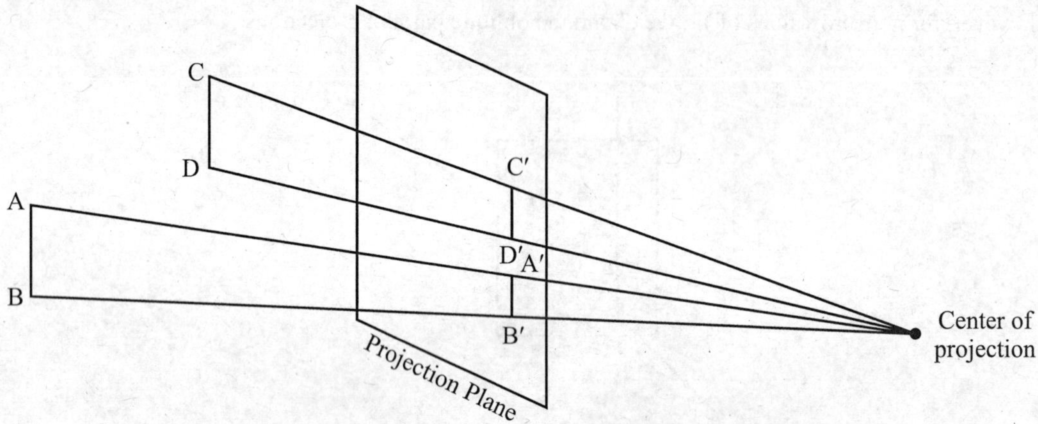

Figure 6.26 Perspective Projections of Equal-sized Objects at Different Distances from the View Plane

18. With respect to the perspective projection, define the following terms:

(a) Perspective foreshortening.

(b) Vanishing point.

(c) Principal vanishing points.

Ans. (a) Perspective foreshortening is defined as the illusion of objects and their lengths to appear smaller as their distance from the observer or center of projection increases. The size of the perspective projection of an object is inversely proportional to the distance of the object from the center of projection. The more is the distance, the smaller will be the object.

(b) A **vanishing point** is a point in perspective drawing at which certain set of parallel lines appears to converge or meet. Depending on the number of sets of parallel lines in a scene, there can be multiple vanishing points—one for each set of projected parallel lines. Such point is often used to help in knowing the curves in the road. If this point is closer or moving towards the observer, then the curve is very sharp, otherwise, the curve is straight.

(c) Principal vanishing point (also known as **axis vanishing point**) is a vanishing point for the set of lines which are parallel to one of the principal axes. Thus, there can be at most three principal vanishing points, corresponding to the three principal axes (x, y and z).

19. Explain the three types of perspective projection.

Ans. The perspective projections are categorized according to the number of principal vanishing points existing in the perspective drawing. These categories are discussed as follows:

- **One-point perspective projection:** It occurs when the line of sight is not perpendicular to one of the principal axes (x, y, or z-axis); rather, it is perpendicular to exactly one principal plane (that is, perpendicular to the other two axes). In this type of projection, exactly one principal axis has a finite vanishing point. The lines parallel to other two axes do not converge, and thus, their vanishing points are at infinity.

- **Two-point perspective projection:** It occurs when the line of sight is not perpendicular to two or three principal axes; rather, it is perpendicular to the remaining principal axis. Thus, in this type of projection, exactly two principal axes have finite vanishing points. The lines parallel to the third axis do not converge and, hence, the vanishing point of the third axis is at infinity. Two-point perspective is commonly used in architectural, engineering, industrial design and in advertising drawings.
- **Three-point perspective projection:** It occurs when the line of sight is not perpendicular to any of the principal axes. Thus, all the three axes have finite vanishing points. That is, there is no set of lines which do not converge.

Figure 6.27 illustrates the three categories of perspective projection.

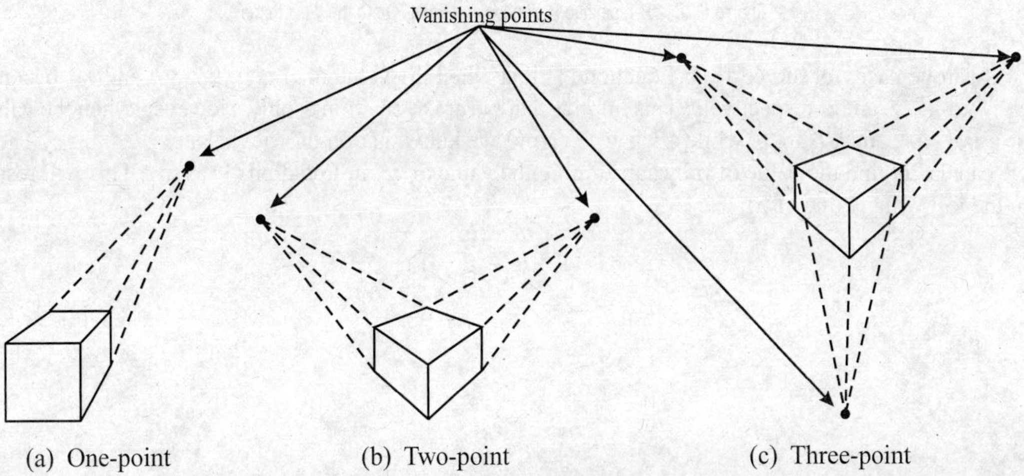

Figure 6.27 Types of Perspective Projections

20. Give the mathematical description for the perspective projection.

Ans. In order to obtain perspective projection one needs to transform positions of an object in such a manner that all of them meet at the projection reference point. Hence, to show this transformation mathematically, we assume z_{prp} to be the projection reference point along the z_v axis and the view plane to be placed at z_{vp} (see Figure 6.28). Moreover, let P be the point having coordinates (x, y, z) for which projection needs to be performed. Then, the coordinate positions (x', y', z') representing any point along this perspective projection line can be written in the parametric form as follows:

$$\begin{aligned} x' &= x - xu \\ y' &= y - yu \\ z' &= z - (z - z_{prp})u \end{aligned} \quad (1)$$

where u is the parameter that can take any value between 0 and 1.

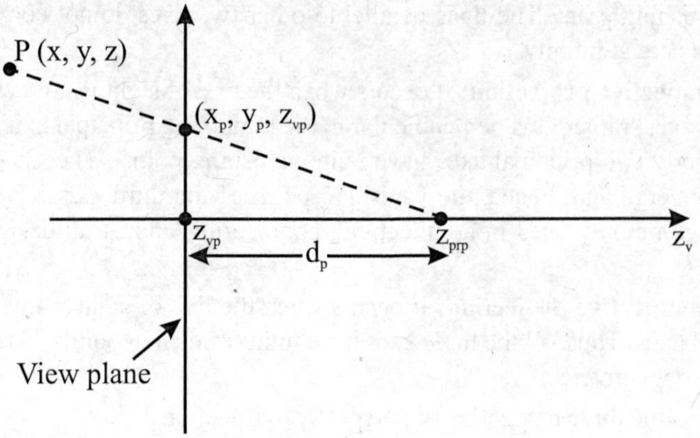

Figure 6.28 Perspective Projection of a Point P onto the View Plane

It can be easily observed from Equation (1) that when the value of u is 0, x', y' and z' become equal to x, y, and z respectively. This implies that we are at position P only. However, when the value of u is 1, x', and y' are 0, while z' is z_{prp}. Now, we know that on the view plane, z' = z_{vp}. Thus, we can easily find the value of u by substituting the value of z' in Equation (1) as z_{vp}. This will result in the following value of u:

$$z_{vp} = z - (z - z_{prp})\,u$$

$$z_{vp} - z = -(z - z_{prp})\,u$$

$$u = \frac{z_{vp} - z}{z_{prp} - z} \qquad (2)$$

To obtain the value of x' and y' on the view plane, we substitute Equation (2) in Equation (1). On this plane, x' is x_p, y' is y_p and z' is z_{vp}. Here, (x_p, y_p, z_p) are the projection coordinates on the view plane. Thus, we obtain:

$$x_p = x\left(\frac{z_{prp} - z_{vp}}{z_{prp} - z}\right) = x\left(\frac{d_p}{z_{prp} - z}\right)$$

$$y_p = y\left(\frac{z_{prp} - z_{vp}}{z_{prp} - z}\right) = y\left(\frac{d_p}{z_{prp} - z}\right) \qquad (3)$$

where $d_p = z_{prp} - z_{vp}$ and refers to the distance of the view plane from the center of projection.

Using a 3D homogeneous coordinate representation, we can rewrite Equation (3) in matrix form as follows:

$$\begin{bmatrix} x_h \\ y_h \\ z_h \\ h \end{bmatrix} = \begin{bmatrix} 1 & 0 & 0 & 0 \\ 0 & 1 & 0 & 0 \\ 0 & 0 & -\frac{z_{vp}}{d_p} & z_{vp}\left(\frac{z_{prp}}{d_p}\right) \\ 0 & 0 & -\frac{1}{d_p} & \frac{z_{prp}}{d_p} \end{bmatrix} \cdot \begin{bmatrix} x \\ y \\ z \\ 1 \end{bmatrix}$$

where h is the homogeneous factor and is evaluated as:

$$h = \frac{z_{prp} - z}{d_p}$$

Thus, we can express x_p and y_p in terms of h as follows:

$$x_p = \frac{x_h}{h}, \quad y_p = \frac{y_h}{h}$$

Note that the original z-coordinate values would be retained in projection coordinates for visible-surface detection and other depth processing.

To simplify the perspective calculations, we can place restrictions on the variables in Equation (3). These are some of the special cases:

Case 1: If the view plane is taken as the uv plane, then $z_{vp}=0$. This alters the value of x_p and y_p as follows:

$$x_p = x\left(\frac{z_{prp}}{z_{prp} - z}\right), \quad y_p = y\left(\frac{z_{prp}}{z_{prp} - z}\right)$$

Case 2: If the projection reference point is taken at the viewing-coordinate origin, then $z_{prp}=0$. Now the values of x_p and y_p become:

$$x_p = x\left(\frac{z_{vp}}{z}\right), \quad y_p = y\left(\frac{z_{vp}}{z}\right)$$

21. What are the various anomalies in perspective projection?

Ans. Although perspective projection helps in increasing the realism of a view in terms of depth cues, this may result in distortions in actual sizes and shapes. This may be due to the following reasons:

- **Perspective foreshortening:** The size of the perspective projection of an object varies inversely with the distance of that object from the center of projection. The farther an object is from the center of projection, the smaller it appears, and hence, its projected size becomes smaller.
- **Vanishing points:** The point at which a set of projected parallel lines appears to converge is called a **vanishing point**. The vanishing point for any set of lines that are parallel to one of the principal axes of an object is called **principal vanishing point** or **axis vanishing point**. For example, an illusion is made for railroad tracks that they are definitely meeting at some point on the horizon.

- **View confusion:** In this, the objects which are placed behind the center of projection are seen upside down and backward onto the view plane.

22. Differentiate perspective and parallel projection.

Ans. Some of the differences between parallel and perspective projections are listed in Table 6.1.

Table 6.1 Differences between Parallel Projection and Perspective Projection

Parallel Projection	Perspective Projection
The distance from the center of projection to the projection plane is infinite.	The distance from the center of projection to the projection plane is finite.
Since the center of projection is at infinity, we need to specify direction of projection (that is, a vector) to define a parallel projection. Such vector is calculated by subtracting coordinates of two points. That is, it is of the form `(x,y,z,1)-(x',y',z',1)=(a;b,c,0).`	We need to specify the center of projection (that is, a point) to define perspective projection. Such point is a homogeneous coordinate of the form `(x,y,z,1).`
It gives less realistic view of objects.	It gives more realistic view of objects because of the presence of perspective foreshortening.
It is useful in measuring the exact shape and length of the objects as it preserves the relative proportions of objects.	It is not very much useful in measuring the exact shape and length of the objects as it does not preserve the relative proportions of objects.

23. Explain the concept of view volumes with respect to 3D viewing.

Ans. The process of 3D viewing involves not just the projections but also a view volume against which a 3D scene is clipped. In 3D viewing, the size of the view window (or projection window) in the view plane determines how much of the scene is displayed. The edges of the view window are parallel to the $x_v y_v$ axes as shown in Figure 6.29. The view window can be placed anywhere on the view plane. This view window plays an important role in defining the view volume.

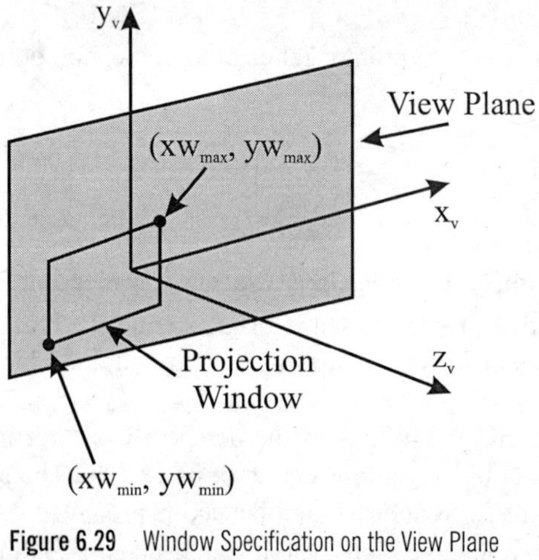

Figure 6.29 Window Specification on the View Plane

For a given specification of view window, we need to set up a **view volume** using the boundaries of the view window. The four sides of the view volume are the planes that pass through the four edges of the window. The objects lying inside the view volume will be displayed, while the objects lying outside the view volume are clipped. The size of the view volume depends on the size of the view window, whereas its shape depends on the type of projection (parallel or perspective). For parallel projections, the four sides of the view volume form an infinite parallelepiped, while for perspective projections, an infinite pyramid is generated with apex at the center of projection.

To obtain a finite view volume, we can limit the z_v extent of the view volume by specifying positions for one or two additional boundary planes. These planes are referred to as **front plane** (or **near plane**) and **back plane** (or **far plane**). These planes allow us to clip those parts of the scene based on the depth. The front and back planes are parallel to the view plane at specified positions z_{front} and z_{back}. By including these planes, the view volume is now bounded with six planes. Now, for a parallel projection, a rectangular parallelepiped is formed (see Figure 6.30a), while for a perspective projection, a **frustum** is generated as shown in Figure 6.30b.

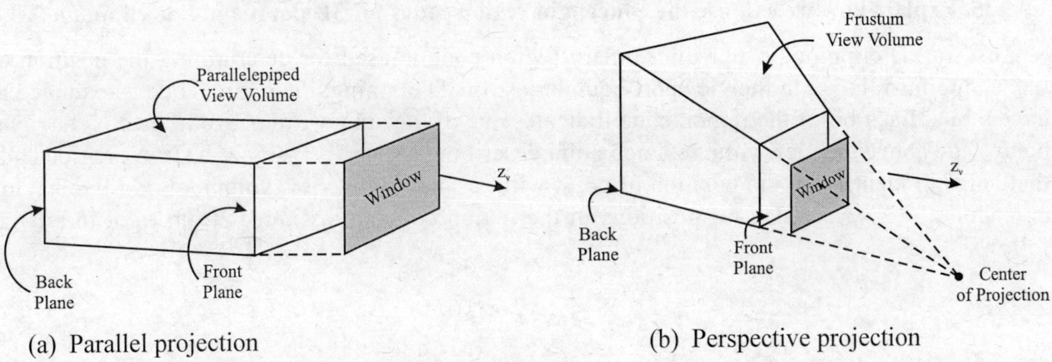

Figure 6.30 View Volumes Bounded by Front and Back Planes

24. Write a short note on 3D clipping.

Ans. We can extend the 2D clipping methods to perform 3D clipping. The only difference is that now the clipping is performed against the boundary planes of the view plane, rather than the straight line window edges. The portions of a 3D scene lying outside the view volume are eliminated. The boundaries of the view volume consist of the boundaries or planes whose orientations are calculated in accordance to the projection type, projection window, and the position of projection reference point. As the view volume has six sides, out of which front and back clipping planes are parallel to the view plane, both these sides have a constant z-coordinate value. However, other four sides of the view volume can have arbitrary spatial orientations.

For clipping a line segment against the view volume, the position of the line is needed to be tested using the view volume's boundary plane equations. To perform this, we need to substitute the coordinates of the line endpoint into the plane equation of each boundary. By doing this, we can easily determine whether the endpoint lies inside or outside the boundary. An endpoint (x, y, z) of a line segment is said to be outside a boundary plane if $Ax+By+Cz+D>0$, whereas the point is said to be inside the boundary plane if $Ax+By+Cz+D<0$. Here, A, B, C, and D are the plane parameters for that boundary. The lines whose both endpoints lie outside the boundary plane are discarded, whereas lines having both endpoints lying inside all boundary planes are saved. The intersection coordinates (x',y',z') of a line with a boundary could be found using the line equations along with the plane equation $Ax'+By'+Cz'+D=0$.

We can simplify the process of determining the intersection of a line with one of the view volume boundaries by converting the view volume to a rectangular parallelepiped before clipping. This makes the clipping process much easier as each surface is now perpendicular to one of the coordinate axes.

For clipping a polygon surface against view volume, the individual polygon edges are eliminated. For determining whether an object is completely outside or inside a boundary, its coordinate extents are tested against each boundary of the view volume. If the coordinate extents of an object are found to be outside all boundaries, then they are discarded and, if the coordinate extents are lying inside all boundaries, then they are saved. If the coordinate extents intersect the boundaries, we apply the intersection calculations. To accomplish this, we determine the polygon edge-intersection positions with the boundary planes of the view volume as done for line clipping.

25. Explain how we can use the concept of region codes for 3D point and line clipping.

Ans. In 2D clipping, a four-digit binary region code is used for determining the position of line endpoints relative to the viewport boundaries. In 3D clipping, the region code is extended to have 6 bits. Each bit of the region code indicates one of the six positions: front, back, left, right, below, and above the view volume. Each point describing a scene is assigned a six-bit region code that helps in identifying the position of point with respect to the view volume. For a line having an endpoint (x,y,z), the bit positions in the region code are assigned (from right to left) as follows:

$$\text{bit } 1 = 1, \text{if } x < xv_{min}\text{(left); otherwise } 0$$
$$\text{bit } 2 = 1, \text{if } x > xv_{max}\text{(right); otherwise } 0$$
$$\text{bit } 3 = 1, \text{if } y < yv_{min}\text{(below); otherwise } 0$$
$$\text{bit } 4 = 1, \text{if } y > yv_{max}\text{(above); otherwise } 0$$
$$\text{bit } 5 = 1, \text{if } z < zv_{min}\text{(front); otherwise } 0$$
$$\text{bit } 6 = 1, \text{if } z > zv_{max}\text{(back); otherwise } 0$$

For example, a region code 010100 signifies that the point is below and at the front of view volume. Similarly, a region code 000000 signifies that the point is inside the view volume. A line segment whose both endpoints have region codes 000000 is completely inside the view volume. In case either of the endpoints of the line segment does not have region code 000000, then we perform the logical OR operation on the region codes of the two endpoints. If all the bits in the resultant code are zero, the line is completely inside the view volume. Otherwise, we perform the logical AND operation on the region codes of the two endpoints. If the result is nonzero, it indicates that the line is completely outside the view volume, and hence it is discarded. For example, in Figure 6.31, the endpoints of the line P_1P_2 have the region codes 010101 and 100110. Since, the logical AND of these region codes produces a nonzero value at bit position 3, it implies that the line is completely below the view volume.

If all these tests fail, we determine the intersection points with the boundary planes of the view volume, and the same procedure is applied until the line segment is either totally discarded or included. For example, for the line segment P_3P_4, we calculate the intersection points to determine how much of the line can be discarded.

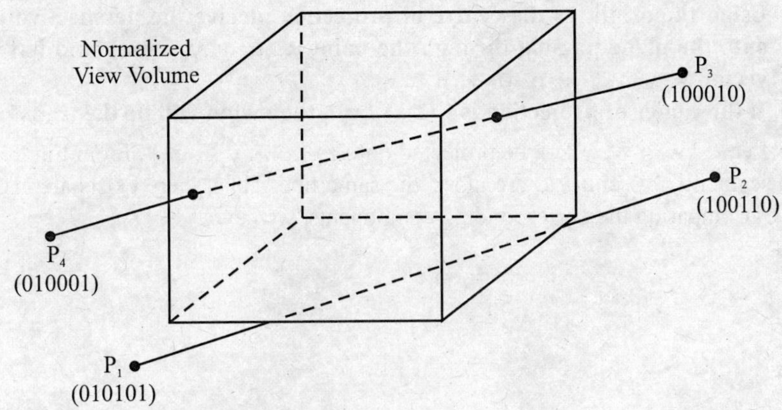

Figure 6.31 3D Clipping Using Region Codes

26. Discuss how Liang-Barsky algorithm can be extended to perform 3D point and line clipping.

Ans. Liang-Barsky algorithm for 2D clipping can be easily extended for 3D clipping. Given a line segment with endpoints $P_1(x_1, y_1, z_1)$ and $P_2(x_2, y_2, z_2)$, the parametric line equations can be written as follows:

$$\begin{aligned} x &= x_1 + (x_2 - x_1)u, \qquad 0 \le u \le 1 \\ y &= y_1 + (y_2 - y_1)u \\ z &= z_1 + (z_2 - z_1)u \end{aligned} \tag{1}$$

where (x, y, z) are the coordinates of a point lying on this line, u is the parameter ranging from 0 to 1—for $u=0$, the point is P_1; and for $u=1$, the point is P_2.

For determining the intersection of a line segment with the view volume plane, the coordinate values for that plane are substituted in Equation (1) to determine the value of u. However, if a line segment is tested against the zv_{min} plane of the view volume, the value for u is given as:

$$u = \frac{zv_{min} - z_1}{z_2 - z_1}$$

If the calculated value of u is not in the range 0 to 1, the line segment does not intersect the plane at any point between endpoints P_1 and P_2. On the other hand, if the calculated value of u is in the range 0 to 1, the intersected x and y coordinates are calculated as follows:

$$x = x_1 + (x_2 - x_1)\left(\frac{zv_{min} - z_1}{z_2 - z_1}\right)$$

$$y = y_1 + (y_2 - y_1)\left(\frac{zv_{min} - z_1}{z_2 - z_1}\right)$$

27. (a) Using the origin as the centre of projection, derive the perspective transformation onto the plane passing through the point $R_0(x_0, y_0, z_0)$ and having the normal vector $N = n_1I + n_2J + n_3K$.

(b) If the center of projection is $C(x_c, y_c, z_c)$, then what will be the transformation?

Ans. (a) Let $P_1(x_1, y_1, z_1)$ be projected onto $P_2(x_2, y_2, z_2)$. From Figure 6.32, it is clear that the line segments P_1O and P_2O are along the same line. Thus, there exists a constant u such that $P_2O = uP_1O$. Comparing the corresponding components, we have

$$x_2 = ux_1$$
$$y_2 = uy_1$$
$$z_2 = uz_1$$

We now find the value of u. Any point $P_2(x_2, y_2, z_2)$ lying on the plane satisfies the equation:

$$n_1x_2 + n_2y_2 + n_3z_2 = d_0 \quad (1)$$

where $d_0 = n_1x_0 + n_2y_0 + n_3z_0$

Putting the values of x_2, y_2 and z_2 in (1), we have

$$n_1(ux_1) + n_2(uy_1) + n_3(uz_1) = d_0$$

$$u = \frac{d_0}{n_1x_1 + n_2y_1 + n_3z_1}$$

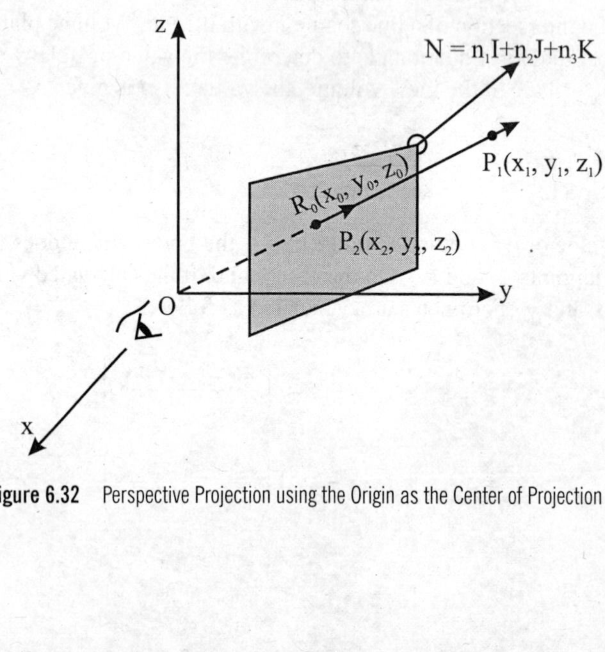

Figure 6.32 Perspective Projection using the Origin as the Center of Projection

Now this projection transformation can be represented using the homogeneous coordinate representation for 3D points as a 4 by 4 matrix as follows:

$$\mathrm{Per}_{N,R_0} = \begin{bmatrix} d_0 & 0 & 0 & n_1 \\ 0 & d_0 & 0 & n_2 \\ 0 & 0 & d_0 & n_3 \\ 0 & 0 & 0 & 0 \end{bmatrix}$$

The application of this matrix to the homogeneous representation $P_1(x_1, y_1, z_1, 1)$ of point P_1 gives $P_2(d_0x_1, d_0y_1, d_0z_1, n_1x_1 + n_2y_1 + n_3z_1)$, which is the homogeneous representation of $P_2(x_2, y_2, z_2)$. Thus, we can express P_2 in matrix form as follows:

$$\begin{bmatrix} x_1 & y_1 & z_1 & 1 \end{bmatrix} \begin{bmatrix} d_0 & 0 & 0 & n_1 \\ 0 & d_0 & 0 & n_2 \\ 0 & 0 & d_0 & n_3 \\ 0 & 0 & 0 & 0 \end{bmatrix} = \begin{bmatrix} d_0x_1 & d_0y_1 & d_0z_1 & n_1x_1 + n_2y_1 + n_3z_1 \end{bmatrix}$$

(b) Now, the center of projection is at $C(x_c, y_c, z_c)$. Therefore, we first translate the center of projection to the origin, then project it onto the plane given using origin as a center of projection and again translate back to its original position. The transformation matrix for this sequence of operations is as follows:

$$P_{N,R_0,C} = T_C \, , \, P_{N,R_0'} \cdot T_{-C}$$

where,

$$R_0' = (x_0 - x_c, y_0 - y_c, z_0 - z_c)$$

such that the plane will now pass through the point $(x_0-x_c, y_0-y_c, z_0-z_c)$.

28. Demonstrate local scaling taking scaling factors along the x, y and z axes as 2, 3 and 1 respectively, for a cube with homogeneous position vectors

$$[X] = \begin{bmatrix} 0 & 0 & 1 & 1 \\ 1 & 0 & 1 & 1 \\ 1 & 1 & 1 & 1 \\ 0 & 1 & 1 & 1 \\ 0 & 0 & 0 & 1 \\ 1 & 0 & 0 & 1 \\ 1 & 1 & 0 & 1 \\ 0 & 1 & 0 & 1 \end{bmatrix}$$

Use the same cube to demonstrate overall scaling by factor 2.

Ans. The transformation matrix for the local scaling will be:

$$[T] = \begin{bmatrix} 2 & 0 & 0 & 0 \\ 0 & 3 & 0 & 0 \\ 0 & 0 & 1 & 0 \\ 0 & 0 & 0 & 1 \end{bmatrix}$$

The resulting figure has the homogeneous position vectors as follows:

$$\left[X^*\right] = [X][T] = \begin{bmatrix} 0 & 0 & 1 & 1 \\ 1 & 0 & 1 & 1 \\ 1 & 1 & 1 & 1 \\ 0 & 1 & 1 & 1 \\ 0 & 0 & 0 & 1 \\ 1 & 0 & 0 & 1 \\ 1 & 1 & 0 & 1 \\ 0 & 1 & 0 & 1 \end{bmatrix} \begin{bmatrix} 2 & 0 & 0 & 0 \\ 0 & 3 & 0 & 0 \\ 0 & 0 & 1 & 0 \\ 0 & 0 & 0 & 1 \end{bmatrix} = \begin{bmatrix} 0 & 0 & 1 & 1 \\ 2 & 0 & 1 & 1 \\ 2 & 3 & 1 & 1 \\ 0 & 3 & 1 & 1 \\ 0 & 0 & 0 & 1 \\ 2 & 0 & 0 & 1 \\ 2 & 3 & 0 & 1 \\ 0 & 3 & 0 & 1 \end{bmatrix}$$

The ordinary physical coordinates will be same as given above because the homogeneous coordinate factor h is unity for each of the transformed position vectors.

Now, applying overall scaling by a factor of 2, we have the following transformation matrix:

$$[T] = \begin{bmatrix} 1 & 0 & 0 & 0 \\ 0 & 1 & 0 & 0 \\ 0 & 0 & 1 & 0 \\ 0 & 0 & 0 & 2 \end{bmatrix}$$

The resulting position vector for the vertices will be:

$$\left[X^*\right] = [X][T] = \begin{bmatrix} 0 & 0 & 1 & 1 \\ 1 & 0 & 1 & 1 \\ 1 & 1 & 1 & 1 \\ 0 & 1 & 1 & 1 \\ 0 & 0 & 0 & 1 \\ 1 & 0 & 0 & 1 \\ 1 & 1 & 0 & 1 \\ 0 & 1 & 0 & 1 \end{bmatrix} \begin{bmatrix} 1 & 0 & 0 & 0 \\ 0 & 1 & 0 & 0 \\ 0 & 0 & 1 & 0 \\ 0 & 0 & 0 & 2 \end{bmatrix} = \begin{bmatrix} 0 & 0 & 1 & 2 \\ 1 & 0 & 1 & 2 \\ 1 & 1 & 1 & 2 \\ 0 & 1 & 1 & 2 \\ 0 & 0 & 0 & 2 \\ 1 & 0 & 0 & 2 \\ 1 & 1 & 0 & 2 \\ 0 & 1 & 0 & 2 \end{bmatrix}$$

Thus, the ordinary physical coordinates will be:

$$[X^*] = \begin{bmatrix} 0 & 0 & 0.5 & 1 \\ 0.5 & 0 & 0.5 & 1 \\ 0.5 & 0.5 & 0.5 & 1 \\ 0 & 0.5 & 0.5 & 1 \\ 0 & 0 & 0 & 1 \\ 0.5 & 0 & 0 & 1 \\ 0.5 & 0.5 & 0 & 1 \\ 0 & 0.5 & 0 & 1 \end{bmatrix}$$

Thus, it can be seen that the size of the resulting cube reduces to half.

MULTIPLE CHOICE QUESTIONS

1. Which of the following is a type of 3D transformation?
   (a) Translation (b) Rotation
   (c) Shearing (d) All of these
2. In 3D ________, the size of an object is changed by compressing or expanding its dimensions.
   (a) Scaling (b) Rotation
   (c) Inverse rotation (d) Reflection
3. A quaternion can be thought as an ordered pair consisting of scalar part and _________ part.
   (a) Non-scalar (b) Vector
   (c) Non-vector (d) Homogeneous
4. Reflection is also known as __________.
   (a) Image reflection (b) Quaternion
   (c) RHVS (d) Mirror reflection
5. The process of viewing a 2D scene is much ________ than the 3D viewing process.
   (a) Complex (b) Simpler
   (c) Composite (d) Tricky
6. _______ vector helps in establishing the positive direction for the z_v-axis and orientation of the view plane.
   (a) VPNV (b) VRP
   (c) VUV (d) VCS
7. What sequence of transformation must be performed to transform objects from world coordinates to viewing coordinates?
   (a) Translate–inverse–rotate (b) Translate–shear
   (c) Translate–rotate (d) Translate–rotate–translate

8. The non-orthographic parallel projections are known as _________ projections.
   (a) Orthographic (b) Isometric
   (c) Oblique (d) Axonometric
9. In _________, coordinate positions are transformed to the view plane along the lines which converge to a point known as center of projection.
   (a) Perspective projection (b) Vanishing point
   (c) Parallel projection (d) Projection reference point
10. Which of the following is not an anomaly (ies) in perspective projection?
   (a) Vanishing points (b) View confusion
   (c) Both (a) and (b) (d) Depth instability

Answers. 1. (d) 2. (a) 3. (b) 4. (d) 5. (b) 6. (a) 7. (c) 8. (c) 9. (a) 10. (d)

7

Three-dimensional Object Representations

1. What are the different ways of representing objects in a three-dimensional scene?

Ans. A three-dimensional scene consists of many different objects like clouds, mountains, trees, walls, paper, river, etc. All these objects cannot be represented using a single method that will include all the characteristics of these different objects. Thus, to produce realistic displays we need to have different methods for different objects so that the object characteristics can be modeled accurately. For example, simple Euclidean objects can be represented using polygons and quadratic surfaces; engineering structures such as beams, domes, arches, etc., can be represented using spline curves and surfaces; natural objects can be represented using fractals; internal features of objects can be represented using octree encodings; and so on.

2. What are the two techniques by which solid objects can be represented? Explain.

Ans. The solid objects can be represented basically by following two representation schemes:

- **Boundary representations (B-reps):** This representation describes a three-dimensional object as a set of surfaces that separates the object interior from the environment. Some examples of such representations are polygon facets and spline patches.
- **Space-partitioning representations:** This representation describes interior properties of 3D objects by partitioning the space containing an object into a set of small, non-overlapping contiguous solids (generally cubes). An example of such representation is octree representation.

3. Discuss how polygon surfaces can be used to represent three-dimensional objects.

Ans. The simplest way of representing 3D graphics objects is to use a set of surface polygons that enclose the object interiors. The polygon description of objects is also referred to as standard graphics objects because many graphics packages store all object descriptions as sets of surface polygons. For each polygon section over the object surface, we specify a set of vertex coordinates and associated attribute parameters such as degree of transparency of the object, its surface reflectivity and texture characteristics. The information about each polygon surface is stored in the form of tables. The information about vertex coordinates and edges of the polygon surface is stored in **geometric data tables**, and the attribute information of an object is stored in the **attribute tables**. Figure 7.1 shows two adjacent polygon surfaces, and vertex table, edge table and polygon table corresponding to these surfaces.

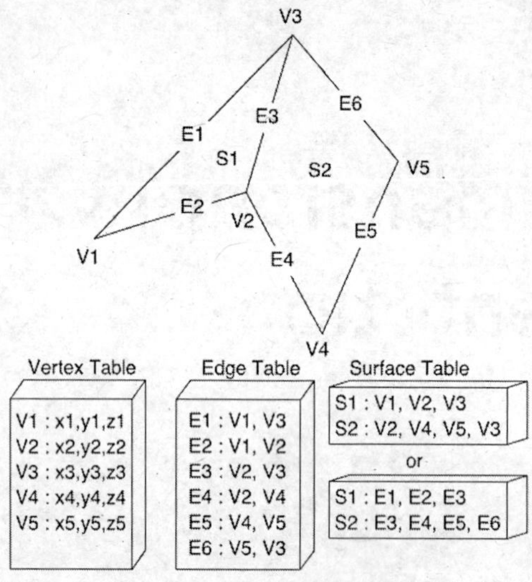

Figure 7.1 Polygon surfaces and associated polygon tables

Some graphics packages provide routines for generating polygon-surface mesh (also known as wire-frame representation) as a set of triangles and quadrilaterals. Such representations are commonly used in the design and solid-modeling applications. Some packages also provide routines for displaying common shapes such as cylinders, cubes, spheres, represented with polygon surfaces.

4. What are quadratic surfaces?

Ans. Quadratic surfaces are the class of objects which are described using quadratic (second-degree) equations. These include ellipsoids, paraboloids, hyperboloids, spheres, and torus. Among these quadratic surfaces, spheres and ellipsoids are the most commonly used components in graphics scenes. Thus, most of graphics packages provide these surfaces as primitives, and from these primitives more complex objects can be constructed.

Mathematically, a sphere with radius r and centered on the coordinate origin can be represented using the following equation:

$$x^2+y^2+z^2=r^2$$

where,

x, y and z are the Cartesian coordinates.

It can also be described in parametric form as follows:

$$x = r\cos\phi\cos\theta$$
$$y = r\cos\phi\sin\theta$$
$$z = r\sin\phi$$

where,

$$-\pi/2 \le \phi \le \pi/2, \qquad -\pi \le \theta \le \pi$$

We can describe an ellipsoidal surface as an extension of a sphere in which the radii in three different directions (axis) can have different values. In Cartesian co-ordinate, the ellipsoid surface can be represented as

$$\left(\frac{x}{r_x}\right)^2 + \left(\frac{y}{r_y}\right)^2 + \left(\frac{z}{r_z}\right)^2 = 1$$

where ,

x, y and z are the Cartesian coordinates.

It can also be represented in parametric form in terms of the latitude angle ϕ and the longitude angle θ as follows:

$$x = r_x \cos\phi \cos\theta$$
$$y = r_y \cos\phi \sin\theta$$
$$z = r_z \sin\phi$$

where,

$-\pi/2 \le \phi \le \pi/2, \quad -\pi \le \theta \le \pi$

Another type of quadratic surface is torus. It is a doughnut-shaped object generated by revolving a circle in three-dimensional space about an axis coplanar with the circle. In Cartesian co-ordinate, equation for torus surface is represented as follows:

$$\left[r - \sqrt{\left(\frac{x}{r_x}\right)^2 + \left(\frac{y}{r_y}\right)^2}\right]^2 + \left(\frac{z}{r_z}\right)^2 = 1$$

where,

r is any given offset value.

It can also be represented in parametric form in terms of the latitude angle ϕ and the longitude angle θ as follows:

$$x=r_x(r+\cos\phi)\cos\theta$$
$$y=r_y(r+\cos\phi)\sin\theta$$
$$z=r_z\sin\phi$$

where,

θ extends over 360° and $-\pi \le \phi \le \pi, \quad -\pi \le \theta \le \pi$

5. Discuss the basic requirements for designing curves and surfaces.

Ans. Some of the basic requirements for designing the curves and surfaces are as follows:

- **Control points:** These are the set of points that are used to specify a curve. They control the shape of the curve interactively. Such points are represented by dots as shown in Figure 7.2a.
- **Coordinate system independence:** It means that when the control points are measured with respect to another coordinate system, then there should be no effect on the shape of the curve or surface.
- **Multi-valued functions:** Generally, the curves are multi-valued with respect to any coordinate system; therefore, one should always consider this requirement when designing any curves or surfaces.
- **Local controllability:** As the shape of the curve is interactively controlled by the control points, the designer always tries to manipulate the shape of the curve by moving the control points in a neighborhood. The control points should be moved in such a way that the shape of the curve is affected only in a small neighborhood of the control points. This property is known as

local controllability. If this property is not maintained, then a small change in the position of a control point can change the shape of the curve abnormally, thereby giving undesirable results (see Figure 7.2b).

- **Order of continuity:** A complex curve or surface is generally modelled by 'tying together' with several curves. This tying up of several curves brings undesirable sharp edges or joints that may have to be smoothened, up to a required degree. This can be done by specifying the various order of continuity such as zero-order, first-order, second-order, and so on.
- **Variation-diminishing effect:** If the curve smoothens small variations in the location of the control points, then a curve is said to have a variation-diminishing effect (see Figure 7.2c).
- **Versatility:** Designing techniques should be flexible enough so as to generate a large set of curves and surfaces.

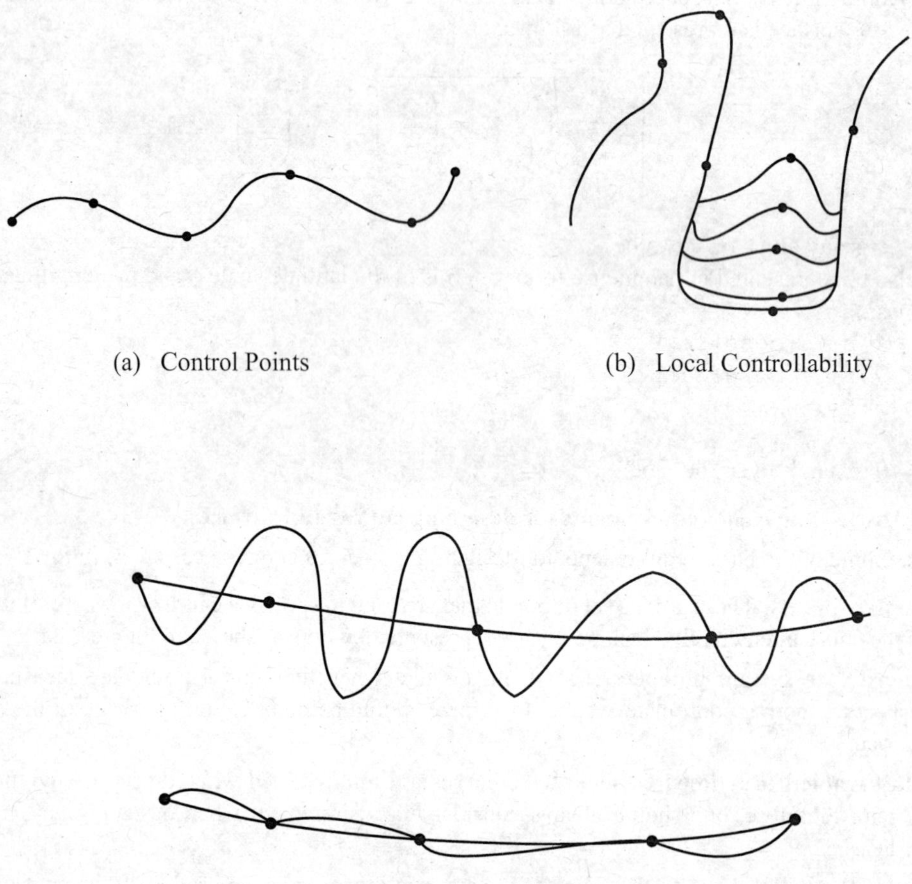

(a) Control Points

(b) Local Controllability

(c) Variation-diminishing Effect

Figure 7.2 Requirements for Designing Curves and Surfaces

6. What are blobby objects?

Ans. Blobby objects are non-rigid objects that do not preserve a fixed shape but tends to change their surface characteristics in certain motions or when in proximity to other objects. These objects include molecular structures, cloth, rubber, melting objects, water droplets, muscles in human body, etc. They also exhibit a certain degree of fluidity. For example, during a chemical reaction, when a molecule comes closer to another molecule, it tends to change its shape (which is originally spherical). This is due to the bonding that occurs between the two molecules.

Blobby objects cannot be described simply with spherical or elliptical shapes. Thus, various models have been developed to handle these kinds of objects. One of the techniques to model these objects is to use a combination of Gaussian density functions (or Gaussian bumps) as shown in Figure 7.3.

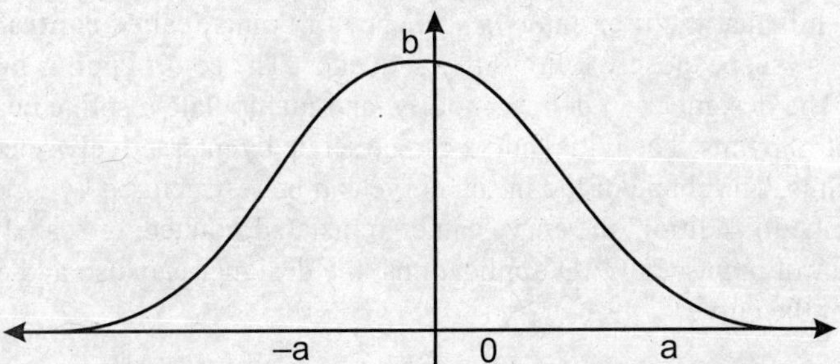

Figure 7.3 Gaussian bump

A surface function is then defined by:

$$f(x, y, z) = \sum_k b_k e^{-a_k r_k^2} - T = 0$$

where,

$r^2_k = \sqrt{x_k^2 + y_k^2 + z_k^2}$

parameter T is some specified threshold, and

parameters a and b adjust the amount of "blobbiness" of the individual objects. Parameter b can also be assigned negative values that will generate dents instead of bumps.

Figure 7.4 shows the surface structure of a composite object modeled using four Gaussian density functions.

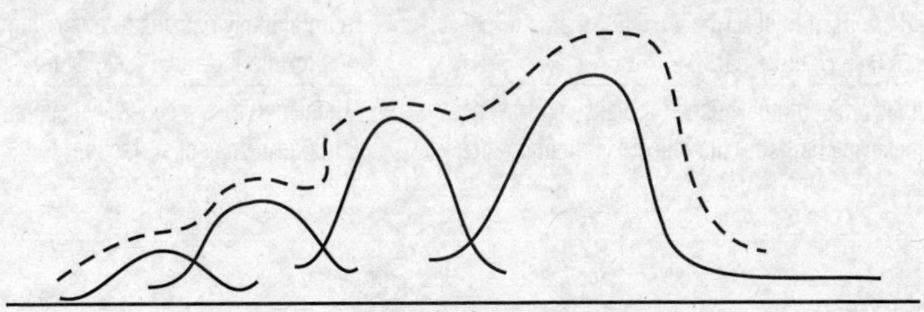

Figure 7.4 A blobby object formed with four Gaussian bumps

Another technique called **metaball technique** is the implicit modeling technique used to describe a blobby object as being made of density functions. These density functions fall off to 0 in a finite interval. It represents the object in the form

$$f(r) = \begin{cases} b\,(1 - 3\,r^2/d^2), & \text{if } 0 < r \le d/3 \\ \dfrac{3}{2}\,b\left(1 - \dfrac{r}{d}\right)^2, & \text{if } d/3 < r \le d \\ 0, & \text{if } r > d \end{cases}$$

7. What is a spline curve? Also, give its uses.

Ans. In computer graphics, a **spline curve** is a mathematical representation for which we can build an interface that will allow us to design and control the shape of complex curves and surfaces. The basic approach is that the user enters a sequence of points (called **control points**), and a curve is constructed whose shape closely follows this sequence. The control points that lie on the curve are known as **knots**. The designer can define, modify, and manipulate a spline curve by applying some operations on control points. The initial curve can be set up by interactively selecting spatial positions for the control points. The shape of the initial curve can be restructured by repositioning some or all of the control points. In addition, the curve can be translated, rotated, or scaled by applying transformations to the control points. In CAD applications, the designer can also add extra control points to adjust the shape of the curve.

Spline curves have numerous uses in graphics and CAD applications. Some of them are as follows:

- Designing curve and surface shapes
- Converting drawings into digital form so that they can stored in a computer
- Specifying paths for the objects in an animation sequence
- Designing automobile bodies, aircraft surfaces, ship hulls, etc.

8. Differentiate between interpolating and approximation spline curves.

Ans. The spline curves are basically divided into two broad categories, namely, *interpolating curves* and *approximation curves*. The differences between these two curves are listed in Table 7.1.

Table 7.1 Differences between Interpolating and Approximation Curve

Interpolating spline curve	Approximation spline curve
❑ A curve that actually passes through all the control points that are used to describe it is known as interpolating curve (see Figure 7.5a).	❑ A curve that passes near to the control points rather than actually passing through them is known as an approximating curve (see Figure 7.5b).
❑ These curves are commonly used for digitizing drawings and for specifying paths for the objects in an animation sequence.	❑ These curves are generally used as design tools for structuring object surfaces.

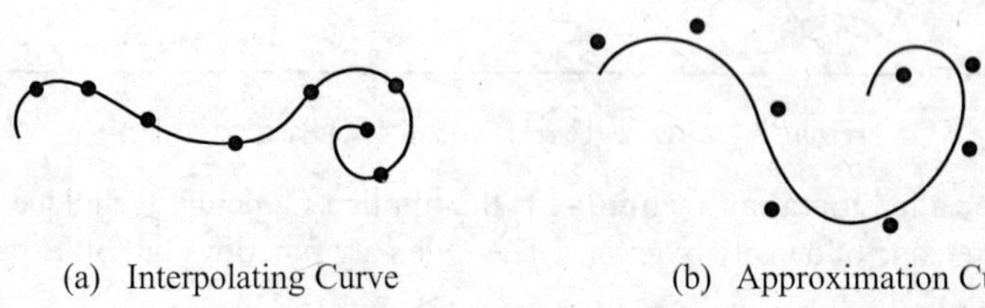

(a) Interpolating Curve (b) Approximation Curve

Figure 7.5 Types of Spline Curves

9. Define the terms convex hull and control graph.

Ans. A **convex hull** is a convex polygon boundary that completely encloses a set of control points, with the minimum number of perimeter nodes. The shape of the convex hull can be imagined as a rubber band stretched around the positions of the control points such that every control point is either on the perimeter of the hull or inside it (see Figure 7.6). It provides a measure for the deviation of a curve or surface from the region bounding the control points. The convex is named so because it possesses an important property that all the points in the polygon must be indented outward, that is convex.

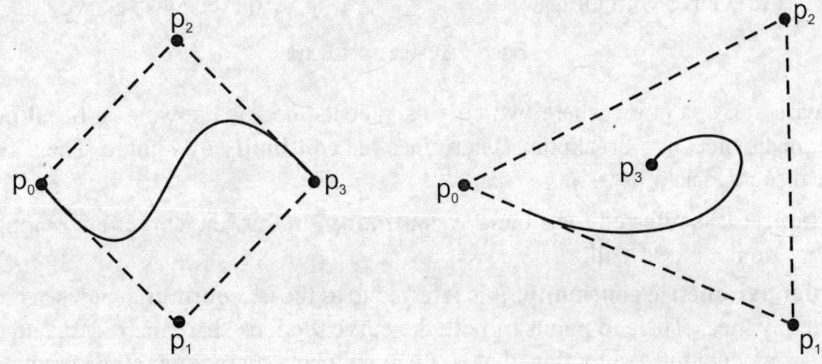

Figure 7.6 Convex Hull Shapes Represented by Cashed Lines

For an approximation curve, we use a polyline to connect the sequence of control points. This set of connected line segments is known as the **control graph** (sometimes known as **control polygon** or **characteristic polygon**) of the curve. It is basically displayed to remind a designer the control-point ordering. The shape of the control graph for two sets of control points in Figure 7.6 is shown in Figure 7.7.

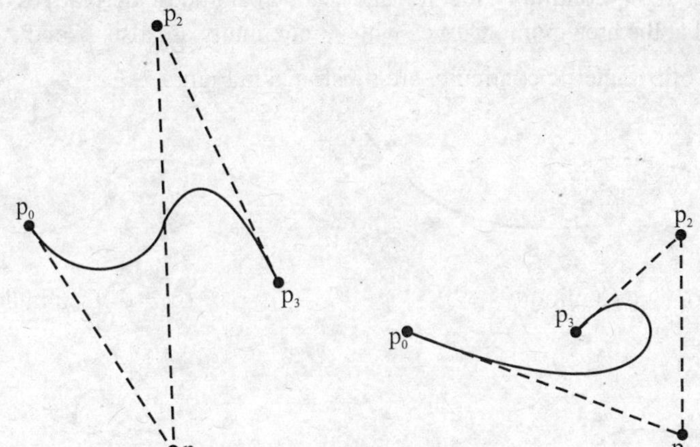

Figure 7.7 Control Graphs

10. Define the term order and continuity of a curve. Explain the different types of parametric continuity conditions?

Ans. The minimum number of control points required to define a curve determines the **order** of the curve. For example, for a curve of order 4, at least four control points must be required. To make curves with more than *order* control points, two or more curve segments can be joined into a piecewise curve as shown in Figure 7.8. The order of the curve also determines how the curve behaves when the control points are moved.

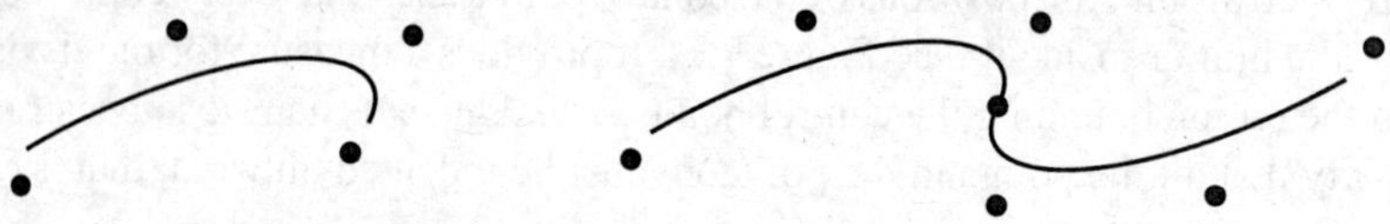

(a) Curve with Order 4 (b) Piecewise Curve

Figure 7.8 Order of a Curve

In a piecewise curve, a point where two curve segments meet is known as a **breakpoint**. The way two curve segments meet at a breakpoint determines the **continuity** of a curve. The different types of continuity are discussed as follows:

- **No continuity:** It is referred to as the C^{-1} **continuity**. In this, the curves are completely disjoint, that is, they do not meet at all.
- **Zero-order parametric continuity:** It is referred to as the C^0 **continuity** and is achieved when the curves simply meet. The end points of both the curve sections share their x, y, and z coordinates. The curves may not meet smoothly, that is, there may be a sharp point at the breakpoint.
- **First-order parametric continuity:** It is referred to as the C^1 **continuity** and is achieved when the curves have identical tangents at the breakpoint. That is, the direction and magnitude of both the tangents are equal. In this, the first parametric derivatives of both the curve sections are equal at the breakpoint. Curves with C^1 continuity also show C^0 continuity.
- **Second-order parametric continuity:** It is referred to as the C^2 **continuity** and is achieved when the curves have identical curvature at the breakpoint. The curvature is defined as the rate of change of the tangents. In this continuity, the first and second parametric derivatives of both the curve sections are equal at the breakpoint. Curves with C^2 continuity are also C^1 and C^0 continuous.

The different types of parametric continuity are illustrated in Figure 7.9.

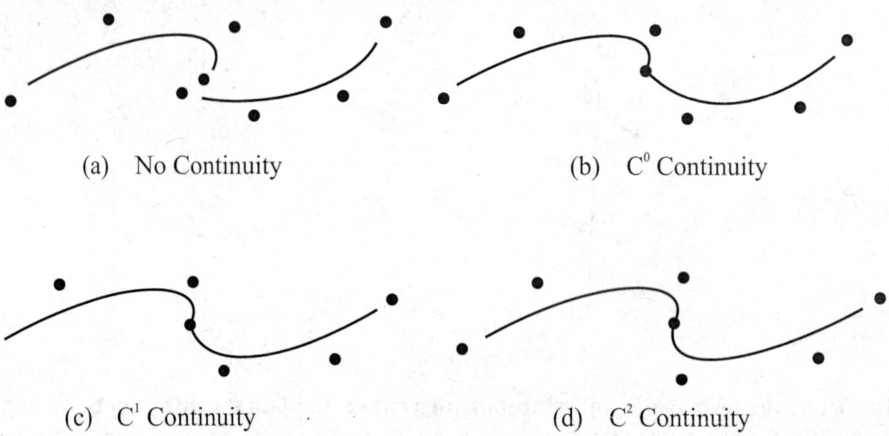

(a) No Continuity (b) C^0 Continuity

(c) C^1 Continuity (d) C^2 Continuity

Figure 7.9 Types of Parametric Continuity

11. Give differences between first-order and second-order parametric continuity.

Ans. Some of the differences between first and second-order parametric continuity are as follows:

- In first-order continuity, the shape of the connecting sections can abruptly change because rate of change of tangent vectors for two adjacent sections can be quite different. On the other hand, in second-order continuity, the tangent line transitions smoothly between the two sections of the curve because the rate of change of the tangent vectors for two adjacent sections are equal at their intersecting point.
- First-order continuity is generally useful for digitizing drawings and some design applications. While second-order continuity fulfills many CAD requirements and is also used for setting up animation paths for camera motion.

12. Explain the different types of geometric continuity conditions?

Ans. In addition to parametric continuity, one can also specify conditions for geometric continuity for joining two piecewise curves. Unlike parametric continuity, which requires the parametric derivates of the two curve sections to be equal to each other at the breakpoint, the geometric continuity requires them to be proportional to each other. The various geometric continuity conditions are discussed as follows:

- **Zero-order geometric continuity:** It is referred to as **G^0 continuity** and is same as zero-order parametric continuity in which the curve simply meet, and the coordinate positions are same at the boundary point for the two curve sections.
- **First-order geometric continuity:** It is referred to as **G^1 continuity**. It means that the parametric first derivatives of the two curve sections are proportional at the intersection point. That is, if the parametric position on the curve is denoted by `P(v)`, then the direction of tangent vector `P'(v)` will be same for the two successive curve sections at their intersection under G^1 continuity. It is to be noted that magnitude of tangent vector `P'(v)` may not be the same for two adjacent curve sections.
- **Second-order geometric continuity:** It is referred to as **G^2 continuity**. It means that both the first and second parametric derivatives of the two curve sections are proportional at their boundary. Also, the curvatures of the two curve sections will match the breakpoint.

The curves generated with geometric and parametric continuity conditions are quite similar with a minor difference in the shape of the curve (see Figure 7.10). That is, with geometric continuity, the curve is pulled towards the section having greater tangent vector.

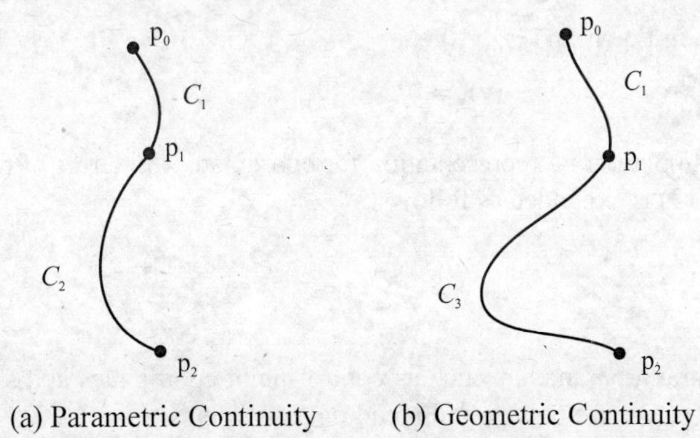

Figure 7.10 Curves Generated with Parametric and Geometric Continuity

13. Illustrate the methods for specifying a spline representation.

Ans. There are three ways to specify a particular spline representation. One way is to state the set of boundary conditions to be imposed on the spline. Alternatively, one can state the matrix that characterizes the spline. Lastly, one can state the set of **basis functions** (or **blending functions**) that determine the way different geometric constraints on the curve are combined to calculate the positions along the curve path. All these three methods are equivalent to each other and one can transform one spline representation to another.

For example, consider the following parametric cubic polynomial representation for the x coordinate along the path of a spline section:

$$x(v) = a_x v^3 + b_x v^2 + c_x v + d_x, 0 \le v \le 1 \quad (1)$$

For this curve, we can set the boundary conditions, say, on the end point coordinates $x(0)$ and $x(1)$ and on the parametric first derivatives at the end points $x'(0)$ and $x'(1)$. These four boundary conditions are sufficient enough to find out the values of the four coefficients a_x, b_x, c_x, and d_x. Equation (1) can also be represented in the form of matrix product, as follows:

$$x(v) = \begin{bmatrix} v^3 & v^2 & v & 1 \end{bmatrix} . \begin{bmatrix} a_x \\ b_x \\ c_x \\ d_x \end{bmatrix} \quad (2)$$

$$= V.C$$

where V is the row matrix of powers of parameter v and C is the coefficient column matrix.

If the values of boundary conditions, $x(0)$, $x(1)$, $x'(0)$, and $x'(1)$ are known, then we can write them in matrix form and solve for the coefficient matrix C as follows:

$$C = M_{spline} \cdot M_{geom}$$

where M_{geom} is a four-element matrix that contains the control-point coordinate values and geometric constraint values (boundary conditions) on the spline.

M_{spline} is known as the **basis matrix**. It is a 4-by-4 matrix that characterizes a spline representation and transforms the geometric constraint values to the polynomial coefficients. It is basically useful for transforming from one spline representation to another. After substituting the value of $C = M_{spline} \cdot M_{geom}$ in Equation (2), we get:

$$x(v) = V.M_{spline} \cdot M_{geom} \quad (3)$$

Finally, to obtain a polynomial representation for coordinate x in terms of the geometric constraint parameters, Equation (3) is expanded as follows:

$$x(v) = \sum_{k=0}^{3} g_k . BF_k(v)$$

where g_k are constraint parameters such as control-point coordinates and slope of the curve at the control points and $BF_k(v)$ are polynomial blending functions.

14. What is cubic spline? How cubic interpolation splines are obtained? Name some methods which help in setting boundary conditions for cubic interpolation splines.

Ans. A spline constructed with the help of piecewise third-order polynomials that pass through a set of n control points is known as a **cubic curve**. It is generally used to set up paths for object motions or to provide a representation for an existing object or drawing. These splines, also known as **interpolating splines**, are sometimes also used to design object shapes. Such splines are preferred over both higher order polynomials and lower order polynomials. When compared with higher order polynomials, cubic splines require fewer calculations, less memory, and are more stable. While compared with lower order polynomials, they are more flexible for modelling arbitrary curve shapes.

Suppose a set of control points is given, then the cubic interpolation spline can be obtained by fitting the input points with a piecewise cubic polynomial curve that passes through each control point of the set. For example, let there be $n + 1$ control points specified with the following co-ordinates:

$$p_i = (x_i, y_i, z_i), i = 0, 1, 2, \ldots\ldots, n$$

Figure 7.11 shows a cubic interpolation fit of these points. Now, the parametric cubic polynomial that is to be fitted between each pair of control points can be described in the form of following equations:

$$\begin{aligned} x(v) &= a_x v^3 + b_x v^2 + c_x v + d_x \\ y(v) &= a_y v^3 + b_y v^2 + c_y v + d_y \qquad (0 \le v \le 1) \\ z(v) &= a_z v^3 + b_z v^2 + c_z v + d_z \end{aligned} \tag{1}$$

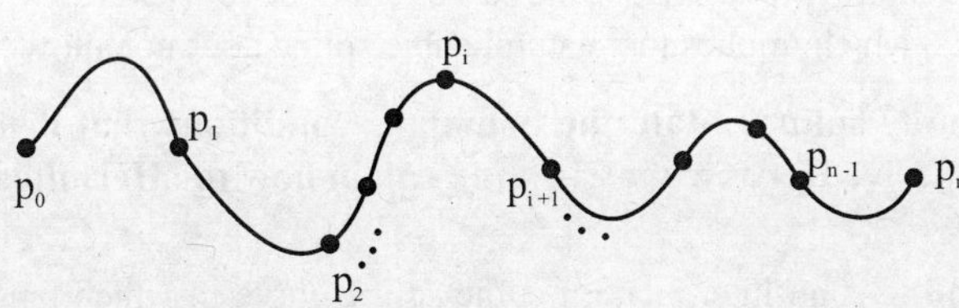

Figure 7.11 A Piecewise Continuous Cubic-Spline Interpolation of $n + 1$ Control Point

To find out the values of coefficients a, b, c, and d, in the polynomial representation for each of the n curve sections between the $n + 1$ control points, one needs to set different boundary conditions at the 'joints' between the curve sections. Some of the methods that can be used for setting these boundary conditions are *natural cubic spline*, *Hermite interpolation*, *cardinal splines*, and *Kochanek-Bartels splines*.

15. Explain natural cubic spline.

Ans. The **natural cubic spline** was the first interpolation spline curve that was developed for graphics applications. This curve is a mathematical model of the original drafting spline that has C^2 order of continuity. In such a spline, if we have $n + 1$ control points to fit, then we have n curve sections each having four polynomial coefficients. Thus, in total we have 4n polynomial coefficients to be determined. For example, suppose we have three control points to fit (p_0, p_1, and p_2) with p_0 and p_2 as end points and p_1 as interior point. Then, we have two curve sections and eight (4*2) polynomial coefficients to be determined (see Figure 7.12).

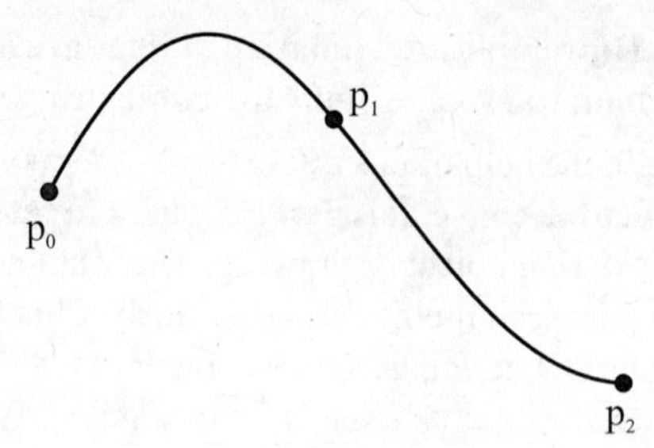

Figure 7.12 Cubic Spline Curve with Three Control Points

At each interior control point, we have four boundary conditions, which are as follows:

- The first and second parametric derivatives of the two curve sections on either side of the control point must be same at that control point, and each curve must pass through that control point.
- We can obtain two additional equations; one from the first control point p_0 and second from the last control point p_n.
- The two more boundary conditions can be obtained with the help of either of the two methods as follows:
  - By setting the second derivatives at end points p_0 and p_n equal to 0.
  - By adding two extra control points (called **dummy points**) one at each end of the cubic curve and labelling them as p_{-1} and p_{n+1} at the beginning and end of the curve, respectively. This will make all the original control points as interior points.

One of the disadvantages of natural cubic spline is that the entire curve gets affected on altering the position of even a single control point. That is, the curve cannot be restructured without specifying a totally new set of control points, which implies that natural cubic spline does not allow 'local control' property.

16. What is Hermite spline? State the boundary conditions that define the Hermite curve section. Also derive Hermite matrix and explain how the Hermite blending functions are derived.

Ans. A **Hermite spline** is an interpolation cubic spline curve in which tangent is specified at each control point. This curve is named after the French mathematician Charles Hermite. The Hermite spline follows local control property as each section of curve is dependent only on its end point constraints. If parametric cubic point function for the curve section in between the control points p_i and p_{i+1} is represented by $P(v)$, (see Figure 7.13), then boundary conditions of Hermite curve section will be as follows:

$$P(0)=p_i$$

$$P(1)=p_{i+1}$$

$$P'(0)=Dp_i \qquad (1)$$

$$P'(1)=Dp_{i+1}$$

Here, Dp_i and Dp_{i+1} specify the values for the parametric derivatives (or slope of the curve) at the control point p_i and p_{i+1}, respectively. Now, for the Hermite-curve section, the parametric point function $P(v)$ can be written as:

$$P(v) = av^3 + bv^2 + cv + d,\ 0 \le v \le 1, \tag{2}$$

where x, y, and z components of P are as follows:

$$x(v) = a_x v^3 + b_x v^2 + c_x v + d_x$$
$$y(v) = a_y v^3 + b_y v^2 + c_y v + d_y$$
$$z(v) = a_z v^3 + b_z v^2 + c_z v + d_z$$

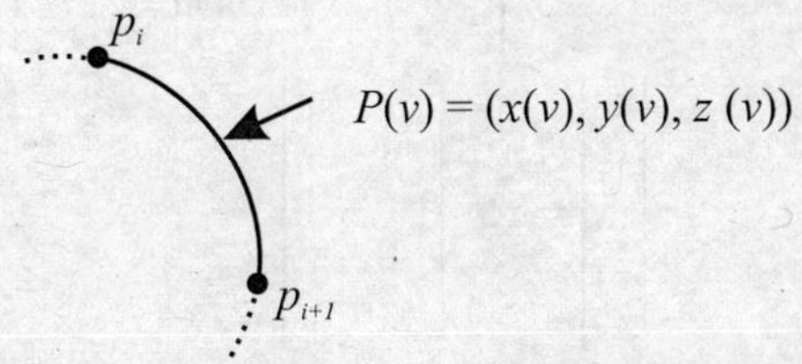

Figure 7.13 Parametric Point Function P(v) for Hermite Curve Section

The matrix equivalent of Equation (2) is

$$P(v) = \begin{bmatrix} v^3 & v^2 & v & 1 \end{bmatrix} \cdot \begin{bmatrix} a \\ b \\ c \\ d \end{bmatrix} \tag{3}$$

The derivative of the point function P (v) can be expressed as:

$$P'(v) = \begin{bmatrix} 3v^2 & 2v & 1 & 0 \end{bmatrix} \cdot \begin{bmatrix} a \\ b \\ c \\ d \end{bmatrix} \tag{4}$$

To express the Hermite boundary conditions [as given in Equation (1)] in the matrix form, we substitute end point values 0 and 1 for parameter v in Equations (3) and (4). The resulting matrix will be as follows:

$$\begin{bmatrix} p_i \\ p_{i+1} \\ Dp_i \\ Dp_{i+1} \end{bmatrix} = \begin{bmatrix} 0 & 0 & 0 & 1 \\ 1 & 1 & 1 & 1 \\ 0 & 0 & 1 & 0 \\ 3 & 2 & 1 & 0 \end{bmatrix} \cdot \begin{bmatrix} a \\ b \\ c \\ d \end{bmatrix} \tag{5}$$

Now, by solving this equation for the polynomial coefficients we get:

$$\begin{bmatrix} a \\ b \\ c \\ d \end{bmatrix} = \begin{bmatrix} 0 & 0 & 0 & 1 \\ 1 & 1 & 1 & 1 \\ 0 & 0 & 1 & 0 \\ 3 & 2 & 1 & 0 \end{bmatrix}^{-1} \begin{bmatrix} p_i \\ p_{i+1} \\ Dp_i \\ Dp_{i+1} \end{bmatrix}$$

$$= \begin{bmatrix} 2 & -2 & 1 & 1 \\ -3 & 3 & -2 & 1 \\ 0 & 0 & 1 & 0 \\ 1 & 0 & 0 & 0 \end{bmatrix} \begin{bmatrix} p_i \\ p_{i+1} \\ Dp_i \\ Dp_{i+1} \end{bmatrix}$$

$$\begin{bmatrix} a \\ b \\ c \\ d \end{bmatrix} = M_H \begin{bmatrix} p_i \\ p_{i+1} \\ Dp_i \\ Dp_{i+1} \end{bmatrix}$$

where M_H is the Hermite matrix or one can say the inverse of the boundary constraint matrix. Now, rewriting Equation (3) in terms of M_H as follows:

$$P(v) = \begin{bmatrix} v^3 & v^2 & v & 1 \end{bmatrix} \cdot M_H \cdot \begin{bmatrix} p_i \\ p_{i+1} \\ Dp_i \\ Dp_{i+1} \end{bmatrix}$$

Or,

$$P(v) = \begin{bmatrix} v^3 & v^2 & v & 1 \end{bmatrix} \cdot \begin{bmatrix} 2 & -2 & 1 & 1 \\ -3 & 3 & -2 & -1 \\ 0 & 0 & 1 & 0 \\ 1 & 0 & 0 & 0 \end{bmatrix} \cdot \begin{bmatrix} p_i \\ p_{i+1} \\ Dp_i \\ Dp_{i+1} \end{bmatrix} \qquad (6)$$

Finally, by performing matrix multiplication in Equation (6), we can find out the expression for Hermite blending functions $H_i(v)$ for $i = 0, 1, 2, 3$. That is,

$$\begin{bmatrix} v^3 & v^2 & v & 1 \end{bmatrix} \cdot \begin{bmatrix} 2 \\ -3 \\ 0 \\ 1 \end{bmatrix} \cdot \begin{bmatrix} p_i \\ p_{i+1} \\ Dp_i \\ Dp_{i+1} \end{bmatrix} = P_i(2v^3 - 3v^2 + 1)$$

Similarly, all other rows are multiplied and following expression is obtained:

$$\begin{aligned} P(v) &= p_i\left(2v^3 - 3v^2 + 1\right) + p_{i+1}\left(-2v^3 + 3v^2\right) + Dp_i\left(v^3 - 2v^2 + v\right) + Dp_{i+1}\left(v^3 - v^2\right) \\ &= p_i H_0(v) + p_{i+1} H_1(v) + Dp_i H_2(v) + Dp_{i+1} H_3(v) \end{aligned}$$

Here, the polynomials $H_i(v)$ for $i = 0,1,2,3$ are referred to as **blending functions**. These polynomials are named so because they blend the boundary constraint values (that is, the end point co-ordinates and slopes) in order to get each coordinate position along the curve. The shape of four Hermite blending functions is shown in Figure 7.14.

As Hermite splines require input values for curve slopes or other geometric information at the control points, they are only useful for some digitization applications where it is easier to specify or approximate the curve slopes.

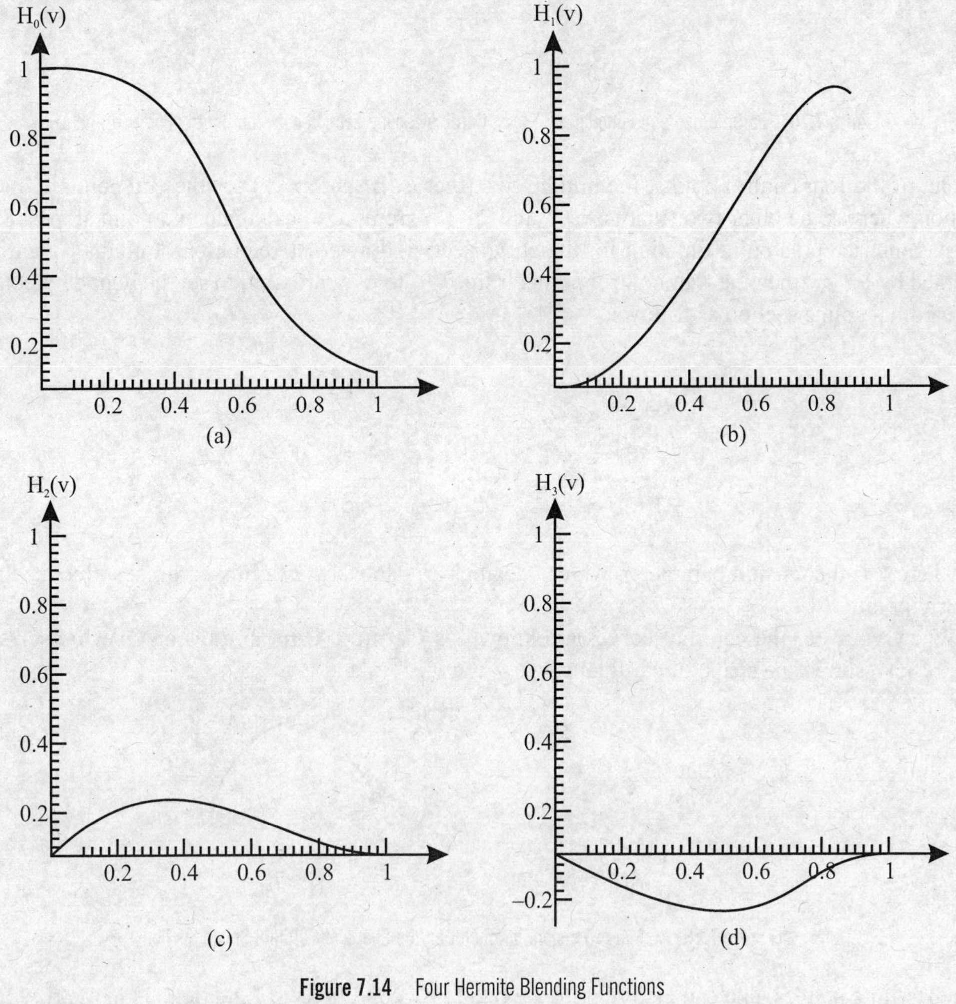

Figure 7.14 Four Hermite Blending Functions

17. Explain the following:

(a) Cardinal spline

(b) Kochanek–Bartels spline

Ans. (a) Cardinal splines are interpolating piecewise cubic polynomials, which are similar to Hermite splines in the sense that they also have specified end point tangents at the boundary of each curve sections. However, unlike Hermite splines, we do not need to input the values for the end point tangents. Instead, the coordinates of the two adjacent control points are used to calculate the slope at a specified control point. In order to completely specify a cardinal spline section, four consecutive control-point positions, p_{i-1}, p_i, p_{i+1}, and p_{i+2}, are required (see Figure 7.15).

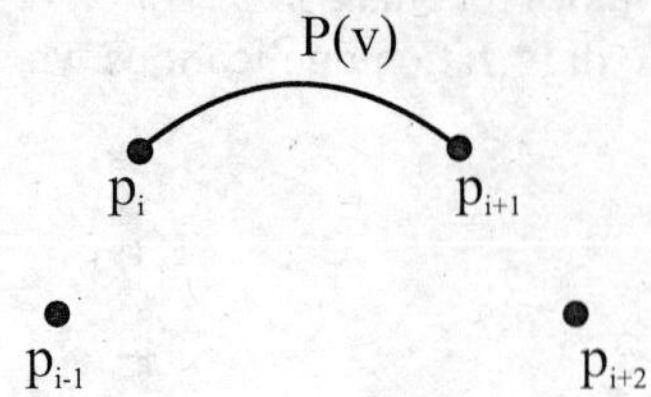

Figure 7.15 Parametric Point Function P(v) for a Cardinal-spline Section between Control Points p_i and p_{i+1}

Out of the four control points, the middle two (that is, p_i and p_{i+1}) are the end points of the curve section whereas the other two (that is, p_{i-1} and p_{i+2}) are used to calculate end point slopes. Suppose the parametric cubic point function for the curve section drawn between control points p_i and p_{i+1} is denoted by $P(v)$, then the four control points from p_{i-1} to p_{i+2} are used to set the boundary conditions for cardinal spline section as follows:

$$\begin{aligned} P(0) &= p_i \\ P(1) &= p_{i+1} \\ P'(0) &= \frac{1}{2}(1-t)(p_{i+1}-p_{i-1}) \\ P'(1) &= \frac{1}{2}(1-t)(p_{i+2}-p_i) \end{aligned} \qquad (1)$$

where t is the **tension** parameter, which specifies how loosely or tightly cardinal spline fits the input control point.

When $t = 0$, the cardinal curves are known as **Catmull–Rom splines** or **Overhauser splines.** Figure 7.16 shows the shape of cardinal curve when $t > 0$ and $t < 0$.

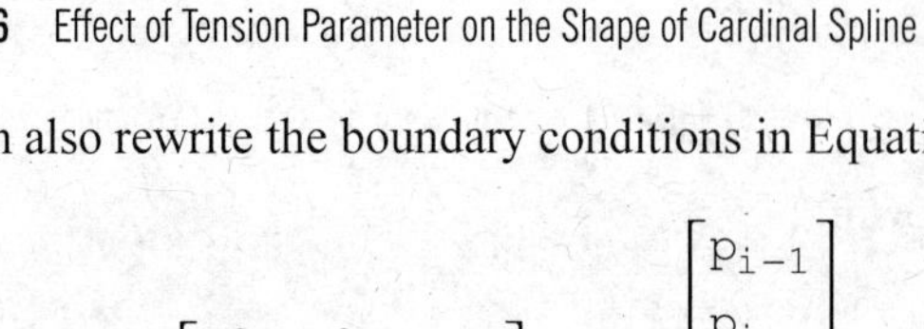

Figure 7.16 Effect of Tension Parameter on the Shape of Cardinal Spline Section

Like Hermite splines, one can also rewrite the boundary conditions in Equation (1) in matrix form as:

$$P(v) = \begin{bmatrix} v^3 & v^2 & v & 1 \end{bmatrix} \cdot M_C \cdot \begin{bmatrix} p_{i-1} \\ p_i \\ p_{i+1} \\ p_{i+2} \end{bmatrix} \qquad (2)$$

where M_c is the cardinal matrix and is represented as follows:

$$M_C = \begin{bmatrix} -s & 2-s & s-2 & s \\ 2s & s-3 & 3-2s & -s \\ -s & 0 & s & 0 \\ 0 & 1 & 0 & 0 \end{bmatrix}$$

where $s = (1-t)/2$.

To convert boundary conditions into polynomial form, we expand Equation (2) as follows:

$$\begin{aligned} P(v) &= p_{i-1}(-sv^3 + 2sv^2 - sv) + p_i[\,(2-s)v^3 + (s-3)v^2 + 1] \\ &\quad + p_{i+1}[\,(s-2)v^3 + (3-2s)v^2 + sv] + p_{i+2}(sv^3 - sv^2) \\ &= p_{i-1}CAR_0(v) + p_iCAR_1(v) + p_{i+1}CAR_2(v) + p_{i+2}CAR_3(v) \end{aligned} \tag{3}$$

where $CAR_i(v)$ are the cardinal blending functions for $i = 0,1,2,3$. Figure 7.17 shows a plot of the basic functions for cardinal splines with $t = 0$.

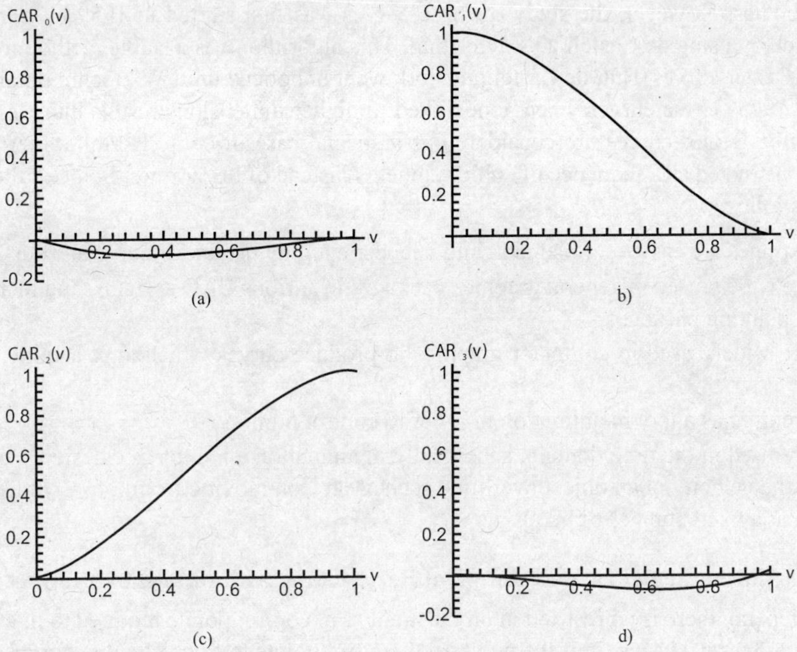

Figure 7.17 Cardinal Blending Functions for t = 0

(b) Kochanek–Bartels splines are the extension of cardinal splines that provide more flexibility in adjusting the shape of the curve sections by introducing two additional parameters in the constraint equations. Given four consecutive control points (p_{i-1}, p_i, p_{i+1}, and p_{i+2}), then the boundary conditions for a Kochanek–Bartels curve section between the control points p_i and p_{i+1} are defined as follows:

$$P(0) = p_i$$

$$P(1) = p_{i+1}$$

$$P'(0)_{in} = \frac{1}{2}(1 - t)[(1 + b)(1 - c)(p_i - p_{i-1}) + (1 - b)(1 + c)(p_{i+1} - p_i)]$$

$$P'(1)_{out} = \frac{1}{2}(1 - t)[(1 + b)(1 + c)(p_{i+1} - p_i) + (1 - b)(1 - c)(p_{i+2} - p_{i+1})]$$

where t is the **tension** parameter, it controls the looseness or tightness of the curve sections; b is the **bias** parameter, it is used to adjust the curvature at each end of a curve section. This enables the curve sections to be skewed towards either of the ends; c is the **continuity** parameter, it is used to control the continuity of the tangent vector across the boundaries of the curve sections. A non-zero value of c shows discontinuity in the slope of the curve across section boundaries. The non-zero values for c are basically used for simulating abrupt changes in the motion of an object such that in cartoon animations.

18. What are Bézier curves? List some of its uses.

Ans. The **Bézier curve** is a spline approximation method that was developed by the French automobile engineer named Pierre Bézier in 1962. He developed this method to be used in the design of Renault automobile bodies. However, the study of these curves was first started in 1959 by a mathematician Paul de Castelijau using de Castelijau's algorithm. This algorithm was a stable method to evaluate and generate 3D Bézier curves. But, de Castelijau work went unnoticed until W. Bochm obtained copies of the report in 1975. These curves when generalized to higher dimensions results into **Bézier surfaces**. Mathematically, Bézier curves are considered as a special case of cubic Hermite interpolation since curves are constructed as a sequence of cubic segments instead of linear ones. Some of the uses of such curves are as follows:

- Bézier splines are easy to implement, and hence are highly useful for curve and surface design.
- They are widely used in general graphics packages in various CAD systems, and in assorted drawing and painting packages.
- They are widely used in computer graphics to produce curves which appear quite smooth at all scales.
- They are used as a tool in animation in order to control motion.
- They are used in the time domain, specifically in animation and interface design. For example, to specify the velocity of an object over time such as an icon moving from X to Y, rather than simply moving at a fixed number of pixels per step.

19. Give the mathematical description of Bézier curve with respect to blending function.

Ans. In general, there is no restriction on the number of control points required to fit a Bézier curve. Still, some graphics packages limit the number of control points to four. The number of control points and their relative position determine the degree of the Bézier polynomial. Like the interpolation splines, Bézier curve path can also be specified using boundary conditions, a characterizing matrix, or blending functions. If there is no limit on the number of control points, then it is convenient to represent the Bézier curve path using blending functions.

Suppose there are $n + 1$ control-point coordinates $p_0, p_1, \ldots, p_n$, where $p_i = (x_i, y_i, z_i)$, for $i = 0, 1, 2, \ldots, n$. By blending these coordinate points, a position vector $P(v)$ can be produced that describes the path of an approximating Bézier polynomial function between p_0 and p_n as follows:

$$P(v) = \sum_{i=0}^{n} p_i BEZ_{i,n}(v), \; 0 \le v \le 1 \tag{1}$$

where x, y, and z components of P are as follows:

$$x(v) = \sum_{i=0}^{n} x_i BEZ_{i,n}(v)$$

$$y(v) = \sum_{i=0}^{n} y_i BEZ_{i,n}(v)$$

$$z(v) = \sum_{i=0}^{n} z_i BEZ_{i,n}(v)$$

Here, $BEZ_{i,n}(v)$ is the **Bézier blending function** (also known as **Bernstein polynomial**) and can be mathematically represented as:

$$BEZ_{i,n}(v) = C(n,i) \; v^i \; (1-v)^{n-i}$$

where $C(n,i)$ is the binomial coefficient and evaluated as:

$$C(n,i) = \frac{n!}{i!(n-i)!}$$

The successive binomial coefficients can be obtained using recursive calculations as follows:

$$c(n,i) = \frac{n-i+1}{i} c(n,i-1), \text{for } (n \ge i)$$

The Bézier blending function also satisfy the recursive relationship:

$$BEZ_{i,n}(v) = (1-v) BEZ_{i,n-1}(v) + vBEZ_{i-1,n-1}(v), \; n > i \ge 1$$

With $BEZ_{i,i} = v^i$ and $BEZ_{0,i} = (1-v)^i$.

In general, a Bézier curve is a polynomial of degree one less than the specified number of control points. For example, three control points generate a parabola; four control points generate a cubic curve, five points generate a curve of order four, and so on. Figure 7.18 shows some Bézier curves in the xy plane (that is, $z = 0$). Note that the placement of control points at a certain locations results in degenerated Bézier polynomials. For example, with three collinear control points, a Bézier curve is a straight-line segment whereas when all the control points lie at the same coordinate position, a curve is a single point.

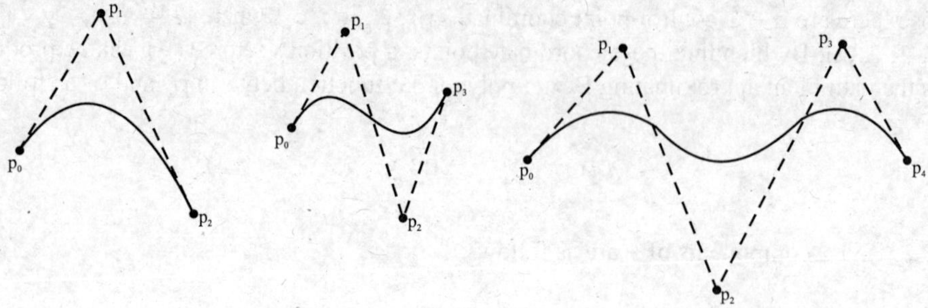

Figure 7.18 Two-dimensional Bézier Curves

20. Explain all three properties of Bézier curves.

Ans. Bézier curve exhibits the following properties:

- **End points geometric property:** According to this property, a Bézier curve always passes through the first and last control points. In other words, first and last control points are the end points of the curve and boundary condition for these two points will be as follows:

$$P(0) = p_0 \qquad (1)$$
$$P(1) = p_n$$

Moreover, the property states that the curve is a tangent at the end points of the control polygon (which is formed by drawing lines between consecutive control points of the curve). This can be observed by calculating the values of the first parametric derivative of a Bézier curve (also called **hodograph**) at the end points using control-point coordinates as:

$$P'(v) = \frac{dP(v)}{dt} = n\sum_{i=0}^{n-1}(p_{i+1}-p_i)\,BEZ_{i,n-1}(v),\ 0 \le v \le 1$$

$$P'(0) = -np_0 + np_1$$
$$P'(1) = -np_{n-1} + np_n \qquad (2)$$

Thus, from Equation (2) it is observed that the slope at the beginning of the curve is along the line joining the first two control points while slope at the end of the curve is along the line joining the last two end points. In the same way, values of the second parametric derivatives of a Bézier curve at the end points can be calculated as follows:

$$P''(0) = n(n-1)[(p_2 - p_1) - (p_1 - p_0)] \qquad (3)$$

$$P''(1) = n(n-1)[(p_{n-2} - p_{n-1}) - (p_{n-1} - p_n)]$$

- **Convex-hull property:** This property states that a Bézier curve always lies within the convex hull (or convex polygon boundary) of the control points. This property is based on the fact that the Bézier blending functions are positive and their sum is always 1.

$$\sum_{i=0}^{n} BEZ_{i,n}(v) = 1$$

It means that any curve position is the weighted sum of the control-point positions. The property of convex hull also makes sure that there are no erratic oscillations, and the polynomial smoothly follows the control points. In other words, curves are stable and do not undulate.

- **Variation-diminishing property:** This property is exhibited by the intermediate part of the curve in which the curve smoothens the control points. The interpolating Bézier curves have intersections only with the first and the last points and not with any other point of the control polygon.

21. Discuss the design techniques for Bézier curves.

Ans. A Closed Bézier curve is constructed by joining the first and last control points. These are the end points of the curve. The curve does not pass through the other control points. The simplest type of Bézier curve is a line segment, which requires only two control points, p_0 and p_1. The line segment starts at point p_0 and ends at point p_1. The number of control points determines the degree of Bézier curve. The degree of curve is one less than the number of control points. For example, two control points are necessary for a linear curve, hence it has the degree one. For quadratic curves, we need three control points, hence they have the degree two. Cubic curves have the degree three, and require four control points (see Figure 7.18).

To construct a closed Bézier curve, we need to set the last control-point coordinates to the first control-point coordinates. For example, Figure 7.19a shows a closed Bézier curve with five control points and $p_0 = p_5$. A particular coordinate position can be given more weight by specifying multiple control points at that position. This allows the resultant curve to be pulled nearer to that point. For example, in Figure 7.19b, a single coordinate position is input as two control points p_2 and p_3. Note that the curve is pulled nearer to this position.

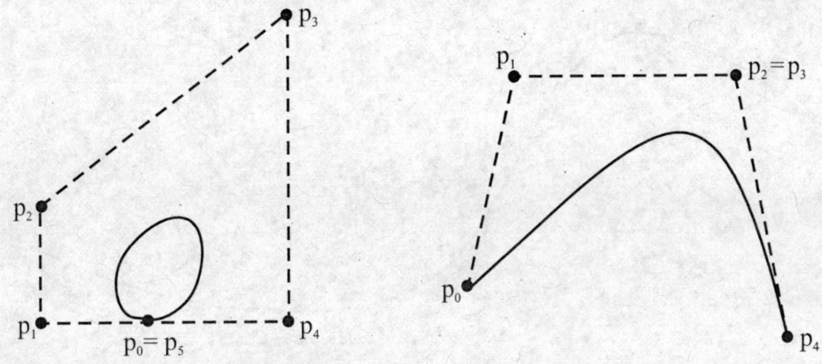

(a) Closed Bézier curve (b) Specifying multiple control points

Figure 7.19 Constructing Bézier Curves

The more complex curves can be generated by piecing together several Bézier curve sections of lower degree. This gives better local control over the shape of the curve. To ensure smooth joining of two curve sections, the first-order and second-order continuity should be maintained.

22. How can one obtain C^1 and C^2 continuity between two Bézier curve sections?

Ans. Bézier curves exhibit an important property that the tangent to the curve at an end point is along the line joining that end point to the adjacent control point. Thus, to obtain first-order or C^1 continuity between two Bézier curve sections, select two control points p'_0 and p'_1 of the new section such that they are along the same straight line as the control points p_{n-1} and p_n of the previous section. The first control point p'_0 is set to the last control point of the previous section, and the second control point p'_1 is positioned at the following location:

$$p'_1 = p_n + \frac{n}{n'}(p_n - p_{n-1}) \tag{1}$$

where n is the number of control points of the first curve section and n′ is the number of control points of the second curve section.

If n = n′, that is, both the curve sections have equal number of control points, then Equation (1) becomes

$$p'_1 = p_n + (p_n - p_{n-1})$$

This makes the three control points collinear and equally spaced.

Second-order or C^2 continuity is obtained between the two Bézier sections by calculating the position of the third control point of a new section in terms of the positions of the last three control points of the previous section as follows:

$$p_{n-2} + 4(p_n - p_{n-1})$$

In case of cubic curves, which have only four control points, C^2 continuity fixes the position of three control points and leaves only one control point that can be used to adjust the shape of the curve segment. Figure 7.20 shows piecewise approximation curve formed with two Bézier curve sections.

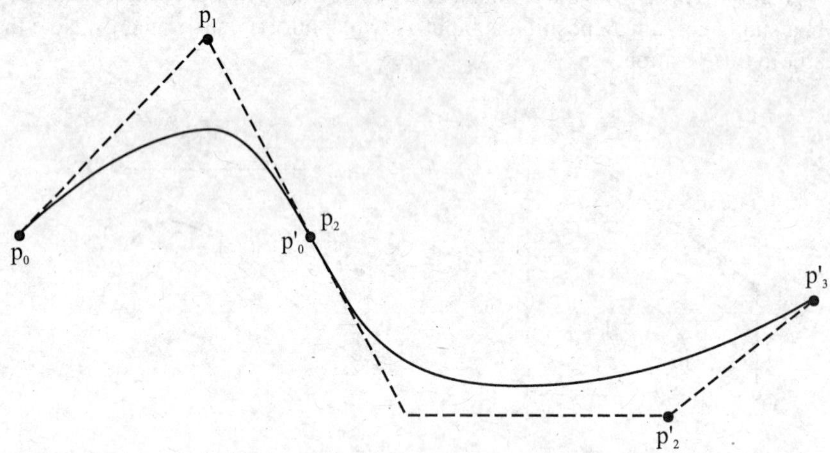

Figure 7.20 Piecewise Approximation Curve Formed with two Bézier Curve Sections

23. Give the mathematical formulation for Cubic Bézier Curves and sketch the blending functions (for n = 3).

or

Derive the parametric equation for a cubic Bézier curves for n = 3.

or

Describe the steps involved in generation of Bézier curve for four control points.

Ans. Though Bézier curve can be constructed with any number of control points, it requires excessive calculations with higher order polynomials. To avoid such situation, most graphics packages provide only cubic spline functions. From such functions, cubic Bézier curves are generated which have four control points. By substituting n = 3 in the following equation:

$$BEZ_{i,n}(v) = C(n,i)v_i(1-v)_{n-i}, \text{ with } C = \frac{n!}{i!(n-i)!}$$

We get four blending functions for such curves as follows:

$$\begin{aligned} BEZ_{0,3}(v) &= (1-v)^3 \\ BEZ_{1,3}(v) &= 3v(1-v)^2 \\ BEZ_{2,3}(v) &= 3v^2(1-v) \\ BEZ_{3,3}(v) &= v^3 \end{aligned} \qquad (1)$$

It can be observed that, at $v = 0$, $BEZ_{0,3}$ is the only blending function which is non-zero, that is, having the value 1 whereas at $v = 1$, $BEZ_{3,3}$ is the only non-zero function which is having a value 1 at that point. Thus, from this one can say that the cubic Bézier curve will always pass through control points p_0 and p_3. The other blending functions, $BEZ_{1,3}$ and $BEZ_{2,3}$, influence the shape of the curve at intermediate values of parameter v that makes the curve to tend towards the control points p_1 and p_2. Blending functions $BEZ_{1,3}$ and $BEZ_{2,3}$ are maximum at $v = 1/3$ and $v = 2/3$, respectively. Moreover, it can be seen that each of the four blending functions in Figure 7.21 is non-zero over entire range of parameter v, which means that the Bézier curves do not allow local control of the curve shape. That is, the entire shape of the curve gets affected on repositioning even a single control point.

The parametric first derivative (slopes) at the end positions of the cubic Bézier curve is calculated as follows:

$$P'(0) = 3(p_1 - p_0), P'(1) = 3(p_3 - p_2)$$

While the parametric second derivatives are calculated as:

$$P''(0) = 6(p_0 - 2p_1 + p_2), P''(1)=6(p_1 - 2p_2 + p_3)$$

These expressions can then be used for the parametric derivatives in order to construct piecewise curves having C^1 and C^2 continuity between sections. Now, to express cubic Bézier point function in the matrix form, we expand the polynomial expression for the blending function. Then, the resultant matrix will be as follows:

$$P(v) = \begin{bmatrix} v^3 & v^2 & v & 1 \end{bmatrix} \cdot M_{Bez} \cdot \begin{bmatrix} p_0 \\ p_1 \\ p_2 \\ p_3 \end{bmatrix}$$

where M_{BEZ} is the Bézier matrix and is represented as follows:

$$M_{Bez} = \begin{bmatrix} -1 & 3 & -3 & 1 \\ 3 & -6 & 3 & 0 \\ -3 & 3 & 0 & 0 \\ 1 & 0 & 0 & 0 \end{bmatrix}$$

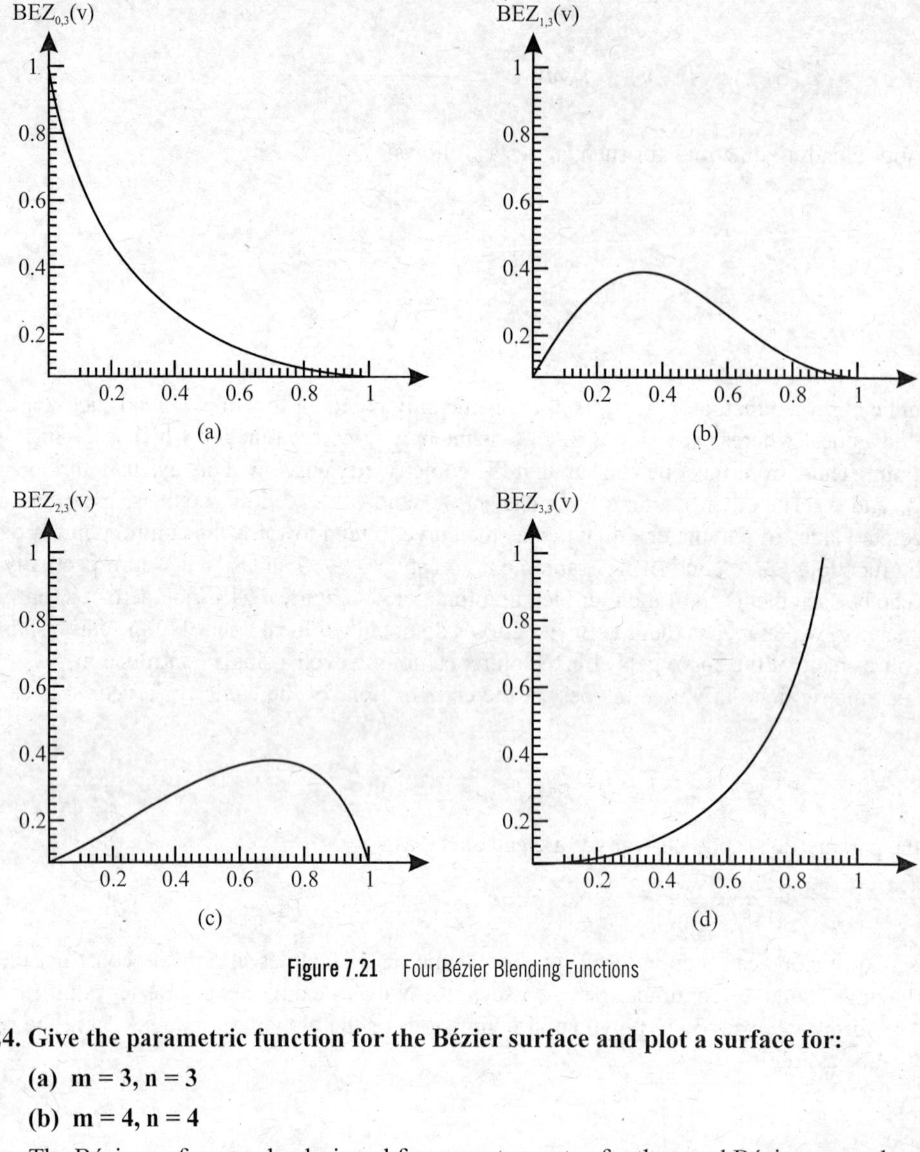

Figure 7.21 Four Bézier Blending Functions

24. Give the parametric function for the Bézier surface and plot a surface for:

(a) m = 3, n = 3

(b) m = 4, n = 4

Ans. The Bézier surface can be designed from any two sets of orthogonal Bézier curves by specifying an input mesh of control points. The parametric vector function for the Bézier surface is formed as a result of Cartesian product of Bézier blending functions as follows:

$$P(u, v) = \sum_{i=0}^{m} \sum_{j=0}^{n} p_{i,j} BEZ_{i,m}(v)\, BEZ_{j,n}(u)$$

where $p_{i,j}$ specifies the location of the $(m + 1)$ by $(n + 1)$ control points.

Figure 7.22a shows Bézier surface plots for $m = 3$ and $n = 3$ while Figure 7.22b shows for $m = 4$ and $n = 4$. Dash lines show control points connectivity whereas the solid lines show curves of constants u and v. Each curve of constant u is plotted by keeping u fixed to any value between 0 and 1 and varying v over this interval. In the same way, curves of constant v can be plotted. Bézier surfaces exhibit same properties as that of Bézier curves and provide a convenient method for interactive design applications. For every surface patch, a mesh of control points can be selected in the xy ground plane and then elevations can be chosen above the ground plane at the grid intersections for the z-coordinate values of the control points. Thereafter, by making use of the boundary constraints, the patches are pieced together to form a Bézier surface.

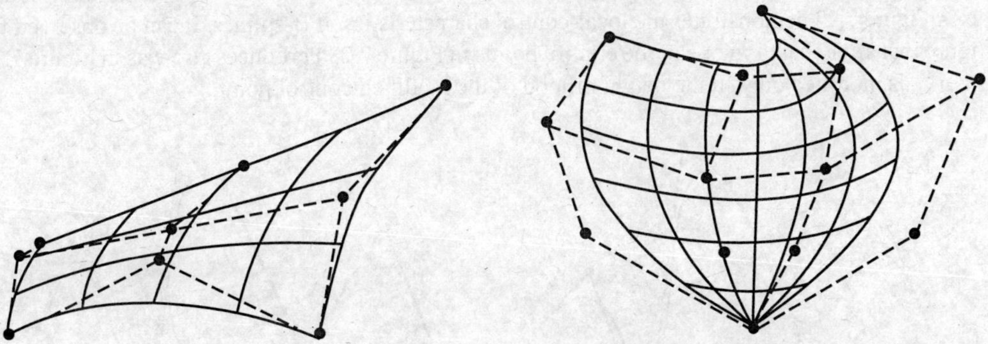

(a) m = 3 and n = 3 (b) m = 4 and n = 4

Figure 7.22 Bézier Surfaces Constructed

25. Write in detail about B-spline curves.

Ans. B-spline curves are the generalization of Bézier curves and are the most widely used class of approximating splines. They consist of curve segments whose polynomial coefficients depend on just a few control points. That is, they allow local control over the shape of a spline curve or surface. Thus, moving a control point does not change the shape of the curve abruptly, rather it affects only a small part of the curve. Moreover, time required to compute the coefficients in B-splines is considerably less. Though B-splines have the same continuity as that of natural splines, they do not interpolate their control points. A general expression to calculate the coordinate positions along a B-spline curve is as follows:

$$P(v) = \sum_{i=0}^{n} p_i B_{i,d}(v), \quad v_{min} \le v \le v_{max}, \quad 2 \le d \le n+1 \qquad (1)$$

where p_i is an input set of n+1 control points; $B_{i,d}$ is the B-spline blending functions of degree d−1, where parameter d (called the **degree parameter**) can be chosen to be any integer value in the range from 2 up to the number of control points, n+1.

Note that we have not chosen the value of d = 1, as in that case the resulting curve will be just a point formed from the set of control points. In B-spline curves, the range of parameter v depends on the way other B-spline parameters are chosen. Each blending function is defined over d subintervals of the total range of v in order to achieve local control property. For B-spline curves, the blending functions are defined by the following Cox-deBoor recursion formulas:

$$B_{i,1}(v) = \begin{cases} 1, & \text{if } v_i \le v \le v_{i+1} \\ 0, & \text{otherwise} \end{cases} \qquad (2)$$

$$B_{i,d}(v) = \frac{v - v_i}{v_{i+d-1} - v_i} B_{i,d-1}(v) + \frac{v_{i+d} - v}{v_{i+d} - v_{i+1}} B_{i+1,d-1}(v)$$

Each subinterval end point v_j is referred to as a **knot** and the entire set of selected subintervals end points is called a **knot vector**. However, any values can be selected for the subinterval end points that satisfy the relation $v_j \leq v_{j+1}$. The values for v_{min} and v_{max} then depend on the selected number of control points, the value selected for parameter d and how the subintervals (knot vector) are set up by the user. Figure 7.23 demonstrates the local-control characteristics of B-splines. It can be observed from the figure that after changing one of the control points in Figure 7.23a produces curve as in Figure 7.23b. This curve is modified only in the neighborhood of the modified control point.

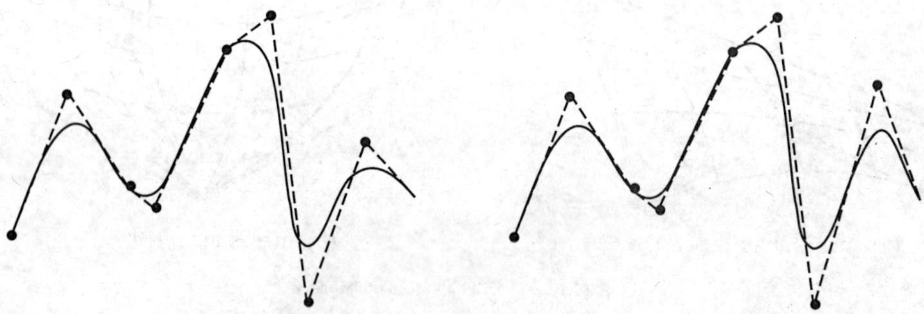

(a) Original Curve (b) Modified Curve

Figure 7.23 Local Modification of a B-spline Curve

The most important feature of B-splines is that they allow us to vary the number of control points used to design a curve without changing the degree of the polynomial. In addition, the curve shapes can be manipulated by adding or modifying the number of control points. Similarly, the number of values in the knot vector can also be increased to aid in curve design. However, for doing this, one also needs to add control points because the size of the knot vector depends on parameter n.

26. Discuss the properties of a B-spline curve.

Ans. A B-spline curve has the following properties:

- The curve is described with n + 1 blending functions for n + 1 control points and each blending function ($B_{i,d}$) is defined over d subintervals of the total range of v, starting from the knot value v_i.
- Over the entire range of v, the polynomial curve is of degree d−1 and has C^{d-2} continuity.
- Just like Bézier curve, a non-periodic B-spline curve also passes through the first and last control points p_0 and p_n, and is tangential to the first $(p_1 - p_0)$ and the last $(p_n - p_{n-1})$ segment of the polygon.
- The range of parameter v is divided into n + d subintervals with n + d + 1 values specified in the knot vector.
- Each section of the spline curve is influenced by d control points.
- Any one control point can affect the shape of at most d curve sections.
- The maximum order of a B-spline curve is equal to the number of control points while the minimum order is 2.

- If the degree of the curve is increased, then the curve becomes more difficult to control and to calculate accurately. Thus, a large number of applications make use of cubic curves.
- B-splines lie within the convex hull of at most d+1 control points. This makes the B-splines tightly bound to the input positions.
- For any value of v in the interval from knot value v_{d-1} to v_{n+1}, the sum over all basis function is 1. That is,

$$\sum_{i=0}^{n} B_{i,d}(v) = 1$$

27. Write in brief on uniform B-spline curves.

Ans. The **uniform B-spline curve** is obtained when the spacing between knot values is constant. For example, consider the following uniform knot vector:

$$\{-2.0, -1.5, -1.0, -0.5, 0.0, 0.5, 1.0, 1.5\}$$

In this knot vector, the spacing between the knot values is 0.5. However, many a times, the knot values are normalized to the range between 0 and 1, as:

$$\{0.0, 0.2, 0.4, 0.6, 0.8, 1.0\}$$

In many applications, the uniform knot values are set to have the difference of 1 and the first value is set to 0. For example:

$$\{0, 1, 2, 3, 4, 5, 6, 7\}$$

The blending functions of uniform B-splines are **periodic**, hence, the curve obtained from such set of knot values are also known as **uniform periodic B-splines**. By periodic, we mean that all the blending functions have the same shape for given values of n and d and each successive blending function is a shifted version of the previous function. That is,

$$B_{i,d}(v) = B_{i+1,d}(v + \Delta v) = B_{i+2,d}(v + 2\Delta v)$$

where Δv is the interval between adjacent knot values.

28. Derive the characteristic matrix for the periodic cubic B-splines.

Ans. To derive the characteristic matrix for a periodic cubic B-spline, we first determine the boundary conditions for periodic cubic B-spline with four consecutive control points, p_0, p_1, p_2, and p_3, as follows:

$$P(0) = \frac{1}{6}(p_0 + 4p_1 + p_2)$$

$$P(1) = \frac{1}{6}(p_1 + 4p_2 + p_3)$$

$$P'(0) = \frac{1}{2}(p_2 - p_0)$$

$$P'(1) = \frac{1}{2}(p_3 - p_1)$$

These boundary conditions state that the curve sections are defined with four control points, and parametric derivatives at the beginning and end of each curve section (that is, P′(0) and P′(1), respectively) are parallel to the chords joining adjacent control points. Moreover, the B-spline curve section starts at a position near p_1 and ends at a position near p_2. A matrix formulation with four control points can then be written as follows:

$$P(v) = \begin{bmatrix} v^3 & v^2 & v & 1 \end{bmatrix} . M_B . \begin{bmatrix} p_0 \\ p_1 \\ p_2 \\ p_3 \end{bmatrix}$$

where M_B is the B-spline matrix (or characteristic matrix) for periodic cubic polynomials. This matrix is represented as follows:

$$M_B = \frac{1}{6}\begin{bmatrix} -1 & 3 & -3 & 1 \\ 3 & -6 & 3 & 0 \\ -3 & 0 & 3 & 0 \\ 1 & 4 & 1 & 0 \end{bmatrix}$$

We can also rewrite the matrix M_B by including a tension parameter t, as follows:

$$M_{Bt} = \frac{1}{6}\begin{bmatrix} -t & 12-9t & 9t-12 & t \\ 3t & 12t-18 & 18-5t & 0 \\ -3t & 0 & 3t & 0 \\ t & 6-2t & t & 0 \end{bmatrix}$$

For $t = 1$, $M_{Bt} = M_B$. Now, to obtain the periodic, cubic B-spline blending functions over the parameter range from 0 to 1, we expand the matrix representation into polynomial form (for $t = 1$) as follows:

$$B_{0,3}(v) = \frac{1}{6}(1-v)^3, \quad 0 \le v \le 1$$

$$B_{1,3}(v) = \frac{1}{6}(3v^3 - 6v^2 + 4)$$

$$B_{2,3}(v) = \frac{1}{6}(-3v^3 + 3v^2 + 3v + 1)$$

$$B_{3,3}(v) = \frac{1}{6}v^3$$

29. Write a short note on open B-spline curves.

Ans. Open B-splines are considered as cross between uniform B-splines and non-uniform B-splines. Sometimes, they are treated as special case of uniform B-splines and other times as non-uniform B-splines. In this class of B-splines, the knot spacing is uniform except at the ends where knot values are repeated d number of times.

For any values of parameters d and n, an open uniform integer knot vector can be generated as follows:

$$v_j = \begin{cases} 0, & \text{for } 0 \le j < d \\ j - d + 1, & \text{for } d \le j \le n \\ n - d + 2, & \text{for } j > n \end{cases}$$

Here, the value of j ranges from 0 to $n + d$. By putting different values of j in the above equation, the first d knots get the value 0, and the last d knots get the value $n - d + 2$.

For example,

For $n = 3$ and $d = 2$, the knot vector will be {0, 0, 1, 2, 3, 3};

For $n = 4$ and $d = 4$, the knot vector will be {0, 0, 0, 0, 1, 2, 2, 2, 2}.

These knot vectors can also be normalized to the range between 0 and 1. This can be done by dividing all the knot values by the last value of the knot vector. For example,

For $n = 3$ and $d = 2$, the normalized knot vector will be {0, 0, 0.33, 0.67, 1, 1};

For $n = 4$ and $d = 4$, the normalized knot vector will be {0, 0, 0, 0, 0.5, 1, 1, 1, 1}.

The main drawback of open B-splines is that the matrix formulation for these curves is not easily generated because the knot vector contains repeated multiple values at the beginning and end.

30. Why Bézier curve is considered as a special case of open uniform B-splines?

or

Discuss the similarities between the Bézier curves and open uniform B-splines.

Ans. When the value of parameter d equals to $n + 1$ (that is, degree of the polynomial is n), the open uniform B-splines reduce to Bézier splines, and the knot vector in this case contains only values either 0 or 1. For example, for $d = 4$ and four control points, the knot vector becomes {0, 0, 0, 0, 1, 1, 1, 1}. In addition, it shows the following properties similar to that of Bézier splines:

- The polynomial curve of such spline passes through the first and the last control points.
- The slope of the parametric curves at the first control point and the last control point is parallel to the line connecting the first two control points and the last two control points, respectively.
- Since open B-spline curve starts from first control point and ends at last specified control point, the closed curves in such class of splines are generated by specifying the first and last control points at the same position.
- Like Bézier curves, specifying multiple control points at a particular position gives more weight to that position, and the result is that B-spline curve is pulled nearer to that point.

31. Write a short note on non-uniform B-spline curves.

Ans. The **non-uniform** B-splines allow choosing multiple internal knot values and unequal spacing between the knot values. For example,

{0, 2, 3, 3, 5, 5}

{0, 1, 2, 3, 3, 6}

{0, 0, 0, 2, 2, 4, 4, 4}

{0.0, 0.1, 0.3, 0.6, 0.9, 1.0}

The unequal spacing between the knot values provides different shapes for the blending functions in different intervals that are used to adjust the spline shapes. Thus, it provides more flexibility in controlling the shape of the curve. If we increase the number of knot values, then we can produce subtle variations in the curve shape and can also introduce the discontinuities in the curve. Moreover, the multiple knot values reduce the continuity by 1 every time a particular value is repeated.

Now, the blending functions for non-uniform B-spline can be obtained in a similar manner as that for the uniform and open B-splines. The procedure is discussed as follows:

1. For a given set of $n + 1$ control points, the degree of the polynomial is set and the knot values are selected.
2. By using recurrence relations, either a set of blending functions are obtained or curve positions are evaluated directly for the display of the curve.
3. A set of characteristic matrices is stored and used to compute values along the spline curve without evaluating the recurrence relations for each curve point to be plotted.

In order to reduce computations, the graphics packages many a times restrict the knot intervals to be either 0 or 1.

32. Give some advantages of B-splines over Bézier splines.

Ans. B-splines offer following advantages over the Bézier splines:

- B-spline curves act more flexibly and intuitively with a large number of control points than Bézier curves.
- B-spline curves are much more useful for designing curves than Bézier curves. This is because B-spline curves are affected by the placement of individual control points whereas Bézier curves are barely affected by such placements.
- The degree of B-spline polynomial is independent of the number of control points.
- B-splines allow local control over the shape of a spline curve or surface however, they are more complex than Bézier splines.

33. Explain sweep representation.

Ans. Sweep representation is one of the construction technique provided by solid-modelling packages to construct three-dimensional objects, which possess translational, rotational, or other symmetries. Such objects are constructed by specifying a two-dimensional shape (such as circles and rectangles) and a sweep that moves the shape through a region of space, hence name of the technique is sweep representation.

A sweep representation requires a set of two-dimensional objects (primitives), such as rectangles and circles, which are used to construct three-dimensional objects. There are several methods of providing these primitives. One way is to provide menu options so that the user can directly select one of the desired options. Alternative methods for obtaining two-dimensional figures are closed spline-curve constructions and cross-sectional slices of solid objects.

There are two types of sweeps, namely, *translation sweep* and *rotational sweep*. In **translation sweep** (also known as **extrusion**), a 2D area is swept along a linear path normal to the plane of the area to create a volume. The volume is computed by simply multiplying the area of the swept object with the length of the sweep. This is the simplest kind of sweep. Figure 7.24 shows a translation sweep in which the periodic spline curve in Figure 7.24a defines the object cross-section. To perform a translational sweep on the object cross-section, the control points p_0 through p_3 are moved along a straight-line path perpendicular to the plane of the cross-section. Then at some fixed intervals along this path, the shape is replicated and a set of connecting lines are drawn in the direction of the sweep so as to obtain the wireframe representation (see Figure 7.24b).

Figure 7.24 Translational Sweep

In **rotational sweep**, an area is rotated about an axis of rotation specified in the plane of the area to produce wireframe representation. Figure 7.25 shows a rotational sweep in which the control points of the periodic spline curve are rotated about the given rotation axis to generate a solid object.

Figure 7.25 Rotational Sweep

34. Write in detail on CSG method. How CSG operations are implemented using ray-casting methods.

Ans. Constructive solid geometry (CSG) is another solid modelling technique, which generates new 3D shapes or objects by applying set operations (union, intersection, and set difference) on two specified 3D objects. The basic idea is to combine the volumes occupied by overlapping 3D objects using set operations to create a new volume. For example, in Figure 7.26a, union operation is applied on two blocks to generate an L-shaped 3D object. In Figure 7.26b, set difference operation is applied on the L-shaped object and a cylinder to generate another 3D object.

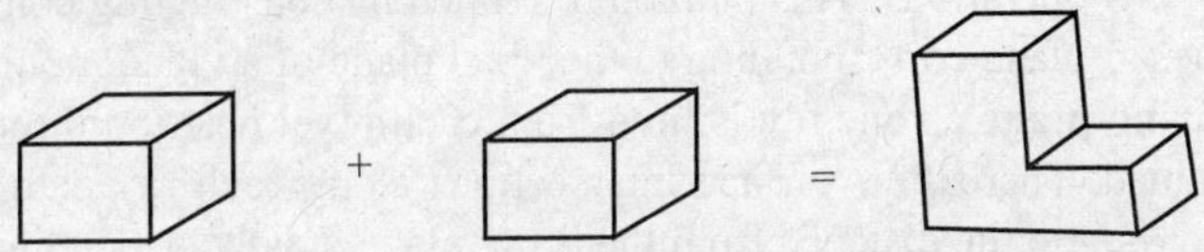

(a) Applying Union Operation

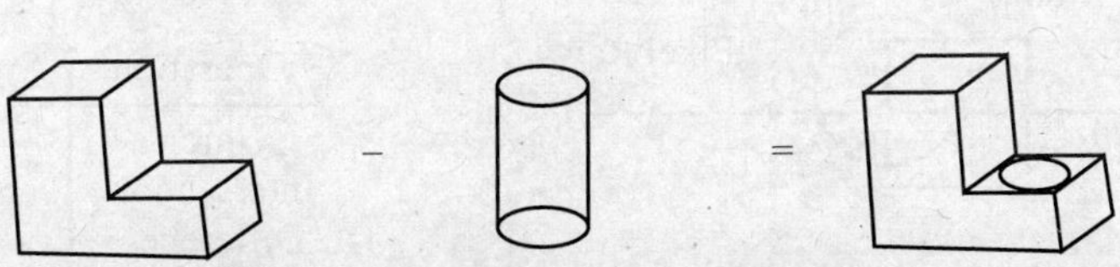

(b) Applying Set Difference Operation

Figure 7.26 Constructive Solid-geometry Methods

A CSG application begins with an initial set of 3D objects (primitives) such as blocks, cylinders, pyramids, cones, spheres, and closed spline surfaces. To create a new 3D object, two desired primitives are first selected. Then the desired set operation is performed on them to combine the volumes of the two primitives to obtain a new 3D object. The resultant 3D object can then be used to form another objects. For example, the 3D object produced in Figure 7.26a is used in Figure 7.26b to create a new 3D object. These steps are repeated until the final 3D object is obtained. An object produced with CSG technique can be represented as a binary tree as shown in Figure 7.27.

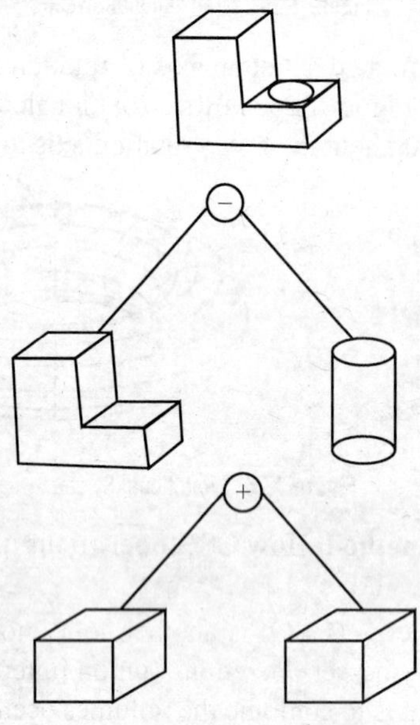

Figure 7.27 CSG Tree Representation

When objects are described with boundary representations, **ray-casting methods** are generally used to implement CSG operations. This method is applied by constructing composite objects in world coordinates with the xy plane corresponding to the pixel plane of a video monitor. The resulting plane is then known as **firing plane** as one ray is fired from each pixel position through the objects that are needed to be combined. Thereafter, surface intersections along each ray path are determined, which are then sorted according to the distance from the firing plane. Lastly, depending on which operation is applied, the surface limits for the object are determined. Figure 7.28 illustrates the ray casting determination of surface limits for a CSG object.

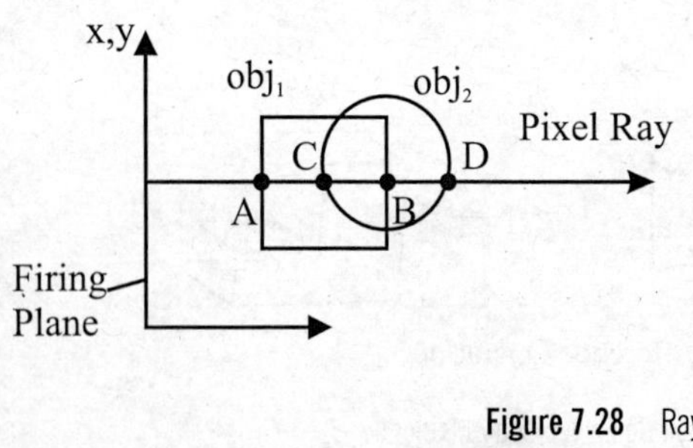

Operation	Surface Limits
Union	A, D
Intersection	C, B
Difference ($obj_2 - obj_1$)	B, D

Figure 7.28 Ray-casting Method

35. How can we determine the volume and mass of a CSG object?

Ans. To determine the volume of the designed CSG object, we first divide the firing plane into any number of small squares (see Figure 7.29). Then, the volume (V_{ij}) of the object for a cross-sectional slice with area (A_{ij}) along the path of a ray from the square at position (i, j) will be approximated as:

$$V_{ij} \approx A_{ij} \Delta z_{ij} \tag{1}$$

where ΔZ_{ij} is the depth of the object along the ray from position (i, j). However, if the object has internal holes, then ΔZ_{ij} is the sum of the distances between pairs of intersection points along the ray. Now, using Equation (1) total volume of the CSG object will be evaluated as follows:

$$V \approx \sum_{i,j} V_{ij}$$

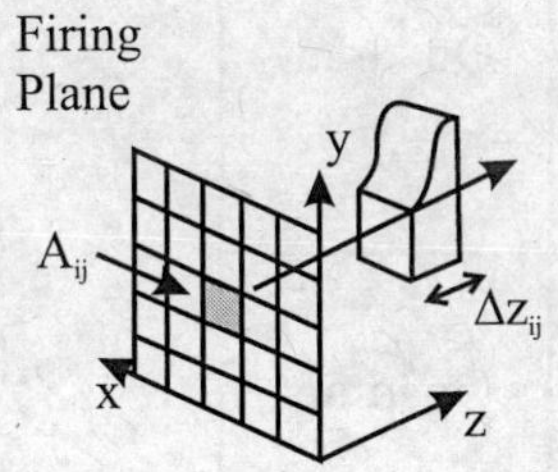

Figure 7.29 Determining Object Volume

For a given density function, $\rho(x, y, z)$ of the CSG object, the mass along the ray from position (i, j) will be approximated as follows:

$$m_{ij} \approx A_{ij} \int \rho\,(x_{ij}, y_{ij}, z)\; dz \tag{2}$$

Note that in Equation (2), the one-dimensional integral is often approximated rather than actually carrying out the integration, depending on the form of the density function. Now, using Equation (2) total mass will be approximated as:

$$m \approx \sum_{i,j} m_{i,j}$$

36. Explain how octrees are used to represent solid objects.

Ans. Octrees are the hierarchical tree structures that represent solid objects in graphics systems. The octree representations are commonly used in those applications which require displays of object cross-sections such as in medical imaging. The tree structure is organized in such a way that each node of it corresponds to a region of three-dimensional space. Representing solids in such a form helps in reducing the storage requirements for the 3D objects as such representation takes advantage of spatial coherence. Moreover, such structures help to store and represent information about object interiors in one of the most convenient way.

37. Discuss an encoding procedure for 2D and 3D space.

Ans. An encoding scheme for 2D space is known as **quadtree encoding** while for 3D space is known as **octree encoding.** Both these encoding schemes are described as follows:

Quadtree Encoding Scheme

To generate quadtrees, a two-dimensional region (usually a square) is successively divided into quadrants. Each node in the quadtree consists of four data elements, one for each quadrant (see Figure 7.30). If the quadrant is homogeneous, means, all the pixels within a quadrant have the same color, then the corresponding data element in the node stores that color. Along with it, a flag is set in data element so as to signal that the quadrant is homogeneous. For example, if all pixels of quadrant 1 are found to be blue, then data element 1 of the node stores the color code for blue.

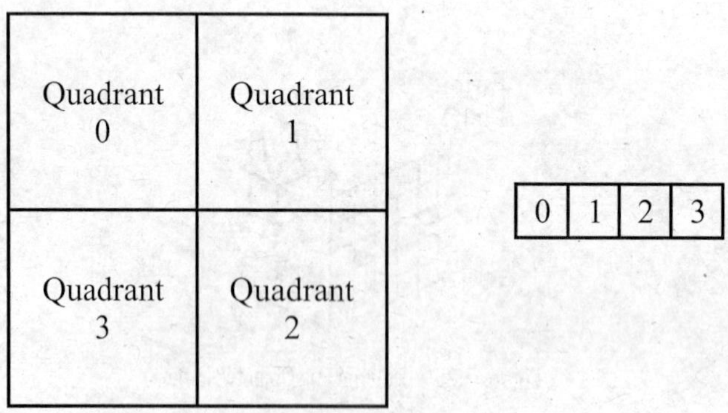

Figure 7.30 Quadtree Encoding Scheme

If all the pixels within a quadrant are note of same color, then the quadrant is said to be heterogeneous and it is subdivided into quadrants (see Figure 7.31). In addition, a flag is set in the data element to indicate that the quadrant is heterogeneous and the data element now stores the pointer to the next node in the quadtree.

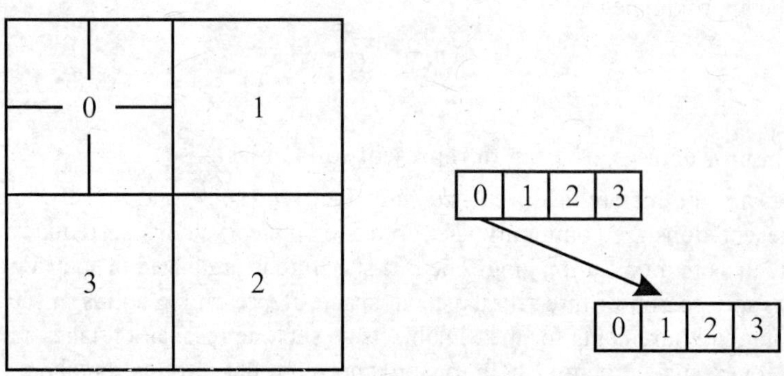

Figure 7.31 Subdividing a Heterogeneous Quadrant

Thus, the algorithm tests pixel intensity values and sets up the quadtree nodes accordingly so as to generate a quadtree. For a homogeneous region of space, the quadtree has only one node, and for a heterogeneous region, the algorithm keeps on dividing quadrants until all of them become homogeneous. Figure 7.32 shows a quadtree representation for a region containing one area with a solid color, which is different from the uniform color specified for all other areas in the region. This quadtree represents a region containing one foreground color pixel on a solid background. When large color areas exist in a region of space, then quadtree encodings considerably help in reducing the storage area as large part of the space can be represented with a single node.

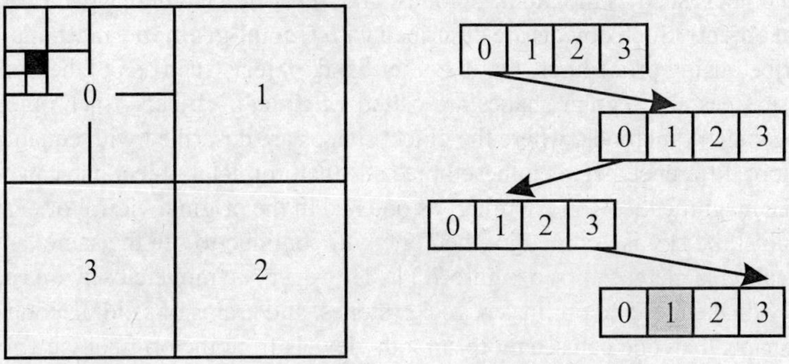

Figure 7.32 Quadtree Representation

Octree Encoding Procedure

This scheme divides a region of three-dimensional space (usually cubes) into octants. Each node in an octree consists of eight data elements—one for each octant (see Figure 7.33). Each subregion of the final subdivided 3D space is referred to as a **volume element** (or **voxel**). In a three-dimensional region, we not only consider the color of the object, but also its other properties like material type, density and other physical characteristics. Thus, a voxel element in the octree representation stores the property values for a homogeneous subregion of the space, and empty regions of the space are represented by voxel type 'void'. Like in quadtree encoding, in octree encoding also, a heterogeneous octant is subdivided into octants until the subdivisions are homogeneous. Each node in an octree can have from zero to eight immediate descendants.

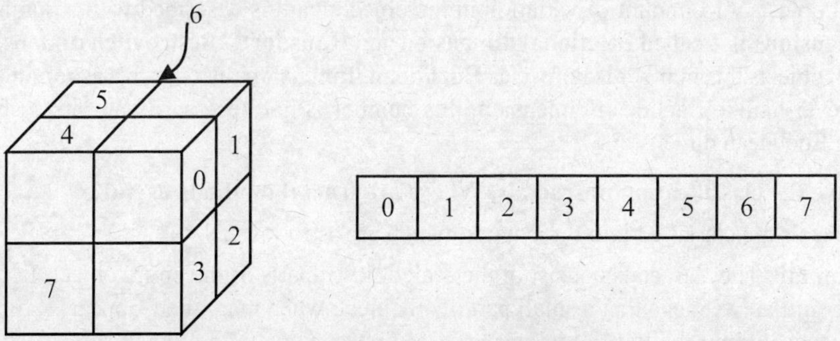

Figure 7.33 Octree Encoding Scheme

Once a solid object is represented in the form of an octree, various manipulations can be performed on it. For example, for the given two octree representations for the same region of space, one can perform various set operations to generate new octree representing a solid object. For example, if we apply union operation on two octree representations, then a new octree is constructed using the octree nodes from each of the input trees. Similarly, for an intersection operation, a new octree is constructed using the octants where the two objects overlap. Finally, for a set difference operation, a new octree is constructed by considering the region occupied by one object and not the other.

38. Compare fractal objects with Euclidean objects.

Ans. Natural objects such as mountains, clouds, and trees, etc., having jagged (or random) surfaces are called **fractal objects**. Such objects are described with **fractal-geometry methods**, where the object shapes are described using procedures. On the other hand, objects such as polyhedrons and ellipsoids, having smooth surfaces and regular shapes are called **Euclidean objects**. Such objects are described with Euclidean-geometry methods, where the object shapes are described with equations.

Another point of difference between these objects is that in fractal object one can continue to see as much detail in the magnification (on zooming) as one had in the original view. For example, if a mountain outlined against the sky is zoomed in, then one will continue to see the same jagged shape as the level of magnification is increased (see Figure 7.34). However, we move closer, we can see smaller details such as individual edges and outlines of rocks, stones, and grains of sand. In contrast, if one zooms on a Euclidean shape, then one can see more smooth view as from the original view.

Figure 7.34 View of a Mountain at Different Level of Magnification

In fractal objects, the amount of variation in the object detail is described with a number called the **fractal dimension** (also called **fractional dimension** and **Hausdorff–Besicovitch dimension**) whereas in Euclidean objects this number is known as **Euclidean dimension** (also known as **topological dimension**). However, unlike Euclidean dimension, this number is not necessarily an integer but is always greater than Euclidean dimension.

39. Give the classification of fractals. Where are fractal methods useful?

Ans. Fractals are classified into three types, which are as follows:

- **Self-similar:** These fractals consist of the scaled-down parts of the entire object. In simple terms, by self-similar, we mean that a small part of an object, when magnified, appears same as the original object. Starting with an initial shape, user first constructs the object subparts by applying a scaling parameter (s) to the overall shape. However, it depends on the user whether to use the same scaling factor for all subparts or to use different scaling factors for different scaled-down parts of the object. If random variations are also applied to the scaled-down subparts, then the fractals are known as **statistically self-similar**. In that case, the parts have the same statistical properties. These fractals are commonly used to model trees, shrubs, and other plants.

- **Self-affine:** These fractals consist of those parts that are formed with different scaling parameters, s_x, s_y, s_z in different coordinate directions. Like self-similar fractals, here also one can include random variations to the parts of object. In that case, fractal is known as **statistically self-affine**. These fractals are commonly used to model water, clouds, and terrain.
- **Invariant fractal sets:** These fractals are formed with non-linear transformations. It includes self-squaring fractals (such as the Mandelbrot set) that are formed with squaring functions in complex space, and self-inverse fractals that are formed with inversion procedures.

The fractal methods are quite useful for modelling a very wide variety of natural phenomena. Fractal representations are also used widely in graphics applications to model terrain, water, clouds, trees, and other plants, fur, feathers and various surface textures, or simply to make pretty patterns. In addition, these methods are helpful in modelling the distribution of stars, moon caters, and river islands. There are other areas also where one can see fractal patterns such as in rain fields, in stock markets, in traffic flow, in music, in urban property utilization, and on the boundaries of convergence regions for numerical-analysis techniques.

40. Give an expression for the fractal dimension of a self-similar fractal.

Ans. Fractal dimension (D) measures the roughness or fragmentation of the objects. More the jagged appearance of the object, larger will be its fractal dimension. Using a given value of D, one can generate fractal objects by setting up some iterative procedures. Though, in general, it is difficult to calculate the value of D, but with the help of some procedures we can determine its value from the properties of the constructed object.

For Euclidean objects like lines, circles, squares, and cubes, the dimension is referred to by the term **Euclidean** (or **topological**) **dimension**, which is simply the least number of parameters required to specify the object. It is always expressed in terms of a whole number (1, 2, 3, etc.). For example, a line has dimension 1, square has dimension 2, and cube has dimension 3. If we divide a line into four sub-parts, where each part is 1/4 of the original, then each subpart looks exactly same as that of the original line, when magnified by a factor of 4 (see Figure 7.35a). This magnification factor is termed as **scaling factor** S. Thus, in this case S=4. Similarly, we can divide a square into subparts, with each side is equal to 1/4 of the original side. However, in this case, we need to 16 (4^2) pieces to get the original square back (see Figure 7.35b). In the same way, a cube can be separated into 64 (4^3) subparts (see Figure 7.35c). Based on this discussion, we have obtained the following formula:

(a) Dividing a Line (b) Dividing a Square (c) Dividing a Cube

Figure 7.35 Subdividing Objects with Euclidean Dimensions

$$N = S^D \quad (1)$$

where N = number of subparts of the shape, S = scaling factor of the shape, and D = dimension of the shape.

If we solve Equation (1) for D, then we get,

$$D = \ln(N) / \ln(S) \quad (2)$$

This expression is used to determine the fractional dimension (also known as **Hausdorff–Besico vitch dimension**) of a self-similar object. From this equation, it is clear that D has a form A/B and hence can take fractional values. Thus, we can say that for self-similar objects, the dimension can be a fraction. Note that the fractal dimension of an object is always greater than the corresponding Euclidean dimension.

41. How one can estimate the fractal dimension of any fractal object?

Ans. For simple shapes such as curves and polygons, one can determine the value of fractal dimension (D) by a method known as **topological covering**, which approximate object subparts with simple shapes. For example, a subdivided curve can be approximated with straight-line sections, and a subdivided polygon can be approximated with small squares or rectangles. However, for complicated shapes, evaluating D with topological covering method is a difficult task. Thus, value of D for these objects is estimated with a method known as **box-covering**, which makes use of rectangles or parallelepipeds to approximate the area inside an object.

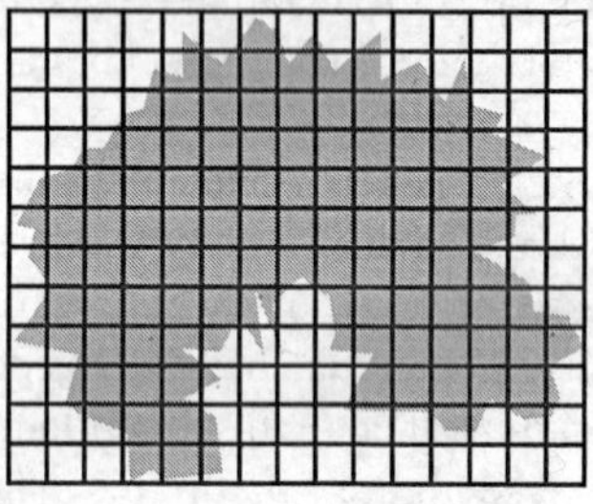

Figure 7.36 Box-covering of an Irregularly-Shaped Object

Box-covering method works by first determining the coordinate extents of an object and then, according to the given scaling factors subdivides the object into a number of small boxes (see Figure 7.36). The total number of boxes (N) required to cover an object is called the **box dimension**, which is then used to estimate the fractal dimension (D) of the object. For statistically self-similar objects (having single scaling factor, S), box-covering method covers an object with n number of squares or cubes and then uses the following equation to estimate the fractal dimension.

$$D = \frac{\ln(n)}{\ln(s)}$$

In case of self-affine fractals, the fractal is covered with N number of rectangular boxes. The value of N along with the affine transformation parameters is then used to estimate the fractal dimension.

42. Give the value or range of D for the following:

(a) Fractal curves

(b) Spatial fractal curves

(c) Fractal surfaces

(d) Fractal solids

Ans. (a) The fractal curves lies completely within a 2D plane. For these curves, the value of D is greater than 1 (say 1.1, 1.2, and so on). The closer D is to 1, the smoother will be the fractal curve. If D equals to 2, then the curve will completely fill a finite region of 2D space and will be known as **Peano curve**. If the value of D lies between 2 and 3, then the curve self-intersects and the area could be covered an infinite number of times. Natural object boundaries such as shorelines are modelled with fractal curves.

(b) The curves that do not lie completely within a single plane are termed as **spatial fractal curve**. Like fractal curves, they also have D greater than 1. However, for $D > 2$, the curve may not be self-intersecting. For $D = 3$, the curve completely fills a volume of space, and lastly for $D > 3$, the curve self-intersects.

(c) Fractal surfaces have following range of fractal dimension:

$$2 < D \leq 3$$

If $D = 3$, then surface fills a volume of space, but if the value of D exceeds 3, there is an overlapping coverage of the volume. Fractal surfaces can be used to model terrain, clouds, and water.

(d) Fractal solids have following range of fractal dimension:

$$3 < D \leq 4$$

If the value of $D > 4$, then there will be self-overlapping object. They are used to model cloud properties such as temperature within a region of space.

43. Describe the geometric construction of deterministic self-similar fractal.

Ans. For constructing a deterministic (non-random) self-similar fractal geometrically, we initiate the procedure with a given geometric shape known as **initiator**. Then subparts of this initiator are replaced with a pattern called the **generator**. For example, the initiator and generator shown in Figure 7.37 can be used to construct the snowflake pattern (or Koch curve) as shown in Figure 7.38.

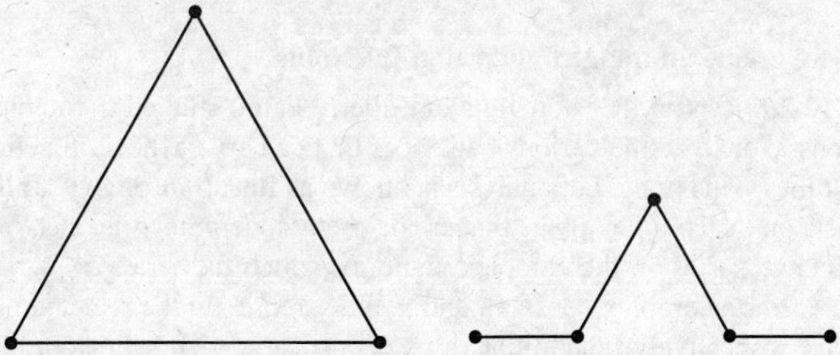

Figure 7.37 Initiator and Generator for the Koch Curve

The initiator is first divided into three parts such that each part is equal to the one-third of the original line segment. Thus, the scaling factor S is 3. Now, each straight line segment in the initiator is replaced with four equal-length line segments at each step, where line segment is one-third of the original. Thus, value of N becomes 4. Now, with the scaling factor S = 3, the fractal dimension would be

$$\ln 4 / \ln 3 \approx 1.2619$$

Note that at each step the length of each side of the Koch curve increases by a factor of 4/3, while the lengths of the line segments are reduced by a factor of 1/3. After the first three iterations, the resultant Koch curve resembles Figure 7.36d. If we repeat this process an infinite number of times, then the length of the fractal curve tends towards infinity.

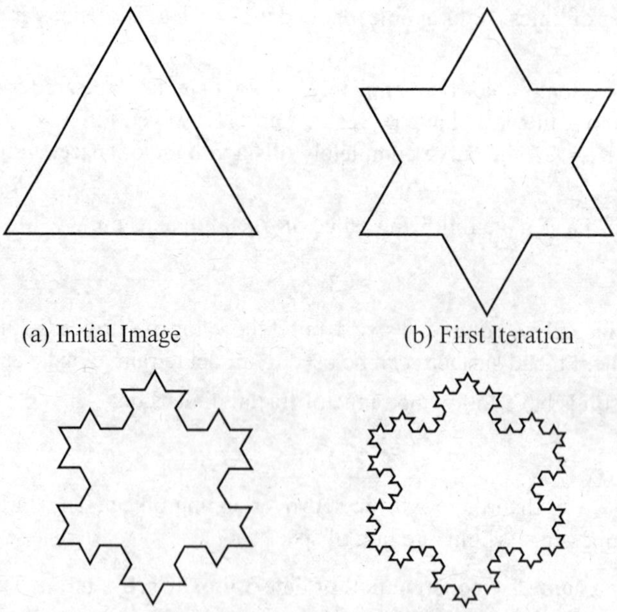

(a) Initial Image (b) First Iteration

(c) Second Iteration (d) Third Iteration

Figure 7.38 First Three Iterations in the Generation of the Koch Curve

44. Write a short note on Julia sets and Mandelbrot sets.

or

How can we create an image by iterated functions?

Ans. In the early 20th century, Gaston Julia and Pierre Fatou studied the iterations of polynomial and rational fractions to analyze the various behaviors that can arise when a function f(x) is iterated infinite number of times. This branch of analysis is known as **iteration theory**. **Julia sets**, named after Gaston Julia, are sets on the complex plane that create pretty indefinitely detailed images. They consist of those set of points $z=x+iy$ on the complex plane for which the series $z_{n+1} = z_n^2 + c$ does not tend to infinity. Here, c is a complex constant, and x and y represent the real and imaginary part of the complex coordinates, respectively. The initial value of z (that is, z_0) is the coordinates of the pixel to which we need to assign some color value.

To generate a Julia set, we iterate the function $z_{n+1} = z_n^2 + c$ for each pixel on the complex plane until it leaves a circle around the origin with radius 2. In each iteration, the z_{n+1} of the previous iteration is now used as z_n. If we keep iterating this function, then depending on the value of z_0, z will either go to infinity, or remain inside or on the boundary of the circle. Thus, we keep on iterating the function until the distance of z from the origin exceeds 2, or we reach maximum number of iterations (say, 256). The points that remain in the circle are the ones that belong to the Julia Set. The number of times we had to iterate the function becomes the color value of the pixel. Thus, we can say that if the iterated z stayed within a given boundary forever (convergence), the point is inside the set and the point is plotted black. On the other hand, if the iteration went out of control (divergence), the point was plotted in a color depending on the number of iterations. Note that for every value of c we get a different Julia set. Some of them are connected and some are in the form of disconnected "islands" [see Figure 7.39(a)].

To understand the generation of Julia set, consider a pixel with coordinates (1,0.5) that we need to color. Let us assign c = (-0.5,0.5). Thus, z_0 becomes 1+0.5i, and c becomes (-0.5+0.5i). Now after first iteration, we get

```
z = z0² + c
  = (1 + 0.5i)² - 0.5 + 0.5i
  = 1 + 2*0.5i + 0.25*i² - 0.5 + 0.5i
  = 0.5 + 1.5i + 0.25*(-1)
  = 0.5 + 1.5i - 0.25
  = 0.25 + 1.5i
```

Thus, z=(0.25, 1.5)

Now, the distance of z from origin is $\sqrt{(0.25)^2 + (1.5)^2}$ = 1.5206 (approx.), which is less than 2. Thus, we again iteration the function and calculate the next value of z.

```
z = (0.25 + 1.5i)² - 0.5 + 0.5i
  = 0.0625 + 2*0.375i + 2.25(i2) - 0.5 + 0.5i
  = -0.4375 + 1.25i + 2.25(-1)
  = -0.4375 + 1.25i - 2.25
  = -2.6875 + 1.25i
```

Thus, z=(-2.6875, 1.25)

Now, the distance of z from origin is $\sqrt{(-2.6875)^2 + (1.25)^2}$ = 7.222+1.5625 = 8.7845(approx.), which is greater than 2, which implies that this point lies outside the Julia set. The number of iterations is 2, thus the pixel gets the color value 2. The more the number of iterations, the more detailed the Julia set will appear when zoom in deeply.

Mandelbrot set

The Mandelbrot set, named after the Benoit Mandelbrot, is one of the most famous fractals in existence. The main difference between the Julia set and the Mandelbrot set is the way we iterate the function. The Mandelbrot set iterates the function by always keeping z at 0 and varying the c value, whereas the Julia set iterates the function for a fixed value of c and varying z values. The Mandelbrot set possesses some important properties, which are as follows:

- The Mandelbrot set is always connected, that is, there is always a path from one point of the set to another point of the set so that all the points in the path are also in the set. It implies that like Julia set there are no disconnected "islands".

- The set has a finite area, which fits inside a circle of radius 2. However, the length of its border is infinite. That is, zooming in any part of the border will take you to more details—you will never find a part where the border is smooth, with a finite length. Thus, if you have made enough iteration on the function, and you have a good resolution monitor, you will always get something new if you start zooming a certain part of the border.
- The border of the set is not random. They are self-similar.

Figure 7.39 shows few examples of Julia set and Mandelbrot set.

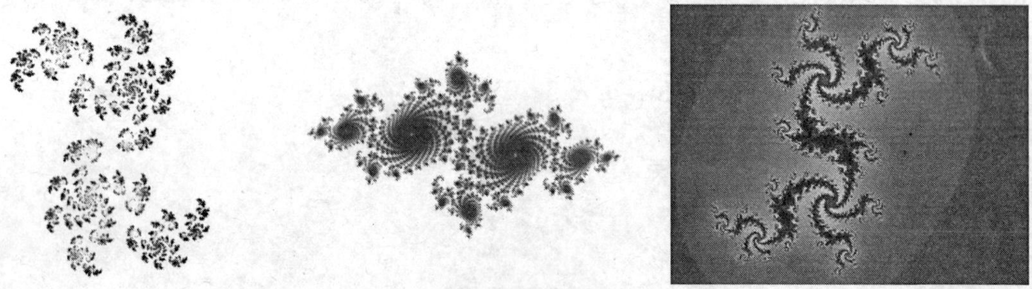

(a) Example of Julia sets

(b) Example of Mandelbrot sets

Figure 7.39 Julia and Mandelbrot sets

45. Construct enough points on the Bézier curve whose control points are $P_0(4,2)$, $P_1(8,8)$ and $P_2(16,4)$ to draw an accurate sketch.

(i) What is the degree of the curve?

(ii) What are the coordinates at v = 0.5?

Ans. **(i)** We know that the degree of Bézier curve is n. We are given three control points, that is, $n + 1 = 3$. Therefore, $n = 2$, thus degree of the curve is 2.

(ii) To find the coordinates, we need to first evaluate blending function for the curve. That is,

$$BEZ_{0,2}(v) = {}^2C_0 v^0 (1-v)^{2-0}$$
$$= (1-v)^2$$
$$BEZ_{1,2}(v) = {}^2C_1 v^1 (1-v)^{2-1}$$
$$= 2v(1-v)$$
$$BEZ_{2,2}(v) = {}^2C_2 v^2 (1-v)^{2-2}$$
$$= v^2$$

Then, the Bézier curve for the given control points is

$$C(v) = P_0 BEZ_{0,2}(v) + P_1 BEZ_{1,2}(v) + P_2 BEZ_{2,2}(v)$$

Solving the curve in x and y coordinates:

$$x(v) = x_0 BEZ_{0,2}(v) + x_1 BEZ_{1,2}(v) + x_2 BEZ_{2,2}(v)$$

$$y(v) = y_0 BEZ_{0,2}(v) + y_1 BEZ_{1,2}(v) + y_2 BEZ_{2,2}(v)$$

Putting the values of Blending functions from above calculations and values of control points from the question as:

$$x_0 = 4,\ y_0 = 2$$
$$x_1 = 8,\ y_1 = 8$$
$$x_2 = 16,\ y_2 = 4$$

Then, $x(v) = 4(1-v)^2 + 8 \times 2v(1-v) + 16v^2$

$= 4v^2 - 8v + 4$ (1)

Now, putting the value of $v = 0.5$ in Equation (1), we get:

$$x(0.5) = 1$$

and $y(v) = 2(1-v)^2 + 8 \times 2v(1-v) + 4v^2$

$= -10v^2 + 12v + 2$

Therefore, $y(0.5) = 5.5$

Therefore, the coordinates at $v = 0.5$ are $(1, 5.5)$.

MULTIPLE CHOICE QUESTIONS

1. __________ is a convex polygon boundary that encloses a set of control points.

(a) Convex hull
(b). Control graph
(c) Characteristic polygon
(d) None of these

2. Which spline is the extension of cardinal spline?
   (a) Kochanek–Bartels (b) Hermite
   (c) Non-uniform (d) Periodic cubic
3. The study of Bézier curve was started by__________.
   (a) Hausdorff–Besicovitch (b) Charles Hermite
   (c) Kochanek–Bartels (d) Paul de Castelijau
4. Which of the following is a property of Bézier curve?
   (a) Convex-hull (b) End points geometry
   (c) Variation diminishing (d) All of these
5. Two sets of _______ Bézier curves are used to design Bézier surface.
   (a) Hexagonal (b) Orthogonal
   (c) Pentagonal (d) Octagonal
6. Which of the following statement is false for B-spline curves?
   (a) The curve is described with n+1 blending functions for n+1 control points.
   (b) Each section of the curve is influenced by d control points.
   (c) It always passes through only first and last control points.
   (d) Any one control point can affect the shape of at most d curve sections.
7. What is the full-form of CSG?
   (a) Common Solid Graph (b) Constructive Solid Geometry
   (c) Constant Solid Graph (d) Constructive Spline Graph
8. Which of the following is/are not a type of fractal?
   (a) Self-invariant (b) Self-similar
   (c) Self-affine (d) Both (b) and (c)
9. The __________ method makes use of rectangles or parallelepipeds to approximate the area inside an object.
   (a) Box-covering (b) Rectangle-covering
   (c) Parallelepipeds-covering (d) None of these
10. The dimension of fractal surfaces is within the range_________.
    (a) $D > 3$ (b) $2 < D \leq 3$
    (c) $2 < D < 3$ (d) $3 < D \leq 4$

Answers. 1. a 2. a 3. d 4. d 5. b 6. c 7. b 8. d 9. a 10. b

8

Illumination and Color Model

1. Write a short note on illumination model.

Ans. In a natural scene, the color of a given point is based on various factors including surface characteristics, its position and orientation relative to light sources illuminating it, and the features of light sources. An **illumination model** (also known as **lighting model**) takes into account these and other relevant factors and calculates the color of a given point on the object's surface. It basically calculates the intensity of the light reflecting from the given point that contributes to its color. To perform its calculations, illumination model often follows the laws of physics describing surface-lighting effects. For example, shiny material reflects more light than dull material. Similarly, transparent material allows transmitting the light through it and we can view the objects behind it..

There are several illumination models that are used today in computer graphics. Some simple models (known as **local illumination models**) take into account the lighting effect created by the light falling on a surface from a light source. However, surrounding objects may also reflect light that falls on the surface and contributes to the light intensity coming from the surface into consideration. Therefore, more accurate, but more complex, models (known as **global illumination models**) have been developed that take into account the light falling from every such source to calculate the intensity of reflected light.

Illumination model is invoked by the **surface-rendering method** (also called **shading method**), while rendering a scene, to determine the color of pixels in the projected portion of scene. Some surface-rendering methods, including scan-line, invoke illumination model for every pixel in the visible portion while others, including ray-tracing, invoke illumination model for small set of pixels and then use interpolation to calculate the color or shade of other pixels.

2. Explain light source.

Ans. Light source is any object that emits electromagnetic radiations with wavelength ranging from 400 to 700 nm, as electromagnetic radiations falling in this range only are visible to human. Example of light source includes the sun and electric bulb. There are many objects in the real world, like table in a room, that are **light reflector** as they reflect light that falls on them. While, some objects behave as both light emitter as well as light reflector. For example, a colored, semitransparent plastic film covering an electric bulb reflects as well as emits light.

In computer graphics, a light source can be specified by several properties including its shape and position and color of light emitted by it. Some light sources emit light in certain directions while some emit light of different colors in different directions. Therefore, we have to specify the properties of light source accordingly to get more realistic display.

3. Explain the following.

(a) Point light source

(b) Distributed light sources

Ans. (a) Point light source: Point light source emits light rays in all the directions as shown in Figure 8.1. It is defined by specifying its position and the color of light being emitted by three components R (red), G (green), and B (blue). It is the simplest light source model and is useful to simulate a light source which is smaller than the objects in the scene. An example of point light source is a small electric bulb illuminating objects in a scene. Notice that when point light source is used in a scene, light on an object falls from single direction only.

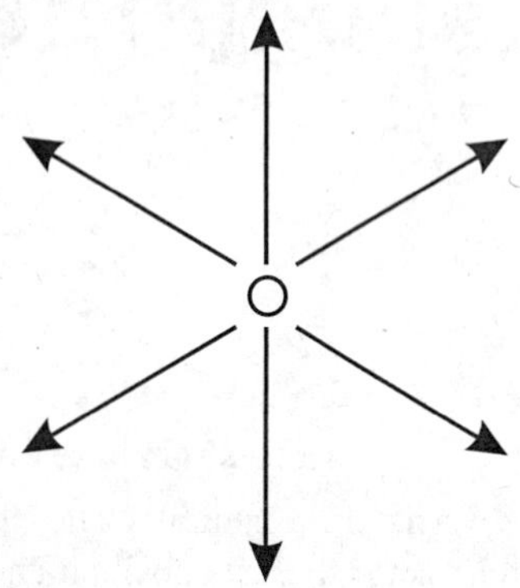

Figure 8.1 Point Light Source

(b) Distributed light source: Distributed (or extended) light source is the one whose surface area that emits light is wide and the light source is placed near to the objects in a scene. An example of distributed light source is fluorescent tube as shown in Figure 8.2. When distributed light source is used in a scene, light on an object falls from multiple directions and multiple points. Therefore, simulating distributed light source model in a scene is complex. One way to simulate this model is to specify the light source as a collection of directional point light sources. Then simply, we can specify the direction of each point light source.

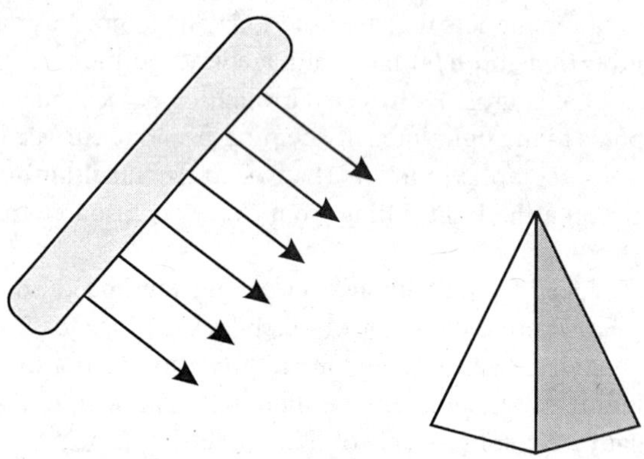

Figure 8.2 Distributed Light Source

4. Explain diffuse reflection in detail.

or

Define diffuse reflection and deduce the expression for diffuse reflection.

or

What are ideal diffuse reflectors? Why they are also known as Lambertian reflectors?

Ans. Opaque objects reflect as well as absorb part of light that falls on them. Some opaque objects, especially those that are having dull surface, reflect light with equal intensity in all the directions. This type of reflection from objects is said to be **diffuse reflection** and such objects are known as **ideal diffuse reflectors**. Since intensity of reflected light is equal in all the directions, object appears equally bright from every view point (see Figure 8.3).

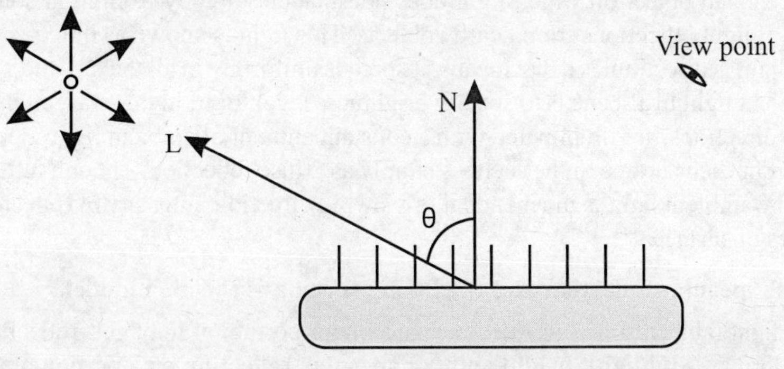

Figure 8.3 Diffuse Reflection

We may want to calculate the amount of radiant energy coming from any point on the surface. For this calculation, **Lambert's cosine law** can be used (that is why ideal diffuse reflectors are also known as **Lambertian reflectors**). This law states that amount of radiant energy coming from any point in a direction D is proportional to $\cos \alpha$, where α is the angle between D and surface normal N.

For a scene in which reflection from all the objects is diffuse, we may specify K_d – a **diffuse-reflection coefficient** – for every object surface. The diffuse-reflection coefficient defines the portion of total incident light to be scattered as diffuse reflection. Typically, value of K_d lies between 0 and 1. Now, we can calculate the diffuse reflection from an object surface as:

$$I_{diff} = K_d \times I \quad (1)$$

where, I is the intensity of total incident light.

The brightness of object's surface also depends on the orientation of object relative to the light source. An object making an angle of 90° with the light source (that is, perpendicular to light source) receives more light rays than an object making any other angle with the light source. Mathematically, the surface area covered by light rays illuminating an object is directly proportional to $\cos \theta$, where θ is the **angle of incidence** between the light rays and the surface normal N. We can calculate the amount of light incident on an object's surface from light source with intensity I_i as:

$$I = I_i \times \cos \theta \quad (2)$$

Now using Equation (2), the diffuse reflection equation can be modified to:

$$I_{diff} = K_d \times I_i \times \cos \theta \quad (3)$$

We can calculate the value of $\cos \theta$ by the dot product N . L. Therefore, Equation (3) becomes:

$$I_{diff} = K_d \times I_i \times N.L$$

Diffuse reflection not only contributes to the brightness, but also to the color of object. Actually, to what we say the color of an object is the color of diffuse reflection. If white light (that is formed by combining lights of equal intensity of all the colors) falls on an object and the color of diffuse reflection is red, we say that the color of object is red. Note that if the light falling on that object is not white, the color of the object may be other than red.

5. Write a short note on ambient light.

Ans. In a scene, an object on which light does not incident directly from light source may still be visible because of light reflections from nearby objects. This light is known as **background** or **ambient light**. Ambient light is directionless, that means, it spreads uniformly in all the directions. One basic way to simulate ambient light in a scene is to specify brightness level for it. In this way, all the surfaces in the scene, in all the directions, are illuminated with a constant amount of ambient light. Because of this, the light reflected from each surface in the scene is simply a diffuse reflection. Though reflection from each surface caused by ambient light is independent of viewing direction, intensity of reflected light depends on the properties of surface.

6. Describe specular reflection and the Phong specular-reflection model.

Ans. When light falls on shiny opaque objects, a major portion of light gets reflected in a particular direction. This forms a **highlight**, **bright spot**, or **specular reflection** on a portion of object's surface; reflection from rest part of the surface remains diffuse. One may observe specular reflection by exposing any object with shiny surface, for example, an apple to white light. The bright, highlighted spot will appear on apple's surface which is the effect of specular reflection. Notice that the color of apple's surface at the highlight spot appears to be white rather than red.

Specular reflection is not visible from every viewpoint. Figure 8.4 illustrates the specular reflection direction R from a point on object's surface. Here, vector L represents the direction of point light source illuminating the object's surface. Notice that vectors L and R form same angle (that is, θ) with the surface normal N but on its opposite side. **Ideal reflector** (or perfect mirror) reflects light exactly in one direction (the direction of R) and the effect of specular reflection will be visible only when angle α between the viewpoint vector V and specular reflection vector R is 0. However, for objects other than perfect mirror, the reflected light energy distributes across a small cone-shaped space centred around R. For shiny surfaces, the cone is narrow while for dull surfaces, the cone is wider.

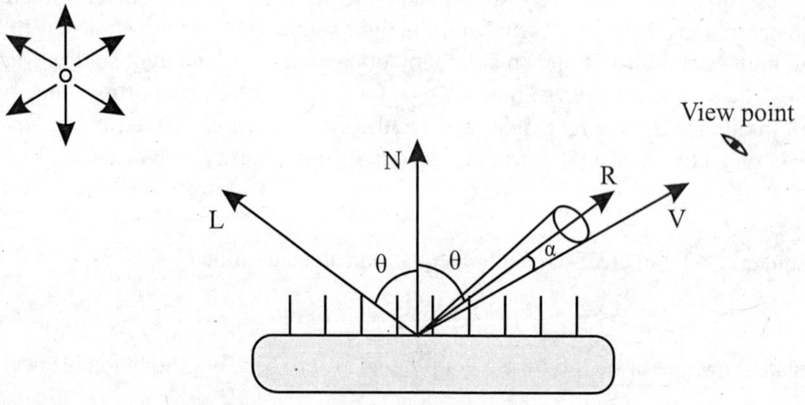

Figure 8.4 Specular Reflection

For calculating the range of space from where specular reflection is visible, **Phong specular-reflection model** is used. This model is based on the fact that intensity of specular reflection is maximum when angle α is 0 and it decreases as α increases. This decrease in intensity is approximated by $\cos^n \alpha$, where n is the **specular-reflection exponent** whose value is determined by the type of surface to be simulated. Value of n typically varies from 1 (for dull surfaces) to several hundreds (for shiny surfaces); for ideal reflector n is infinite. Angle α is assigned a value in the range from 0° to 90°, which makes $\cos^n \alpha$ to vary from 0 to 1.

The intensity of specular reflection highly depends on the angle of incidence θ and the surface-material properties. To model the specular intensity variation, we can use a **specular-reflection coefficient** $W(\theta)$, which tends to increase as the angle of incidence increases. Using $W(\theta)$, we can express the Phong specular-reflection model by the following equation.

$$I_{ispec} = W(\theta) \times I_i \times \cos^n \alpha \tag{1}$$

where I_i is the intensity of light source. Value of $\cos \alpha$ can be calculated by the dot product V.R. Note that if viewpoint and direction of point light source are on the same side of surface normal or light source is behind the surface, there will be no specular reflection. Experimentally, it has been observed that specular reflection is constant for most opaque materials for all angles of incidence. Therefore, we can typically set $W(\theta)$ to a constant specular-reflection coefficient, say K_s. Value of K_s ranges from 0 to 1 depending upon the surface of object. Now, Equation (1) can be modified as following to calculate the intensity of specular reflection.

$$I_{ispec} = \begin{cases} 0, & \text{if } V.R < 0 \text{ or } N.L \le 0 \\ K_s \times I_i \times (V.R)^n, & \text{if } V.R > 0 \text{ and } N.L > 0 \end{cases}$$

7. Write a short note on transparency.

Ans. A transparent object allows seeing through it and the objects located behind it are visible. Actually, when light is incident on a transparent object, part of light gets transmitted and a part gets reflected. The amount of light that is transmitted through a transparent surface depends on two factors.

- degree of transparency of the transparent surface
- whether there is any light source behind the transparent surface

Assume that a transparent object lies between us and an opaque surface. When light falls on opaque surface, it reflects part of incident light. This reflected light transmitting through transparent object reaches to our eyes and we are able to view the opaque object located behind the transparent surface. We can observe both diffuse as well as specular transmission on transparent surface. If the surface is semi-transparent, diffuse transmission takes place. In this case, the transmitted light gets scattered and the object behind the transparent surface seems little blurred.

Transparent objects not only transmit, but also reflect a part of light. Therefore, while modelling transparent surfaces, intensity equations should combine reflected intensity I_{refl} through opaque object and transmitted intensity I_{trans} from transparent surface using transmission coefficient K_T. Parameter K_T measures the transparency of the surface and is assigned a value ranging from 0 (for opaque surfaces) to 1 (for perfect transparent surfaces).

$$I = (1 - K_T)\, I_{refl} + K_T\, I_{trans}$$

where $(1 - K_T)$ is the opacity factor. Notice that when light is transmitted through a transparent object, it gets refracted (or bent) as shown in Figure 8.5. The direction of refracted light is specified by the angle of refraction θ_R, which depends on various factors including index of refraction of both incident material and transparent material. According to Snell's law, one can calculate the angle of refraction as follows:

$$\sin\theta_R = \frac{I_i}{I_R}\sin\theta_i$$

where I_i is the index of refraction of incident material, I_R is the index of refraction of reflecting material, and θ_i is the angle of incidence.

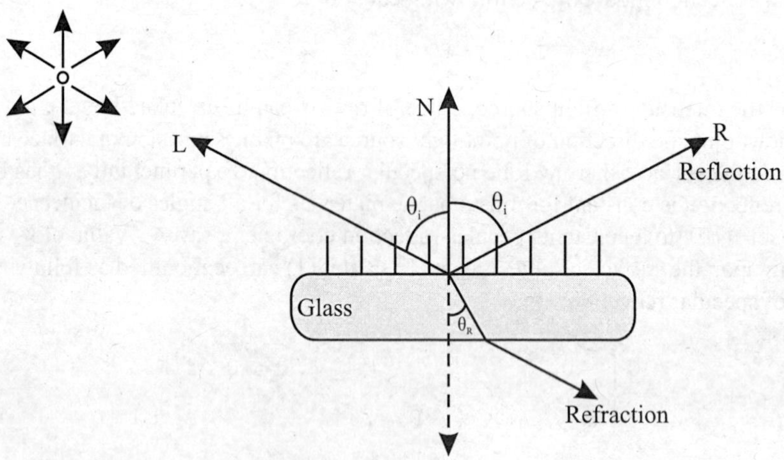

Figure 8.5 Refraction of Light

Some simple algorithms for modelling transparent surfaces ignores bent when light rays pass through them. However, modelling realistic scenes requires considering the angle of refraction.

8. What is a color model?

Ans. A color model specifies a 3D color coordinate system and a visible subset of the coordinate system in which all the colors of a particular color gamut lie. There is a wide variety of color models each of which explains the properties or behaviour of color from a different aspect; some explains how color is displayed on video monitor, while some describe color output on printers and plotters. For example, the color model RGB is used with color CRT monitors, YIQ for broadcast TV color system and CMY for various color-printing devices.

Color models like RGB, YIQ, and CMY are not easy to use. Therefore, some more models including HSV, HLS, and HVC have been developed. In addition, a conversion from all of these models to RGB is specified. Since RGB model can be converted to the worldwide standard, that is, CIE, we can convert any of HSV, HLS, and HVC models to RGB and then to the CIE standard.

9. Define electromagnetic spectrum. Also explain the relationship between wavelength and frequency of electromagnetic wave.

Ans. Objects like the sun, earth, light lamp in house, and radio station emit electromagnetic radiations of different frequencies and wavelengths. Varying frequencies or wavelengths of electromagnetic radiations contribute to their distribution on **electromagnetic spectrum**. Figure 8.6 shows the electromagnetic spectrum expressed in terms of frequency, which is measured in hertz (Hz). Notice that only a narrow portion of spectrum is visible to human eye. Every frequency in the narrow visible band (ranging from approximately 3.8×10^{14} to 7.9×10^{14} Hz) in the spectrum corresponds to a distinct **spectral** color. At the lower end in the visible band are the red color and its shades including orange and yellow while, at the high-frequency end, the colors including blue and violet lie.

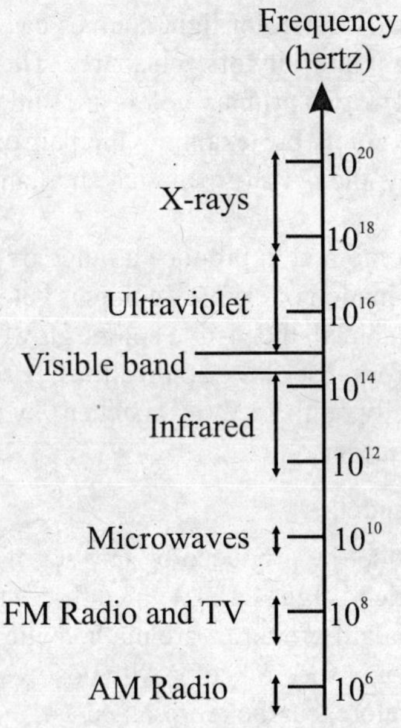

Figure 8.6 Electromagnetic Spectrum and a Sinusoidal Wave

Electromagnetic radiation travels in the form of sinusoidal wave with the speed of light and emits energy while travelling. The distance between any two consecutive wave-crests in the sinusoidal wave is its wavelength (denoted by λ). The wavelength of any wave is inversely proportional to its frequency `f`, with the speed of light, say, `c` as the proportionality constant. This can be expressed as

$$c = \lambda f$$

Notice that the frequency of a spectral color is same in all the materials including air, water, and vacuum. However, the speed of light and wavelength vary depending on the material.

10. Explain the characteristics used to describe the different properties perceived in a light.

Ans. When white light – containing all the frequencies within narrow visible band – falls on an opaque object, it absorbs some frequencies of light while reflects others. Different properties perceived in the light are described by using the following three characteristics.

- **Dominant frequency:** The combination of frequencies in the light reflected by the object contributes to its color. When high frequencies are predominant in the reflected light, the object appears to be of violet color. Basically, the perceived light in this case has the dominant frequency (also known as **dominant wavelength** or **hue**) at the high-frequency end in the narrow visible band of the electromagnetic spectrum.

- **Brightness:** It defines the total light energy and can be measured as the amount or intensity of light. If the intensity of light is increased, the object will appear brighter.
- **Purity** (or **saturation**)**:** It defines how close the light appears to be a pure spectral color. Less pure colors, including pale and some shades of grey, appear almost white.

The characteristics purity and dominant frequency together are called **chromaticity**.

11. Explain the terms complementary colors and color gamut.

Ans. Light from two or more different color light sources can be combined to produce a range of colors by selectively varying the light intensity of each source. The chosen hues of the light sources are referred to as the **primary colors**. The two primary colors are said to be **complementary colors** if they can be combined to produce **white color**. For example, the pair of primary colors red and cyan is the complementary color pair. Similarly, the pairs (green, magenta) and (blue, yellow) are complementary color pairs.

In general, primary colors are combined to produce a range of colors for an application. The set of all the colors produced by the combination of primary colors is **color gamut**. Notice that color gamut of any set of primary colors cannot contain all the visible colors. However, three primary colors are usually sufficient to produce all the colors for most of the applications. A color that is not in the color gamut of the three primary colors can generally be formed (or matched) by mixing any fourth color with one or more colors in the set of chosen primary colors.

12. Discuss the XYZ color model.

Ans. All the possible colors cannot be produced by any set of primary colors. Therefore, in 1931, **Commission Internationale de l'Éclairage (CIE)** defined three standard primaries, generally referred to as **XYZ color model**. These standard primaries are mathematically defined positive-color matching functions that can be used to match any spectral color with positive amount of each primary. Any color, say, C in the XYZ color space, therefore, can be represented as:

$$C = (X, Y, Z)$$

where the parameters X, Y, and Z specify the amount of each primary needed to match the given color. The values for these parameters are calculated using the color-matching functions X_λ, Y_λ, and Z_λ as follows.

$$X = k\int P(\lambda)\, X_\lambda d\lambda \qquad (1)$$

$$Y = k\int P(\lambda)\, Y_\lambda d\lambda \qquad (2)$$

$$Z = k\int P(\lambda)\, Z_\lambda d\lambda \qquad (3)$$

where the parameter k has the value of approximately 680 lumens/watt for CRT and $P(\lambda)$ is the selected light intensity in a particular direction. The value of parameter Y defines the luminance of the color and for white color it is 100. For other colors, its value lies in the range of 0 to 100.

To derive the chromaticity values, Equations (1), (2), and (3) can be normalized against the sum S of X, Y, and Z that represents the total amount of light energy.

$$x = \frac{X}{S}$$

$$Y = \frac{Y}{S}$$

$$Z = \frac{Z}{S}$$

Clearly, $x + y + z = 1$. Therefore, any color can be represented by specifying the values of x and y. Further, parameters x and y depend only on the hue and purity and hence they are called **chromaticity values**.

Notice that if a color is represented by specifying values of x and y only then z can be determined by subtracting the sum of x and y from 1, that is, $z = 1 - (x + y)$. However, values of X, Y, and Z cannot be obtained from x and y only. Therefore, we may say that values of x and y do not describe all the properties of color. To describe a color completely, we need value of luminance Y also. Given x, y, and luminance Y, we may calculate values of each CIE primary, that is, X, Y, and Z parameters as

$$X = \frac{x}{y} \times Y, \qquad Y = Y, \qquad Z = \frac{z}{y} \times Y$$

13. Draw a neat diagram of CIE chromaticity and explain it. Also mention its uses.

Ans. The **CIE chromaticity diagram** can be obtained by plotting the normalized values x and y for all the colors in the spectrum as shown in Figure 8.7. The points on the boundary of this curve represent the pure spectral colors while points in the interior region represent all the visible colors; the points on the dotted line joining the red and violet colors are not part of the visible spectrum. Notice that the luminance of color is not part of the CIE chromaticity diagram. Therefore, all the colors with same chromaticity but different luminance map to the same point in this diagram. In the interior region, a point C is formally defined to represent the standard white light source known as **illuminant C**. The point C is very near to the point where all normalized values x, y, and z are 1/3.

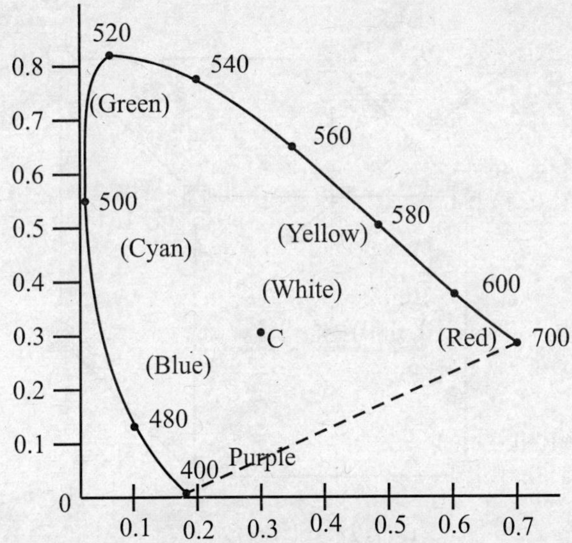

Figure 8.7 The Chromaticity Diagram

The CIE chromaticity diagram has many uses. First, it allows determining the dominant wavelength and purity of a color by matching the given color with the color produced by mixing the three CIE primaries. Second, it allows defining and comparing the color gamuts of various sets of primary colors. Third, it can be used to identify the complementary colors, that is, the pair of colors that can be mixed to produce white light.

14. What are the different intuitive color concepts used by artists?

Ans. Artists often use intuitive color concepts and create different tints, shades, and tones of a color by increasing or decreasing its saturation and lightness while keeping its hue unchanged. For this, they mix pigments of white and black color with the pigment of original color. As pigment of white color is mixed with the pigment of given color, saturation of color decreases and different **tints** of color are obtained. To obtain different **shades**, its lightness has to be varied, which can be achieved by mixing the pigment of black color with the pigment of original color. While by mixing pigments of both white and black color to the pigment of original color, different **tones** of color are produced.

The above explained color concept is more intuitive than the idea of specifying the amount of different primary colors needed to produce a given color. That is why most graphics packages employ a color model to provide intuitive color interfaces to the user and one or more color models to describe amount of color components for monitor or other output devices to display a color.

15. Explain the RGB color model.

Ans. Three primary colors red, green, and blue are used to display colors on CRT monitors as mixing different intensity levels—ranging from 0 to 1—of these colors produce a wide range of colors. This model is referred to as **RGB color model**; R for red, G for green, and B for blue. All the colors that can be produced by this color model define the RGB color space, which can be represented by a cube on R, G, and B axes as shown in Figure 8.8. Colors on the vertices of the cube's axes are primary colors and colors on other vertices are complementary colors.

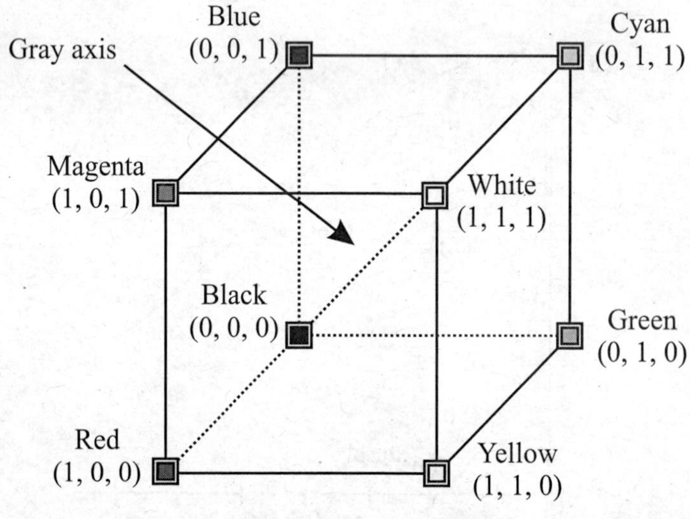

Figure 8.8 The RGB Color Space

Each vertex of this cube is labelled with a triple, say, (1,1,1) and a color. The numbers in the triple correspond to the intensity of red, green, and blue color, respectively, needed to yield the color associated with the vertex. For example, white color is obtained by mixing maximum and equal amount of red, green, and blue color, thus, the triple (1,1,1) with white color. Notice that the origin of this cube, that is, (0,0,0) representing black color is connected diagonally with vertex representing white color through a dotted line. This dotted line is named **gray axis** as the points along this axis represent various shades of gray color.

RGB color model is additive and to specify an arbitrary color, we begin with black color (for which intensity of all primaries is zero) and add appropriate amount of red, green, and blue color to yield the desired color. A color in RGB color model is, therefore, sum of the amount of all the three primaries, that is, a color, say, C, can be represented as:

$$C = (R, G, B) = r \times R + g \times G + b \times B$$

where r, g, and b are the intensities of red, green, and blue color, respectively, in C.

16. Explain the YIQ color model.

Ans. The RGB color model which is used in color CRT monitor provides red, green, and blue components separately. However, color television requires composite signal for displaying color and they use YIQ color model. The YIQ color model uses the parameter Y to carry the luminance information and parameters I and Q carry chromaticity information, that is, hue and purity. This is much like the use of X, Y, and Z parameters to carry luminance and chromaticity information in CIE XYZ color model.

The National Television System Committee (NTSC) encodes the luminance (Y) and chromaticity (I and Q) information within a bandwidth 6 MHz. Since human can detect changes in luminance more easily than changes in hue or saturation, NTSC encodes Y at much higher bandwidth than that of I and Q. Typically, 4.2 MHz is assigned to Y value and 1.8 MHz to I and Q collectively. Nevertheless, the encoded signal contains luminance as well as color information in it. This signal is received by the television set, which displays the picture according to the information. Note that black-and-white television set shows only Y component of signal ignoring I and Q components of signal.

The YIQ color model is a linear transformation of the RGB color model and the following transformation matrix can be used to map YIQ model to RGB model.

$$\begin{bmatrix} Y \\ I \\ Q \end{bmatrix} = \begin{bmatrix} 0.299 & 0.587 & 0.114 \\ 0.701 & -0.587 & -0.114 \\ -0.299 & -0.587 & 0.886 \end{bmatrix} \begin{bmatrix} R \\ G \\ B \end{bmatrix}$$

Clearly, one can take the inverse of above transformation matrix to map RGB color model to YIQ color model.

17. Explain the CMY color model.

Ans. The CMY color model is defined on the primary colors cyan (C), magenta (M), and yellow (Y), which are the complement colors of red, green, and blue, respectively, on which the RGB color model is defined. Like the RGB model, the color space of the CMY model can be represented by a unit cube. However, instead of R, G, and B as the axes and black color at the origin, the unit cube of the CMY model has C, M, and Y axes and white color at the origin as shown in Figure 8.9. The points along the gray axis represent various shades of gray color.

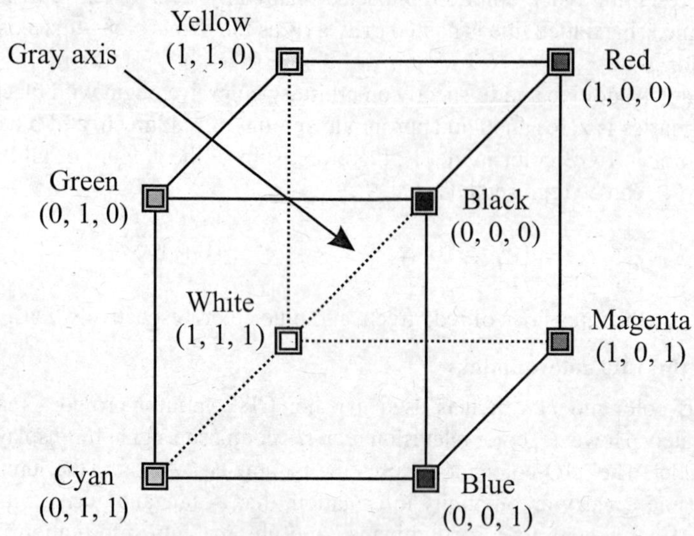

Figure 8.9 The CMY Color Space

The CMY model is subtractive. That means, to specify an arbitrary color, we begin with white color and subtract the appropriate amount of cyan, magenta, and yellow components to yield the desired color. Because of this property, the CMY model is used with hardcopy devices such as printers and plotters. Color patterns on a surface are produced by coating it with color pigments and what we perceive depends on the light reflected by the color. For example, consider a surface coated with cyan color, which is complementary color of red. When white light (which consists of red, green, and blue lights) falls on this surface, it absorbs red light and reflects green and yellow. In other terms, we say cyan color subtracts red from white light. Since green and yellow forms cyan, we perceive the color of surface as cyan. Similarly, magenta subtracts green while yellow subtracts blue from the white light. In case, surface is coated with the equal component of cyan, magenta, and yellow colors, the red, green, and blue are subtracted from white and we perceive the color of surface as black. The conversion from CMY space to RGB space can be performed using following transformation.

$$\begin{bmatrix} R \\ G \\ B \end{bmatrix} = \begin{bmatrix} 1 \\ 1 \\ 1 \end{bmatrix} - \begin{bmatrix} C \\ M \\ Y \end{bmatrix}$$

where, unit column vector represents white color in RGB space. The conversion from RGB to CMY space can be performed using following transformation.

$$\begin{bmatrix} C \\ M \\ Y \end{bmatrix} = \begin{bmatrix} 1 \\ 1 \\ 1 \end{bmatrix} - \begin{bmatrix} R \\ G \\ B \end{bmatrix}$$

where, unit column vector represents black in CMY space.

In practice, the CMY model generally uses black ink in addition to cyan, magenta, and yellow inks because the combination of cyan, magenta, and yellow inks produces shades of gray rather than pure black. This modified CMY model is known as the **CMYK model**; K is used to represent black rather than B as letter B may confuse between black and blue. Conversion from CMY to CMYK space can be performed by assigning minimum of C, M, and Y to K and then subtracting K from C, M, and Y components.

18. Explain the HSV color model.

Ans. The HSV color model is user-oriented model as it provides interface that allows artists to select colors based on the intuitive color concepts. The three color components of the HSV model are hue, saturation, and value. The color space of this model is defined by a hexcone as shown in Figure 8.10. At the top of this hexcone is the hexagon that can be derived by viewing the unit cube of the RGB model along the main diagonal. The points on the boundary of hexagon correspond to bright colors.

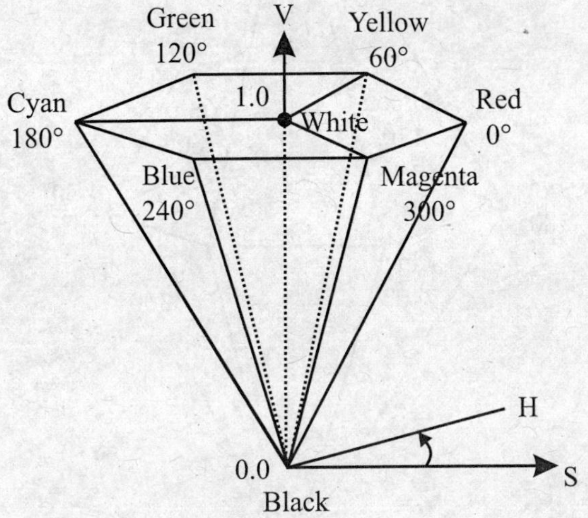

Figure 8.10 The HSV Color Space

In the color space, hue (H) is represented by an angle relative to the vertical axis; red color is at 0°, yellow at 60°, green at 120°, and so on. Notice that the vertices of hexagon representing primary colors are separated by an interval of 60° and complementary colors lie 180° apart from one another. Saturation (S) defines the purity of color. Its value ranges from 0 (at the vertical axis) to 1 (at the boundary of hexcone). Value (V) varies from 0 to 1. The point at the apex of hexcone is black with V = 0; S and H are irrelevant at this point. At the centre of the hexcone is the white color with V = 1 and S = 0; H is irrelevant at this point.

To select a color, artist specify angle for H and values for V and S that specify the amount of white and black components to be added to the spectral color to produce its various tints, shades and tones. Note that for any pure spectral color, V and S are 1 and H specifies the spectral color. For example, for cyan color, H is at 180° and both V and S are 1. If V is decreased keeping S constant, shades of the selected color are produced. To produce tints of a color, S is decreased keeping V constant. When both S and V are decreased, tones of the selected hue are produced.

19. Explain the HLS color model.

Ans. The HLS color model is also a user-oriented model, like the HSV model, with hue (H), lightness (L), and saturation (S) as the three color components. Its color space can be defined by a double hexcone as shown in Figure 8.11.

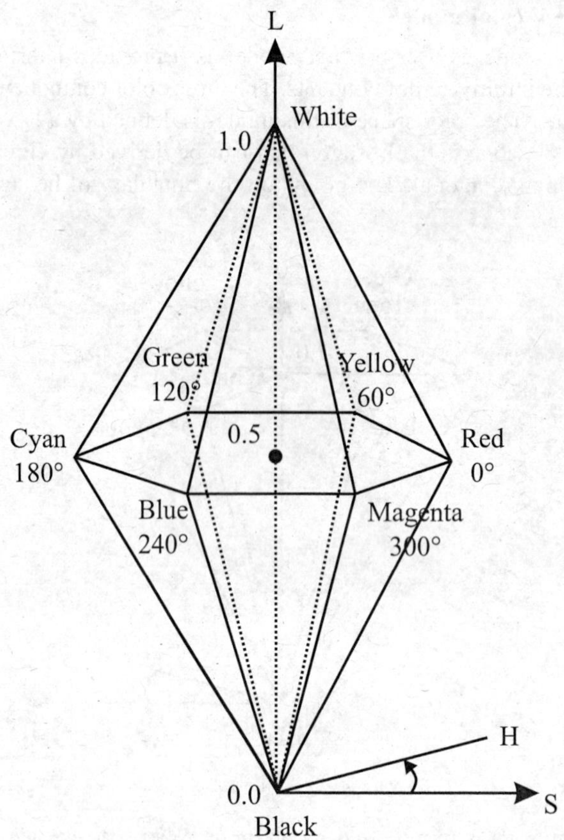

Figure 8.11 The HLS Color Space

The components H and S have the same meaning in the HLS model as in the HSV model. This implies that component H is represented by an angle relative to the vertical axis and corresponds to a spectral color. Vertices of the hexagon represent primary colors and are separated by an angle of 60°, starting with red at 0°. Complementary colors are 180° apart on the hexagon as in HSV. Component S defines the purity of color with value ranging from 0 (at vertical axis) to 1 (at the boundary of hexcone).

Component L in this model defines the lightness and is represented by the vertical axis in the double hexcone. It can have values ranging from 0 (for black color) to 1 (for white color). The axis itself represents shades of gray color.

To select a color, artist specifies the angle for H representing a desired spectral color. Then, he adjusts the values of L and S to produce various tints, shades, and tones of selected spectral color. Note that for any pure spectral color, L is 0.5 and S is 1.

MULTIPLE CHOICE QUESTIONS

1. Illumination model is also known as __________.
   (a) Surface-rendering (b) Shading method
   (c) Lighting model (d) None of these
2. Light source is any object that emits electromagnetic radiations with wavelength ranging from __________ to __________ nm.
   (a) 300, 600 (b) 400, 700
   (c) 500, 800 (d) 600, 900
3. Which of these is known as Lambertian reflector?
   (a) Any light reflector (b) Perfect mirror
   (c) Light source (d) Ideal diffuse reflector
4. For which of these, Phong specular-reflection model is used?
   (a) To calculate the range of space from where specular reflection is visible
   (b) To convert specular reflection into diffuse reflection
   (c) To eliminate the effect of specular reflection
   (d) None of these
5. On which of the following, direction of refracted light depends?
   (a) Index of refraction of incident material
   (b) Index of refraction of transparent material
   (c) Both (a) and (b)
   (d) None of these
6. __________ is used for broadcast TV color system.
   (a) RGB (b) CMY
   (c) YIQ (d) CMYK
7. __________ and __________ together are called chromaticity.
   (a) Purity, saturation (b) Purity, brightness
   (c) Brightness, hue (d) Purity, dominant frequency
8. Which of the following is not a part of CIE chromaticity diagram?
   (a) Luminance (b) Spectral colors
   (c) Both (a) and (b) (d) None of these

9. In CMYK, C represents cyan, M represents magenta, Y represents yellow, and K represents __________.

   (a) Blue (b) Black
   (c) Grey (d) Any fourth color

10. In the HSV model, V is specified as __________.

   (a) Value ranging from 0 to 1.0 (b) Value ranging from 0 to 100
   (c) Value ranging from 0 to 0.5 (d) Value in angle

Answers. 1. c 2. b 3. d 4. a 5. c 6. c 7. d 8. a 9. b 10. a

9

Hidden-surface Elimination and Surface Rendering Methods

1. What are hidden-surface elimination algorithms? Discuss their two categories.

Ans. In Generally, in a three-dimensional (3D) scene, all the objects are not visible. The objects may be obstructed by a part of their own body or by some of the surrounding objects. Thus, while displaying objects in a 3D space, it is very important to identify those parts of an object which are visible from a chosen-viewing position. One way to accomplish this is to represent all the objects starting from the farthest to the nearest in such a way that the faces of the objects which need not be represented are hidden by the faces of the objects lying in front of them. However, in some cases like for wireframe displays, the hidden surfaces are not actually eliminated; rather they are represented with dashed lines so as to retain the information about their shape. Thus, depending on the complexity of the scene and type of objects to be displayed, several methods have been developed. These methods are referred to as **hidden-surface elimination** (or **visible-surface detection**) methods. The main aim of these methods is to remove all those parts (surfaces and lines) which are not to be displayed in a 3D scene.

Another objective of these algorithms is to form the shadows of the objects in the scene depending on the direction of light. To achieve this objective, the objects which lie farther from the light source are shadowed by the objects lying in front of them. In such a situation, the algorithm is applied twice, once to remove the hidden surfaces based on the viewing position, and second to form the shadows based on the direction of the light source.

Depending on whether these algorithms deal with object definitions directly or with their projected images, these methods are divided into two categories, namely, *object-space methods* and *image-space methods*.

- **Object-space methods**: The algorithms in this category compare the objects and their parts to each other within the 3D scene so as to determine the visible surfaces. These methods work directly on the objects before they are converted into pixels in the frame buffer. Thus, the resolution of the display device is irrelevant as the calculations are done at the mathematical level of objects. Back-face detection, BSP tree method, area-subdivision method, octree method, and ray-casting method follow the object-space approach.

- **Image-space methods:** The algorithms in this category determine the visibility point-by-point at each pixel position on the projection plane. That is, these algorithms work while the objects are being converted into pixels in the frame buffer. The resolution of the display device plays an important role as the calculations are done on a pixel-by-pixel basis. Most of the visible-surface detection algorithms make use of image-space methods. Depth-buffer method, A-buffer method, scan-line method, and area-subdivision method follow the image-space approach.

Though the basic approach taken by the various algorithms is different, most of the algorithms use sorting and coherence methods for better performance. Sorting helps in depth comparisons by ordering the individual surfaces in a scene according to their distance from the viewing position. Coherence methods, on the other hand, are used to take advantage of regularities in a 3D scene.

2. Explain the back-face detection algorithm for visible-surface detection.

Ans. In a solid object, such as a polyhedron, the surfaces which are facing the viewer are referred to as **front faces**, and those which are opposite to the viewer are referred to as **back faces**. These back faces contribute to approximately half of the total number of surfaces. Since back faces of a surface are not visible, we can remove them before the clipping process in order to save the processing time. The **back-face detection** algorithm is a fast and simple object-space algorithm which is used to identify the back faces of a polyhedron. It is based on the inside–outside test, which is performed to identify the interior regions of an object. Any point (x, y, z) is considered as an interior point of polygon surface if

$$Ax+By+Cz+D < 0$$

where, A, B, C, and D are the plane parameters.

If the point (x, y, z) is along the line-of-sight to the surface, the polygon must be back face. To simplify this test, we can consider the normal vector N to each polygon surface of the polyhedron, which has the Cartesian components (A, B, C). Now, consider a vector V in the viewing direction from the eye or camera position. If

$$V.N > 0$$

then the surface is considered as a back face.

However, if the object descriptions are transformed into projection coordinates and our viewing direction is parallel to the viewing z_v axis, then, we have

$$V = (0,0,Vz)\text{, and}$$

$$V.N = V_z C$$

It is clear from the above Equations that we only need to consider the sign of the z component of the normal vector N, which is, C.

In a left-handed viewing system (LHVS), where the viewing direction is along the positive z-axis, the polygon will be back face if $C > 0$. That is, the z component of the normal vector is positive. In addition, if $C = 0$, then also we cannot see that face. Thus, in an LHVS any polygon surface is considered as a back face if its normal vector has a z-component value $C \geq 0$ (see Figure 9.1).

Similarly, for a right-handed viewing system (RHVS), in which the viewing direction is along the negative z-axis, the polygon will be back face if $C < 0$. That is, the z-component of the normal vector is negative. In addition, if $C = 0$, then also we cannot see that face. Thus, in an RHVS, any polygon surface is considered as a back face if its normal vector has a z-component value $C \leq 0$.

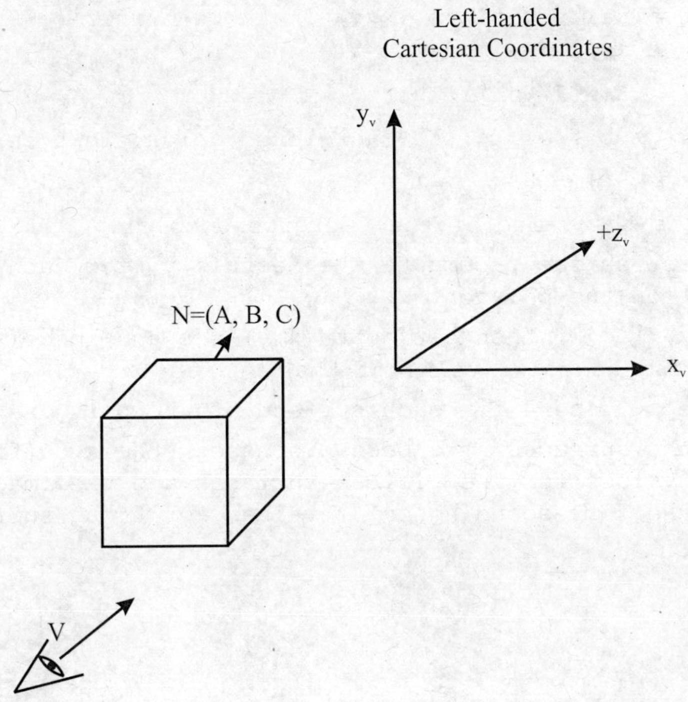

Figure 9.1 In an LHVS, a Polygon Surface with C $\geq$ 0 is Considered as Back Face

Thus, by examining the value of C for the different planes defining an object, we can easily identify all the back faces. For single and non-overlapping convex polyhedra, this test easily and correctly identifies all the hidden surfaces. However, for concave and overlapping polyhedra, more tests need to be carried out to identify additional faces which are completely or partially hidden.

3. Explain the depth-buffer method in detail.

Ans. Depth-buffer method (also known as **z-buffer method**) is the simplest and most commonly used image-space approach used for detecting visible surfaces. This algorithm was originally proposed by Catmull. It compares surface depths at each pixel position on the projection plane. The depth of the object is usually measured from the view plane along the z-axis of a viewing system; hence, the name of the method is z-buffer. This method works by processing every surface of a scene individually, that is, one point at a time across the surface. This method works well for the scenes containing polygon surfaces as the depth values of such surfaces can be computed very quickly and easily. However, one can use this method for non-planar surfaces also.

To implement this method, two buffers are required, namely, *image* (or *refresh*) *buffer* and *z-buffer* (or *depth buffer*). The **image buffer** is used to store the color (or intensity) values of each pixel position and the **z-buffer** is used to store the depth (or z-values) values for each (x, y) position. Thus, for each pixel position (x, y) on the view plane, the objects depths can be compared by comparing their z-values. The surface with the smallest depth from the view plane is visible at that position. Figure 9.2 shows three surfaces at varying distance from position (x, y) on a view plane. These surfaces can be processed in an arbitrary order. The algorithm for the depth-buffer method is given as follows:

1. Initialize pixel positions (x,y) in the z-buffer to 0 (minimum depth). That is,

   depth(x,y)=0

2. Set the image buffer to the background color. That is,

   $\text{image}(x,y)=I_B$

   where, I_B is the value of the background color.
3. For the first surface, compute the depth(x,y) for each pixel position (x,y) on the polygon.
4. If depth(x,y) < z, then set depth(x,y) = z and $\text{image}(x,y)=I_S$. where, I_S is the color value of that surface.
5. Repeat steps 3 and 4 for each surface of the polygon.
6. Once all the surfaces have been processed, the z-buffer contains the depth values for the visible surfaces and the image buffer contains the corresponding color values for those surfaces.

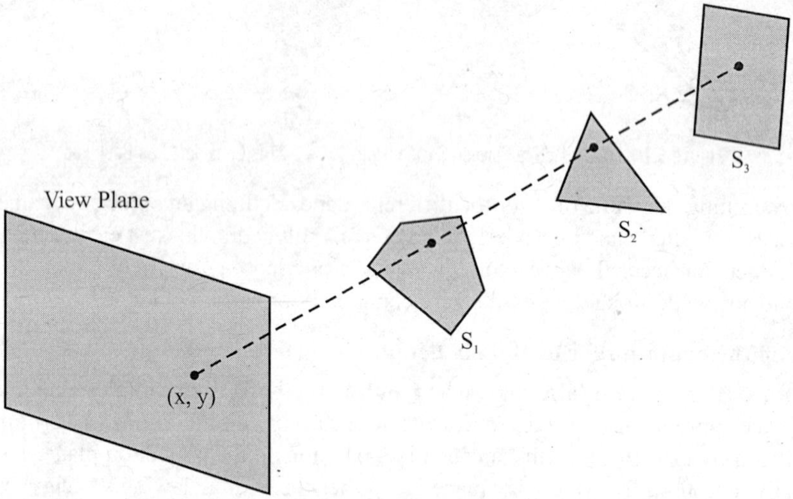

Figure 9.2 Three Surfaces Overlapping the Pixel Position (x, y) on the View Plane. The Visible Surface S_1 has the Minimum Depth Value

4. How can we calculate the depth (z) for polygon surfaces?

Ans. In general, the depth (z) for a surface position (x, y) can be calculated by using the plane Equation, $Ax + By + Cz + D = 0$ as follows:

$$z = \frac{-Ax - By - D}{C}$$

For any scan line, adjacent horizontal x values across a scan line and vertical y values on adjacent scan lines differ by 1 (see Figure 9.3). Thus, the depth value z' of the next position $(x + 1, y)$ across a scan line is obtained as follows:

$$z' = \frac{-A(x+1) - By - D}{C}$$

$$z' = \frac{-Ax - A + By - D}{C}$$

$$z' = \frac{-Ax - By - D}{C} - \frac{A}{C}$$

$$z' = z - \frac{A}{C}$$

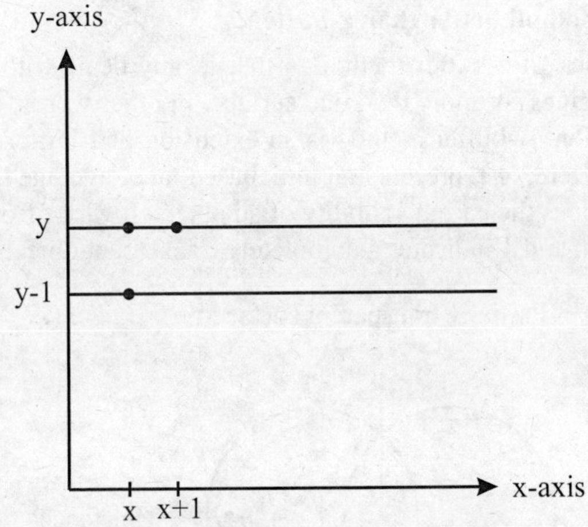

Figure 9.3 From Position (x, y) on a Scan Line, the Next Position Horizontally is (x + 1, y) and Vertically (x; y – 1)

In the same way, we can obtain the depth value `z'` of the next position `(x, y - 1)` along the adjacent scan lines as follows:

$$z' = \frac{-Ax - B(y-1) - D}{C}$$

$$z' = \frac{-Ax - By + B - D}{C}$$

$$z' = \frac{-Ax - By - D}{C} + \frac{B}{C}$$

$$z' = z + \frac{B}{C}$$

5. What are the advantages and disadvantages of using a z-buffer algorithm?

Ans. Some of the most significant benefits of z-buffer algorithm are as follows:

- For polygon surfaces, this method is very easy to implement as it does not require any sorting of the surfaces in a scene.

- It is useful in displaying complex surface intersections easily.
- It does not require depth sorting of objects, hence provides linear computational complexity.

Apart from these advantages, it also has some shortcomings. Some of them are as follows:

- It may paint the same pixel several times and hence, computing the color of the pixel may prove to be expensive.
- It requires large storage requirements, which arises the need of additional buffer along with the refresh buffer.
- It is a time-consuming process and can only find one visible surface at each pixel position.
- It requires recalculations, when changing the scale.

6. How is A-buffer method better than z-buffer?

Ans. The main drawback of z-buffer method is that it only deals with opaque surfaces and cannot accumulate intensity values for more than one surface. In other words, it can find only one visible surface at each pixel position. A-buffer method is an extension of z-buffer method that can deal with transparent surfaces also. Here, ***A*** represents an antialiased, area-averaged, accumulation-buffer. The transparency factor determines the partial visibility of an object. It varies from 0 to 1, where 0 indicates a completely opaque object, and 1 indicates a completely transparent object (see Figure 9.4).

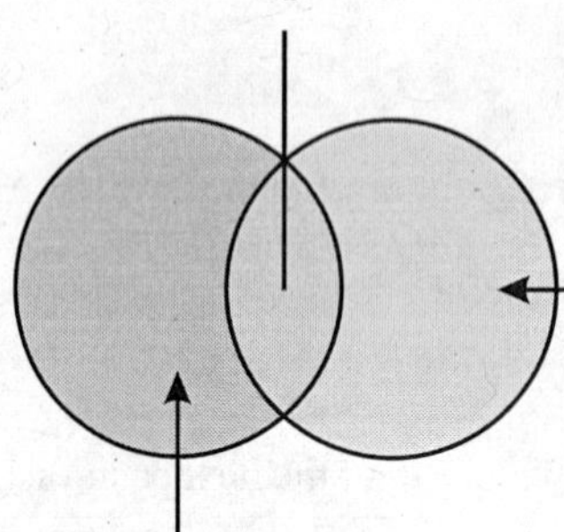

Figure 9.4 Partially Transparent Surface

A-buffer method was developed by Lucasfilm to be implemented in the surface-rendering system named **REYES** (**R**enders **E**verything **Y**ou **E**ver **S**aw). A-buffer method expands the z-buffer method by creating a linked list of surfaces for each pixel position. It allows each pixel position to reference a linked list of surfaces overlapping that pixel. Thus, it considers more than one surface intensity at each pixel position and computes a pixel color as a combination of different surface colors for transparency or anti-aliasing effects. This makes the A-buffer method better that the z-buffer method.

7. Give an organization of an A-buffer pixel position.

Ans. Figure 9.5 illustrates two possible organizations of an A-buffer pixel position in which each position comprises two fields, namely, *depth field* and *intensity field*. **Depth field** stores a positive or negative real number while **intensity field** stores surface intensity information or a pointer value. If the depth field contains a positive value, it indicates the depth of a single surface overlapping the corresponding pixel area. The intensity field in this case will store the RGB components of the surface color at that point with the percentage of pixel coverage (see Figure 9.5a). On the other hand, if the depth field contains a negative real number, it indicates the depth of multiple surfaces overlapping the corresponding pixel area. In this case, the intensity field stores a pointer that points to a linked list of surface data (see Figure 9.5b). Each node of the linked list contains the following data for each surface:

- surface depth
- percentage of transparency
- RGB intensity components
- surface identifier
- percentage of area coverage
- other surface-rendering parameters
- pointer to next surface

The pixels in A-buffer algorithm are processed using the methods similar to those used in depth-buffer algorithm. The scan lines are processed to determine the surface overlaps of pixels across individual scan lines. Each surface is subdivided into a polygon mesh and clipped against the pixel boundaries. The opacity factors and percentage of surface overlaps can be used to calculate the intensity of each pixel. The intensity in this case would be an average of the contributions from the overlapping surfaces.

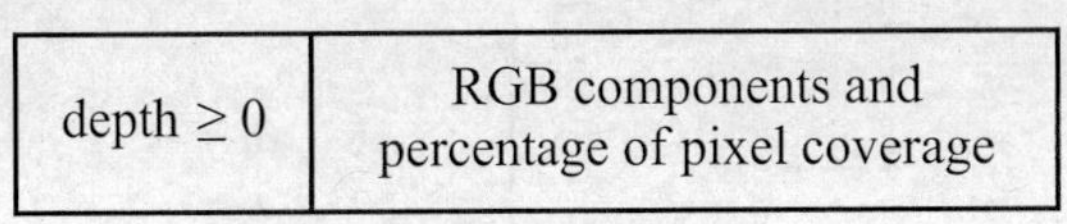

(a) Organization 1

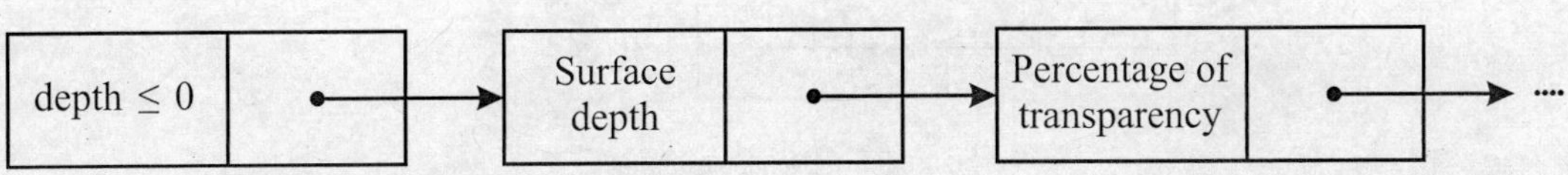

(b) Organization 2

Figure 9.5 Two Possible Organizations of A-buffer Pixel Position

8. Explain the method which is a combination of image space and object space methods with the help of an example.

Ans. The method which makes use of both image-space and object-space methods is **depth-sorting method**. The basic idea behind this method is to draw the objects in the frame buffer in the decreasing order of the distance from the viewpoint. That is, the farther objects are drawn first and the objects which are nearer are drawn over the top of the already drawn objects. The algorithm can be easily understood by comparing it with an artist's painting. Just like an artist creates an oil painting by first painting the background colors, then drawing the most distant objects, then the nearer objects, and so on. Finally, the artist paints the foreground objects over the canvas background and the other distant objects. In this way, as soon as the painter paints the current layer, the previous layer is hidden. Thus, this algorithm is also referred to as the **Painter's algorithm**.

Based on this technique, the algorithm follows a simple algorithm:

1. All the surfaces are first sorted based on their distance from the view plane.
2. Ambiguities are resolved – ambiguities arise when the z-coordinates of the surfaces overlap.
3. Surfaces are drawn (scan converted) in order from back to front.

The algorithm is very simple if the surfaces do not overlap. However, if the surfaces overlap, additional processing is required. For each surface that overlaps, a depth order is created, which is expressed in the form of a linked list containing pointers to those surfaces that are in front of it. In addition, a `behind_counter` is maintained to record the number of surfaces that are behind the surface under consideration. The surfaces having `behind_counter` equals to 0 are drawn first, and the value of `behind_counter` is set to –1 to make sure that these surfaces are not drawn again. This process is repeated recursively until all the surfaces are drawn with their respective color intensities. To understand this concept, consider Figure 9.6 containing several overlapping surfaces.

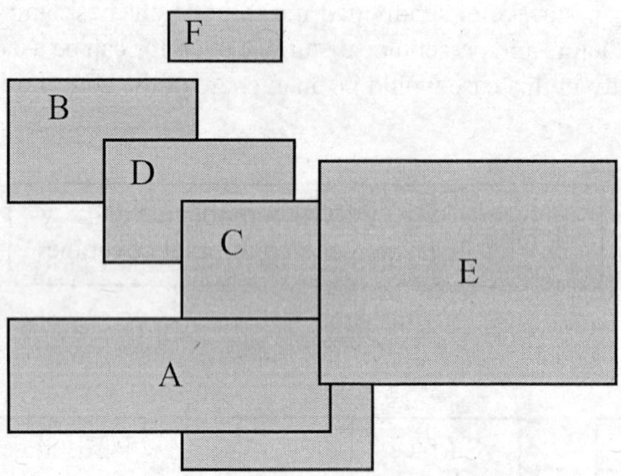

Figure 9.6 Overlapping Surfaces

All these surfaces are sorted based on their distance from the view plane. The depth order table for these surfaces is shown below:

Surface	`behind_counter`	Front list
A	1	E
B	0	D
C	1	A, E
D	1	C
E	2	
F	0	

The status of depth order table after each iteration is shown as follows:

Iteration 1: Surfaces B and F have `behind_counter` 0, so they are drawn first.

Surface	`behind_counter`	Front list	Surfaces drawn	New `behind_counter`
A	1	E	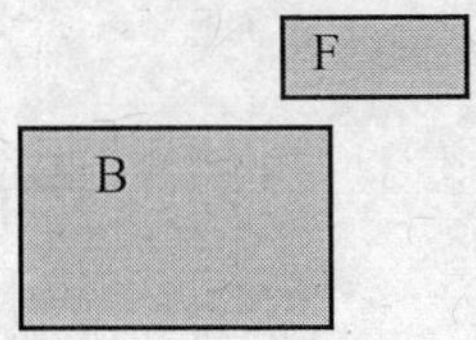	1
B	0	D		-1
C	1	A, E		1
D	1	C		0
E	2			2
F	0			-1

Iteration 2: Surface D has `behind_counter` 0, so it is drawn next.

Surface	`behind_counter`	Front list	Surfaces drawn	New `behind_counter`
A	1	E	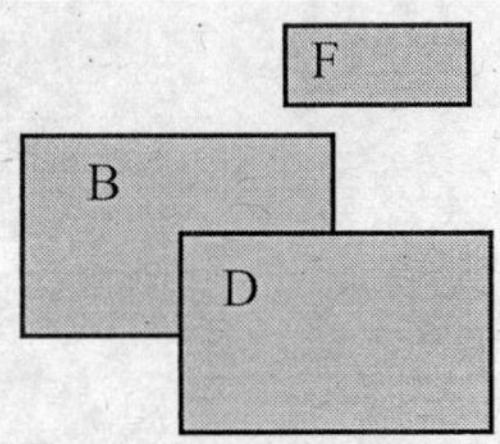	1
B	–1	D		-1
C	1	A, E		0
D	0	C		-1
E	2			2
F	–1			-1

Iteration 3: Surface C has `behind_counter` 0, so it is drawn next.

Surface	`behind_counter`	Front list	Surfaces drawn	New `behind_counter`
A	1	E	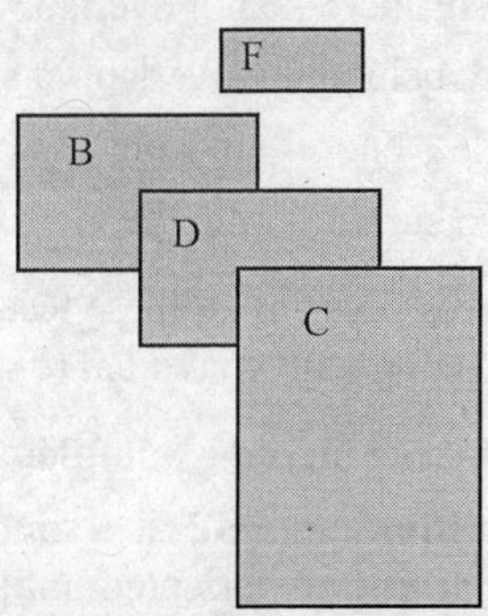	0
B	–1	D		-1
C	0	A, E		-1
D	–1	C		-1
E	2			1
F	–1			-1

Iteration 4: Surface A has `behind_counter` 0, so it is drawn next.

Surface	`behind_counter`	Front list	Surfaces drawn	New `behind_counter`
A	0	E	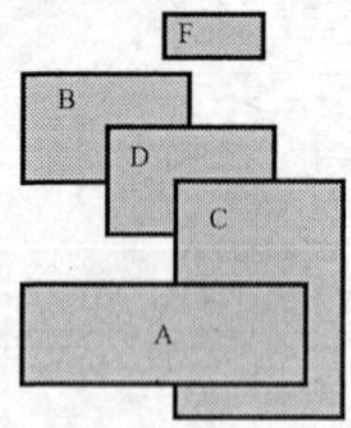	-1
B	-1	D		-1
C	-1	A, E		-1
D	-1	C		-1
E	1			0
F	-1			-1

Iteration 5: Surface E has `behind_counter` 0, so it is drawn at the end.

Surface	`behind_counter`	Front list	Surfaces drawn	New `behind_counter`
A	-1	E	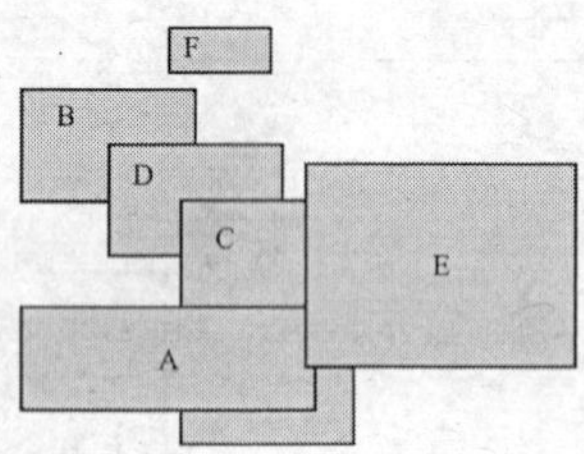	-1
B	-1	D		-1
C	-1	A, E		-1
D	-1	C		-1
E	0			-1
F	-1			

Note that the algorithm is discussed by taking an example of simple polygon surfaces. However, to apply this algorithm on complex curved surfaces, we first represent the surfaces using polygons, and then apply the algorithm on those polygons.

Alternatively, we can perform the following tests on each surface that overlaps the surface `S` under consideration.

1. The `x`-extents of the two surfaces do not overlap.
2. The `y`-extents of the two surfaces do not overlap.
3. The surface `S` lies entirely behind the overlapping surface relative to the viewpoint.
4. The overlapping surface lies entirely in front of `S` relative to the viewpoint.
5. The projections of the two surfaces onto the view plane do not overlap.

If all the overlapping surfaces pass any of these tests, none of them is behind `S`. This implies that no reordering is required and `S` can be scan converted (drawn).

9. Explain how the BSP-tree method is implemented for visible surface detection.

Ans. A **binary space partitioning** (**BSP**) is a simple technique which recursively divides a space into subspaces by choosing arbitrarily oriented splitting planes. Then for each splitting plane we identify the surfaces which are in 'front' or in 'back' of that particular plane, relative to the viewing direction. This subdivision allows a user to represent the scene by means of a tree data structure known as a **BSP tree**. This technique is particularly useful when only the view positions change and the objects remain at their fixed positions. This technique overcomes the limitation of Painter's algorithm in which the time is wasted while drawing the background objects which are overdrawn later by the foreground objects. In BSP tree method, the order of the objects is determined in advance before drawing them on the screen. Thus, this technique is considered to be more fast and efficient than the Painter's algorithm.

To understand the BSP tree method, consider a region of space containing several polygon surfaces shown in Figure 9.7a. Initially, plane P_1 is set up to partition the space into two halves so that one set of objects is in front of P_1 and other set of objects is in the back of P_1. It is clear from Figure 9.7b that objects 2 and 3 are in front of P_1 and objects 1 and 5 are in back of P_1. Since object 4 is lying on the plane P_1, it is divided into two separate objects 4a and 4b, with 4a in front of P_1 and 4b in back. The process of subdivision is recursively performed until each part contains a single polygon as shown in Figure 9.7c.

Now, we construct the binary tree representation as shown in Figure 9.7d. In this tree, the objects are represented as nodes of the tree with front nodes as the left branches and back nodes as right branches. Once the BSP tree is complete, the objects are drawn in order from back to front. This method requires fast hardware implementations for constructing and processing BSP trees.

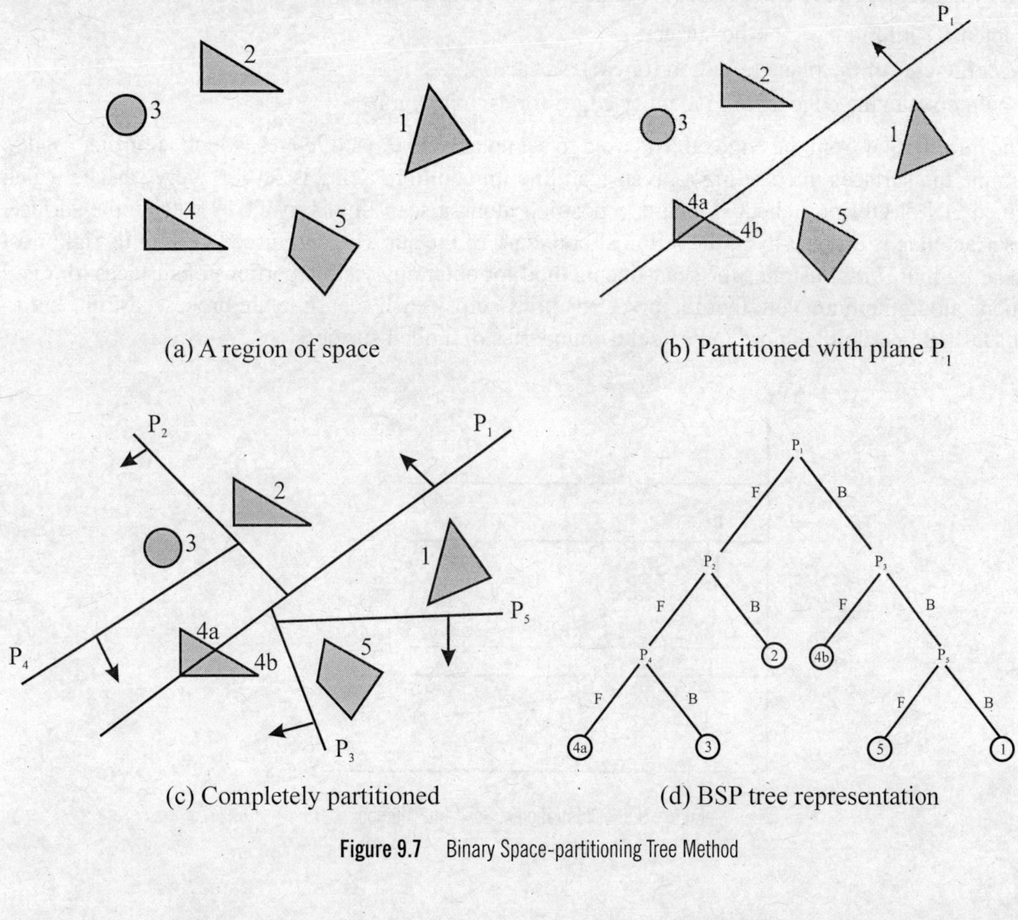

Figure 9.7 Binary Space-partitioning Tree Method

10. Explain the scan-line method for removing hidden surfaces with the help of an example. Is it image space or object space method?

Ans. A scan-line method is an image-space method for removing hidden surfaces. It is an extension of the scan-line algorithm which was used for filling polygon interiors. That is, the algorithm now deals with multiple surfaces rather than just one surface. When a scan line is processed, the algorithm examines all polygon surfaces which intersect that line in order to determine which ones are visible. In case the surfaces overlap, depth calculations are performed across each scan line in order to determine the nearest visible surface to the view plane. Once visible surface is determined, the intensity value for that surface is entered into the refresh buffer.

The implementation of scan-line method for hidden-surface removal is a bit different from that used in polygon filling. The scan-line method when used for polygon filling requires only an edge list (or edge table) to be maintained. However, if it is used for hidden-surface removal, then it requires an additional table known as **polygon table**. The edge table in this case contains the following information:

- coordinate endpoints for each edge
- the inverse slope of each edge (`1/m`), and
- pointers to the polygon table to determine the surfaces bounded by each edge.

The polygon table, on the other hand, contains the following information:

- intensity information for the surfaces
- coefficients of the plane Equation for each surface
- pointers into the edge table to identify edges for each polygon

The information from the edge table is used to set up an active list of edges, which is further used to determine the surfaces intersecting a given scan line. In addition, a flag is set for every surface which is turned ON or OFF to indicate whether a position along a scan line is inside or outside the surface. The surface flag is turned ON at the leftmost boundary of the surface, and turned OFF at its rightmost boundary. Figure 9.8 illustrates the scan-line method for obtaining visible portions of surfaces for pixel positions along the line. Note that the pixel positions across each scan line are processed from left to right. Dashed lines in the figure indicate the boundaries of hidden surfaces.

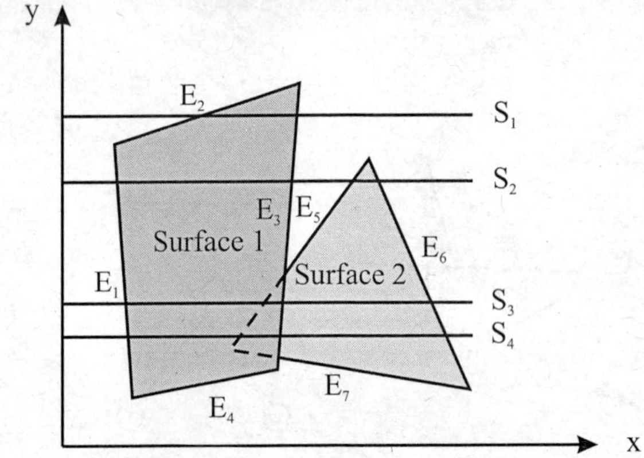

Figure 9.8 Illustration of Scan-line Method

For scan line S_1, the active edge list contains edges E_2 and E_3. For pixel positions along this scan line between edges E_2 and E_3, only the flag for Surface 1 is turned ON. Hence, the intensity information for Surface 1 is entered from the polygon table into the refresh buffer. For scan line S_2, the active edge list contains edges E_1, E_3, E_5, and E_6. Along this scan line, first the flag for Surface 1 is turned ON when edge E_1 is encountered, and turned OFF when edge E_3 is encountered. Hence, during this interval, the intensity information for Surface 1 is entered from the polygon table into the refresh buffer. Similarly, when edge E_5 is encountered, the flag for Surface 2 is turned ON, and when edge E_6 is encountered, the flag for Surface 2 is turned OFF. Hence, during this interval, the intensity information for Surface 2 is entered from the polygon table into the refresh buffer. However, no depth calculations are required as the surfaces do not overlap.

For scan line S_3, the active edge list contains the same edges as for S_2, but in different order, that is, E_1, E_5, E_3, and E_6. Along this scan line, from edge E_1 to E_5, only the flag for Surface 1 is ON. However, between edges E_5 and E_3, the flags for both surfaces are ON. Therefore, during this interval, the depth order needs to be calculated. The plane coefficients for the two surfaces are used to compute the depth of both planes. In our figure, the *z*-depth of Surface 1 is assumed to be less than that of Surface 2, which indicates that it is closer to the screen. Therefore, the intensity information for Surface 1 is loaded into the refresh buffer until edge E_3 is encountered. Then, the flag for Surface 1 is turned OFF, and intensity information for Surface 2 is stored until edge E_6 is encountered.

For scan line S_4, we can take the advantage of coherence along the scan line as we pass from one scan line to the next. Since the scan line S_4 has the same active list as that of scan line S_3, and there are no changes in the line intersections, we do not have to make depth calculations again between the edges E_3 and E_5. Hence, the same intensities for Surface 1 can be entered without further calculations. Note that this method can be readily extended to any number of overlapping polygon surfaces.

11. Explain how Warnock's algorithm is used to remove hidden surfaces.

Ans. Warnock's algorithm (also known as **area-subdivision algorithm**) was developed by John Warnock. It is basically an image-space method but can sometimes make use of object-space operation to accomplish depth comparison. This algorithm exploits area coherence by finding those view areas which represent part of a single surface. The algorithm follows the divide-and-conquer strategy. That is, it divides the total viewing area into smaller and smaller rectangles until every small area showcases a projection of part of a single visible surface or a blank space. The subdivision can also be continued until we left with a single pixel for checking.

The method can be implemented by first performing the tests on a particular area so as to determine whether the area is a part of single surface or too complex to analyze easily. Initially, the tests are applied to determine whether the process of subdividing the total area into smaller rectangles is required. If the test reflects the high complexity of a view, then it must be subdivided. After this, each smaller area is tested again and if the tests still indicate complexity of the surface, the given area is subdivided again. This recursive process is continued until the subdivisions are properly analyzed as belonging to a single surface or they are reduced to a single pixel.

The easiest way to perform the recursive division of the area is to divide the area into four equal parts at each step. The subdivisions can be in the form of rectangles or any similar shape. To determine whether a single surface is visible within a specified rectangular area, the surfaces can be compared to the boundary of that area. There are four possible relationships that a surface can have with the boundary of a specified rectangular area, which are as follows:

- **Surrounding surface:** The surface which completely surrounds the rectangular area.
- **Intersecting surface** (also called **overlapping surface**): The surface which is partially inside and partially outside the rectangular area.
- **Contained surface** (also called **inside surface**): The surface which is completely inside the rectangular area.
- **Disjoint surface** (also called **outside surface**): The surface which is completely outside the rectangular area.

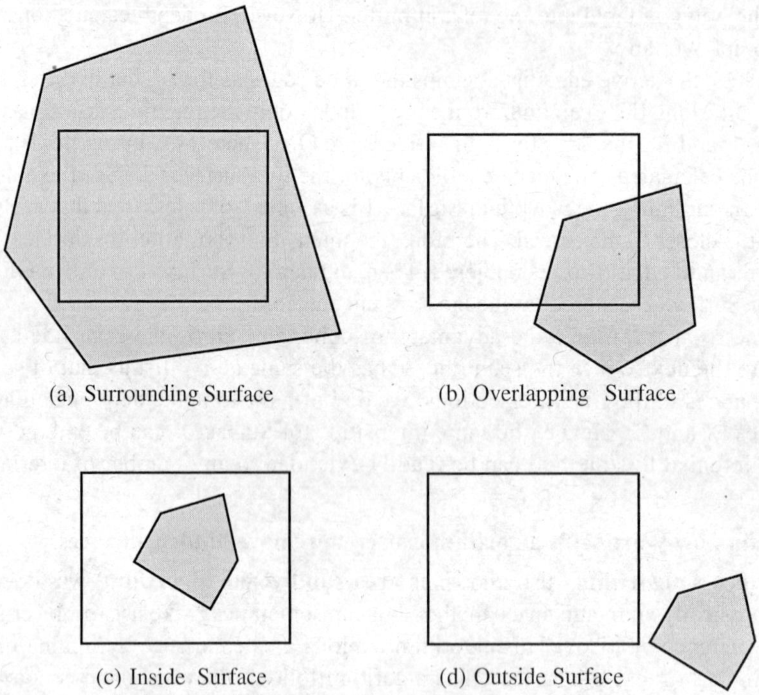

Figure 9.9 Relationships between Polygon Surfaces and a Rectangular Area

All the tests for determining the surface visibility within an area are completely based on these four classifications. The subdivision of a specified area is not required if any one of the following conditions exists:

- All the surfaces lie completely outside the rectangular area. In this case, the color of the window is set to the background color.
- If only one inside, overlapping, or surrounding surface is in the area. Then independent of the type of surface, the area is filled with the background color and only the part of the surface within the area is rendered.
- When there is a single surrounding surface which completely blocks all other surfaces within the area boundaries. One way to test this condition is to sort the surfaces according to minimum depth from the view plane. Then for each surrounding surface, the maximum depth within the area under consideration is computed. If the maximum depth for one of these surrounding surfaces is closer to the view plane than the minimum depth of all other surfaces within the area, this implies that

the surface probably blocks all other surfaces. Another way to test this condition is to compute the depth values at the four vertices of the area for all inside, overlapping, and surrounding surfaces. If all four depths for one of the surrounding surfaces is less than the computed depths for all other surfaces, then it is also assumed that the surface blocks all other surfaces. In such a case, the area is filled with the color of the surrounding surface.

Figure 9.10 shows an example of area-subdivision method in which the viewing area is recursively divided into rectangular areas until every small area represents a projection of a part of single visible surface, or a blank surface.

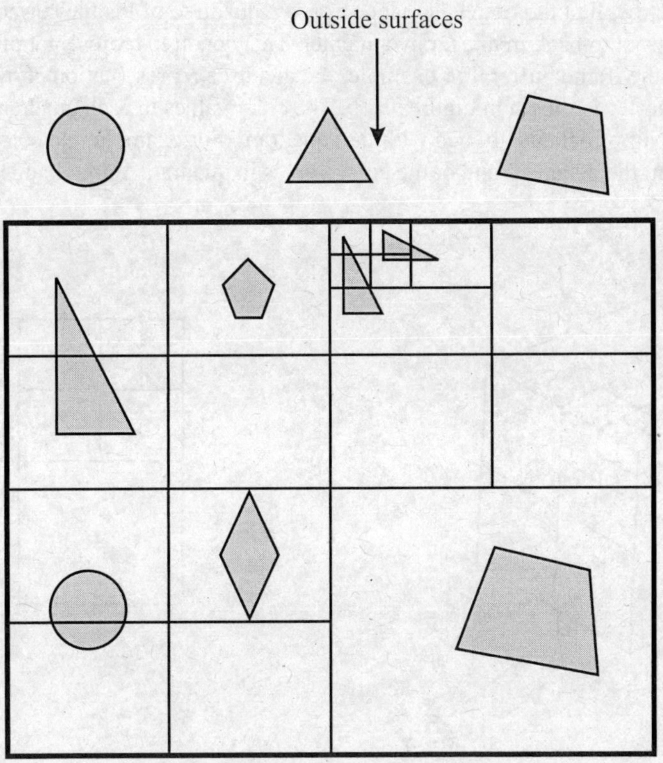

Figure 9.10 Area-subdivision Method

12. Explain the procedure how hidden-surface elimination is done using octree representation.

Ans. In addition to representing solid objects, the octree representation can also be used for hidden-surface elimination. It is accomplished by projecting the octree nodes onto the viewing surface in a front-to-back order. As shown in Figure 9.11a, the octants numbered 0, 1, 2, and 3 represent the front faces of a region of space and are visible from the viewer's side. Thus, all the polygon surfaces which lie in front of these octants are clearly visible to the viewer. On the other hand, the octants numbered 4, 5, 6, and 7 represent the back faces. The surfaces lying on the back side of the front octants or in the back octants are probably hidden by the front faces, and hence, not visible. These surfaces can be eliminated by traversing the octree nodes in depth-first order, that is, in the order 0, 1, 2, 3, 4, 5, 6, and 7. While following this order, we ensure that the nodes representing the octants 0, 1, 2, and 3 for the entire region are visited before the nodes representing octants 4, 5, 6, and 7. The same order is followed while traversing the nodes of suboctants of each octant. For example, the nodes for the front four suboctants of octant 0 are traversed before the nodes for the four back octants.

While traversing an octree node, when a color value is encountered, the pixel area in the frame buffer corresponding to this node will be set to this color value, if there is no other value already stored in this area. This ensures that only the front colors will be stored into the frame buffer. For blank areas, nothing will be stored in the frame buffer. In addition, once a node of the octree is found to be hidden, it is completely eliminated from further processing, that is, its subtrees are ignored.

To display an octree, first the octree is mapped onto a quadtree of visible surfaces by traversing the octree nodes from front to back in a recursive manner. This quadtree representation for visible surfaces is then loaded into the frame buffer. For example, the quadtree representation corresponding to the octants in a region of space is shown in Figure 9.11b. The color values in each quadrant of the quadtree are obtained from the pair of octants aligned with that quadrant. For example, the color values in quadrant 0 are generated from the octants 0 and 4; the color values in quadrant 1 are obtained from the octants 1 and 5, and so on.

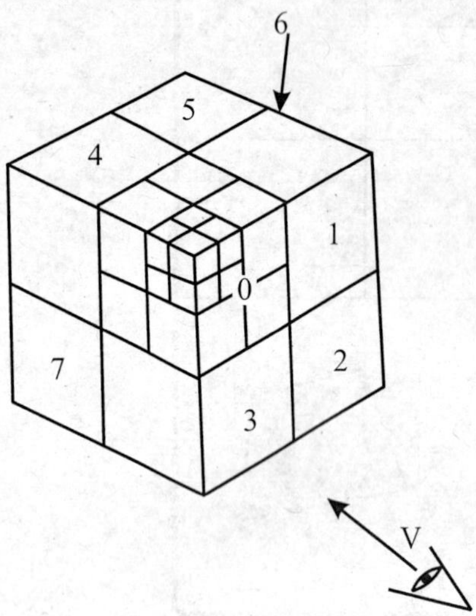

(a) Octants in space

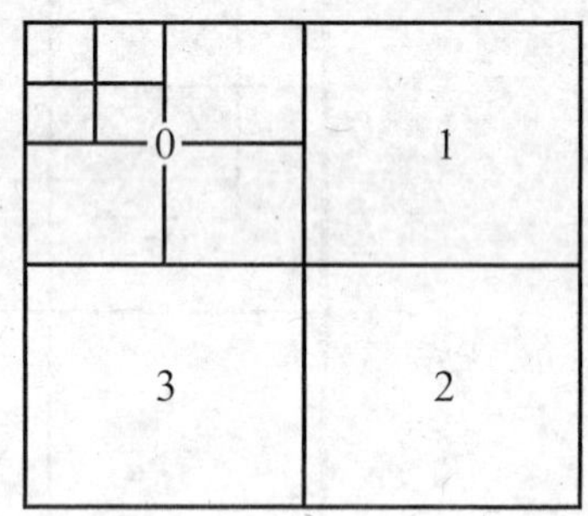

(b) Quadrants for the view plane

Figure 9.11 Octant Divisions for a Region of Space and the Corresponding Quadrant Plane

13. Explain the ray-casting method for visible surface detection.

Ans. The **ray-casting method** is a visible-surface detection method that uses the ray-casting methods similar to those used to implement constructive solid-geometry(CSG) methods. This method is based on geometric optics methods, which trace the paths of light rays. The ray-casting method considers the line of sight from a pixel position on the view plane, and determines which objects in the scene intersect this line. Once all ray-surface intersections are determined, the surface whose intersection point is closest to the pixel is considered as the visible surface (see Figure 9.12). Since there can be an infinite number of rays in a scene and we are interested in only those rays which pass through the pixel positions, we can trace the light-ray paths backward from the pixels through the scene. This method is very much effective for the scenes containing curved surfaces, especially spheres.

The ray-casting method can be considered as the variation of depth-sorting method for visible surface detection. In depth-sorting method, the surfaces are processed one at a time. The depth values for all projection points over the surface are calculated, and the calculated depth values are then compared to the already stored depth values to determine which surfaces are visible at each pixel. Whereas, in ray-casting method, the pixels are processed one at a time, and the depth values for all surfaces along the projection path to that pixel are then calculated.

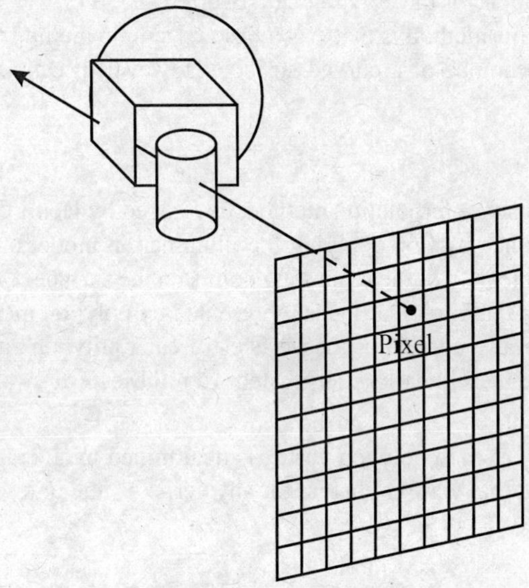

Figure 9.12 Ray-casting Method

14. Discuss the four polygon rendering methods.

Ans. An illumination model can be applied to the rendering of standard graphics objects, which are formed with polygon surfaces. We can shade any surface by calculating the surface normal (a vector perpendicular to the surface) at each visible point and applying an illumination model at that point. However, applying illumination model at each visible point is computationally expensive. Thus, we can use more efficient methods for shading surfaces defined by polygons and polygon meshes, which are as follows:

- By rendering every polygon with a single intensity
- By making use of an interpolation scheme so as to obtain the intensity at each point of the surface

Both these ways lead to four different types of shading methods, which are described as follows:

Constant-intensity Shading

Constant-intensity shading (also known as **flat shading** or **faceted shading**) is the simplest method for rendering an object with polygon surfaces. This method applies an illumination model once to determine a single intensity value, which is then used to shade each polygon surface. This implies that all points over the polygon surface are displayed with the same intensity value. This method gives an accurate rendering if the following assumptions are true:

- The light sources illuminating the object are at infinity, so that `N.L` and the attenuation function is constant across the polygon surface. Here, `N` is the normal vector (perpendicular) to the surface and `L` is the light source vector (direction) striking the surface.

- The viewer is at infinity, so that V.R is constant across the polygon surface. Here, V is the viewpoint vector looking at the surface and R is the specular-reflection vector.
- The polygon represents the actual surface being modelled, and is not an approximation of an object with a curved surface.

Even if all these assumptions are wrong, then also the constant-intensity shading gives approximate surface-lighting effects by using small polygon facets and calculating the intensity for each facet, say, for the centre of the polygon or for the polygon's first vertex.

The main advantage of this method is that it is a fast and simple method that can be used for quickly displaying the general appearance of a curved surface. However, it cannot produce the variations in shade across the polygon.

Gouraud Shading

Gouraud shading is an intensity interpolation method, developed by Henri Gouraud in 1971. The method renders the polygon surface by first applying the illumination model on a subset of surface points and then interpolating the intensity of the remaining points on the surface. Gouraud shading is generally used to produce continuous shading of surfaces represented by polygon meshes. Thus, in this case, the illumination model is generally applied at the vertices of each polygon surface and the colors in the interiors of the surfaces are then linearly interpolated from these vertex values. The Gouraud shading works as follows:

1. The unit normal vector at each polygon vertex is determined by averaging the surface normals of all polygons meeting at that vertex. That is, for any vertex V, the unit vertex normal N_v can be calculated as follows:

$$N_V = \frac{\sum_{i=1}^{n} N_i}{\left|\sum_{i=1}^{n} N_i\right|}$$

where, n is the total number of surface normals of all the polygons sharing that vertex.

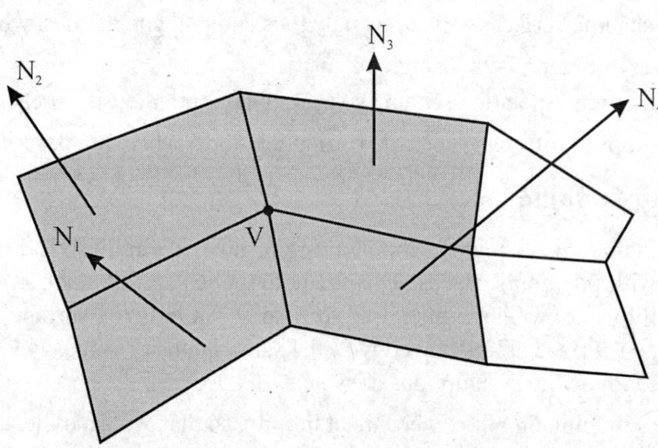

Figure 9.13 Surface Normals of Polygons

2. The light intensity at each polygon vertex is then determined by applying an illumination model at that vertex.
3. The color intensities of the vertices are linearly interpolated to obtain the intensities of the border pixels (pixels at the edges of the polygon) along each scan line that intersects the polygon. For each scan line, the intensity at the intersection of the scan line with a polygon edge is linearly interpolated from the intensities at the endpoints of that edge. To understand this step, consider a polygon surface shown in Figure 9.14.

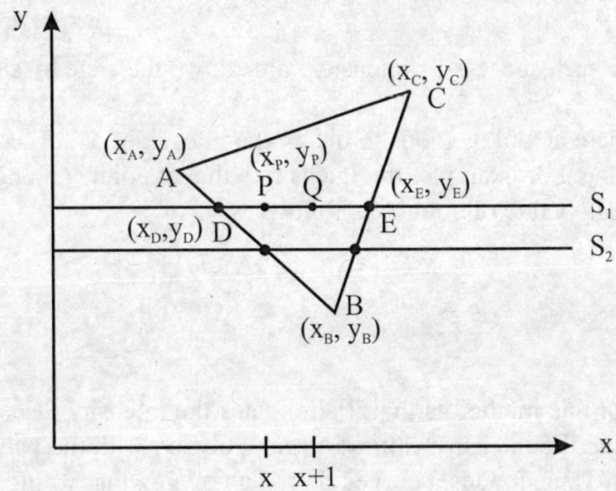

Figure 9.14 Gouraud Surface Rendering of a Polygon Surface

In this figure, the scan line S_1 intersects the edges AB and BC at points D and E, respectively. The intensity at point D can be obtained by interpolating the intensity values at vertices A and B as follows:

$$I_D = \frac{y_D - y_B}{y_A - y_B} I_A + \frac{y_A - y_D}{y_A - y_B} I_B \tag{1}$$

where, I represents the intensity for one of the RGB color components.

In the same way, we can obtain the intensity at point E by interpolating the intensity values at vertices B and C as follows:

$$I_E = \frac{y_E - y_B}{y_C - y_B} I_C + \frac{y_C - y_E}{y_C - y_B} I_B \tag{2}$$

Equations (1) and (2) give the intensities of the border pixels at points D and E for the scan line S_1. By interpolating the intensities of boundary pixels, we can obtain the interior pixel intensities. For example, the intensity for one of the RGB color components at point P in Figure 9.14 can be calculated from the values of I_D and I_E as follows:

$$I_P = \frac{x_E - x_P}{x_E - x_D} I_D + \frac{x_P - x_D}{x_E - x_D} I_E$$

We can apply an incremental procedure to obtain the intensity values on successive scan lines. We start from a scan line that intersects one of the polygon vertices, and then incrementally obtain the intensity values for other scan lines that intersect an edge connected to that vertex. For example, we can use the intensity I_A of endpoint A to compute the intensity I along the edge AB for the scan line S_1 as follows:

$$I = I_A + \Delta I_y$$

where, $\Delta I_y = \dfrac{I_B - I_A}{y_A - y_B}$ is a constant term.

Similarly, we can compute the intensity I' along the same edge AB for the next scan line S_2 as follows:

$$I' = I + \Delta I_y$$

Thus, we can compute each successive intensity value down the edge by simply adding ΔI_y to the previous intensity value.

We can also use the incremental methods to obtain the intensities at successive horizontal pixel positions along each scan line. For example, the intensity value at point Q along the scan line S_1 can be calculated from the intensity value of point P as follows:

$$I_Q = I_P + \Delta I_x$$

where, $\Delta I_x = \dfrac{I_D - I_E}{x_E - x_D}$

The main advantage of this method is that it eliminates the intensity discontinuities that can occur in flat shading by matching the intensity values of each polygon with the values of adjacent polygons along the common edges. Thus, it adds a curved feel to a polygon that would otherwise appear flat. In addition, it allows you to specify a different shade for each vertex of a polygon, and the rendering engine then smoothly interpolates the shade across the surface. However, it has some disadvantages also, which are as follows:

- The specular highlights (for example, a glint of reflected light on the surface of an apple) are not rendered correctly. They are displayed with anomalous shapes.
- It suffers from the problem of **Mach banding**, in which the bright and dark intensity streaks (called **Mach bands**) appear on the surface due to linear intensity interpolation. These effects can be reduced by dividing the surface into a large number of polygon faces or by using precise intensity calculations.

Phong Shading

Phong shading, also known as **normal vector interpolation shading**, is a more accurate interpolation method, developed by Phong Bui Tuong. Unlike Gouraud shading, Phong shading interpolates normal vectors rather than interpolating intensity values. Then the illumination model is applied to each surface point. Phong shading renders a polygon surface in the following manner:

1. The unit normal vector at each polygon vertex is determined by averaging the surface normals of all polygons meeting at that vertex as done in Gouraud shading.
2. The vertex normals are then linearly interpolated over the surface of the polygon.
3. Finally, an illumination model is applied at each pixel position along a scan line to determine the pixel intensities using the interpolated normal vectors.

We can use the similar interpolation methods for normal vectors as used for intensity values in the Gouraud shading method. For example, for the polygon surface shown in Figure 9.15, we can obtain the normal vector N_D at point D by interpolating the normal vectors N_A and N_B at endpoints A and B, respectively, as follows:

$$N_D = \frac{y_D - y_B}{y_A - y_B} N_A + \frac{y_A - y_D}{y_A - y_B} N_B$$

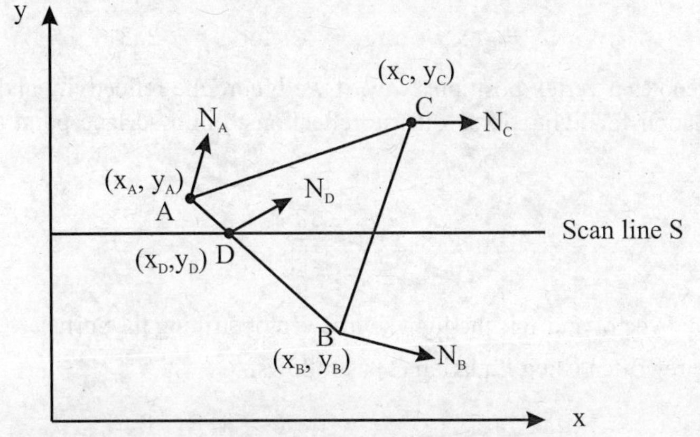

Figure 9.15 Interpolation of Surface Normals along a Polygon Edge

Like Gouraud shading, here also incremental methods can be applied to evaluate normals on successive scan lines and at successive horizontal pixel positions along each scan line.

The Phong shading gives more accurate shading as compared to Gouraud shading. It also reduces the problem of Mach bands to great extent since it displays more realistic highlights on a surface as compared to Gouraud shading method. However, the processing time and cost of shading a surface using Phong shading is more as compared to other shading techniques because of excessive calculations (Figure 9.16).

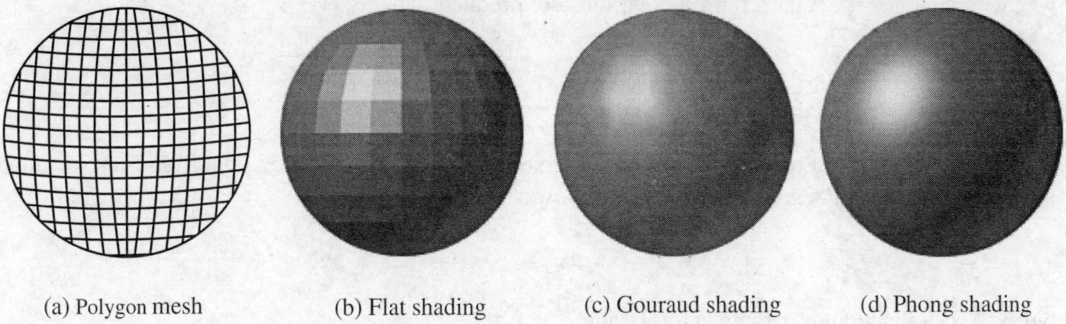

Figure 9.16 Surface Rendered through Flat, Gouraud, and Phong Shading

Fast Phong Shading

Fast Phong shading method speeds up the Phong shading method by approximating some of the illumination-model calculations. It basically restricts the polygon facets to triangular surface patches, and performs the intensity calculations using a truncated Taylor-series expansion. As Phong shading interpolates normal vectors from vertex normals, one can express the surface normal N at a point (x, y) over a triangle as:

$$N = Ax + By + C \tag{1}$$

where A, B, and C can be determined from three vertex Equations as follows:

$$N_i = Ax_i + By_i + C, \text{ for } i = 1, 2, 3$$

Here, (x_i, y_i) denotes a vertex position. Now, if we ignore the reflectivity and attenuation parameters, then the Equation for light-source diffuse reflection from a surface point (x, y) can be given as:

$$I_{diff}(x, y) = \frac{L \,.\, N}{|L|\,|N|} \tag{2}$$

where N is the normal vector and L is the light source vector striking the surface.

Equation (2) can be rewritten using Equation (1) as follows:

$$\begin{aligned} I_{diff}(x, y) &= \frac{L \,.\, (Ax + By + C)}{|L|\,|Ax + By + C|} \\ &= \frac{(L \,.\, A)x + (L \,.\, B)y + L \,.\, C}{|L|\,|Ax + By + C|} \end{aligned} \tag{3}$$

Equation (3) can also be written as follows:

$$I_{diff}(x, y) = \frac{ax + by + c}{(dx^2 + exy + fy^2 + gx + hy + i)^{1/2}} \tag{4}$$

where parameters a, b, and c represent various dot products. That is,

$$a = \frac{L.A}{|L|}, \; b = \frac{L.B}{|L|}, \; c = \frac{L.C}{|L|}$$

The denominator of Equation (4) can be expressed as an expanded form of Taylor series by retaining the terms upto second degree in x and y, as follows:

$$I_{diff}(x, y) = T_5x^2 + T_4xy + T_3y^2 + T_2x + T_1y + T_0 \tag{5}$$

where T_i is a function of parameters a, b, and c.

Once the initial forward-difference parameters have been evaluated, Equation (5) can be evaluated by performing only two additions for each pixel position (x, y), thereby, reducing the calculations. Even after these simplifications, the fast Phong shading method still takes approximately double processing time to shade a surface as compared to Gouraud shading.

15. Describe the ray tracing algorithm for surface rendering.

Ans. Ray-tracing algorithm is a simple and powerful technique used for surface rendering developed by Turner Whitted in 1979. It is an extension of basic ray-casting method in a sense that it not only looks for visible surfaces for each pixel, but also collects various intensity contributions by repeatedly bouncing the pixel ray around the scene (as shown in Figure 9.17). In ray-casting method, as soon as a ray hits a surface in a scene, it is not traced further. However, in case of ray-tracing method, when a ray hits a surface, we do not stop; rather, the reflection and refraction rays generated after the intersection are also taken into account. Thus, the ray-tracing algorithm not only detects visible surfaces, but also obtains global reflection and transmission effects, identifies shadow areas, generates perspective-projection views, and identifies illumination effects from multiple light sources.

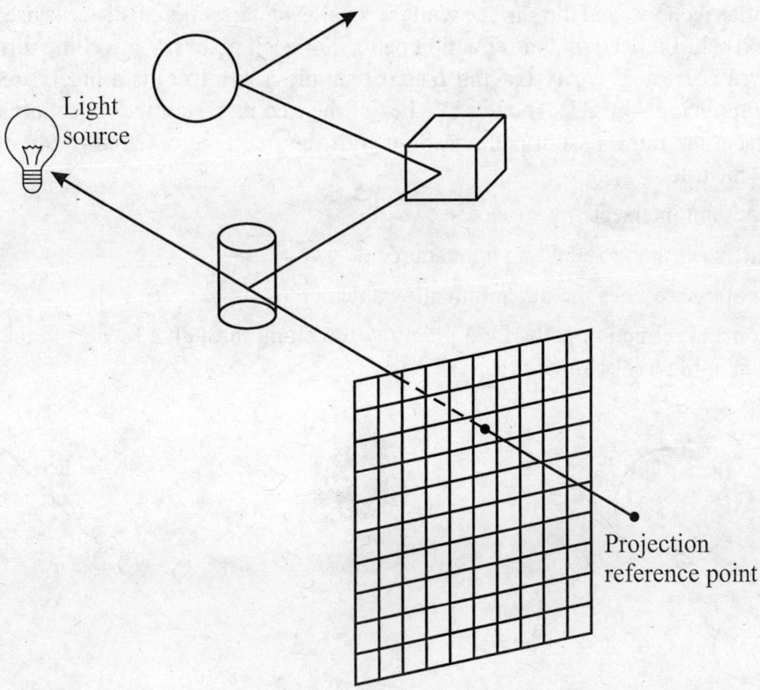

Figure 9.17 Ray-tracing Method

Like ray-casting method, the basic ray-tracing algorithm is also based on the concept of geometric optics. Light rays from the surfaces in a scene originate in all directions, and few of them pass through the pixel positions on the projection plane. Since there can be an infinite number of rays in a scene and we are interested in only those rays which pass through the pixel positions, we can determine the intensity contributions for each pixel by tracing the light-ray path backward from that pixel position through the scene.

As shown in Figure 9.17, the pixel positions in a ray-tracing method lie on the xy-plane and the projection reference point lie on the z-axis. The geometry of the scene is described in this coordinate system and the pixel rays are generated. Each ray originates at the projection reference point, passes through pixel centre, and continues through the scene forming the various branches along reflection and transmission paths. This generates a perspective-projection view of the scene.

For each pixel ray, all the surfaces in the scene are processed to determine whether there are any ray-surface intersections. If the ray intersects a surface, the distance from the pixel to the surface intersection point is calculated. Once all the surfaces have been processed, the surface with the smallest intersection distance is considered to be the visible surface for that pixel. From each visible surface, the ray is reflected off along the specular-reflection path. For a transparent surface, a ray is sent through the surface in the refraction direction. These reflected and refracted rays are known as **secondary rays**.

Now, the same ray-processing method is repeated for the secondary rays. Surfaces are tested for the secondary ray intersections, and the surface with the smallest intersection distance is used to recursively produce the next set of reflection and refraction paths. For each pixel ray travelling through the scene, a ray-tracing tree is created. A **ray-tracing tree** (or simply a **ray tree**) is a binary tree whose nodes represent the intersected surfaces. The left braches of the tree represent the reflection paths, and right branches represent the transmission paths. A branch of the tree is terminated if any of the following conditions become true:

- The ray does not intersect any surface.
- The ray intersects a non-reflecting light source.
- The depth of tree reaches the maximum allowable depth.

The reflection and refraction paths for a pixel ray travelling through a scene and the corresponding ray tree is shown in Figure 9.18.

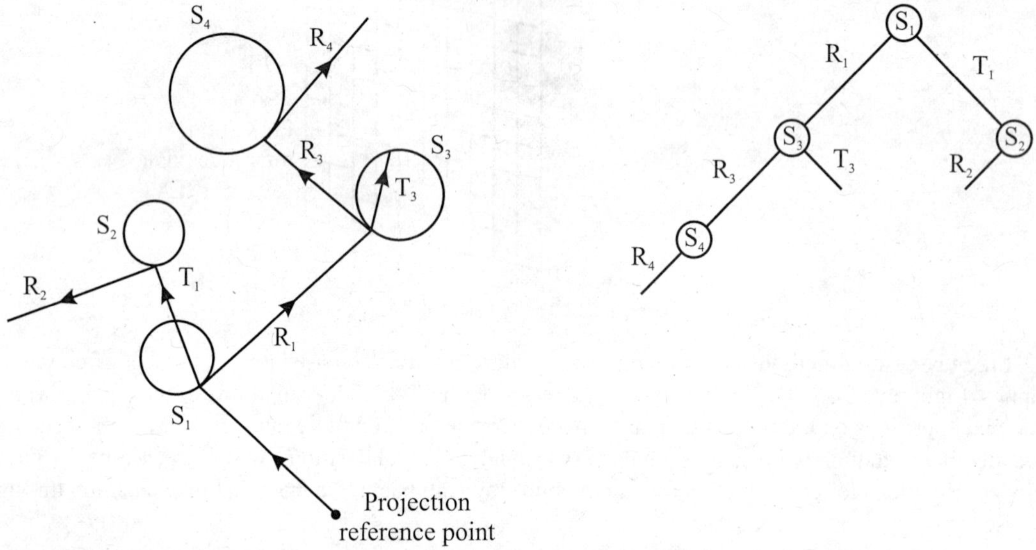

(a) Reflection and refraction paths (b) Ray-tracing tree

Figure 9.18 Constructing a Ray-tracing Tree

16. How can we determine the intensity of a pixel in ray-tracing method?

Ans. Once the binary tree for a pixel is complete, we need to determine the intensity contributions at that pixel position. The ray tree is evaluated in the bottom-up manner, starting from the leaf nodes of the tree. The surface intensity from each node of the tree is attenuated by the distance from the parent node and added to the intensity of the parent node. Thus, the intensity at the root node would be the sum of the attenuated intensities of its child nodes. The intensity at the root node is assigned to the pixel.

The surface intensity contribution at each surface intersection is determined by invoking the basic illumination model. This intensity value is stored at the surface-node position in the pixel tree. A ray that intersects the non-reflecting light source can be assigned the intensity of the light source. If the primary ray does not intersect any surface, the ray-tracing tree is empty and the pixel is assigned the background intensity. If the ray intersects a reflecting surface, then we use unit vectors to calculate the reflected light intensity. Consider a reflecting surface shown in Figure 9.19, which is intersected by a ray. For ray-tracing calculations, we consider the following unit vectors:

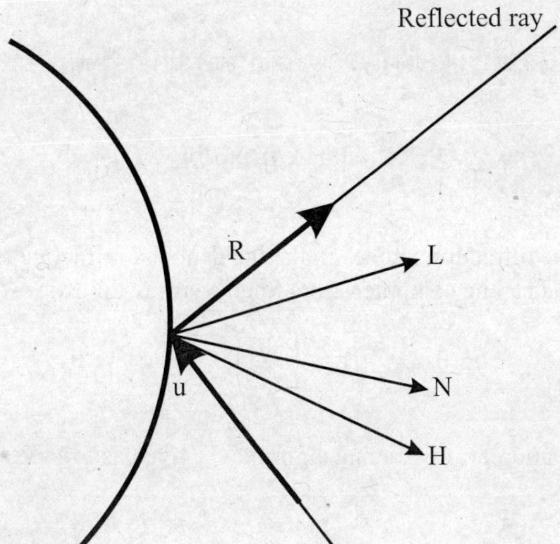

Figure 9.19 Unit Vectors at the Surface of an Object.

- u is the unit vector in the direction of the incoming ray path
- N is the unit surface normal vector
- R is the unit reflection vector, R = u - (2u.N)N
- L is the unit vector indicating the direction of the point light source
- V is unit viewpoint vector in the viewing direction, V = -u
- H is the unit vector halfway between L and V.

For a transparent surface, we also need to determine the intensity contributions from the light refracted through the surface. The source of this contribution can be located by tracing a secondary ray along the transmission direction T as shown in Figure 9.20. We can obtain the unit transmission vector T from vectors u and N as follows:

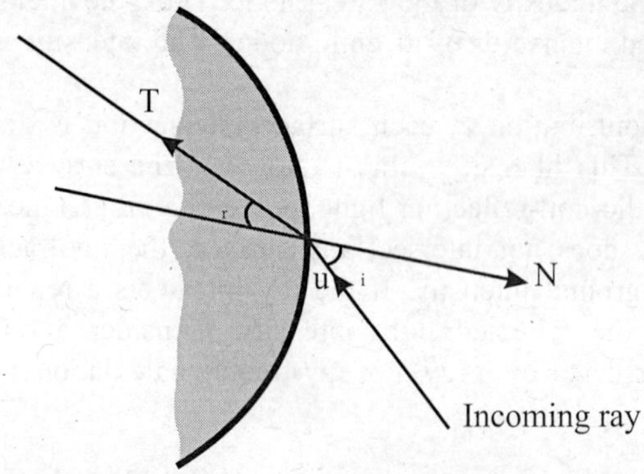

Figure 9.20 Refracted-ray Transmission Path T through a Transparent Object

$$T = \frac{\eta_i}{\eta_r} u - \left(\cos \theta_r - \frac{\eta_i}{\eta_r} \cos \theta_i \right) N$$

where η_i and η_r are the refraction indices in the incident and refracting material, respectively. θ_r is the angle of refraction, and can be computed from Snell's law as follows:

$$\cos \theta_r = \sqrt{1 - \left(\frac{\eta_i}{\eta_r} \right)^2 (1 - \cos^2 \theta_i)}$$

Now, the intensity Equation for ray tracing algorithm is given as follows:

$$I = I_{local} + (1 - k_t) I_{refl} + k_t I_{trans}$$

where

I_{local} is the intensity at the intersection, $1-k_t$ is the opacity factor – ranges from 0 to 1, I_{refl} is the reflected intensity, k_t measures the transparency of the surface – ranges from 0 (for opaque surfaces) to 1 (for perfect transparent surfaces), and I_{trans} is the transmitted intensity.

The local intensity can be computed from any illumination model as follows:

$$I_{local} = k_a I_a + I_{light} \left[k_d (N \cdot L) + k_s (V \cdot R)^n \right]$$

where k_a is the ambient-reflection coefficient – ranges from 0 to 1, I_a is the ambient light intensity, I_{light} is the intensity of light source, k_d is the diffuse-reflection coefficient – ranges from 0 to 1, k_s is the specular-reflection coefficient – ranges from 0 to 1, and n is the specular-reflection exponent – varies from 1 (for dull surfaces) to several hundreds (for shiny surfaces).

17. Explain mathematically how ray-surface intersection can be calculated for spheres.

Ans. If a ray is described with an initial position P_0 and unit direction vector, u (see Figure 9.21), then the coordinates of any point, say P, which are along the ray at a specific distance d from P_0 can be calculated from the following Equation:

$$P = P_0 + du \tag{1}$$

This Equation is termed as **ray Equation**. The initial value of P_0 can either be set as the pixel position on the projection plane, or could be selected as a projection reference point. And, the initial value of unit vector (u) can be calculated as follows:

$$u = \frac{P_{pixel} - P_{prp}}{|P_{pixel} - P_{prp}|} \tag{2}$$

where P_{pixel} refers to the position of the pixel through which the ray passes and P_{prp} refers to the projection reference point.

Now at each intersected surface, values of P_0 and u are updated for both reflection and refraction rays (i.e., secondary rays) at the ray-surface intersection point. For such rays, reflection direction for u is R while the transmission direction is T. Therefore, in case of secondary ray-surface intersection, we need to simultaneously solve both the ray Equation and the surface Equation for each individual object in the scene.

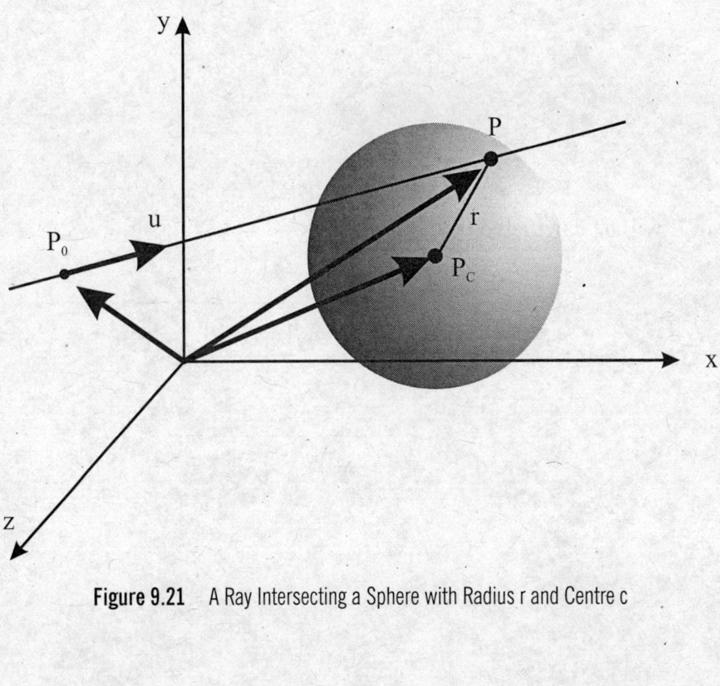

Figure 9.21 A Ray Intersecting a Sphere with Radius r and Centre c

The simplest object that can be ray traced is a sphere. To find surface intersection coordinates for a sphere, consider a sphere of radius r and center position P_c. Then any point, say P, on that surface must meet the following sphere Equation:

$$|P - P_c|^2 - r^2 = 0 \tag{3}$$

Substituting the value of P of Equation (1) in Equation (3), we get:

$$|P_0 + du - P_c|^2 - r^2 = 0 \tag{4}$$

Let $\Delta P = P_c - P_0$ and then expanding Equation (4) to obtain quadratic Equation as:

$$d^2 - 2(u \cdot \Delta P)d + \left(|\Delta P|^2 - r^2\right) = 0 \tag{5}$$

Now, to find the solution of d, we first calculate discriminant (D) as:

$$\begin{aligned} D &= \sqrt{b^2 - 4ac} \\ &= \sqrt{4\,(u \cdot \Delta P)^2 - 4(|\Delta P|^2 - r^2)} \\ &= \pm 2\sqrt{(u \cdot \Delta P)^2 - |\Delta P|^2 + r^2} \end{aligned}$$

where,

$$\begin{aligned} a &= 1 \\ b &= -2\,(u \cdot \Delta P) \\ c &= |\Delta P|^2 - r^2 \end{aligned}$$

Finally, value of d will be calculated from the formula $\dfrac{-b \pm \sqrt{D}}{2a}$ as follows:

$$\begin{aligned} d &= \frac{-\left[-2\,(u \cdot \Delta P)\right] \pm 2\sqrt{(u \cdot \Delta P)^2 - |\Delta P|^2 + r^2}}{2 \times 1} \\ &= u \cdot \Delta P \pm \sqrt{(u \cdot \Delta P)^2 - |\Delta P|^2 + r^2} \end{aligned} \tag{6}$$

If the value of D is negative, the ray does not intersect the sphere. If $D = 0$, the ray touches the sphere. If $D > 0$, two intersection points are possible. In this case, we put the smaller of the two values in ray Equation (1) to obtain the surface-intersection coordinates.

In case of small spheres which are far from initial ray position, Equation (6) may result in round off errors. That is, if, $r^2 << |\Delta P|^2$ then we could lose the r^2 term in the precision error of $|\Delta P|^2$. Such situations can be avoided by rearranging the calculation for distance d as follows:

$$d = u \,.\, \Delta P \pm \sqrt{r^2 - |\Delta P - (u - \Delta P)\, u|^2}$$

18. Explain texture mapping.

Ans. Texture mapping (also known as **pattern mapping**) is a way to map patterns onto the geometric description of the object. Unlike shading an object where the same basic color in lighter or darker shade is assigned to every pixel on the object, texture mapping maps the entire image onto the object surface. An image or a picture that is placed on the surface of the objects is known as **texture map**. Texture mapping gives realism to the object by adding more detail to it. The textures can be defined as one-dimensional, two-dimensional or three-dimensional. A one-dimensional texture pattern (also known as **linear texture pattern**) can be specified in a one-dimensional array of color values, which defines a sequence of colors in a linear texture space. A two-dimensional texture pattern (also known as **surface texture pattern**) can be specified with two-dimensional array that defines the color values and position in this texture space. The three-dimensional texture patterns (also known as **volume texture patterns** or **solid textures**) are specified using three-dimensional texture-space coordinate, which can designate a set of colors for positions throughout a 3D region of space.

For texture mapping, we need a texture routine `texture(u,v)`, that produces a color or intensity value for each value of u and v. Here, u and v are the horizontal and vertical locations of the point in the image, respectively. The values of u and v lie between 0 and 1. The most common source of texture is bitmap representations of images (such as clip art, digital camera image, image produces using some program, etc.). In this case, the texture consists of a 2D array of color values, called **texels**. All we have to do is to associate the proper item in the array with the given values of u and v between 0 and 1.

Another method of adding texture pattern to an object is to define a mathematical function for the color variations that are to be applied. In this method, the programmer is free to describe his or her own function. Any function that can be computer for each value of u and v can provide a texture. The value produced by `texture(u,v)` can be used in different ways, such as to color the face itself to show the glowing effect on the face, to modulate the amount of light reflected from the face, or to alter the normal vector to the surface to add the bumpy appearance to the object.

The texture can be pasted onto a flat surface (like square, pentagon, etc.), or it can also be wrapped on curved surfaces (like cylinder or spheres). It is easier to paste texture on a flat surface as compared to wrapping it on a curved surface. For wrapping texture on a sphere, we define v to be the latitude of the point, and u to be the longitude of the point on the sphere. Figure 9.22 shows example of texture mapping on a flat surface and curved surface.

(a) Pasting an image of a wall on a cube surface

(b) Wrapping image of globe around a sphere

Figure 9.22 Texture mapping

19. Write briefly about adding shadows of objects.

Ans. Shadows give further more realism to the objects in a scene, and provide additional depth to the scene. With the help of shadows, one can determine the position of the light source and the objects in the scene. For example, if an object A casts a shadow on surface B, then it is clear that A is between B and a point light source. A point on the object is in shadow relative to a given light source if rays from that light source cannot directly reach the point. In simple words, shadowed points are the points that are not visible from the light source.

There are several methods for generating shadows in an image. The simplest way is to generate shadows as texture. This technique displays the shadows that are cast onto a flat surface by a point light source. The main problem with this technique is to determine the shape of the shadow that is cast. To determine the shape of the shadow, each of the faces of the object is projected onto the plane of the floor, using the source as the center of projection. In fact the shadow is the union of the projections of all the faces. The main drawback of this technique that it is restricted to casting shadows onto planar surfaces only.

Another technique of drawing shadows uses an auxiliary second depth buffer known as **shadow z-buffer**, for each light source. Though this technique requires a lot of memory, it is not restricted to casting shadows onto planar surfaces only. The basic idea behind this technique is that all those points which are hidden from the light source must be in shadow; whereas if no object lies between a point and the light source, the point must not be in shadow. The shadow buffer basically contains a depth picture of the scene from the point of view of light source. Each element of shadow buffer records the distance from the light source to the closest object in the scene in associated direction.

20. Write the steps for rendering shadows in a scene.

Ans. There are two steps for rendering shadows in a scene:

1. **Loading shadow buffer:** Each element in the shadow buffer is first initialized with value 1.0, which indicates the largest pseudodepth possible. Then, with the help of camera positioned at the light source, each face in the scene is scan converted to only test the pseudodepth of a point on the face. Now, each element in the shadow buffer records the smallest pseudodepth seen so far. Note that calculations in shadow buffer are performed independent of the eye position. That

is, change in the position of eye does not affect the elements in the shadow buffer—the shadow buffer is loaded only once. However, in case objects are moved relative to the light source, the shadow buffer must be recalculated.

2. **Rendering the scene:** Once the shadow buffer is loaded, each face is rendered in the scene using the eye camera as usual.

MULTIPLE CHOICE QUESTIONS

1. Which of these hidden-surface elimination algorithms is not an object-space method?
   (a) Back-face detection (b) Octree method
   (c) Depth-buffer method (d) Ray-casting method
2. Which of these statements is not true for A-buffer algorithm?
   (a) It is an extension of z-buffer method.
   (b) It can deal with only opaque surfaces.
   (c) It was developed by Lucasfilm to be implemented in the surface-rendering system named REYES.
   (d) It creates a linked list of surfaces for each pixel position.
3. Which algorithm is also known as Painter's algorithm?
   (a) Depth-sorting algorithm (b) Ray-casting algorithm
   (c) Depth-buffer algorithm (d) None of these
4. Which data structure is used in binary space partitioning algorithm?
   (a) Linked list (b) Graph
   (c) Tree (d) Array
5. Which of these hidden-surface algorithms is based on geometric optics?
   (a) Ray-casting method (b) Light intensity method
   (c) Depth-sorting method (d) Back-face detection
6. Which of these is a surface rendering method?
   (a) Constant-intensity shading (b) Gouraud shading
   (c) Phong shading (d) All of these
7. Which of these statements is invalid for ray-tracing algorithm?
   (a) This technique is used for surface rendering.
   (b) It is based geometric optics.
   (c) It only looks for visible surfaces for each pixel position.
   (d) All of these
8. Which of these rays are also known as secondary rays?
   (a) Reflected rays (b) Refracted rays
   (c) Both (a) and (b) (d) None of these
9. In which algorithm a ray tree is generated?
   (a) Ray-casting algorithm (b) Ray-tracing algorithm
   (c) Both (a) and (b) (d) None of these

10. Which of these surface rendering algorithms suffers from Mach banding problem?
    (a) Phong shading
    (b) Gouraud shading
    (c) Fast Phong shading
    (d) Constant-intensity shading

Answers. 1. c 2. b 3. a 4. c 5. a 6. d 7. c 8. c 9. b 10. b

10

Graphics Programming

1. What is OpenGL? Describe the OpenGL libraries. Which header files need to be included for writing an OpenGL program?

Ans. OpenGL is an application programming interface that consists of library of routines for specifying graphics primitives, attributes, geometric and viewing transformations, and many other graphical operations. OpenGL library is specifically designed for drawing images of complex three-dimensional scenes; however, it can also be used for drawing two-dimensional scenes as a special case of three-dimensions where all the `z` coordinate values are 0. Since OpenGL is designed to be device independent, input and output routines are not included in its library. In order to use input/output functions in OpenGL programs, additional libraries need to be included.

The **OpenGL basic library** (also known as **OpenGL core library**) is fundamental OpenGL library which forms the permanent part of OpenGL. The functions in basic OpenGL library are named in such a manner that each function name is prefixed with `gl` followed by the name of function with its first letter in capitals. For example, `glBegin()`, `glEnd()`, `glClear()`, `glFlush()`, `glClearColor()`, etc. In addition, the symbolic constants are named in such a way that they begin with letters `GL` followed by an underscore (_) and the name of the constant in capitals. For example, `GL_POINTS`, `GL_LINES`, `GL_POLYGON`, `GL_RGB`, etc.

In addition to core library, three other libraries of utility functions are also available. The functions in these libraries are used for handling special operations. These libraries are as follows:

- **GLUT:** It is the OpenGL Utility Toolkit that provides routines for opening and closing windows, developing and managing menu items and managing events. The functions in GLUT library are prefixed with `glut`.
- **GLU:** It is the OpenGL Utility Library that provides high-level routines for handling certain matrix operations, drawing quadratic surfaces (such as ellipsoids, paraboloids, hyperboloids and spheres), processing surface-rendering operations, and other complex tasks. In addition, it provides a number of routines that assist in decomposition of complex shapes into simpler ones such as triangles. The functions in GLUT library are prefixed with `glu`.
- **GLUI:** It is the OpenGL User Interface Library that provides functions to add advanced controls and menus to OpenGL programs. This library can operate properly only if GLUT is available.

For writing a program in OpenGL, certain header files must be included in the program. These header files are as follows:

```
#include <windows.h>   //for writing programs for Windows
#include <gl/gl.h>     //for OpenGL basic library
#include <gl/glu.h>    //for GLU library
#include <gl/glut.h>   //for GLUT library
```

Note that the header file `windows.h` must be included before OpenGL and GLU header files because it contains macros which are required by Microsoft Windows version of the OpenGL libraries. In addition, if we include `glut.h` header file, we can omit the `gl.h` and `glu.h` header files as `glut.h` makes sure that the functions of `gl.h` and `glu.h` are included correctly.

2. Discuss the various data types supported by OpenGL.

Ans. The various data types supported by OpenGL are signed and unsigned char, short and unsigned short, int and unsigned int, float, and double. These data types along with their size and OpenGL type name are listed in Table 10.1.

Table 10.1 OpenGL Data Types

Data type	Size	OpenGL type name
integer	8 bits	`GLbyte`
short	16 bits	`GLshort`
integer	32 bits	`GLint`
float	32 bits	`GLfloat`
double	64 bits	`GLdouble`
unsigned integer	8 bits	`GLubyte`
unsigned short	16 bits	`GLushort`
unsigned integer	32 bits	`GLuint`

3. What are callback functions? What is the need of registering the callback functions?

Ans. One of the most important properties of Windows-based programs is that they are event driven. That is, the programs respond when some event occurs such as keyboard hit, mouse click, etc. The system automatically manages the events on the first-come, first-serve basis. To implement event-driven programming, the programmer organizes the program as a collection of **callback functions** that are executed when an event occurs. While writing the code for the callback function, the programmer only needs to specify what should happen when an event occurs, but no need to specify when the function is to be called. The system automatically handles it.

Only writing the code for the callback function is not enough, the programmer must associate each type of event with callback function. This is known as **registering** the callback function. For example, whenever the system determines that a screen window should be redrawn (when the window is opened for the first time, or when it is resized), it issues the redraw event. In that case, the `glutDisplayFunc()` of GLUT library is called, which needs to be registered with a callback function say `display()`. This function tells the system what should happen when the redraw event is triggered. The code for the `display()` function is written by the programmer. The callback function is registered by the event type using the following statement.

```
glutDisplayFunc(display);
  /*the name of the callback function is chosen by the
programmer*/
```

4. Describe the OpenGL basic primitives.

Ans. OpenGL provides tools for drawing various output primitives such as points, lines, circles, polygons, etc. Most of the output primitives are specified using a set of vertices (or corners). Thus, to draw such objects in OpenGL, a list of vertices is specified between two OpenGL functions calls `glBegin()` and `glEnd()`. The object which needs to be drawn is passed as an argument to the `gl-Begin()`, and `glEnd()` command terminates the list of primitives. For example, to draw a straight line segment with integer Cartesian endpoints (100, 30) and (10, 100), the code segment is as follows:

```
glBegin(GL_LINES);
 glVertex2i(100,30);
 glVertex2i(10,100);
glEnd();
```

Similarly, to draw other primitives such as points and polygons, `GL_POINTS` and `GL_POLYGON` are passed as an argument to `glBegin()`.

The function `glVertex2i()` can be used in different ways. It basically depends on the number and type of arguments passed to the function. For example, if instead of integer coordinates, floating-point coordinates need to be specified, then the following form is used.

```
glBegin(GL_LINES);
 glVertex2f(100.5,30.5);
 glVertex2f(10.5,100.5);
glEnd();
```

If you want to draw a line in 3D space, then you also need to specify the `z` coordinate. For this, the following code is written:

```
glBegin(GL_LINES);
 glVertex3i(100,30,50);
 glVertex3i(10,100,50);
glEnd();
```

In addition to drawing objects, you can also change the current size of points, current background color, current color of drawing, current size of the window, and so on. These are called **state variables**. The value of a state variable remains active as long as it is not changed by giving another command. The point size can be changed using `glPointSize()`, which accepts one floating-point value specifying the size of the point.

To change the background color of the display window, `glClearColor()` is used. It is written as follows:

```
glClearColor(1.0,1.0,1.0,0.0);//setting drawing color to white
```

The first three parameters specify RGB components, and last parameter is called **alpha value**, which specifies a degree of transparency of the objects. An alpha value of 0.0 indicates a completely transparent object, and an alpha value of 1.0 indicates an opaque object. The alpha values can also be used to determine the resulting color for two overlapping objects. Note that the command `glClearColor()` only assigns the color to the display window, it does not put the display window on the screen. To do so, following OpenGL function is used.

```
glClear(GL_COLOR_BUFFER_BIT);
```

This command can also be used to clear the screen. In addition to setting the background color, we can also set different color schemes for drawing different objects on the screen. To change the color of the drawing, the function `glcolor3f()` is used, which takes three parameters—one for each red, green and blue color. The values lie between 0.0 and 1.0. For instance, to set the drawing color to red, the following command is given.

```
glColor3f(1.0,0.0,0.0);     //setting drawing color to red
```

Similarly, other colors can also be set as follows:

```
glColor3f(0.0,1.0,0.0);     //setting drawing color to green
glColor3f(0.0,0.0,1.0);     //setting drawing color to blue
glColor3f(0.0,0.0,0.0);     //setting drawing color to black
glColor3f(1.0,0.0,1.0);     //setting drawing color to magenta
glColor3f(0.0,1.0,1.0);     //setting drawing color to cyan
glColor3f(1.0,1.0,1.0);     //setting drawing color to bright white
```

Before drawing any object on the screen it is necessary to establish the coordinate system. Since OpenGL is mainly designed for drawing 3D objects, in which 2D object is treated as a special case of 3D viewing it processes even a simple 2D drawing through the full 3D viewing operations. To set up the coordinate system, following OpenGL commands are used.

```
glMatrixMode(GL_PROJECTION);
gluOrtho2D(0.0, 640.0, 0.0, 480.0);
```

These two statements specify that an orthogonal (parallel) projection is to be used to map the contents of a 2D rectangular area of world coordinates to the viewing coordinates. The first statement determines how a scene is to be projected onto the screen, and second statement sets the coordinate reference frame within the display window which is 640 pixels wide and 480 pixels high. The coordinates (0.0, 0.0) represent the lower-left corner of the display window and (640.0, 480.0) represent the upper-right corner of the window.

In case, we want to produce a perspective projection of the objects, we can use the `gluPerspective()` in place of `gluOrtho2D()`, which has the following prototype.

```
gluPerspective(angle,aspect,dnear,dfar);
```

where `angle` represents the field-of-view angle—the angle between the top and bottom clipping planes. Its value ranges from 0° to 180°; `aspect` is the aspect ratio (width/height) of the clipping window; `dnear` is the distance of the view point to the near clipping plane; `dfar` is the distance of the view point to the far clipping plane.

5. How to open the initial window for drawing? Is it possible to create multiple display windows for an application? If yes, how?

Ans. Since OpenGL functions are device independent and opening a screen window for drawing is device system dependent, we therefore use GLUT that provides functions for opening a window on any system. The statements for opening the display window is written in `main()` function. The code segment for opening the window for drawing is as follows:

```
//header files and callback functions
...
void main(int argc, char** argv)
```

```
{
    glutInit(&argc, argv);        //initializing GLUT library
    glutInitDisplayMode(GLUT_SINGLE|GLUT_RGB)
                                  //setting display mode
    glutInitWindowPosition(30,20);     //setting window position
    glutInitWindowSize(640,480);  //setting window size
    glutCreateWindow("The window is opened"); //opening the window
    ...   //statements for drawing objects on the screen
    glutMainLoop();   //continue displaying the objects
}
```

The explanation of the functions is as follows:

- **`glutInit(&argc, argv)`** : This function is used to initialize the GLUT library. It takes the command-line arguments as its parameters.
- **`glutInitDisplayMode(GLUT_SINGLE|GLUT_RGB)`** : This function is used to set the buffering and color mode options for the display window. The symbolic constant `GLUT_SINGLE` specifies that a single refresh buffer is to be used for display window, and `GLUT_RGB` specifies that the RGB color mode is to be used for selecting color modes.
- **`glutInitWindowPosition(30,20)`** : This function is used to set the top-left corner (origin) of the window. In our example, the window will be placed at the position which is 30 pixels right from the left edge of the screen and 20 pixels down from the top edge of the screen. The user can move this window wherever required, while the program is running.
- **`glutInitWindowSize(640,480)`** : This function is used to set the initial size of the window. The user can resize the window, when the program is running.
- **`glutCreateWindow("The window is opened")`** : This function actually opens and displays the screen window, and puts the text "`The window is opened`" on the title bar.
- **`glutMainLoop()`** : This function must be the last statement in the OpenGL program. It basically displays all the graphics on the display window and continues to display until user closes the display window or gives some input from the keyboard or mouse (in case of interactive applications).

One can also create multiple display windows for an application. In that case, each window is assigned a positive integer starting from 1. It is known as **display-window identifier**. The identifier is assigned at the time of initiation of display window, as shown here.

```
windowID=glutCreateWindow("A display window");
```

The variable `windowID` stores the unique identifier for the display window. It can be used to change the display parameters of the window. In addition, it can be used to delete the display window using the following statement.

```
glutDestroyWindow(windowID);
```

When multiple windows are created for an application, we can set any window as the current display window using the following statement.

```
glutSetWindow(windowID);
```

We can query the system to determine which window is the current display window using the following statement.

```
currentwindowID=glutGetWindow();
```

6. How to draw dots using OpenGL?

Ans. To draw dots or points in OpenGL, the following code is written.

```
glBegin(GL_POINTS);
  glVertex2i(100,80);      //coordinates of the first dot
  glVertex2i(50,80);       //coordinates of the second dot
  glVertex2i(100,100);     //coordinates of the third dot
glEnd();
```

7. Write the OpenGL code for drawing an open and a closed polyline of thickness 4.0, and in blue color.

Ans. A polyline consists of line segments joined end to end. To draw a polyline, the following code is written:

```
glBegin(GL_LINE_STRIP);
  glColor3f(0.0,0.0,1.0);     //setting the drawing color to blue
  glLineWindth(4.0);     //setting the line thickness to 4.0
  glVertex2i(10,20);
  glVertex2i(70,20);
  glVertex2i(10,60);
  glVertex2i(70,60);
glEnd();
```

The resulting polyline is shown in Figure 10.1(a).

If the endpoints of the last line are joined to the starting coordinates, the polyline results into a closed polyline. For this, the coding will be same; only the symbolic constant `GL_LINE_STRIP` is replaced with `GL_LINE_LOOP`, as shown here.

```
glBegin(GL_LINE_LOOP);
  glColor3f(0.0,0.0,1.0);     //setting the drawing color to blue
  glLineWindth(4.0);     //setting the line thickness to 4.0
  glVertex2i(10,70);
  glVertex2i(50,70);
  glVertex2i(10,10);
  glVertex2i(50,10);
glEnd();
```

The resulting closed polyline is shown in Figure 10.1(b).

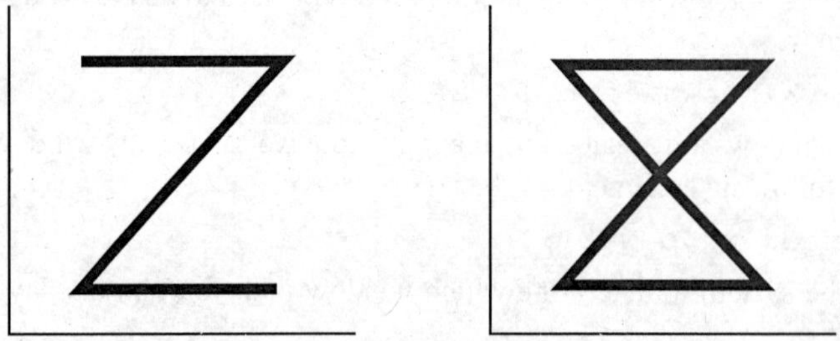

(a) Polyline of thickness 4.0 (b) Closed polyline of thickness 4.0

Figure 10.1 Drawing Open and Closed Polyline

To draw a polygon, the symbolic constant `GL_LINE_LOOP` is replaced with `GL_POLYGON`, as shown here.

```
glBegin(GL_POLYGON);
 glVertex2i(10,70);
 glVertex2i(50,70);
 glVertex2i(10,10);
 glVertex2i(50,10);
glEnd();
```

Note that `GL_POLYGON` can only be used to draw simple and convex polygon. Hence, the closed polyline shown in Figure 10.1(b) cannot be drawn using `GL_POLYGON` constant.

8. Describe the OpenGL glRect() function.

Ans. A rectangle is a special case of polygon in which the sides are aligned with the coordinate axes. One can draw a rectangle or a square using the `GL_POLYGON` symbolic constant, as follows:

```
glBegin(GL_POLYGON);
 glVertex2i(10,10);
 glVertex2i(40,10);
 glVertex2i(40,40);
 glVertex2i(10,40);
glEnd();
```

However, OpenGL provides the in-built function `glRecti ()`, which accepts the coordinates of opposite corners as parameters, as shown below.

```
glRecti(10,10,40,40);
```

where first two values are the coordinates of lower-left corner, and second two values are the coordinates of upper-right corner.

9. What is use of passing parameters to a function in OpenGL? Write the OpenGL code for drawing pentagon of different sizes.

Ans. Parameters allow user to draw same figure in different sizes depending on the values of the parameters. They give more flexibility in drawing group of objects of varying sizes. To draw a pentagon, we need to pass the height and width of the pentagon, and the coordinates of the starting point, as shown below.

```
void pentagon(GLintPoint top, GLint width, GLint height)
{
   //top specifies the coordinates of the top vertex of the pentagon
 glBegin(GL_LINE_LOOP);
    glVertex2i(top.x, top.y);
    glVertex2i(top.x+width/2, top.y-3*height/8);
    glVertex2i(top.x+width/2, top.y-height);
    glVertex2i(top.x-width/2, top.y-height);
    glVertex2i(top.x-width/2, top.y-3*height/8);
 glEnd();
}
```

If we specify `top` at (70, 120), `width`=60 and `height`=80, the coordinates of the resulting pentagon will be as follows:

...

```
glVertex2i(70, 120);
glVertex2i(100, 90);
glVertex2i(100, 40);
glVertex2i(40, 40);
glVertex2i(40, 90);
    ...
```

10. Describe the OpenGL GL_TRIANGLES and GL_QUADS symbolic constants.

Ans. `GL_TRIANGLES` accepts the listed vertices three at a time and draws a separate triangle for each. On the other hand, `GL_QUADS` accepts four vertices at a time and draws a separate quadrilateral for each.

11. How window-to-viewport mapping is done in OpenGL?

Ans. We need to set up the window coordinates and viewport coordinates in our OpenGL program. OpenGL automatically clips off the parts of the objects lying outside the world window. OpenGL `glViewport()` function is used to set up the coordinates for the viewport. The syntax of `glViewport()` is as follows.

```
void glViewport(GLint x, GLint y, GLint width, GLint height);
```

To set up the window and viewport, the following code is written.

```
//setWindow callback function for setting the world window
void setWindow(GLdouble left, GLdouble right, GLdouble bottom, GLdouble top)
{
 glMatrixMode(GL_PROJECTION);
 glLoadIdentity();
 gluOrtho2D(left, right, bottom, top);
}
//setViewport callback function for setting the viewport
void setViewport(GLint left, GLint right, GLint bottom, GLint top)
{
 glViewport(left, bottom, right-left, top-bottom);

//right-left specifies the width and top-bottom specifies the height
}
```

12. Discuss the various types of modes that can be used with the glMatrixMode() function of OpenGL.

Ans. `glMatrixMode` function is used for specifying the current matrix for projection transformations, geometric-viewing transformations, texture transformations, or color transformations. OpenGL provides four types of modes that can be used with the `glMatrixMode` function. These modes are as follows:

- **Projection mode:** This mode designates the matrix that is to be used for the projection transformations, which determine how a scene is to be projected onto the screen. To set up the projection mode, the matrix `GL_PROJECTION` is passed as parameter to `glMatrixMode()` function, as shown below.

```
glMatrixMode(GL_PROJECTION);
```

This matrix is used to define the frustum, which determines the objects or the portions of objects to be clipped.

- **Modelview mode:** This mode sets up a matrix used to store and combine the geometric transformations. The modelview mode can be specified using the following statement.

```
glMatrixMode(GL_MODELVIEW);
```

- **Texture mode:** This mode sets up a matrix used for mapping texture patterns to surfaces. To set up the texture mode, the following statement is used.

```
glMatrixMode(GL_TEXTURE);
```

- **Color mode:** This mode sets up a matrix used to convert from one color model to another. To set up the texture mode, the following statement is used.

```
glMatrixMode(GL_COLOR);
```

13. Describe the OpenGL functions used for performing 3D geometric transformations.

Ans. OpenGL provides routines for performing basic transformations (translation, scaling and rotation). These routines are as follows:

- **`glTranslated(dx, dy, dz)`**: This function translates an object by `dx` in `x` axis, by `dy` in `y` axis and by `dz` in `z` axis. In case of 2D transformation, the value of `d z` is set to 0. For example, to move an object 20 units in *x* direction and 10 units in *y* direction, the following statement is written.

```
glTranslated(20.0, 10.0, 0.0);
```

The suffix `d` in `glTranslated()` specifies the data type of the argument (which is, double). There is also the version `gltranslatef()`, which takes float arguments.

- **`glScaled(sx, sy, sz)`**: This function scales an object by a factor of `sx` in `x` direction, by a factor of `sy` in *y* direction and by a factor of `sz` in *z* direction. In case of 2D, the value of `sz` is set to 1.0. For example, to scale an object by a factor of 3 in *x* direction and by a factor of 2 in `y` direction, the following statement is written.

```
glScaled(3.0, 2.0, 1.0);
```

There is also the version `glScalef()`, which takes float arguments.

- **`glRotated(angle, x, y, z)`**: This function rotates an object by an `angle` (specified in degrees) about one of the axis. For example, to rotate an object by an angle of 45° about the `z` axis, following statement is written:

```
glRotated(45.0, 0.0, 0.0, 1.0);
```

There is also the version `glRotatef()`, which takes float arguments.

For performing geometric transformations, we first need to set up the modelview matrix using the following statement.

```
glMatrixMode(GL_MODELVIEW);
```

14. What does gluLookAt() function do?

Ans. The `gluLookAt()` function is basically used for setting the camera position and orientation. It accepts nine values as parameters. The first three values specify the camera position or an eye point, the next three values indicate the point we are looking at (that is, the reference point indicating the center of the scene) and the last three values defines the up vector. The up vector is most often set to (0, 1, 0), which implies that the direction described by the up vector projected onto the viewing plane is mapped to the positive `y` axis so that it points upward in the viewport. The syntax of `gluLookAt()` is as follows:

```
void gluLookAt(GLdouble eyex, GLdouble eyey, GLdouble eyez, GLdouble
lookx, GLdouble looky, GLdouble lookz, GLdouble upx, GLdouble upy,
GLdouble upz);
```

15. Discuss the pushMatrix() and popMatrix() functions of OpenGL.

Ans. Today's graphics programs demand complex scenes with many objects, each rendered under its own transform. To facilitate this, as mentioned, OpenGL stores transformations in a stack. OpenGL provides two functions for processing the matrices in a stack, which are `glPushMatrix()` and `glPopMatrix()`.

- **`glPushMatrix`:** This function copies the current matrix at the top of the active stack and stores that in the second stack position also. In this way, we get two copies of the same matrix at the top two positions of the stack. This duplication is required because when we pop the top of the stack, then there must be at least two matrices in the stack; otherwise an error is generated.
- **`glPopMatrix`:** This function pops the matrix stored at the top position of the stack, and the matrix at the second position becomes the top of the stack.

16. Discuss the OpenGL glOrtho() function.

Ans. The `glOrtho()` function of OpenGL describes a perspective matrix that produces a parallel projection. In parallel (or orthogonal) projection, no adjustments are made for the distance of the objects from the camera. All the objects on the screen appear the same size irrespective of their distance from the camera. The function is used as follows:

```
glOrtho(GLdouble left, GLdouble right, GLdouble bottom, GLdouble
top, GLdouble near, GLdouble far);
```

where `left` and `right` are the coordinates for the left and right vertical clipping planes, respectively; `bottom` and `top` are the coordinates for the bottom and top horizontal clipping planes, respectively; `near` and `far` are the distances to the nearer and farther depth clipping planes, respectively. A negative value indicates that the plane is behind the viewer.

17. Discuss the OpenGL functions used to create basic 3D objects.

Ans. GLUT provides several built-in functions to create basic 3D shapes such as cube, sphere, torus, teapot, and many more. These objects can be represented as a wireframe model as well as a solid model. GLUT provides functions to represent the objects in both ways. These functions are discussed as follows:

- **Cube:** A cube has four faces, where each face is a square. To represent the wireframe model of a cube, the following function is used.

```
glutWireCube(GLdouble size); //size is the length of each side
```

To represent the solid model of a cube, the following function is used.

```
glutSolidCube(GLdouble size);
```

- **Sphere:** To represent the wireframe model of a sphere, the following function is used.

```
glutWireSphere(GLdouble r, GLint nLongitudes, GLint nLatitudes);
```

where `r` is the radius of the sphere; `nLongitudes` and `nLatitudes` represent the number of longitude and latitude lines that will be used to approximate the spherical surface as a quadrilateral mesh.

To represent the solid model of a sphere, the following function is used.

```
glutSolidSphere(GLdouble r, GLint nLongitudes, GLint nLatitudes);
```

- **Cone:** The wireframe model of a cone can be represented using the following function.

```
glutWireCone(GLdouble br, GLdouble height, GLint nLongitudes,
GLint nLatitudes);
```

where `br` is the radius of the cone base; `height` is the height of the cone; `nLongitudes` and `nLatitudes` represent the number of longitude and latitude lines that will be used to approximate the conical surface as a quadrilateral mesh.

To represent the solid model of a cone, the following function is used.

```
glutSolidCone(GLdouble br, GLdouble height, GLint nLongitudes, GLint nLatitudes);
```

- **Torus:** A torus is described as a surface generated by revolving a circle in 3D space about the coplanar `z` axis. The wireframe model of a torus can be represented using the following function.

```
glutWireTorus(GLdouble inRad, GLdouble outRad, GLint nConcen,
GLint nRadial);
```

where `inRad` is the inner radius of the torus; `outRad` is the outer radius of the torus; `nConcen` is the number of concentric circles centered on the `z` axis to be used on the torus surface; `nRadial` is the number of radial slices through the torus surface.

To represent the solid model of a torus, the following function is used.

```
glutSolidTorus(GLdouble inRad, GLdouble outRad, GLint nConcen, GLint nRadial);
```

- **Teapot:** The teapot can be displayed as a mesh of over one thousand bicubic surface patches using the following function.

```
glutWireTeapot(GLdouble size);
```

where `size` is the maximum radius of the teapot bowl.

The surface of the teapot is generated using the OpenGL bezier curve functions. To represent the solid model of a torus, the following function is used.

```
glutSolidTeapot(GLdouble size);
```

- **Tetrahedron:** A regular tetrahedron is a triangular pyramid with four faces. The wireframe model of a tetrahedron is represented using the following function.

```
glutWireTetrahedron();
```

To represent the solid model of a tetrahedron, the following function is used.

```
glutSolidTetrahedron();
```

- **Octahedron:** A regular octahedron is a kind of polyhedron having eight equilateral triangular faces. The wireframe model of an octahedron is represented using the following function.

```
glutWireOctahedron();
```

To represent the solid model of an octahedron, the following function is used.

```
glutSolidOctahedron();
```

- **Dodecahedron:** A regular dodecahedron is a kind of polyhedron having 12 pentagonal faces. The wireframe model of a dodecahedron is represented using the following function.

```
glutWireDodecahedron();
```

To represent the solid model of a dodecahedron, the following function is used.

```
glutSolidDodecahedron();
```

- **Icosahedron:** A regular icosahedron is a kind of polyhedron having 20 equilateral triangular faces. The wireframe model of an icosahedron is represented using the following function.

```
glutWireIcosahedron();
```

To represent the solid model of an icosahedron, the following function is used.

```
glutSolidIcosahedron();
```

18. Describe various OpenGL illumination and surface rendering functions.

Ans. OpenGL provides various functions for setting up and using the light sources as well as for specifying the surface properties of objects in a scene. Some of these functions are discussed here.

`glLight*()`

This function is used to set the properties of a point light source. OpenGL allows you to define eight light sources, which are referred to by names `GL_LIGHT0`, `GL_LIGHT1`, `GL_LIGHT2`, and so on. The prototype of this function is as follows:

```
glLight*(lightName, lighProperty, propertyValue);
```

where

`*` can be replaced by `i` or `f` depending on the data type and property value;

`lightName` can be assigned one of the values from `GL_LIGHT0`, `GL_LIGHT1`, ..., `GL_LIGHT7`; `lightProperty` can be assigned one of the ten symbolic property constants which are used to set various properties of light source such as its position, type, color, attenuation and spotlight effects; `propertyValue` is the value for the `lightProperty`.

For example, to set the light source at a particular position, the following statements are written.

```
GLfloat lightPos [] = {2.0, 0.0, 3.0, 1.0};

glLightfv(GL_LIGHT0, GL_POSITION, lightPos);
```

The first statement specifies the position vector of the light source which is (2.0, 0.0, 3.0), and the last parameter indicates that the light source is local such as desk lamp, bulb, etc. For infinitely remote light source such as the sun, this value is 0.0, and (`x`, `y`, `z`) specifies the direction vector. The second statement sets the light source at this particular position. Figure 10.2 shows the effect of different positions of a light source.

Figure 10.2 Effect of Different Positions of Light Source

In addition to specifying the position of light source, we can also specify the colors of the light source. The three light-source colors (RGB) provide options for varying the lighting effects in a scene.

We can assign a different color to three types of light that a source emits: ambient, diffuse and specular. Thus, we can use three symbolic constants, namely, `GL_AMBIENT`, `GL_DIFFUSE` and `GL_SPECULAR`, along with the RGB components as shown here.

```
GLfloat lightColor1 [] = {1.0, 1.0, 1.0, 1.0};

glLightfv(GL_LIGHT0, GL_AMBIENT, lightColor1);
```

The first statement specifies the light-source color in RGB format. The fourth parameter is the alpha component which is used only if color-blending routines are activated. The second statement sets the light source as white ambient light. Figure 10.3 shows the effect of different colors of a light source.

Figure 10.3 Effect of Different Colors of Light Source

`glEnable()`

This function is used to activate the lighting effects and a particular light source. The function is used as follows:

```
glEnable(LIGHTING);

glEnable(GL_LIGHT0);
```

`glShadeModel()`

This function is used to specify whether flat shading or smooth (Gouraud) shading is to be used for surface rendering. The function is used as follows:

```
glShadeModel(GL_FLAT);

glShadeModel(GL_SMOOTH);
```

Figure 10.4 shows the effect of both types of surface rendering.

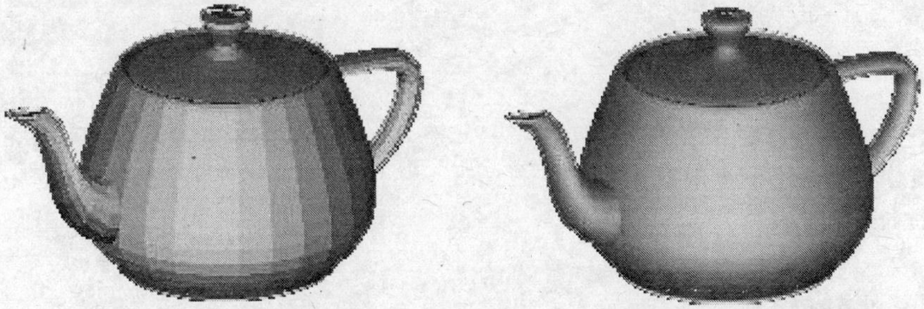

Figure 10.4 Effect of Flat and Smooth Surface Rendering

19. Write an OpenGL code for creating a scene containing 3D wireframe objects.

Ans. The following OpenGL code displays wireframe models of 3D objects placed on the corners of a big cube.

```
##include<windows.h>
#include<gl/gl.h>
#include<gl/glu.h>
#include<gl/glut.h>
void myInit()
{
 glClearColor(1.0, 1.0, 1.0, 1.0);
 glColor3f(0.0, 0.0, 0.0);
}
void display()
{
 glMatrixMode(GL_PROJECTION);
 glLoadIdentity();
 glOrtho(3.0, -3.0, -2.0, 2.0, 0.1, 10.0);
 glMatrixMode(GL_MODELVIEW);
 gluLookAt (2.5, 2.0, 2.5, 1.0, 1.0, 0.0, 0.0, 1.0, 0.0);

 glClear(GL_COLOR_BUFFER_BIT|GL_DEPTH_BUFFER_BIT);

 glPushMatrix();
 glTranslated(1.0, 1.0, 1.0);
 glutWireCube(2.0);
 glPopMatrix();

 glPushMatrix();
 glTranslated(2.0, 2.0, 0);
 glutWireSphere(0.3, 20, 20);
 glPopMatrix();

 glPushMatrix();
 glTranslated(2.0, 2.0, 2.0);
 glutWireTeapot(0.3);
 glPopMatrix();

 glPushMatrix();
 glTranslated(0, 2.0, 0);
 glRotated(90.0, 1, 0, 0);
```

```
 glutWireCone(0.3, 0.5, 10, 10);
 glPopMatrix();
 glPushMatrix();
 glTranslated(2.0, 0.0, 0.0);
 glScaled(0.2, 0.2, 0.2);
 glRotated(45.0, 1, 0, 0);
 glutWireDodecahedron();
 glPopMatrix();

 glPushMatrix();
 glTranslated(0, 2.0, 2.0);
 glutWireTorus(0.2, 0.2, 20, 20);
 glPopMatrix();
 glPushMatrix();
 glTranslated(2.0, 0, 2.0);
 glutWireCube(0.2);
 glPopMatrix();
 glPushMatrix();
 glTranslated(0, 0, 2.0);
 glScaled(0.3, 0.3, 0.3);
 glRotated(60, 1, 0, 0);
 glutWireTetrahedron();
 glPopMatrix();
 glFlush();
}
void main(int argc, char** argv)
{
 glutInit(&argc, argv);              //initializing GLUT library
 glutInitDisplayMode(GLUT_SINGLE|GLUT_RGB);
                                           //setting display mode
 glutInitWindowPosition(50,50);    //setting window position
 glutInitWindowSize(800,600);      //setting window size
 glutCreateWindow("The window is opened");    //opening the window
 glutDisplayFunc(display);
 myInit();
 glutMainLoop();       //continue displaying the objects
}
```

The output of the program is shown in Figure 10.5.

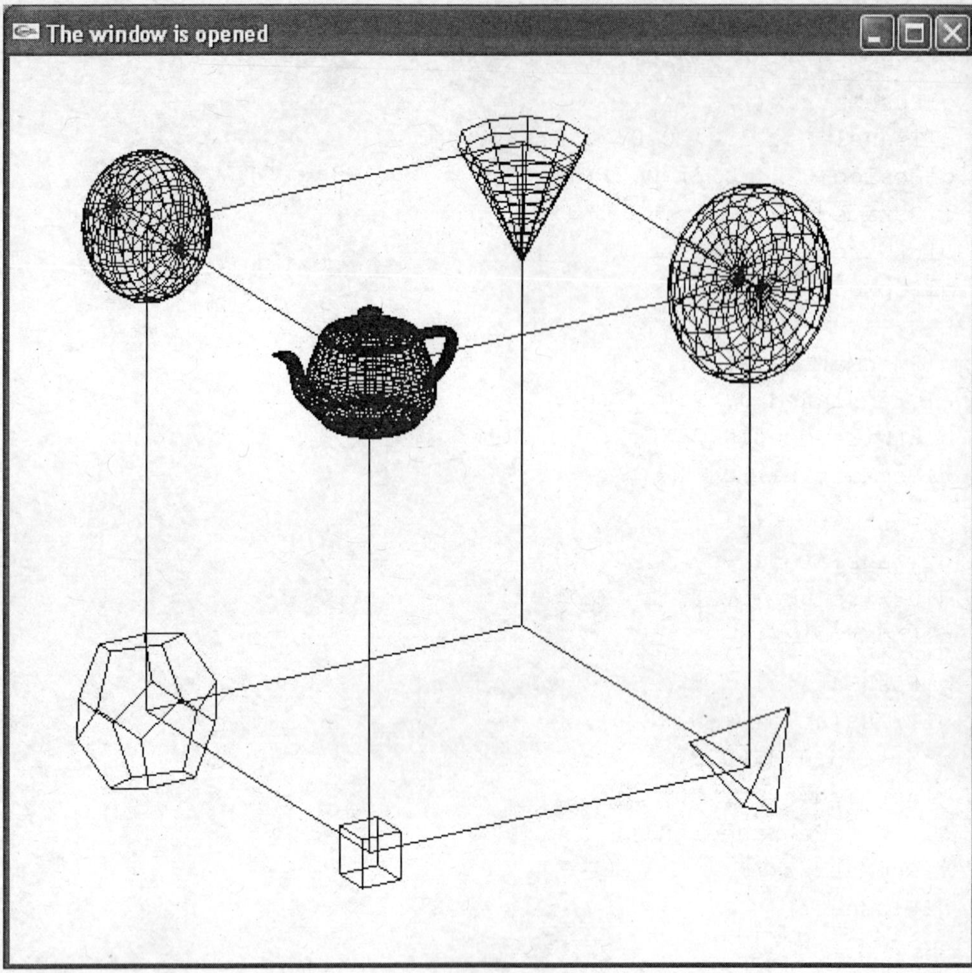

Figure 10.5 3D Scene Containing Wireframe Models of 3D Objects

20. Write an OpenGL code for creating a 3D scene rendered with shading.

Ans. The following OpenGL code displays solid 3D objects placed on the corners of a big solid cube.

```
#include<windows.h>
#include<gl/gl.h>
#include<gl/glu.h>
#include<gl/glut.h>

void Init()
{
 glClearColor(1.0, 1.0, 1.0, 0.0);
 glColor3f(0.0, 0.0, 0.0);
```

```
 glViewport(0,0,800,600);
}
void solidDisplay()
{
 glMatrixMode(GL_PROJECTION);
 glLoadIdentity();
 glOrtho(3.0, -3.0, -2.0, 2.0, 0.1, 10.0);
 glMatrixMode(GL_MODELVIEW);
 gluLookAt (2.5, 2.0, 2.5, 1.0, 1.0, 0.0, 0.0, 1.0, 0.0);

 glClear(GL_COLOR_BUFFER_BIT|GL_DEPTH_BUFFER_BIT);

 glPushMatrix();
 glTranslated(1.0, 1.0, 1.0);
 glutSolidCube(2.0);
 glPopMatrix();

 glColor3f(0.0, 1.0, 0.0);
 glPushMatrix();
 glTranslated(2.0, 2.0, 0);
 glutSolidSphere(0.3, 20, 20);
 glPopMatrix();
 glPushMatrix();
 glTranslated(2.0, 2.0, 2.0);
 glutSolidTeapot(0.3);
 glPopMatrix();

 glPushMatrix();
 glTranslated(0, 2.0, 0);
 glRotated(90.0, 1, 0, 0);
 glutSolidCone(0.3, 0.5, 10, 10);
 glPopMatrix();
 glPushMatrix();
 glTranslated(2.0, 0.0, 0.0);
 glScaled(0.2, 0.2, 0.2);
 glRotated(90.0, 1, 0, 0);
 glutSolidDodecahedron();
```

```
 glPopMatrix();

 glPushMatrix();
 glTranslated(0, 2.0, 2.0);
 glutSolidTorus(0.2, 0.2, 20, 20);
 glPopMatrix();

 glPushMatrix();
 glTranslated(2.0, 0, 2.0);
 glutSolidCube(0.2);
 glPopMatrix();

 glPushMatrix();
 glTranslated(0, 0, 2.0);
 glScaled(0.3, 0.3, 0.3);
 glutSolidTetrahedron();
 glPopMatrix();
 glFlush();
}
void main(int argc, char** argv)
{
 glutInit(&argc, argv);           //initializing GLUT library
 glutInitDisplayMode(GLUT_SINGLE|GLUT_RGB|GLUT_DEPTH);
                                  //setting display mode
 glutInitWindowPosition(50,50);   //setting window position
 glutInitWindowSize(800,600);     //setting window size
 glutCreateWindow("The window is opened");    //opening the window
 glutDisplayFunc(solidDisplay);
 glEnable(GL_LIGHTING);
 glEnable(GL_LIGHT0);
 glShadeModel(GL_SMOOTH);
 glEnable(GL_DEPTH_TEST);    //for hidden surface removal
 glEnable(GL_NORMALIZE);     //normalize vectors for proper shading
 Init();
 glutMainLoop();             //continue displaying the objects
}
```

The output of the program is shown in Figure 10.6.

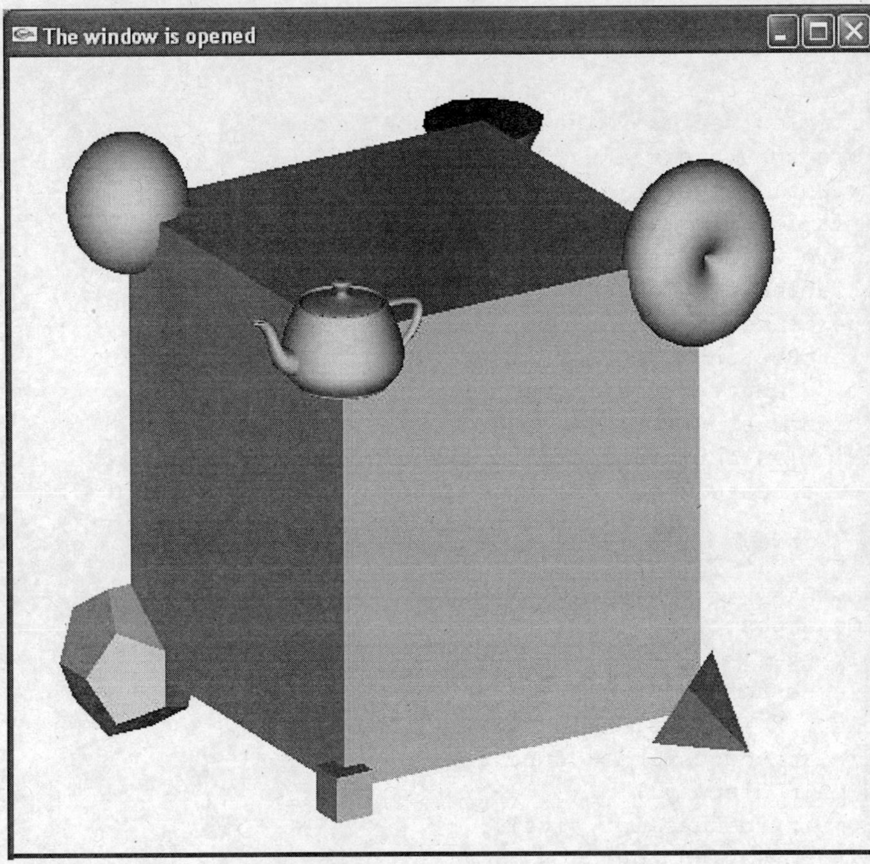

Figure 10.6 3D Scene Containing Solid 3D Objects

21. How can we specify camera in an OpenGL program?

Ans. In any graphics application, there is no physical existence of a camera; rather, what you see on the screen is the view of the camera. Thus, adjusting the camera lens or rotating or moving it implies changing the view of the scene. In OpenGL, there is no built-in function to specify the camera. Thus, to simulate the camera we can apply the inverse of the camera transformations on the objects in the scene.

The following OpenGL program implements the concept of camera. In this program, the mouse actions are used to rotate, scale and translate the object. The left mouse button is used to rotate the object in different directions through different angles, middle button (or scroll wheel) is used to scale the object, and right button is used to translate the object to different positions. The initial position of the camera is set such that the front view of the object is visible.

```
#include <windows.h>
#include <stdio.h>
#include <stdarg.h>
#include <stdlib.h>
#include <gl/glut.h>
```

```
//define the window position on screen
int window_x;
int window_y;
//variables representing the window size
int window_width = 400;
int window_height = 400;
//variables for main window and subwindow
int main_window, subwindow;
//variables for mouse buttons
//true if corresponding buttons clicked, and false otherwise
int leftButton = 0;
int middleButton = 0;
int rightButton = 0;
//variables for transforming the objects in the scene
float translate_x = 0.0f, translate_y = 0.0f, translate_z = 0.0f;
float rot_x = 0.0f, rot_y = 0.0f, rot_z = 0.0f;
float scale_x = 1.0f, scale_y = 1.0f, scale_z = 1.0f;
float previousX = 0.0f, previousY = 0.0f, previousZ = 0.0f;
//Camera position, look at position, up vector
double eyeX = 0, eyeY = 0, eyeZ = 0;
double centerX = 0, centerY = 0, centerZ = 0;
double upX = 0, upY = 1, upZ = 0;
//main window callback functions
void main_display();
void main_reshape(int, int);
void keypress(unsigned char, int, int);
//subwindow display functions
void displayFrontView();
void display();
void redisplay();
void mouseClick(int, int, int, int);
void motion(int, int);
//initialization function
void init();
//support functions
void ScreenInCenter ();
void drawObject ();
//reset object transformations in the scene
void reset()
{
 translate_x = translate_y = translate_z = 0.0f;
 rot_x = rot_y = rot_z = 0.0f;
 scale_x = scale_y = scale_z = 1.0f;
```

```
 previousX = previousY = previousZ = 0;
 redisplay();
}
//main window display function
void main_display()
{
 glClearColor(0, 0, 0, 0);
 glClear(GL_COLOR_BUFFER_BIT);
 glutSwapBuffers();
}
//main window reshape function
void main_reshape(int w, int h)
{
 //Disallow window re-sizing
 glutReshapeWindow(window_width, window_height);
}
//main window keypress function
void keypress(unsigned char key, int x, int y)
{
    switch(key)
    {
          case '0':
                reset();
                break;
    }
}
//redisplays the subwindow
void redisplay()
{
 glutSetWindow (subwindow);
 glutPostRedisplay ();
}
//display the subwindow
void display()
{
    //clear subwindow
    glClearColor(1, 1, 1, 1);
    glClear(GL_COLOR_BUFFER_BIT|GL_DEPTH_BUFFER_BIT);
    //set perspective
    glMatrixMode(GL_PROJECTION);
    glOrtho(-1, 1, -1, 1, -2, 2);
    //set camera position and view vector
    glMatrixMode(GL_MODELVIEW);
```

```
    gluLookAt(eyeX, eyeY, eyeZ, centerX, centerY, centerZ,
                upX, upY, upZ);
    //apply translation
    glTranslatef(translate_x, translate_y, translate_z);
    //apply rotation
    glRotatef(rot_x, 1.0f, 0.0f, 0.0f);
    glRotatef(rot_y, 0.0f, 1.0f, 0.0f);
    glRotatef(rot_z, 0.0f, 0.0f, 1.0f);
    //apply scaling
    glScalef(scale_x, scale_y, scale_z);
    //draw object
    drawObject();
    //make the current ModelView matrix an identity matrix
    glLoadIdentity();
    //make the current Projection matrix an identity matrix
    glMatrixMode(GL_PROJECTION);
    glLoadIdentity();
    glutSwapBuffers();
}
//display front view
void displayFrontView()
{
    glColor3f (0.5, 0.5, 0.5);
    eyeX = 0;
    eyeY = 0;
    eyeZ = 1;
    upX = 0;
    upY = 1;
    upZ = 0;
    display();
}
//draw the object
void drawObject()
{
    glutSolidTeapot(0.4);
}
//mouseClick function
void mouseClick(int button, int state, int x, int y)
{
    //checks if the user presses the left button
    if (button == GLUT_LEFT_BUTTON)
    {
          leftButton = state == GLUT_DOWN;
```

```
    }
    //left button allows user to rotate the object
    else if (button == GLUT_MIDDLE_BUTTON)
    {
          middleButton = state == GLUT_DOWN;
    }
    //middle button allows user to scale the object
    else if (button == GLUT_RIGHT_BUTTON)
    {
          rightButton = state == GLUT_DOWN;
    }
    //right button allows user to translate the object
    previousX = x;
    previousY = y;
    previousZ = y;
}
//function used when the user drag the mouse
void motion(int x, int y)
{
    //translate
    if (rightButton)
    {
          translate_x += (x - previousX) * 0.005;
          translate_y -= (y - previousY) * 0.005;
    }
    //scale
    if (middleButton)
    {
          scale_x -= (y - previousZ) * 0.005;
          scale_y -= (y - previousZ) * 0.005;
          scale_z -= (y - previousZ) * 0.005;
    }
    //rotate
    if (leftButton)
    {
          if ((y - previousY) >= 0)
                rot_x += (y - previousY);
          else
                rot_x += (y - previousY);
          if ((x - previousX) >= 0)
                rot_y += (x - previousX);
          else
                rot_y += (x - previousX);
```

```
    }
    //reset the previousX, previousY, and previousZ to the current
    //position of the mouse
    previousX = (float)x;
    previousY = (float)y;
    previousZ = (float)y;
    redisplay();              //redisplaying the subwindow
}
//This function sets the window x and y coordinates
//such that the window appears in the center of the screen
void ScreenInCenter()
{
    window_x = (glutGet (GLUT_SCREEN_WIDTH) - window_width)/2;
    window_y = (glutGet (GLUT_SCREEN_HEIGHT) - window_height)/2;
}
void main(int argc, char **argv)
{
    glutInit(&argc, argv);
    glutInitWindowSize (window_width, window_height);
    ScreenInCenter();
    glutInitWindowPosition (window_x, window_y);
    glutInitDisplayMode (GLUT_RGB | GLUT_DOUBLE);
    main_window = glutCreateWindow ("OpenGL Camera-Press 0 to reset
    the window");
    //set the callback functions for main window
    glutDisplayFunc(main_display);
    glutReshapeFunc(main_reshape);
    glutKeyboardFunc(keypress);
    //set the position and dimensions of subwindow
    subwindow = glutCreateSubWindow(main_window, 25, 25, 300, 300);
    glutDisplayFunc(displayFrontView);
    glutMouseFunc(mouseClick);
    glutMotionFunc(motion);
    glutKeyboardFunc(keypress);
    //applying lighting and shading on the object in the scene
    glEnable(GL_LIGHTING);
    glEnable(GL_LIGHT0);
    glShadeModel(GL_SMOOTH);
    glEnable(GL_DEPTH_TEST);
    glEnable(GL_NORMALIZE);
    glutMainLoop();
}
```

The outputs of the program after applying different transformations are shown in Figure 10.7.

(a) Front view

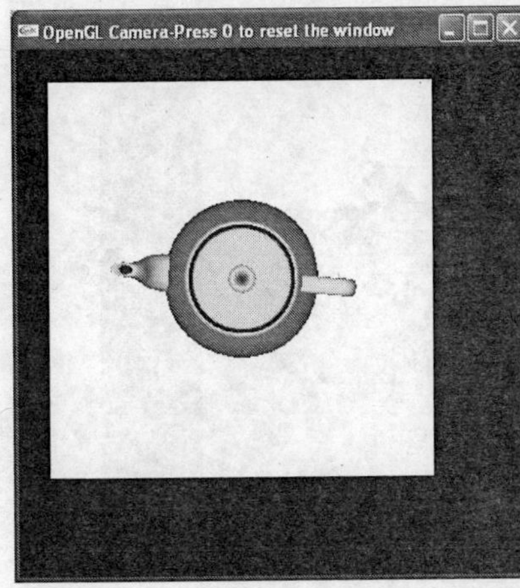

(b) Top view

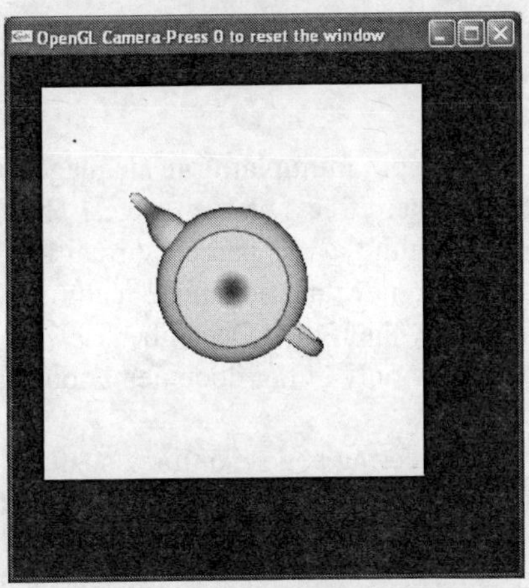

(c) Bottom view

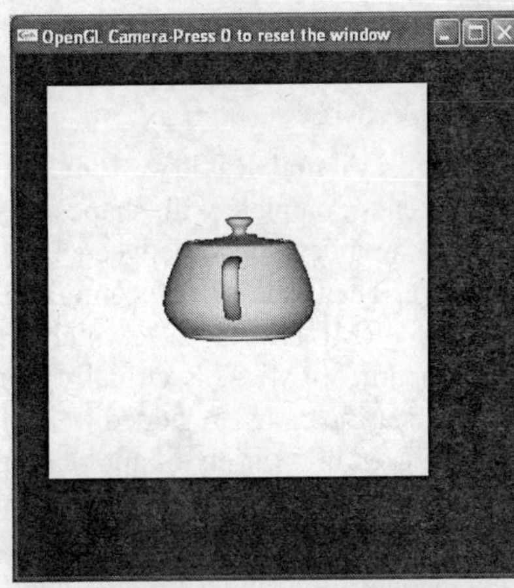

(d) Left view

(e) Side view

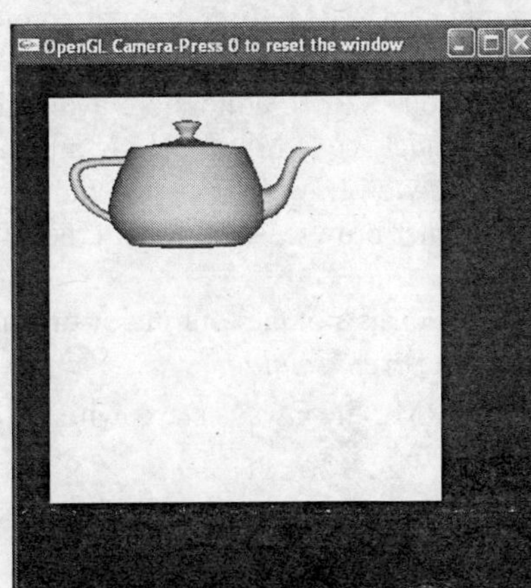

(f) Translated image

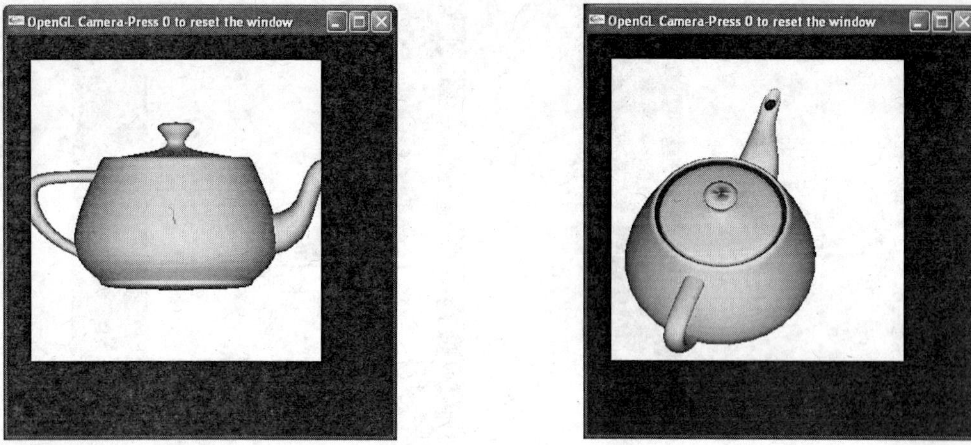

(g) Scaled image (h) After applying all translations

Figure 10.7 Specifying Camera in a Program

22. What is VRML?

Ans. VRML, or **Virtual Reality Modeling Language**, is a simple multiplatform language used to describe 3D scenes complete with shapes, lights, textures, and other effects on web pages. The first version of VRML was developed between 1994 and 1995, and that time it was named Virtual Reality Markup Language. Then, VRML 2.0 came into existence with some new and advanced features. The current version of VRML is VRML97, which is formally approved by the ISO in December 1997, as an international standard. VRML97 is virtually identical to VRML 2.0—only minor documentations have changed and few clarifications are added.

VRML can be used in a variety of application areas such as engineering and scientific visualization, architecture, advertising, multimedia presentations, entertainment and education, business, manufacturing and design, and shared virtual worlds (virtual communities).

VRML documents allow hyperlinking, that is, we can associate URLs with 3D objects so that a web browser can fetch a webpage or a new VRML file from the Internet when the user clicks on the specific graphical component. VRML files are written in plain text format, that is, VRML code is an ASCII type code. The VRML files are commonly known as "worlds" and have the `*.wrl` extension (e.g.,, `scenery.wrl`). Various VRML editors are available which can be used for writing VRML code such as *VrmlPad2.1*, *Blender 2.64*, *Alteros 3d 2.8*, and many more. To view VRML worlds in a browser, we can install *Cortona3d* viewer, which is a fast and highly interactive 3D viewer. It works as a VRML plug-in for popular Internet browser such as Internet Explorer, Google Chrome, Opera, Netscape Navigator, etc.

A VRML file consists of the four major functional components, namely, *the header*, *the scene graph*, *the prototypes* and *event routing*.

❑ **Header:** A VRML file always starts with the header, which is written as follows:

```
#VRML V2.0 utf8
```

Here, `utf8` indicates that the internal characters in your VRML files are interpreted using UTF-8 encoding. The character # is used to insert a comment anywhere in the VRML document except for the first line.

- **Scene graph:** Scene descriptions in VRML are made up of entities called **nodes**. The nodes can be 3D shapes, properties, transformations, cameras and lights. These nodes are not randomly placed in a VRML description; rather they are organized in a hierarchical structure known as **scene graph**. The top-level node is the **root node**, which may contain other nodes called **children**.
- **Prototypes:** Prototypes allows the user to extend the set of VRML node types. The user can define the prototypes in terms of either built-in node types or already defined prototypes. Prototype interface can be declared by using `PROTO` statement in which we can define the event interface as well as default values for prototype's fields.
- **Event routing:** Event routing mechanism allows you to build the connection between the node generating an event and the node receiving an event. Thus, it acts as an interface of a model to interact with a user. The main advantage of event routing is that it separates event from the scene graph hierarchy.

VRML defines the unit of measures of the world coordinate system in meters. The angles are measured in radians instead of degrees, time in seconds, and colors in RGB values ranging from 0.0 to 1.0. In addition, a Cartesian, right-handed, 3D coordinate system is used in VRML models.

23. Give the syntax to define a node in VRML with the help of an example.

Ans. A VRML file is basically collection of nodes which can be physical objects such as box, sphere, cylinder, etc., or abstract objects such as viewpoints, hyperlinks, transformations, sound, etc. Each node consists of fields, which hold the data for the node. These nodes are arranged in hierarchical structure forming a scene graph. The syntax to declare a node is as follows:

```
node type
{
    fields
    children[list of child nodes]
}
```

where `fields` override the default values of the properties of a node; `children` allow to add children nodes in the scene graph.

The `Shape` node is generic node in VRML that can be used to draw all objects. It consists of two child nodes: `Appearance` and `geometry`. The `Shape` node is declared as follows:

```
Shape {
 appearance Appearance {
    material Material{
          diffuseColor 1.0 0.0 0.0
    } #end of material
  } #end of appearance
 geometry Box {
    size 2 2 2
  } #end of geometry
} #end of Shape
```

The `Appearance` node controls the way a shape looks. It can contain the `Material` node, which specifies the object's surface properties such as its color and transparency. The `Material` node can have six fields: *diffuseColor, emissiveColor, ambientIntensity, shininess, specularColor* and *transparency.* All these fields have an RGB value associated with them ranging from 0.0 to 1.0. The syntax of `Material` node is as follows:

```
material Material{
 diffuseColor 1.0 0.0 0.0
 emissiveColor 0.0 0.0 0.0
 ambientIntensity 0.2
 shininess 0.2
 specularColor 0.0 0.0 0.0
    transparency 0.0
}
```

VRML provides various primitive shapes such as box, cone, cylinder and sphere. These shapes are declared as the `geometry` node. For example, to draw a generic cylinder with default values, following VRML code is written:

```
#VRML V2.0 utf8
# cylinder with default values
Shape {
 geometry Cylinder {
 } # end of Cylinder
} # Shape
```

To draw a cylinder with some specific values, the following code is written:

```
#VRML V2.0 utf8
# cylinder with specified values
Shape {
 appearance Appearance {
    material Material{
          diffuseColor 0.5 0.5 0.0
    } #end of material
 } #end of appearance
 geometry Cylinder {
    height 3.5
          radius 1.0
          side TRUE
          top FALSE
          bottom TRUE
 } #end of geometry
} #end of Shape
```

The output of the above code is shown in Figure 10.8(a).

24. Write the VRML code for drawing the following objects:

a. Sphere of radius 1.5

b. Cone with bottom radius 2.0 and height 3.5, and all sides visible.

Ans. a. The VRML code for drawing a sphere is as follows:

```
#VRML V2.0 utf8
```

```
# sphere
Shape {
 appearance Appearance {
    material Material{
          diffuseColor 0.5 0.5 0.0
    } #material
 } #appearance
 geometry Sphere {
    radius 1.5
 } #geometry
} #Shape
```

The output of the above code is shown in Figure 10.8(b).

b. The VRML code for drawing a cone is as follows:

```
#VRML V2.0 utf8
# cone
Shape {
 appearance Appearance {
    material Material{
          diffuseColor 0.5 0.5 0.0
    } #material
 } #appearance
 geometry Cone {
    bottomRadius 2.0
    height 3.5
    side TRUE
    bottom TRUE
 } #geometry
} #Shape
```

The output of the above code is shown in Figure 10.8(c).

25. Write the VRML code for adding text in the document.

Ans. Text can be added in the VRML document using `Text` node. We can specify the text to be included, the font style, font size, alignment, and so on using the `fontStyle` node. By default, the text is placed in the positive *y* direction. The VRML code for adding text is as follows:

```
#VRML V2.0 utf8
# text
Shape {
 appearance Appearance {
    material Material{
          diffuseColor 1.0 0.0 0.0
    } #material
 } #appearance
 geometry Text {
    string ["This is the first line of the text",
    "This is the second line of the text"]
```

```
        fontStyle FontStyle {
        family "Arial"
        size 0.5          #default value is 1.0
        justify    "MIDDLE"
        horizontal TRUE
        leftToRight TRUE
    } #fontStyle
  } #geometry
} #Shape
```

The output of the above code is shown in Figure 10.8(d).

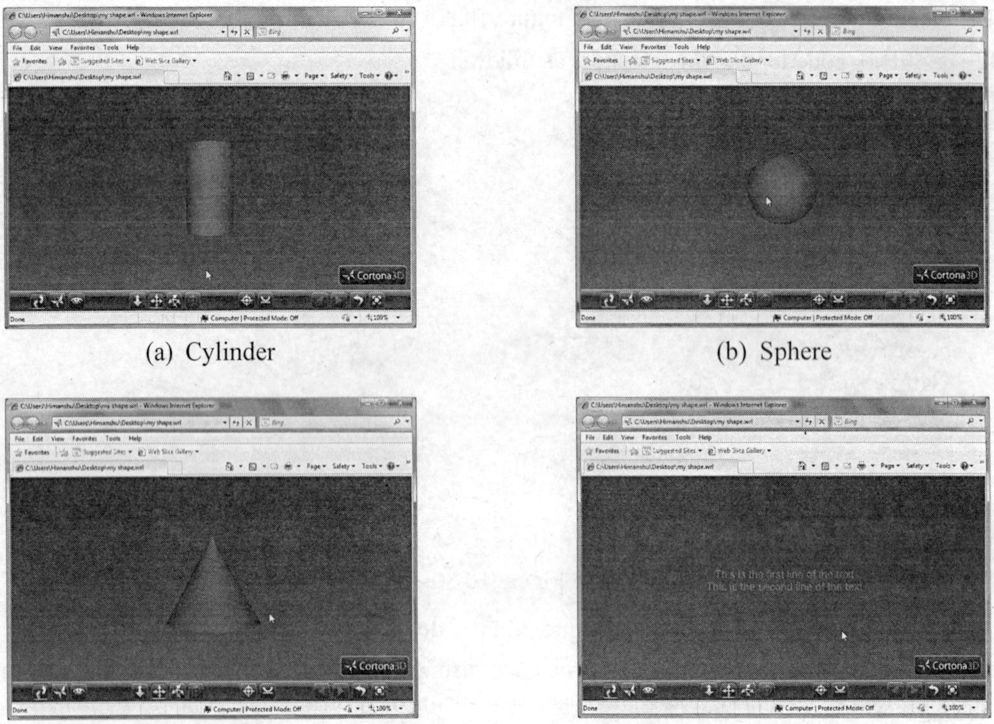

(a) Cylinder (b) Sphere

(c) Cone (d) Adding text

Figure 10.8 Drawing Various 3D Objects Using VRML

26. How can we group nodes in VRML?

Ans. VRML allows you to group a set of nodes to form a single node so that it is treated as a single entity. Grouping is a kind of encapsulation, which allows you to bind all those nodes together for which you want same properties, same material, same appearance and same transformation. For example, suppose we want to group a cylinder and sphere shape to form a single node. This can be accomplished as follows:

```
#VRML V2.0 utf8
# Grouping of nodes
```

```
Group {
 children [
         Shape {
         appearance Appearance {
              material Material{
                    diffuseColor 0.5 0.5 0.0
              } #material
         } #appearance
         geometry Cylinder {
              radius 0.5
              height 5.0
         } #geometry
 } #Shape
 Shape {
         appearance Appearance {
              material Material{
                    diffuseColor 1.0 0.0 0.0
              } #material
         } #appearance
         geometry Sphere {
                    radius 1.0
         } #geometry
      } #Shape
 ] #end of children
} #end of Group
```

The output of the above code is shown in Figure 10.9.

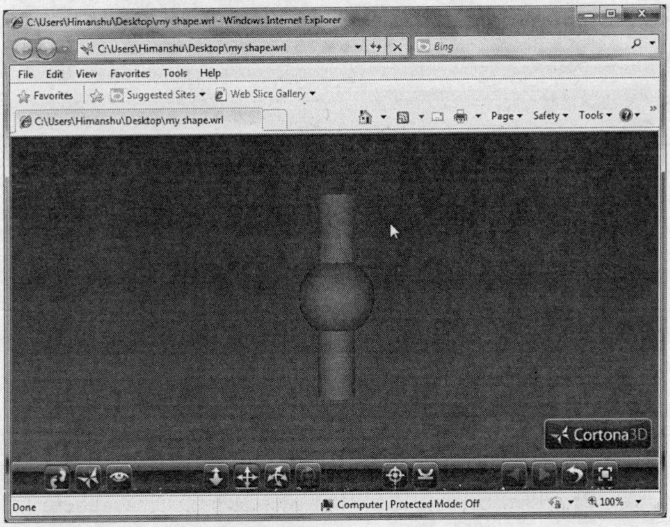

Figure 10.9 Grouping of Nodes

27. Write the VRML code for performing 3D geometric transformations.

Ans. We can use the `Transform` node of VRML for performing geometric transformations. Transform node is a group node which allows you to define a new local coordinate system for the nodes within the group. We can apply translation, rotation and scale transformations to all the nodes within the `Transform` node. The syntax of using the `Transform` node is as follows:

```
Transform {
    rotation x y z angle
    translation x y z
    scale x y z
  children [ Shape {} , Shape {}, .... ]
}
```

For example, to apply the transformations on a cone of radius 0.5 and height 2.0, the VRML code is as follows:

```
#VRML V2.0 utf8
#Transformations on a cone
Transform {
      translation 0.0 -1.0 0.0      #translation in X Y Z direc-
                                    tions
      rotation 0.0 0.0 1.0 3.14     #angle specified in radians
                                    #rotation around z axis by 180o
      scale 0.5 1.0 0.5             #scale factor in X Y Z dimen-
                                    sions
      children [ Shape{
                              appearance Appearance{
                              material Material { }
                              }
                              geometry Cone{
                                    bottomRadius   0.5
                                    height         2.0
                                    side TRUE
                                    bottom TRUE
                              }
                  }
      ]
}
```

28. How can we name the nodes in VRML? What is advantage of naming the nodes?

Ans. As we know, the shapes are the building blocks of VRML worlds. We can create complex drawings using the basic shapes provided by VRML such as box, cone, sphere and cylinder. Sometimes it is required to use the same shape many times in the same VRML file. This can be achieved using the `DEF` and `USE` structure. The syntax of using these structures is as follows:

```
DEF newShape Shape {
  . . .
              }
  . . .
      USE newShape
  . . .
      USE newShape
```

Suppose we want to draw a pattern in which four cubes are placed at the corner of a cube. Each cube is of grey color and 2.0 units in size. For this, we can define a node to draw one cube, and then use it four times after applying transformations. To do this, the following code is written.

```
#VRML V2.0 utf8
DEF cube Shape {
                     appearance Appearance {
                     material Material{
                             diffuseColor 0.5 0.5 0.5
                     } #end of material
             } #end of appearance
      geometry Box {
             size 2 2 2
      } #end of geometry
} #end of Shape

Transform {
      translation 2 2 0
      children [ USE cube ]
}

Transform {
      translation -2 2 0
      children [ USE cube ]
}

Transform {
 translation -2 -2 0
 children [ USE cube ]
}

Transform {
 translation 2 -2 0
 children [ USE cube ]
}
```

The output of the above code is shown in Figure 10.10.

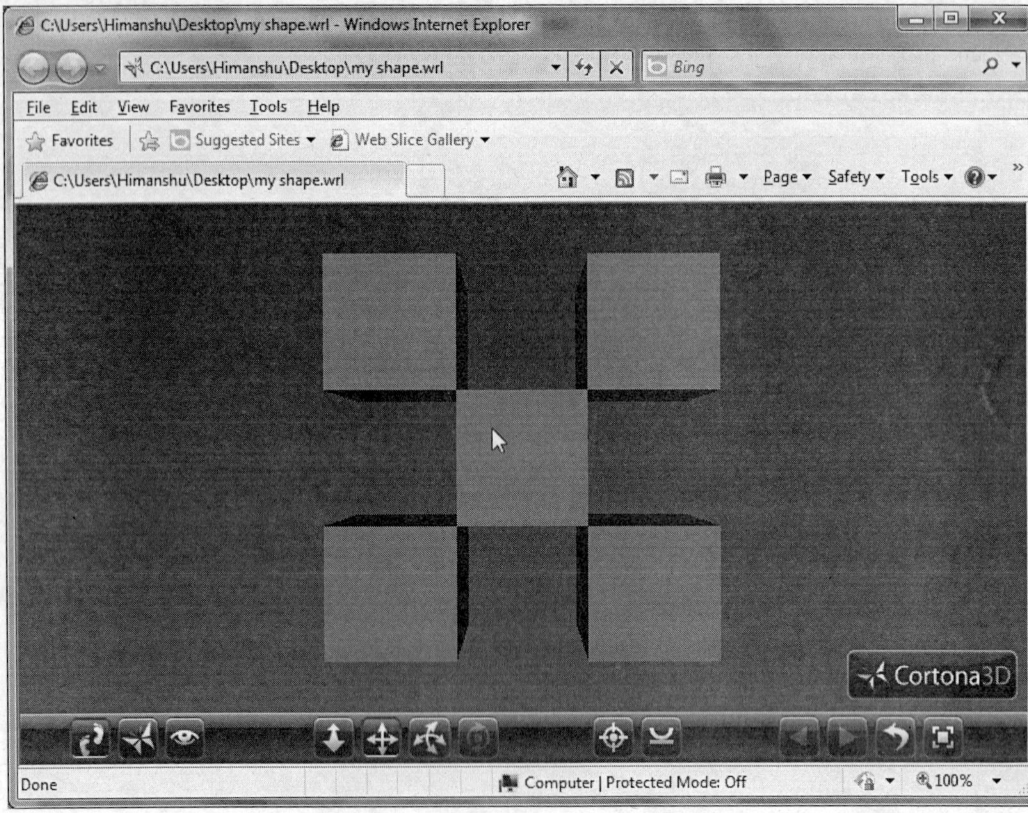

Figure 10.10 Reusability of a Node to Draw a Pattern

MULTIPLE CHOICE QUESTIONS

1. Which of these is known as the core library of OpenGL?
   (a) GLUT (b) GLU
   (c) GLUI (d) None of these
2. Which of these header files must be included in an OpenGL program for using OpenGL core library?
   (a) `gl.h` (b) `opengl.h`
   (c) `glu.h` (d) `glut.h`
3. What is the size of `GLdouble` data type in OpenGL?
   (a) 8 bits (b) 32 bits
   (c) 16 bits (d) 64 bits
4. Which of these OpenGL command is used to terminate the list of primitives?
   (a) `End();` (b) `glEnd();`
   (c) `glend();` (d) `glEnd;`

5. Which OpenGL command is used to clear the screen?
   (a) `glClear(GL_COLOR_BUFFER_BIT);`
   (b) `glClearColor(1.0,1.0,1.0,0.0);`
   (c) `glClearScreen();`
   (d) None of these
6. Which of these functions continues to display the output on the display window until user closes the display window?
   (a) `glLoop();` (b) `glMainLoop();`
   (c) `glutMainLoop();` (d) `glutLoop();`
7. Which of the following symbolic constants is a valid parameter for `glMatrixMode()`?
   (a) GL_PROJECTION (b) GL_MODELVIEW
   (c) GL_COLOR (d) All of these
8. Which of these is not a component of a VRML file?
   (a) Header (b) Scene graph
   (c) Prototypes (d) Functions
9. Which of these nodes is used to insert text in a VRML document?
   (a) `Appearance` (b) `Text`
   (c) `Title` (d) `String`
10. Which of these is used to implement reusability in VRML?
   (a) `DEF` and `USE` (b) `DEFINE` and `USE`
   (c) `DEF` and `REUSE` (d) None of these

Answers. 1. d 2. a 3. d 4. b 5. a 6. c 7. d 8. d 9. b 10. a

11

Multimedia

1. Define the terms multimedia and multimedia system.

Ans. The word multimedia is made up of two separate words, *multi* means many, and *media* means ways through which information can be transmitted. Therefore, **multimedia** can be described as an integration of multiple media elements (such as text, graphics, audio, video, and animation) together to emphasize the given information so that it can be presented in an attractive and interactive manner. In simple words, multimedia means being able to communicate in more than one way. The main advantage of integrating all media in the computer is that it allows using the existing computer power to represent information interactively. This information can also be transmitted over the computer networks.

A **multimedia system** is a system capable of processing multimedia data and applications. It deals with the generation, manipulation, storage, presentation, and communication of information in digital form. It is important to note that multimedia-based applications put tremendous demands on the system hardware, in terms of both computing performance and storage. Thus, computer hardware plays a vital role in supporting multimedia-based applications. A very high-speed processor is essential for the processing of multimedia elements. In addition, high-capacity storage devices like CD and DVDs are required to keep digitized information for the future retrieval and use. Multimedia also requires a large amount of computer's main memory (RAM) and large amount of bandwidth when distributed on a network. Multimedia-based applications also demand for efficient input/output devices such as a high-resolution graphics display, audio speakers, sound card, and microphone to allow display, playback, and recording of data.

2. What are the data objects used in a multimedia system?

or

What are the basic elements of a multimedia system?

or

What are the building blocks of a multimedia system?

Ans. Multimedia is mainly concerned with the computer-controlled integration of text, graphics, drawings, still or moving images (video), animation, and audio where every type of information can be represented, stored, transmitted, and processed digitally. Thus, text, graphics (images), audio (sound), video, and animation are the basic elements of a multimedia system.

- **Text:** Words and symbols in any form, spoken or written, are the most common means of communication. The on-screen display of words, that is text, is the base of most applications. Different styles, fonts, and colors can be used to emphasize specific points. With the recent explosion of the Internet and World Wide Web, text has become more important than ever. Nowadays, the text is not only capable of displaying information, but it has also gained interactivity; things like an electronic annotation, which assist in navigating through all the information presented on the Web by means of *hypertext*. A **hypertext** can be defined as an object in the text that allows the user to jump from one web page to another at a click of the mouse button. It acts like electronic footnotes and assists you in navigating through all the information. The amount of text to be included in an application, the type of font selection, the size, style, and color of the font make the application more meaningful.
- **Images (graphics):** It is said that a picture is worth a thousand words; as a result, every multimedia presentation is predominantly based on graphics. By nature, human beings comprehend concepts more easily through graphics than textual information. Adding a graphic element into a text-based document can change the user's perception towards the document. Integration of the graphics element into the application makes it more elegant and understandable. Growing technology has produced a wealth of graphics and visual imagery for a multimedia project. For the development of multimedia project, various images are captured from different sources like scanners, digital cameras, and through the Internet. Once the images are transformed into digitized form, they can be edited and modified with the help of image editing software like Adobe Photoshop, CorelDraw, and Freehand. Graphics can be presented in various modes such as animated and colorful background, bitmaps and clip art images, photographs or captured video frames, charts and graphs, and flowcharts.
- **Audio (sound):** It is perhaps the most powerful element of multimedia. This includes speech, audio effects, ambient sound (for example, the background sound of the sea), and music. Audio means the sensation resulting from stimulation of the auditory mechanism by airwaves or vibrations. It is the vibration of air molecules in the atmosphere that can be sensed by the ear. Today, a computer can play back most complex parts of a melody with great precision. Computers and digital technology have changed the face of music industry. Today, digital music is used to produce special effects in televisions, films, in recording studios, and in games. Music and sound effects not only add interactivity with the user, but also play with the user's perception and emotions.

  Music is probably the most obvious form of sound. It can be used to set a mood, convey an idea, and even tell a story. Music influences how we think and feel and how we perceive other forms of information. Speech is also a perfect way for teaching users the pronunciation of words as done by the speech learning software. Non-speech sound effects can be used in the user interface to inform users about background events. Sounds can be embedded into a web page and can be played. Common types of sound formats are Musical Instrument Digital Interface (MIDI) and WAV.
- **Video:** The term video refers to the moving picture recorded using digital video recorder accompanied by sound, for example, a movie on the television. It adds richness to content and enhances the user's experience. Integrating video element in a multimedia application provides a great deal of information in a short time. Digital video is useful in multimedia applications for showing real-life objects, such as people talking or real-life illustrations of concepts. There are three main types of video files that are used: QuickTime, AVI, and MPEG. QuickTime and MPEG are the most commonly used file formats, whereas AVI is a Windows-oriented video format which is not used commonly because of the synchronization problem between audio and video.

- **Animation:** It is the process of sequencing still images in rapid succession to give the effect of live motion. The sequence of images is shown one after the other very quickly so that the human eye and brain blend the images to produce the effect of motion. Animation adds visual impact to your multimedia presentation. It is a powerful tool capable of communicating complex ideas. Animation is viable because of a natural phenomenon known as **persistence of vision**. An object seen by the human eye remains mapped on the eye's retina for a short time interval after viewing. This makes it possible for a series of images that are changed very slightly and very rapidly, one after the other, to seemingly merge into a visual illusion of movement. In other words, if we just change slightly the location or shape of an object rapidly enough, the eye will perceive the changes as motion. An animated sequence has to show a certain number of frames every second. For professional animation, one needs to have at least 30 frames per second.

3. Discuss the two categories of a multimedia system.

Ans. A multimedia system is broadly categorized into two categories, namely, *linear* and *non-linear.*

- **Linear:** In linear (also known as **passive**) multimedia system, the user simply plays a sequence of sound, video, and images without having any control over the application's content. A TV documentary, business presentations are some of the examples of this type of system.
- **Non-linear:** In non-linear (also known as **interactive**) multimedia system, the user is allowed to control the sequence by selecting different options, thus involving interaction with the multimedia application. These systems achieve a higher degree of information transfer because they allow users to receive data or information and actively participate in the process. Video-on-demand (VoD), digital libraries, electronic games, etc., are some of the examples of this type of system.

4. Discuss the various application areas of multimedia.

Ans. The growing technology of computer hardware and software, to hold several types of media, had made multimedia suitable for a wide range of applications and users. Here are some of the possible areas where the use of multimedia applications has replaced the conventional system with new technology.

- **Education:** The usage of multimedia in the field of education is increasing rapidly. Currently, multimedia is used to develop a wide range of computer-based training (CBT) software and reference books such as encyclopaedia and almanacs. A CBT allows the user to go through a series of presentations, text about a particular topic, and associated illustrations in various information formats. The use of multimedia in education has given rise to an informal term *edutainment*, which is a combination of education and entertainment. It is based on the idea of learning with fun. Many products for home learning such as story telling CDs fall into this category. The graphical user interface (GUI) allows students to interact with the learning module, thus allowing them to experience the simulated real life environment. Students prefer this new technology instead of the traditional text-based approach because of the multi-sensory experience they undergo, making them feel to have a game-like interface. Multimedia has the ability to accommodate different learning styles and can present material in a non-linear manner. It is motivating, highly interactive, and can provide feedback and evaluate skills.
- **Entertainment:** The entertainment industry is probably one of the most important application areas where multimedia is used. The integration of both audio and video effects in a multimedia system has made it useful in the field of entertainment. Nowadays, multimedia is extensively being used in the field of television broadcasting, movies, and animations. For example, while watching

a live match on television, we are habitual of seeing replays, slow motion, charts analysis, and other statistical information. These kinds of integrations on the sports make a novice understand and predict the sports in a better way. In movies and animations, it is used to develop special audio and video effects.

Another important application of multimedia is in the field of video games. In fact, game developers were the pioneers in the use of multimedia and they still provide the most innovative and interactive applications of multimedia. A game is one of those multimedia domains where all the elements of multimedia play an equally important role in making it realistic and interactive. In order to attract, engage, captivate, and challenge the user, multimedia provides fast action, vivid colors, 3D animations, and elaborate sound effects that are essential for entertainment. Today, many games have moved from the physical (hand/eye coordination) to the mental (solving the mystery or outwitting the opponent).

- **Training:** In a corporate world, many multinational organizations need to train their employees on a wide range of subjects from personnel policy to equipment maintenance. With the boom in multimedia, the nature of CBT has undergone revolutionary changes. The widespread use of multimedia in training programs has helped people in carrying out their tasks in a much better way. For example, an automobile mechanic can learn to repair the engine of a car; security personnel can learn to tackle a bank robbery through simulation, and so on. These days, many companies are producing their own in-house multimedia training products. For instance, the Boeing Company has an entire training division dedicated for developing multimedia titles that instruct mechanics and pilots on new aircraft systems. Using multimedia tools, the trainee can perform a simulated job function in order to develop an advanced level without having touched the actual unit. The integration of audio and video permits this training technology to be a highly effective medium in areas such as flight and driving simulators. Similarly, NASA uses multimedia extensively for flight control training for astronauts.
- **Business:** The use of multimedia application in the business world has created a boom among the business industry around the world. One can now run his/her business in a much organized and professional manner. Multimedia offers a wide variety of options for conducting business presentations, marketing, advertising, and communications via videoconferencing. As compared to a conventional presentation, a multimedia presentation can make the audience come alive with the presence of ambient sound and visual effects. Multimedia can also be used at trade shows or to produce electronic catalogues. The marketing of new products can greatly be enhanced by using multimedia; these products can be marketed in such a manner which provides more detailed and stimulating information than print media can provide. Auto manufacturers such as Nissan also provide interactive test drives of new vehicles on the Web or on CD.
- **Marketing and advertising:** Multimedia technology has also greatly affected the advertising industry. Its power to boost communication on an affordable cost opened the way for the marketing and advertising personnel. Today, almost all the advertisement and marketing agencies are well equipped with authoring tools and workstations. Some of the elements such as flying banners, video transitions, animations, and sound effects are used in composing a multimedia-based advertisement. Incorporation of such elements presents the advertisement to the consumer in a better way, and thus helps in increasing the overall sales of the products. In addition, multimedia has incalculably increased the creativity of the marketing institutions. Today's computer has replaced high-priced sound and video editing facilities with reasonably priced equipment. The same computer can now be used with a number of elements: sound, video, animation, and so on.

- **Multimedia interactive kiosks:** A multimedia kiosk is a kind of an automated information centre where one can get necessary information related to a particular context. Some of the common services provided by the kiosk include searching for necessary information, performing financial transactions, taking online shopping orders, and many more. These kiosks are located near the public places such as hotels, railway stations, museums, historical monuments, bus stops, and grocery stores, round the clock for the convenience of people thereby eliminating the need for conventional-based information booths and staff members. In such kiosks, printers are often attached so that a user can walk out with the printed copy of the information. For example, a kiosk on the bus stop can be useful in providing a list of all the bus numbers plying on the respective routes, the arrival and departure time of the buses, fare for the different destinations, and so on.
- **Electronic encyclopaedia:** Nowadays, the multimedia technology is being used for developing electronic encyclopaedias that contain textual as well as visual information. The visuals may be either still images or a movie. In addition, these encyclopaedias can have audio clips to explain or narrate a part of the text. Some of the common examples of electronic encyclopaedias are electronic catalogues providing information about the products of companies, electronic encyclopaedia related to science and technology, and so on. Since electronic encyclopaedias contain information of different dimensions, they are more "lively" as compared to the print media.
- **Medicine:** In the field of medicine, the doctors can use the multimedia technology to get training by looking at a virtual surgery or they can simulate how the human body is affected by diseases spread by viruses and bacteria, and then develop techniques to prevent it.

5. What are the various types of multimedia system architectures?

Ans. There are three types of multimedia system architectures:

- Multimedia workstation architecture.
- The interactive multimedia association (IMA) architectural framework.
- Network architecture for multimedia systems.

6. Explain the multimedia workstation architecture in detail.

Ans. The multimedia system encompasses a wide variety of technologies and integration of multiple architectures interacting in real time. Another important aspect of multimedia system is that all the multimedia capabilities must integrate with the standard GUIs such as Microsoft Windows and X windows. To design and develop multimedia applications, we need to extend the existing non-multimedia hardware and software. The typical multimedia workstation architecture consists of four layers:

- The topmost layer consists of the application programs that provide interface to the user to interact with the multimedia system. For applications to function with a wide range of hardware components, interface standards are necessary. These interface standards are device independent and are known as **application programming interfaces (APIs)**. The applications are designed in such a way that they can operate with any hardware component or operating environment that supports the API. In addition, the use of common file formats allows data files to be exchanged between different hardware architectures and operating environments. Standard APIs and common file formats allow various developers to publish applications that can interact in a cohesive manner.
- The second layer consists of the basic GUI provided by Windows, and multimedia extensions to support multimedia applications such as full-motion digital video and remote desktop.

- The third layer consists of the operating system, software drivers, and multimedia driver support. A software driver is required for each hardware device. It acts as an interface between the application and the device. The user can interact with a much wider range of peripherals using software drivers. Multimedia drives, on the other hand, support add-on multimedia devices and peripherals.
- The last layer consists of system hardware and add-on multimedia devices and peripherals. A multimedia application demands for high computing performance, storage capacity, and high-resolution display technologies. Moreover, such systems also demand for parallel processing so that multiple applications can be operated simultaneously. Thus, additional hardware resources are needed to fulfil such requirements. In addition, add-on multimedia devices and peripherals such as video camera, microphone, scanner, digital camera, audio equipments, printer, etc., are needed. Each device requires its own device controller to provide an interface from an application to the device.

Figure 11.1 shows the multimedia workstation architecture. In this architecture, the shaded portion is very much similar to a non-multimedia system, and the white area shows the new architectural components required to support multimedia applications.

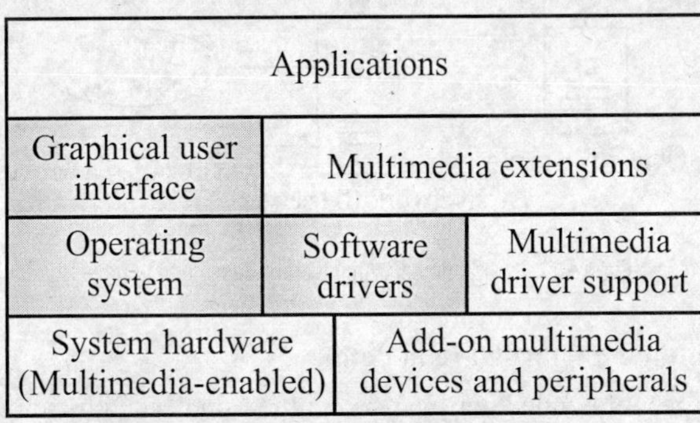

Figure 11.1 Multimedia Workstation Architecture

7. Discuss the IMA architectural framework for multimedia.

Ans. The IMA (Interactive Multimedia Association) has a task group which has a licence to define the architectural framework of multimedia to provide interoperability for multimedia products. Its role is to provide the technological specifications rather than products. The task group mainly focuses on two areas, namely, *desktops* (*clients*) and *servers*.

- **Desktops:** In this area, the main focus is to define the interchange formats so that the multimedia objects can be displayed on any workstation or personal computer (PC).
- **Servers:** In this area, the focus is to define the class libraries for multimedia objects so as to enable distributed multimedia applications across multivendor platforms.

The architectural approach followed by IMA is based on defining the interfaces to a multimedia interface bus. The **multimedia interface bus** acts as the interface between the systems and multimedia sources. It also provides streaming I/O services, which include filters and translators. Figure 11.2 shows the generalized architectural approach.

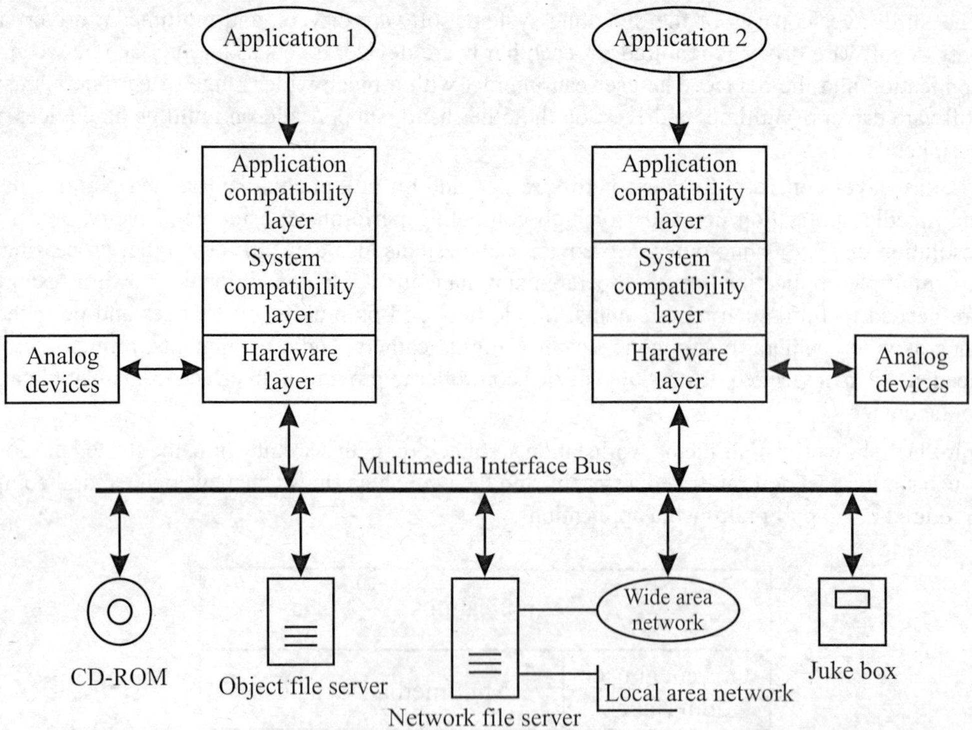

Figure 11.2 Multimedia Architecture Based on Interface Bus

8. Discuss the multimedia hardware in detail.

Ans. The minimum recommended hardware configuration needed by a multimedia PC to support a good multimedia application is as follows:

- **High processing power:** A multimedia system requires high processing power to deal with large data processing and real-time delivery of media. A multimedia system should have a processor having a minimum of 500 MHz (or higher) of processing speed.
- **Bus interface:** It plays a very important role in a multimedia system and provides interconnections among various hardware devices. The three most important interfacing components are Small Computer System Interface (SCSI), Integrated Drive Electronics (IDE), and Media Control Interface (MCI). These interface standards have been modified from time-to-time to cope up with the technological advancements.
- **Memory and storage devices:** Typically, all multimedia presentations are memory hungry, and hence require storage devices with large capacity and lots of RAM (128 MB, 256 MB, or more). The storage devices include hard disk, CDs, DVDs, and pen drives. In addition, large cache memory is required of Level 2 and 3 hierarchies for efficient management.
- **Operating system:** Every multimedia system requires a special operating system that allows access to file system and process data efficiently and quickly. It is also needed to support direct transfers to disk, real-time scheduling, fast interrupt processing, I/O streaming, and so on.

- **Software tools:** User-friendly software tools are needed to handle media and design, develop applications, and to deliver the media. In addition, data representations/file formats should be easy to handle and should also allow for compression/decompression in real-time.
- **Sound and display cards:** Since audio and video are basic components of any multimedia presentation, a good sound and color display card (at least 8-bit) is necessary for any multimedia system.
- **Efficient input/output (I/O) devices:** Efficient I/O devices are needed to allow real-time recording as well as playback of data. Typically, a multimedia system should be equipped with a high-resolution color monitor, a CD-ROM drive (24× or higher), keyboard, scrollable mouse, color printer (300 dpi or more), scanner (300–500 dpi or more), digital and video cameras, audio and video recorders, amplifiers and speakers, and an audio microphone.
- **Network support:** In a business conference, where a multimedia presentation is on, we may require associated peripherals connected to a main computer via communication devices (modems, hubs, and so on) to carry out the supportive role in running an application. In addition for higher transmission speeds, it is required to use ISDN, DSL, ATM, or any other digital switched network service.

9. Explain the following.

(a) SCSI

(b) IDE

(c) MCI

Ans. (a) SCSI (pronounced "scuzzy") is the abbreviation for small computer system interface. SCSI bus refers to the standard adopted by ANSI for I/O bus type in 1986. It connects devices like disk drives, CD/DVD drives, printers, modem, scanner, and other peripherals. A total of eight devices (ID numbers from 0 to 7) can be connected to the SCSI port. However, as per the recommendation of IT community, SCSI ID 0 is assigned to the bootable hard disk, ID 2 to the floppy disk drive, and ID 3 to CD-ROM drive.

The SCSI bus is smaller and simpler than a system bus. The original SCSI standard SCSI-1 was designed to transfer data at the rate up to 5 MB/s, and has an 8-bit data line (called **narrow bus**). This standard was subsequently modified to SCSI-2 that allows data transfer rate up to 10 MB/s and has 16-bit wide data bus. A wide SCSI bus has 16 data lines and can transfer 16 bits at a time. The control functions are performed by 10 additional lines. The SCSI-2 standard allows you to connect maximum of 16 devices. However, with recent developments, SCSI bus now has wider data buses, more control features, and higher data transfer rates. The Ultra SCSI (SCSI-3) allows you to connect as many as 32 devices, achieve speeds of 40 MB/s.

(b) IDE is a 16-bit bus standard based on IBM PC Industry Standard Architecture (ISA). Unlike SCSI which can connect both internal components and external devices, IDE connections are typically internal and connect hard disks, CD-ROM drives, and other hardware components inside the PC. IDE drive controller is often built into the PC motherboard. A PC motherboard can support two IDE controllers, and each controller in turn can support two devices (a master and a slave). In this way, you can install a combination of four hard disks, CD-ROM drives, or other components inside your PC. Though the circuitry for IDE is less expensive and less complex than that of SCSI, it has some limitations, which are as follows:

- It supports only up to 9 GB drive capacity.
- It allows only one drive to be active at a time from the master/slave pair.
- Since the master drive manages the operations and if both drives are connected to the controller, then a failure of master will halt the operations of both drives.

Like SCSI, IDE also comes in various forms, namely, *simple IDE* (with a data transfer rate of 2.5 MB/s), *Enhanced IDE*, with a data transfer rate of 16.6 MB/s, and *Ultra IDE* with data transfer rate of 33 MB/s.

(c) The MCI is a high-level API provided by Windows to allow software to interact with multimedia peripherals such as CD player, audio controllers, AVI video, etc. With MCI, you can connect any hardware device to a computer running Windows. Each MCI multimedia device provides a set of MCI commands. For example, *play* command is used to play an already opened file or a track. To start using any device, it is necessary to initialize that device by sending appropriate commands. The MCI has now been phased out in favour of the DirectX interface. DirectX is a collection of APIs for handling multimedia-related tasks.

10. Discuss different types of multimedia software used for various purposes.

Ans: The different multimedia software used for various purposes are discussed as follows:

- **Text-editing and word-processing software:** These software are used to store data in textual form as a document. Most of the word processors come as a part of Office Suite that also includes spreadsheet software, presentation software and database software. Most of the word-processing software possess useful features such as spelling and grammar checker, text and table formatters, thesaurus, etc. In addition, they also include built-in templates for letters, resumes, and other important documents. Word-processing software also allow the user to embed multimedia elements such as images, sounds and videos with the textual data. Some of the most commonly used word-processing software are Microsoft Word, WordPerfect, and OpenOffice.org Writer.
- **Painting and drawing software:** Any multimedia project is incomplete without the images. Images make your project more interesting, presentable, and easy to understand. Painting software are used for creating bitmap (or raster) images and drawing software are used for creating vector-based images. Some of the commonly used painting software are Adobe Photoshop, Microsoft Paint, Corel PhotoPaint, and the GIMP. And some of the commonly used drawing software are Adobe Illustrator, CoralDraw, Aldus FreeHand, and Macromedia Fireworks. Some software applications are capable of creating both bitmap as well as vector images.
- **3-D modeling and animation software:** These software have raised the standard of multimedia projects. They provide 3D and other animation effects to an image that it looks so realistic and presentable. They allow you to add realism to a 3D scene by adding lighting and surface rendering effects. These software also bundled with some commonly used 3D clip art objects such as people, buildings, furniture, trees and plants, vehicles, and animals and birds. Some of the 3-D modeling and animation software are Macromedia Extreme 3D, AutoDesk 3D Studio Max, StrataVision 3D, and Specular Infini-D.
- **Image-editing software:** These software are used for editing the existing bitmapped images. Many painting and drawing software can be used as image editing software. The scanned images, clip art images, and images from digital cameras can also be edited using these software applications. Some image-editing software are Photoshop, Corel PhotoPaint, etc.
- **Sound-editing software:** These software are basically used for editing digital as well as MIDI sound files. They allow the user to actually see the music in a score or waveform. The users can cut, copy or paste the portions of the audio file according to their need. They can also add special effects such as echo, amplifications, and noise reduction to create their own sound effects. Some sound-editing software are Creating WaveStudio, WavePad, Macromedia SoundEdit 16, etc.

- **Video and animation software:** Video and animation are nothing but sequence of still images which when played back at a fast speed, display a continuous scene. Some software allow you to edit and assemble the video clips captured from camera, tape or other digitized movie segments, audio clips, scanned images, or animation to form a new video clip with your own audio and animation effects. One can also add transition and visual effects to the generated clip. Some movie making software are Adobe Premiere Pro, VideoPad, Corel VideoStudio Pro, and MediaStudio Pro.

11. Present an architectural framework for VoD.

Ans. Nowadays, many companies provide VoD that allows an individual user to select and watch desired videos at anytime. In addition, the viewer can play, pause, or stop the running video. The video must be delivered to the user's computer in real time, reliably, and inexpensively. The existing database systems do not provide real-time response that these applications require. Thus, the server in such database systems must contend with specialized real-time constraints. In addition, the video delivery rates must be synchronized both at the server and the client side, taking into account the characteristics of the communication network. The basic architecture of a VoD system comprises the following:

- **Video server:** Since the storage requirements of multimedia data are very high, the multimedia data are generally stored on several disks (usually in a RAID configuration). Moreover, the systems containing large volume of data can use tertiary storage for less frequently accessed data.
- **Terminals:** The devices through which the people view multimedia data are collectively known as *terminals*. The PCs and televisions attached to the set-top box are the examples of terminals.
- **Network:** A high-capacity network is required to transmit a large volume of multimedia data from a server to multiple terminals.

12. Write a short note on multimedia databases.

Ans. With the technological advancements in computing, multimedia data such as images, audio, video, text or document, and other graphic objects are being used in a wide variety of software applications. Examples of such applications are Internet video, video conferencing, art and entertainment, digital libraries, journalism, and many more. The databases that allow users to store different types of multimedia objects and also provide support for efficient querying and indexing of multimedia data are known as **multimedia databases**. These databases not only provide almost all the functionalities, a traditional database provides, but also provide some new and enhanced functionalities. They provide unified frameworks for storing, processing, retrieving, transmitting, and presenting a variety of media data types in different formats. In addition, they adhere to numerical constraints that the traditional databases generally lack.

Since, multimedia data need a huge amount of storage space, it is mandatory to store and transmit multimedia data in compressed form in order to save the storage space. For example, to compress images to a lesser number of bytes, different compression standards like JPEG (Joint Picture Experts Group) or GIF (Graphical Image Format) are used. For compressing video data, a different series of standard MPEG (Moving Picture Experts Group) is used as it exploits the common features and thus, reduces the size to a greater extent. Different standards used for encoding audio data are MP3, Real Audio, Windows Media Audio, etc.

In addition to multimedia objects, multimedia databases require to store several aspects related to the multimedia objects. The various contents of multimedia data are described as follows:

- **Media data:** It includes the actual multimedia object such as an image or an audio clip or a video clip stored in the database. This object is usually in a compressed form so as to save the storage space.

- **Format data:** It includes information related to format of multimedia data such as encoding scheme used, resolution, sampling rate, etc. Format data are used to represent the retrieved information.
- **Keyword data:** It includes keyword description usually related to the creation of multimedia data. For example, date, time, place, creator, etc. This information is also referred to as **content descriptive data**.
- **Feature data:** It includes information that characterizes multimedia data. For example, shapes, colors, textures used in an image. This information is also referred to as **content-dependent data**.

The last three types of contents are known as **metadata** as they describe several aspects of the multimedia data. The keyword and the feature data are used as indices for searching purposes, whereas the format data are used to present the retrieved information.

13. State and explain the desirable characteristics of multimedia databases.

Ans. Multimedia databases should not only provide inherent characteristics such as huge size, support for multimedia data types, temporal nature, richness of content, complexity of representation, and subjective interpretation, but in addition must also posses some additional characteristics, which are listed as follows:

- They should be able to manage different types of input and output devices. For example, data input can be from various devices such as scanners, digital cameras, microphones, MIDI devices, or video cameras while typical output devices include high-resolution monitors and speakers.
- They should be able to support different data compression techniques and storage formats.
- They must be able to integrate different data models. For example, the textual and numeric data can be best represented using a relational data model, whereas video documents are better represented using an object-oriented data model. Thus, the multimedia database systems should support the integration of both these models.
- They should provide a device-independent and format-independent interface. That is, multimedia databases should hide details of device control as well as the internal storage format. In addition, they must allow conversion of one format to another (for example, gif, tiff, etc.) without affecting the multimedia applications.
- They must perform read and write operations of continuous-media data in real time. In addition, the data transfer of continuous data must be given a higher priority than other database management actions.
- Due to the inexact and subjective nature of multimedia data, the keyword-based searches, and exact and range searches used in traditional databases are not sufficient in multimedia databases. For example, in traditional databases the retrieval of records based on the social security number is precisely defined; however, in a multimedia database containing facial images, the retrieval of records could be based on certain facial features. Thus, the multimedia databases must support similarity-based and content-based queries, which require indices that are content dependent, in addition to keyword-based indices.
- They must support different computing platforms and operating systems.
- Since the transfer of large amount of data takes a long time, the multimedia databases must handle long transactions in a reliable manner.
- As a query for the same item can be written in different forms, a multimedia database must offer a variety of user-friendly query systems suited to different kinds of media. In addition, they must offer easy-to-use queries, and fast and accurate retrieval of information.

- It is quite possible that different media data corresponding to a single multimedia object are stored in different formats, on different devices, and have different rates of transfer. Thus, it is desirable for multimedia databases to periodically synchronize the media data before presenting it to the user.

14. What is the key limitation of relational database in implementing multimedia applications? Discuss the extensions made to RDBMS to support multimedia.

Ans. The relational database system is the dominant database paradigm; however, it lacks the ability to support multimedia databases. The key limitation of RDBMS for implementing multimedia applications comes from two areas: the relational data model and relational computational model. The relational database systems have been designed to manage only alphanumeric and date type data in the form of tables. That is, the traditional relational database systems cannot store multimedia objects such as graphics, images, audio, and full-motion video with recorded audio and annotated voice components.

To support multimedia applications, most of the leading relational databases have adapted a data type known as **Binary Large Object** (**BLOB**) for storing binary and free-form text. BLOBs are used for storing objects such as images or other binary data types. The tables in the relational database store the information about the location of the BLOBs, which may be actually stored outside the database on separate image or video servers.

15. Discuss various multimedia data structures used for storing multimedia data.

Ans. Certain applications such as Geographical Information Systems (GIS), Computer-aided-design (CAD), Computer-aided-manufacturing (CAM), etc., require to store data related to objects like points, lines, rectangles, polygons, cubes, maps, satellite images and other geometric objects, in multidimensional space. These objects cannot be stored using simple data structures such as arrays, linked lists, etc. For these objects, we need some advanced data structures such as k-d trees and R-trees.

- **K-d trees:** The k-d tree (stands for **k-dimensional tree**) is a space partitioning data structure that organizes points in a k-dimensional space. It is a multi-dimensional binary search tree where each node consists of a 'record' that contains data and two pointers. These pointers are either null or point to another node in the tree. Like B-trees, k-d trees organize points by successively dividing space into smaller parts. Every node of a k-d tree stores a point, which in turn contains a key expressed as k-coordinates and an associated value. Each level of a k-d tree splits the space into two parts (known as **half-spaces**) such that both contain approximately equal number of points. The partitioning is done along one dimension at the top level that is root node, along another dimension at the next level nodes, and so on. The partitioning process continues as long as any node contains more than a given maximum number of points.

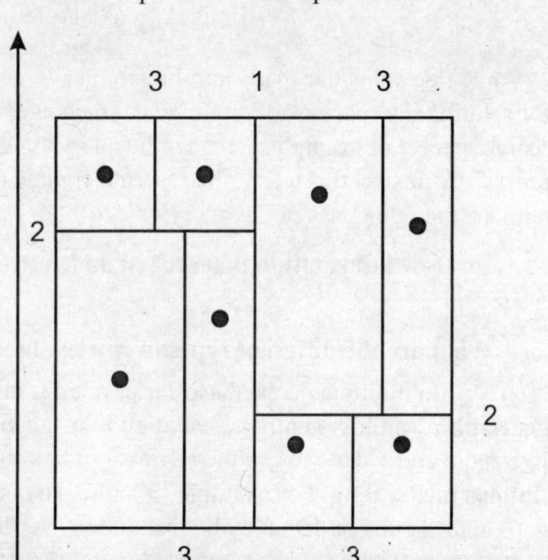

Figure 11.3 k-d Tree Representation of a Set of Points in 2-D Space

Figure 11.3 shows the k-d representation of a set of points in two-dimensional space. Here, each line represents a node in the tree and the line numbers show the level of the tree at which a particular node appears. Note that the maximum number of points in a leaf node has been set to one.

- **R-trees:** An R-tree (where R stands for a rectangle) is a balanced tree structure used for indexing of objects such as points, lines, rectangles and other polygons. Like B^+-tree, the objects to be indexed (say, polygons) are stored in the leaf nodes; however, each node of an R-tree is associated with a rectangular bounding box called **minimum bounding rectangle (MBR)** rather than a range of values. The bounding box of each internal node stores the bounding boxes of its child nodes along with the pointers to child nodes. The bounding box of each leaf node contains the indexed objects and sometimes the bounding boxes of the objects. Note that the bounding box of an object stores the object itself. Figure 11.4 shows an R-tree representation of a set of rectangles (represented by solid lines) and the bounding boxes of the nodes of R-tree (represented by dotted lines) for the set of rectangles.

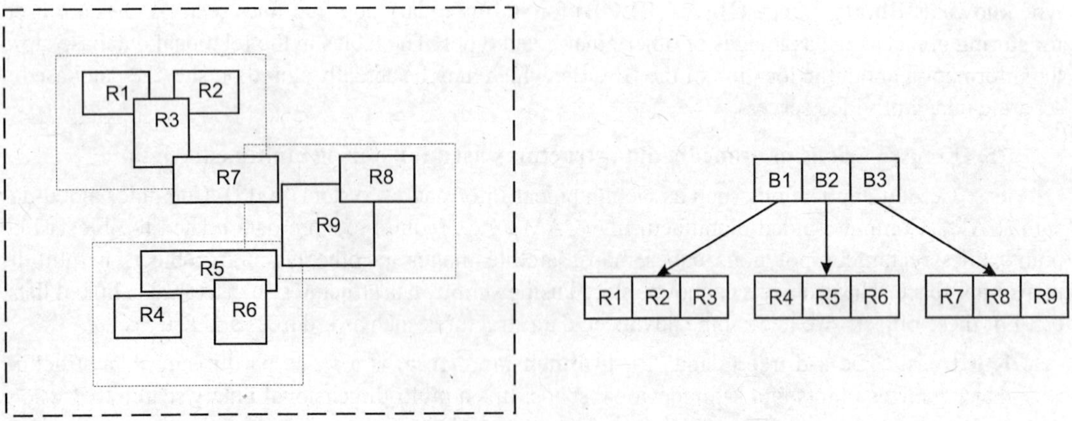

Figure 11.4 An R-tree Representation of a Set of Rectangles

An R-tree splits the space into hierarchically nested and overlapping bounding boxes. The criterion for splitting the space is to minimize the rectangular area that results in faster searching by limiting the search space. For example, consider the query "find all the objects in a given area that intersect the query object". To answer this query, the search is limited only to those subtrees whose bounding boxes overlap with the bounding box of the query object.

16. How information is searched and retrieved from multimedia databases?

or

What are the different types of retrieval techniques for multimedia databases?

Ans. In multimedia databases, user queries not always result in textual form; rather it may require generating a multimedia representation that satisfies the user queries. Some types of multimedia data like audio and video require the retrieval of data from the database at a constant rate, thus, called **continuous media data**. For example, if audio data is retrieved at a variable rate, then either there will be gaps in the sound or data may be lost due to overflow of system buffers.

The main type of queries imposed on multimedia databases request for multimedia data containing certain objects or activities. For example, a user might want to search an image based on its color or texture or shape, or any other information that can be derived from the image from a web-based photo gallery. Such type of queries that retrieve multimedia objects from multimedia databases based on their contents are referred to as **content-based queries or content-based retrieval**.

In some cases, the user may also need to find the images in the database that are similar to a given image. These types of queries can be answered by comparing the given image with each image in the database on the basis of visual attributes. Since it is rare to find the exact match, the matching of two images is based on similarity measuring function for visual attributes. To check the similarity between two images, different approaches can be used. In one of the most widely used approach, each visual attribute is assigned a particular weight, and a similarity measuring function calculates the relative distance (known as **score**) between the two images being compared. The score for each visual attribute determines the degree of similarity between the two images and the image with a least score reflects the closest match. This type of retrieval is also referred to as **similarity-based retrieval** and most often used in fingerprints matching systems, retailing stores, medical imaging, etc.

Synchronization between multiple media streams is one of the most important requirements for some multimedia applications. For example, during retrieval of a movie, there must be synchronization between audio and video data so that lips movement of the person must match with the voice of the person.

17. List and explain the three basic issues of multimedia synchronization.

Ans. In a strict sense, **multimedia synchronization** refers to the temporal relationship between media objects in a multimedia document. However, in a broader sense, it could be extended to content or spatial relationships. Synchronization between multiple media streams is one of the most important requirements for some multimedia applications. The multimedia synchronization addresses three basis issues, which are as follows:

- **Content relationship (or content synchronization):** It deals with the maintenance of a media object's relationship to (dependency on) a particular piece of data. In simple terms, it defines dependencies of media data units on some data. A typical example of content synchronization is a graph linked to a spreadsheet. In this case, when data in the spreadsheet are edited, the graph linked to it is also updated. The graph linked to the data is generated automatically and cannot be edited directly.
- **Spatial relationship (or spatial synchronization):** It refers to the physical arrangement (that is, layout) of the multimedia objects and the corresponding relationships between them on a particular output device (for example, monitor) at a certain point of time. Thus, it is also known as **layout relationship**. It basically defines the location where the media objects should be placed in space (usually the two-dimensional display screen). For example, tables in HTML, layout managers in Java, and so on.
- **Temporal relationship (or temporal synchronization):** It defines how different media objects are coordinated in time. For example, during retrieval of a movie, there must be synchronization between audio and video data so that lips movement of the person must match with the voice of the person. For the audio/video pairing, if the media are not synchronized, their intended meaning could be degraded to the point of being completely lost. Another example could be a PowerPoint presentation containing voice narration and animated images or graphics. The clarity of the presentation is often determined by the appropriate ordering, timing, and layout of objects on the slide. The incorrect ordering or timings of the objects on the slide make the presentation difficult to understand, or possibly even convey incorrect information.

18. What is the difference between time-dependent and time-independent media objects?

Ans. A **time-dependent** media object is always presented as a media stream. The media stream can be divided into units and temporal relationship exists between consecutive units of the media stream.

If the presentation durations of all units of a time-dependent media object are equal, it is said to be a **continuous media object**. A typical example of a continuous media object is video as all units (frames) in it are of equal durations. A **time-independent** media object, on the other hand, is any traditional kind of media like image, graphics, or text.

A time-independent media object can be transmitted and updated in any order, that is, from top to bottom (which is the usual way), or left to right, or right to left, or bottom to top. In any case, the semantics of the content do not change. However, for a time-dependent media object such as a video or an audio, the order is important. If a video or an audio presentation is run in the reverse order, the semantics will be lost.

19. Differentiate between intra-object and inter-object synchronization.

Ans. Intra-object synchronization refers to the time relationships between various presentation units of one time-dependent media object. One good example is the time ratio of individual frames of a video sequence. If a video has a refresh rate of 25 frames per second, then each frame has to be shown for at least 40 ms (see Figure 11.5a). If this is not the case, the synchronization will be lost. Lack of intra-object synchronization results in pauses or jerks.

Inter-object synchronization, on the other hand, refers to the temporal relationships between different media objects, which may be time-independent or time dependent. An example of an inter-object synchronization is a video, which has a synchronized audio with it. This is followed by several images, which is again followed by an animation, synchronized with audio commentary (see Figure 11.5b).

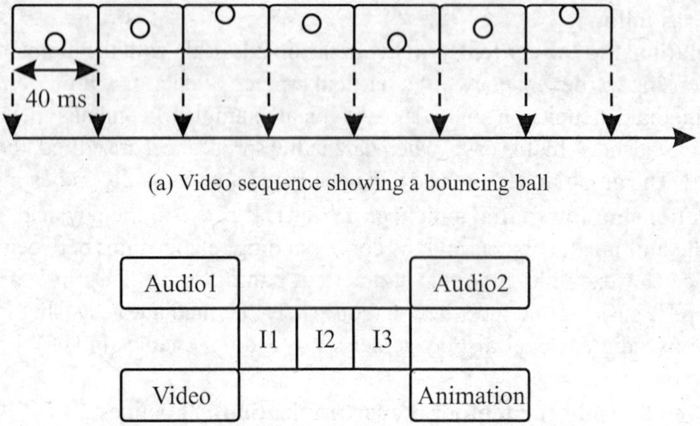

(a) Video sequence showing a bouncing ball

(b) Inter-object synchronization of image

Figure 11.5 Intra and Inter-object Synchronization

20. What is the difference between hypertext and hypermedia?

Ans. The term hypertext was first invented by Ted Nelson around 1965. In **hypertext systems**, the documents contain links to other related documents on the Internet. These links are called **hyperlinks**. A hyperlink is used to jump to another part of the same page or to load a different web page. A hypertext system provides a non-linear way of accessing documents, by following links that point to other parts of the document or indeed to other documents. In simple terms, it is text with links, links and more links. Usually hypertext links appear in a different color (typically in blue and underlined) from the rest of the text. When the mouse pointer is moved over a text link or over a graphic link, it will change from an arrow to a hand.

When this link is clicked, a page containing information related to the hypertext is displayed. A hypertext system provides a simple and consistent way to organize large data available on the Internet. In addition, it allows fast and easy searching of some information in the documents spanned up to thousands of pages.

Hypermedia is an extension of the concept of hypertext. It is not constrained to be text based. It can contain other media objects also, such as images, graphics, audio, and video. The World Wide Web is the best example of hypermedia application. It contains not only text links, but also links of images, audio clips, animated videos, and even full-motion videos.

21. Write a short note on virtual reality.

Ans. Virtual reality can be described as an artificial environment that is created by using special computer hardware and software, which is presented to the user in such a manner that it appears and feels like a real three-dimensional world. Virtual reality, also referred as **artificial reality** or **synthetic reality**, is an interactive technology which totally controls sensory input and creates the convincing illusion that one is completely immersed in a computer-generated world.

To enter in virtual reality, a user wears special gloves, earphones, and head-mounted display (HMD) device, all of which receive input from the computer system. In this way, at least three of the five human senses are controlled by the computer. In addition to feeding sensory input to the user, the devices also monitor the user's actions. The HMD, for example, tracks how the eyes move and respond accordingly by sending new video input.

In virtual reality, cyber space is made up of thousands of geometric objects and points plotted in a three-dimensional space; the more the number of objects and points that describe the objects, the higher the resolution; therefore, a more realistic view will be seen. Each motion or action requires the computer to perform recalculation on the position, angle, and shape. Note that a virtual environment can represent any three-dimensional world that is either real or abstract. This includes real systems like buildings, landscapes, underwater shipwrecks, spacecrafts, archaeological excavation sites, human anatomy, sculptures, crime scene reconstructions, solar systems, and so on. Of special interest is the visual and sensual representation of abstract systems like magnetic fields, turbulent flow structures, molecular models, mathematical systems, auditorium acoustics, stock market behaviour, population densities, information flows, and so on. These virtual worlds can be animated, interactive, shared, and can expose behaviour and functionality.

Since virtual reality systems require very expensive hardware and software, and tremendous computing power, they are mainly used in research laboratories. However, there are several other areas where virtual reality is used. These areas include *health care* (surgery, diagnostics, and rehabilitation), *mass entertainment* (video games arcades, theme parks), *education* (training simulators, teaching aids), *architecture*, *design*, *marketing*, *insurance*, *finance*, *sports*, and *telecommunications*.

22. What are bitmap images? How they are different from vector images?

Ans. A *bitmap* or *raster* graphics is made of small blocks of color called **pixels** (the smallest element of a digital image). Each pixel has a numerical color value as well as a position in the picture. The bitmaps are resolution dependent and look good at their actual size. While they are scaled, they either appear jagged or lose image quality. Some of the most commonly used bitmap formats include BMP, GIF, JPEG, TIFF, and PNG.

A **vector image**, on the other hand, is made of geometrical shapes such as lines, curves, ellipses, polygons, etc., which can be defined by algebraic Equations. For example, two end points for a line. The vector images are resolution independent, that is, they can be printed or displayed at any resolution, scaled up (enlarged) and down (reduced) to any size without losing details and quality. Thus, they are well suited for creating logos and illustrations. One can also create sharp and crisp outlines with the help of vector graphics. Some of the most commonly used vector formats include CDR (CorelDRAW) and AI (Adobe Illustrator).

23. Define compression. What is the difference between lossy and lossless compression?

Ans. In terms of computers, the only limitation of using a multimedia presentation is that it consumes a lot of storage space. In order to manage large multimedia data objects efficiently, these data objects need to be compressed to reduce the file size for storage of these objects. **Compression** of a file refers to the process of cutting down the size of the file by using special compression algorithms. Compression tries to remove the redundancies in the pattern of data. For example, if a white pixel is followed by 25 black pixels, then instead of storing all the black pixels, only the count of black pixels can be stored by using some coding mechanism. After removing such redundancies, the object takes less storage space. In addition, the components of multimedia such as audio and video take significantly less time for transmission over the Internet when they are compressed. There are two types of compression techniques, namely, *lossy* and *lossless*.

In **lossy** compression technique, some data are deliberately discarded in order to achieve massive reductions in the size of the compressed file. In this compression format, we cannot recover all of its original data from the compressed version. JPEG image files and MPEG video files are examples of lossy compressed files. On the other hand, in **lossless** compression technique, the size of the file is reduced without permanently discarding any information of the original data. If an image that has undergone lossless compression is decompressed, the original data can be reconstructed exactly, bit-for-bit, that is, it will be identical to the digital image before compression. PNG image file formats use lossless compression.

24. Describe Huffman encoding algorithm used for compressing text files.

Ans. Huffman coding is statistical based coding. This algorithm is named after its inventor David Huffman. The main idea behind this algorithm was to replace fixed-length codes (such as ASCII) by variable-length codes, assigning shorter code words to the more frequently occurring symbols and thus decreasing the overall length of the data. The basic algorithm is as follows:

1. The text to be compressed is scanned and the total number of occurrences of all the characters is determined.
2. The characters are sorted based on the number of occurrences in the text.
3. The Hufffman code tree is built based on the sorted list using bottom-up approach.
4. The tree is traversed to determine new code words. While traversing we follows a rule, which is, going left is a 0 and going right is a 1. The code word is only completed when a leaf node is reached.
5. The text is scanned again and a new text file is created using the Huffman codes.

25. Describe Run Length Encoding (RLE) algorithm used for compressing text files.

Ans. RLE is a simple compression technique which is more suitable for the data with strings of repeating symbols. The main idea behind this algorithm is that the string of repeated characters is represented as pair of string length and the character. For example, if the given string is '*aaaaabbbbaabbabbaaaa*' then it will be encoded as '*5a4b2a2b1a2b4a*'. Thus a string of 20 bytes is reduced to 14 bytes. However, the main drawback of this algorithm is that if they are no or less repeating symbols then the length of encoded string may become double the input string. For example, the output string for '*ababaababcd*' is '*1a1b1a1b2a1b1a1b1c1d*' where the length of input string is 11 bytes and the length of output string is 20 bytes which is almost double of the input string. To overcome this problem, the output string obtained using RLE can further be encoded using Huffman encoding.

26. Explain the difference between JPEG and MPEG standard.

Ans. JPEG is the standard compression technique used to compress still images. It is designed to compress either full-color or grey-scale images. It works well with naturalistic artwork, photographs, and similar material; however, it does not work well with lettering, simple cartoons, or line drawings. JPEG is lossy in the sense that the decompressed image differs slightly from the original one. It is especially useful for transmitting files across networks, and for archiving libraries of images. The fundamental advantage of JPEG is that it stores full-color information, that is, 24 bits/pixel (16 million colors), as compared to GIF, which can only store 8 bits/pixel (256 or fewer colors). However, the main disadvantage of JPEG standard is that it takes longer to decode and view the JPEG image as compared to GIF file format. JPEG method is a symmetrical algorithm in the sense that decompression is the exact reverse process of compression.

MPEG is a method devised for the compression of a wide range of video and motion pictures. It is available in two versions: MPEG-1 and MPEG-2. The former version has been designed for CD-ROM with a data rate of 1.5 Mbps while the latter version has been designed for digital TV broadcast and DVD with a data rate of 3–6 Mbps. The MPEG-2 standard allows the transmission of MPEG data across television and cable network systems. Each video is composed of a set of frames where each frame is actually a still image. The frames flow so rapidly (for example, 50 frames per second in TV) that the human eye cannot notice the discrete images. This property of human eye forms the basis of motion pictures. To handle and play large MPEG video files, it is required to have sufficient processor speed, internal memory, and hard disk space.

MPEG uses an asymmetric compression method, that is, compression and decompression are performed using two different processes. Compression under MPEG is more complicated as compared to decompression. This makes MPEG a good choice for applications that need to write data only once, but need to read it many times. An example of such an application is an archiving system. However, the systems requiring audio and video data to be written many times (such as an editing system) are not good choices for MPEG. This is because they will run more slowly when using the MPEG compression scheme.

27. Give the basic steps/algorithm of JPEG compression.

Ans. Following are the steps involved in the JPEG image compression (lossy) process.

1. **Color sub-sampling:** This step is performed only if the image to be compressed is colored; for grey-scale images, this step is not required. The RGB color space of the image is changed to YUV color space and its chrominance component is down-sampled.
2. **Blocking:** The image is divided into a series of 8 × 8 pixel blocks. Blocking also reduces the number of calculations needed for an image.
3. **Discrete cosine transformation** (DCT): Each block of 8 × 8 pixels goes through the DCT transformation to identify the spatial redundancy in an image. The result of DCT transformation for each 8 × 8 block of pixels is 8 × 8 block of DCT coefficients (that is, 64 frequency components in each block).
4. **Quantization:** In this phase, the DCT coefficients in each block are scalar quantized with the help of a quantization table (Q-table) in order to wipe out the less important DCT coefficients. Each value in the block is divided by a weight taken from the corresponding position in Q-table with ignoring the fractional part. The changes made in this phase cannot be undone. That's why this JPEG method is considered lossy.
5. **Ordering:** The output of quantization is then ordered in a zigzag manner to distinguish the low-frequency components (usually non-zero) from the high-frequency components (usually,

zero). Ordering results in bit stream in which zero frequency components are placed close to the end.

6. **Run-length encoding:** The run-length encoding is applied to zeros of zigzag sequence to eliminate the redundancy. This encoding replaces each repeated symbol in a given sequence with the symbol itself and the number of times is repeated. For example, the text "*cccccccbbbbuffffff*" is compressed as "*c7b4u1f6*". Thus, redundant zeros are removed after this phase.
7. **Variable-length encoding:** The variable-length encoding is applied on the output of the previous phase to get the compressed JPEG bit stream. In variable-length encoding, a variable number of bits are used to represent each character rather than a fixed number of bits for each character. Fewer bits are used to represent the more frequently used character; the most frequently used character can be represented by one bit only. This helps in reducing the length of compressed data.

28. Differentiate among the different types of encoded frames used in MPEG video compression.

Ans. In MPEG video compression, the encoded frames fall under three categories, namely, *intra-coded (I) frames*, *predicted (P) frames*, and *bidirectional* (*B*) frames, which are described as follows:

- **I-frame:** This frame is not associated with any other frame (previous or next). It is encoded independently of other frames in the video and contains all the necessary information that is needed to recreate the entire frame. Thus, I-frames cannot be constructed from any other frames. I-frames must appear in a movie at regular intervals to indicate the sudden changes in the frame.
- **P-frame:** This frame relates to the frame preceding to it whether it is an I-frame or a P-frame. It contains small differences relative to its preceding I-frame or P-frame but it is not useful for recording major modifications, for example in case of fast moving objects. Thus, P-frames carry only a small amount of information as compared to other frames and even more less number of bits after compression. Unlike I-frames, a P-frame can be re-constructed from its preceding frame.
- **B-frame:** This frame relates to its preceding as well as succeeding I-frame or P-frame. However, a B-frame cannot relate to any other B-frame. Such frames provide improved motion compensation and the best compression.

29. What is the difference between intra-frame and inter-frame video compression?

Ans. MPEG uses two types of compression methods to encode video data, namely, *inter-frame* and *intra-frame* encoding. The differences between inter-frame and intra-frame compression are listed in Table 11.1.

Table 11.1 Differences between Inter-frame and Intra-frame Compression

Inter-frame (or temporal) compression	Intra-frame (or spatial) compression
❑ It uses one or more preceding or succeeding frames in a sequence to compress the current frame.	❑ It compresses each frame separately and independently of the surrounding frames (such as JPEG).
❑ It looks for patterns across the frames. For example, in a movie, there are certain scenes where the background is same and stationary and only some portion such as hand movement is changing. In such cases, most consecutive frames will be almost similar except the portion of frame covering the hand movements.	❑ It looks for patterns within the same frame. For example, the intensity value of a pixel can be guessed from that of its neighbouring pixels. Thus, it is not necessary to represent each pixel in an image frame independently—rather, one can predict a pixel from its neighbours.

❑ Since inter-frame compression copies data from one frame to another, if the original frame is lost in the transmission (or simply cut out), it is difficult to reconstruct the following frames.	❑ Making cuts in the intra-frame compression is almost as easy as editing in uncompressed video. The user finds the beginning and ending of each frame, and simply copies bit-for-bit each frame that needs to be kept; and discards the unwanted frames.
❑ Since inter-frame compression attempts to remove redundant information across different frames, some unique information may be lost.	❑ It offers better quality than inter-frame as the integrity of each frame is maintained.
❑ It works well for programs that can simply be played back by the user. It causes problems if the video sequence needs to be edited.	❑ It is used for purposes such as video editing where frames need to be randomly accessed.

30. Write a short note on audio compression.

Ans. Before the audio data can be transmitted over the Internet, it needs to be compressed. Audio compression can be applied on speech or music. There are two categories of techniques that can be used to compress audio, namely, *predictive encoding* and *perçeptual encoding*.

- **Predictive encoding:** In digital audio or video, successive samples are usually similar to each other. Considering this fact, the initial frame and the difference values in the successive samples for all the samples are stored in the compressed form. As the size of the difference values between two samples is much smaller than the size of sample itself, this encoding technique saves much space. While decompressing, the previous sample and the difference value are used to reproduce the next sample. Predictive encoding is generally used for speech.
- **Perceptual encoding:** The human auditory system suffers from certain flaws. Exploiting this fact, the perceptual encoding technique encodes the audio signals in such a manner that they sound similar to human listeners, even they are different. This technique is generally used for compressing music as it can create CD-quality audio. MP3, a part of MPEG standard, is the most common compression technique based on perceptual encoding.

31. Discuss the digitization principle of audio.

Ans. Audio plays a very important role in a multimedia system. Any multimedia application is incomplete without the use of audio effects. Whether it is an academic presentation or any video game, the effects added by audio are of utter importance. There are basically two types of audio that can be played on the multimedia systems, namely, *digitized audio* and *MIDI*. When voice or music is captured by a microphone, it generates an electrical signal, which consists of a fundamental sine wave of a certain amplitude and frequency. The amplitude represents the intensity of the sound, whereas the frequency represents the pitch of the sound.

If we want to store the digital version of sound waves, we need to form the digitized representations of audio information. The digitization of sound necessarily implies *sampling* and *quantization* of signals. The digitized representation of sound waves consists of a binary code that stores a massive amount of numbers used to represent a signal. An **analog-to-digital converter** (**ADC**) is a computer chip used to convert an analogue signal into digital information. This process is called **sampling**. The rate at which sampling is performed is called **sampling frequency**. Once the signal is converted into digital form, it can be manipulated with processes like combining sounds, slicing, truncation, looping, reversing a sound and other digital signal processing. The signal can then be converted back to an analogue signal through a **digital-to-analog converter** (**DAC**). The digital waveform to be reconstructed depends on the selected sampling frequency. If the sampling frequency selected is very low, then it becomes difficult to reconstruct the waveform.

When sampling is performed in the amplitude or voltage dimension, it is called **quantization**. During quantization, each sample value is round off to the nearest integer to create the waveform. However, the quantization process can create unwanted noise.

32. Write a short on MIDI.

Ans. With the advancement in synthesizer technology, the relationship between music and computers has become more and more important. A synthesizer can generate or play sounds of multiple instruments such as piano, trumpet, violin, guitar, etc., simultaneously. The interface between the synthesizer and the computer is provided by a hardware setup called **MIDI**. MIDI (Musical Instruments Digital Interface) is a small piece of equipment that is connected to the serial port of the computer and allows the transmission of music signals. It forms a protocol adopted by the electronic music industry that enables computers, synthesizers, keyboards, and musical instruments from different manufacturers to communicate with each other. In addition, it allows the direct recording of musical notes from the musical instruments into the computer.

MIDI—instead of storing the actual sound components—records events such as pressing of a key, the time when the key is pressed, the duration for which the key is pressed, and with how much pressure the key is pressed. This musical information is stored in a data file called **MIDI file**, which consists of a list of commands which when executed produces the sound. For example, the pressing of a piano key can be represented as a computer command, which when processed by the MIDI device, results in the sound from the piano. The MIDI file can easily be edited to add any sound effects or change the voice of an instrument.

The MIDI hardware setup consists of a 31.25 kbps serial connection with 10 bits transmitted per byte (including a start bit, 8 data bits, and one stop bit). The MIDI interface consists of three *MIDI ports* (5-pin connectors), labelled as *IN, OUT*, and *THRU*. The **IN** port accepts all the MIDI data coming from an individual instrument. The **OUT** and **THRU** ports send data out to the rest of the MIDI set up. The only difference is that the data coming out of the THRU port is an exact copy of the data received at the IN port. That is, no change is made to the data from the time it arrives at the IN port to the time it leaves the THRU port. In simple terms, the MIDI THRU is the connector by which the device echoes that it receives from MIDI IN. The MIDI THRU connector is basically used for daisy-chaining multiple instruments. The chaining of multiple instruments is done by connecting the MIDI THRU of instrument 1 to the MIDI IN of instrument 2, and MIDI THRU of instrument 2 to the MIDI IN of instrument 3, and so on. The MIDI information is transmitted through a MIDI cable that has DIN-type male plug connectors with five pins to connect the synthesizer ports.

33. What are the advantages and disadvantages of using MIDI over digital audio?

Ans. The advantages of using MIDI over digital audio are discussed as follows:

- MIDI files are smaller in size than digital audio files, and hence can be embedded while loading of Web pages and promptly played. In general, MIDI files are 200 to 1000 times smaller than the CD-quality digital audio.
- The size of MIDI files is completely independent of the playback quality. One can alter the length of the MIDI file (by varying its tempo) without changing the pitch of the music or degrading the signal quality.
- Due to their small size, MIDI files require lesser amount of RAM, disk space, and CPU resources.

- In some cases, when the MIDI sound source is of high quality, MIDI files may sound better than digital audio files.

In spite of these advantages, MIDI has some disadvantages also, which are discussed as follows:

- Since the signals are stored as the notes played on the musical instrument, the user needs to have the knowledge of the music theory while working on the MIDI files.
- MIDI cannot easily be used to play back spoken dialogues.
- Since MIDI data itself are not an audio signal (or sound), you can be certain that playback will be accurate only if the MIDI playback device and the device used for production are identical. The same MIDI file may sound different, if played on different synthesizers.

34. Discuss the various data and file formats.

or

What are the various audio file formats and video file formats?

Ans. These days, a large number of different formats, standards as well as proprietary data and file formats are available. The file formats which are primarily used in the Microsoft Windows-based systems are discussed as follows:

- **Rich-text format (RTF):** The early text editors used to allow carrying only textual information in the form of ASCII (or EBCDIC), but did not allow carrying any formatting information. This limited the data interchange because when text was moved from one application to another, all the formatting information was lost. The user had to re-apply all the formatting to the document. The use of RTF has overcome this problem. With the help of RTF, the range of information that can be carried from one application to another has been extended. The key format information that can be carried across in the RTF document files includes the following:
    - Character set
    - Font table
    - Color table
    - Document formatting (document margins)
    - Section formatting (section breaks and page breaks)
    - Paragraph formatting (justification, tab positions, left, right, and first indents, style sheets)
    - General formatting (footnotes, bookmarks, annotation, and pictures)
    - Character formatting (bold, italic, underline, strikethrough, shadow text, etc.)
    - Special characters (hyphens, non-breaking spaces, backslashes, etc.).
- **Tagged image file format (TIFF):** It is an industry-standard file format which is designed to represent raster image data generated by scanners, frame grabbers, and paint/photo retouching applications. It allows describing the raster images in several color models with different data compression schemes. TIFF is available in several versions, the latest version is 6.0. It allows much wider range of specifications as compared to its previous versions 5.0. TIFF is compiler, processor, and device-independent file format, and hence allows interchanging files across different file formats. The TIFF file format provides tags that store information about various aspects such as color, resolution, the compression scheme used for capturing, date and time of capture, and even information about the creator of the file.

Searching in a tagged file is fast as tag locations are found through pointers, and tags are identified using 32-bit ASCII strings. If some modifications or changes need to be made to a specific type of information, more space is allocated, and the pointer to the new block is inserted into the pointer field provided by the tagged block. Thus, a TIFF file format allows you to add new information at any time. A TIFF file consists of a header containing three fields: byte-ordering flag (Intel or Motorola), TIFF file format version number, and a pointer to a table called an **image file directory**. An image file directory consists of a table of entries of the various tags in the file and their associated information. An important feature of a tagged image is that if an application is not able to handle a new feature (such as higher resolution), it can skip the tag and walk through the rest of the tags.

- **Resource interchange file format (RIFF)**: It is a multimedia file format created by Microsoft for use with Windows GUI. RIFF itself is not a new file format; rather it is a container file format that may contain other existing data formats. That is, it provides a framework or an envelope for multimedia file formats. For example, a MIDI file format is converted to RIFF by adding the RIFF structure in the form of RIFF chunks to a MIDI file. A **chunk** is coded blocks of information. It is similar to the image file directory of a TIFF file. Like TIFF, RIFF is also tagged file format and uses tags to tag information.

  A chunk is the basic building block of a RIFF file. Each chunk consists of a chunk ID, chunk size, and chunk data. The RIFF specification defines the following kinds of chunks:

  - **RIFF chunk:** defines the contents of the RIFF file.
  - **List chunk:** allows storing metadata (additional information) about the file such as copyright information, creation date, archival location, and so on.
  - **Subchunk:** allows adding more information to a primary chunk if the primary chunk is not sufficient

- **Device-independent bitmap (DIB):** DIB, also known as, **BMP file format**, or simply a **bitmap,** is the graphics format supported by Microsoft Windows and other OS. It is used to define device-independent bitmaps in various color resolutions. The main purpose of DIB is to allow bitmaps to be moved from one device to another so that bitmaps can be displayed and printed on different devices (hence, the name device-independent). When a DIB image is output to a specific device, the device driver translates the DIB colors into actual colors that the output device can display. In addition to .BMP files, DIBs can also be embedded in Windows .WMF metafiles and clipboard or .CLP files.

  A DIB structure consists of a bitmap information header called **BITMAPINFOHEADER**, a color table called **RGBQUAD** and an array of bytes for the pixel bitmap. In addition to a DIB structure, a DIB file also consists of a **BITMAPFILEHEADER** which is appended before the DIB structure. The DIB file format is shown as follows:

BITMAPFILEHEADER	BITMAPINFO=BITMAPINFOHEADER+RGBQUAD	PIXELS

  The `BITMAPFILEHEADER` structure specifies the type and size of the bitmap file, whereas the `BITMAPINFOHEADER` structure specifies the dimensions, compression type, and color format for the bitmap. The number of elements in the array RGBQUAD represents the total number of colors in the bitmap. For bitmaps containing 24 color bits per pixel, the color table is not used because the 24-bit value itself contains the RGB color value.

- **MIDI:** The MIDI file format, like the RIFF file format, consists of chunks of data. MIDI specifies two types of chunks: *header chunks* and *track chunks*. The **header chunk** is 14 bytes long, where
  - the first four bytes contain a four-character string "MThd"
  - the next four bytes contain the data size for the header chunk
  - the last six bytes contain the data for the header chunk

  The **track chunk**, on the other hand, is organized as follows:
  - the first four bytes contain a four-character string "MTrk"
  - the next four bytes contain the track length
  - the remaining bytes consist of the MIDI messages
- **JPEG:** *Refer question 26*
- **MPEG:** *Refer question 26*

35. Explain various multimedia authoring systems.

Ans. Authoring systems are the systems that allow users to create multimedia objects and embed or link them in other objects such as documents or database records. Authoring tools provide an integrated environment for binding together the different multimedia objects. Authoring systems for multimedia applications are designed by keeping two target users in mind: *professionals* who design multimedia objects for wide distribution, and *ad hoc users* who prepare multimedia objects for presentations or stored messages. The ad hoc users require simple authoring tools whereas professional users require more comprehensive and flexible authoring tools. Depending on their complexity, the role they are intended to play, and the functionality they must support, the authoring systems are divided into various categories, which are discussed as follows:

- **Dedicated authoring systems:** These systems are the simplest type of authoring systems that are designed to handle only one kind of an object for a single user. The dedicated authoring systems are basically designed for the end users workstations, and authoring is performed on the objects captured by local video camera and image scanner. The authoring can also be performed on some kind of stored multimedia object such as inventory presentation about a product. The user can use the authoring tools to customize the presentation according to his or her requirement. Dedicated systems must be designed to cater the novice users who may not be having much knowledge about multimedia composition management. The user interfaces provided by such systems are extremely intuitive and follow real-world metaphors.
- **Timeline-based authoring systems:** These systems use a timeline along which the multimedia objects are placed. The timeline can either be drawn graphically on the screen in the window, or it can be created using a script. In cases, the resource object and its position in the timeline is specified by the user. When the user plays back the multimedia application, the object starts playing at that point in the timescale. Most of the traditional authoring systems are based on this approach. The main drawback of timeline-based authoring systems is that once the multimedia object has been captured in the timeline, it is fixed in location and cannot be manipulated directly. This makes the editing of a component a difficult task, as editing a single component requires reassignment of all the objects. In addition, copying a portion of the timeline becomes difficult as it is difficult to predict the start of a new section.

  In some implementation, this limitation has been overcome by defining the timing relations directly between the objects; that is, the start from one object and the end of another object. The clear boundaries of the start and end of each object make the insertion and deletion of objects much easier. If the timeline is too long, the selected objects can be trimmed and re-inserted; and, if the timeline is not too long, new objects can be inserted. In such authoring systems, the user can work at the object composition level instead of timeline composition level. This provides much greater ease of use and flexibility.

- **Icon-based multimedia authoring system:** In this approach, each multimedia element is represented as an icon, where each icon does a specific task (for example, plays a sound). These icons are then linked to form complete applications. The user can select objects, timing, and sequencing in the form of icons and organize them on a layout screen in a structural framework. The main advantage of icon-based approach is that it provides the ability to graphically design complex interactions for repetitive applications.
- **Structured multimedia authoring system:** Structured multimedia authoring is performed in two stages, first, the structure of a presentation is constructed, and then the detailed timing constraints are assigned. The basic timing information is derived from the structures and the timing constraints are derived from the constituent data items. A well-structured authoring system must provide some capabilities in order to navigate through the structure of the final presentation. These capabilities are as follows:
  - Ability to view the complete structure, or specific components in part or from start to finish
  - Capable of maintaining a hierarchy of objects
  - Ability to zoom down to any specific component
  - Capable of showing the timing relations between the various components
  - Capability to provide a running status of the presentation
  - Ability to address all types of multimedia objects such as text, images, audio, video, and animations

  The most important aspect of a structured authoring system is that it allows the user to define *object hierarchy* and to specify the *relative location* of each object within that hierarchy. Another important feature of a structured design is that the user does not have to determine the absolute timing of each object. The object hierarchy is created by defining only the relative location for each object in time and space within the object hierarchy; the playback engine automatically computes the absolute locations.
- **Programmable authoring systems:** The main drawback of structured authoring tools is that the authors (users) are not able to express the automatic functions for handling certain routine tasks. Programmable authoring systems allow the users to write small programs, which can be associated with multimedia objects. For example, the user can write a program to make an image to move across the screen or to play an audio clip when an item is clicked. These systems have also improved on direct manipulations systems by providing powerful functions based on image processing and analysis, and by embedding program interpreters to use image-processing functions.

36. Discuss various 2D and 3D authoring tools.

Ans. 2D authoring tools are used for creating multimedia objects in two-dimensional space. Some of the commonly used 2D authoring tools are discussed as follows:

- **Microsoft Word:** It is used for creating and editing text files. Bitmapped as well as vector images can be embedded in it. It provides you with many effects such as font effects, font colour, text and table formatting features and many more. There are built-in images (known as clipart) that you can embed with textual data. This tool is widely used for creating advertisement brochures, public notice, letters, etc.

- **PowerPoint:** It is used to create 2D slides that include text and images. You can provide animation, sound and other effects to it that make your data more presentable and understandable. Numerical data can be easily representing in the form of charts, bar graphs, etc., to make the presentation more attractive. It is widely used in giving public presentations for product advertisements.
- **Adobe Premiere:** It is a timeline-based video editing software application, which comes as a part of Adobe Creative Suite. It allows you to edit and assemble different video clips to generate a new video clip with your own audio and animation effects. In addition, it allows you to add transition and visual effects to the generated clip.
- **PageMaker**: It is a simple desktop publishing software used to type the textual data as well as insert images. It is used to create books, novels, articles, etc.

3D authoring tools, on the other hand, are used for creating multimedia objects in three-dimensional space. Some of the commonly used 3D authoring tools are discussed as follows:

- **Autodesk Maya:** It is used to create interactive 3D applications, including video games, animated films, and television series with special visual effects. The product is named after the Sanskrit word Maya—the Hindu concept of illusion. It provides a virtual workspace to the users to create and edit multimedia components for their project. It allows you to save scenes in variety of formats and the default file format is Maya Binary (.mb).
- **Macromedia Director (version 8.5):** It provides an environment for creating interactive movies and provides 3D effects to them. Note that Macromedia Director can be used as 2D as well 3D authoring tool. The latest version of Macromedia Director (which is 8.5) is used to create interactive 3D applications. In Macromedia Director a window known as 'Stage' is used where the actual scene is created and edited (where action takes place). The other two main windows that are used are cast and score.
- **3Ds Max:** It is developed and produced by Autodesk Media and Entertainment. It provides powerful 3D modeling, rendering and animation tools that allow users to focus on creative challenges rather than technical challenges. It has flexible plug-in architecture that can be used on Microsoft Windows platform. This tool is used by TV commercial studios, video game developers and architectural designers. The latest version of 3Ds includes additional features such as shaders, global illumination, dynamic simulation, and on top of it a customizable user interface and its own scripting language.
- **AutoCAD:** It is especially designed in CAD/CAM and drafting applications. Like Macromedia Director, it can also be used as 2D as well as 3D authoring tool. It is available in different languages including English, French, German, Japanese, Korean, Spanish, Chinese, Dutch, Swedish, Urdu, etc. The modern AutoCAD provides powerful and interactive 3D tools, and a full set of basic solid modeling elements. It is available in different versions (each designed for specific platforms). In 2010, Autodesk released its first AutoCAD mobile application AutoCAD WS for iPhone, iPad and Android phones. The mobile application comes with of complete set of AutoCAD tools that allow users (only registered) to view, edit, and share their AutoCAD (DWG) drawings with the help of a web browser. The users do not have to install the AutoDAD software into their mobile phones.
- **Solid Works:** It is 3D mechanical computer-aided design (CAD) program which is used as a parasolid-based modeler and runs on Windows operating system. It follows a parametric-feature approach to create models and assemblies. **Parameters** are the constraints whose values determine the shape or geometry of the model or assembly. They can be either numeric parameters, or

geometric parameters. Numeric parameters include line lengths or circle diameters, and geometric parameters include tangent, parallel, concentric, horizontal or vertical.

37. Discuss Macromedia Flash used as an authoring tool.

Ans. Macromedia Flash is a popular software developed by Macromedia. It is an authoring tool used to develop high quality animations, animated cartoons, website navigation controls, animated logos, interactive Flash movies and visually stunning websites which are entirely based on the Flash platform. The Macromedia Flash window has many parts such as title bar, menu bar, stage, toolbox, panel, and property inspector panel. These parts are discussed as follows:

- **Title Bar:** The title bar displays the name of the software (for example, Macromedia Flash Professional 8) and the name of the document on which you are currently working. Before we save a document, it is titled as Untitled-1.
- **Menu Bar:** The menu bar contains several menus such as File, Edit, View, etc., that categorize various functions and commands available in Flash.
- **Stage:** The white rectangular area in the center of the window is known as the stage. All the animations, objects and scenes for a Flash movie are created, edited, placed and played back in the stage. An object is any graphical feature drawn on the stage (text, circle, square, rectangle, lines, etc.). The grey area surrounding the stage is known as the **Work area**. You can create and edit objects in the work area also but they will not be visible in the final movie. Only the graphical objects kept inside the stage are visible in the final movie. The intersecting horizontal and vertical lines on the stage is called **grid**. The grid helps in aligning the objects to a particular position on stage.
- **Toolbox:** The toolbox contains tools that help in drawing, coloring and modification of objects. You can select one tool at a time from the toolbox and use it on the stage or work area. The toolbox is divided into four sections: Tools, View, Colors and Options.
    - **Tools:** This section contains the basic drawing and editing tools. For example, Brush Tool, Pencil tool, Eraser Tool, etc.
    - **View:** This section contains the tools that help you to view the stage area more conveniently as per the requirement. For example, Hand Tool, Zoom Tool, etc.
    - **Colors:** This section contains the tools that allow you to select and modify the stroke (border) or fill (foreground) colours of various objects.
    - **Options:** This section contains the modifiers for the selected tool. The modifiers are used to change the properties of the selected tool. For example, reshaping lines and shape outlines, optimizing curves, etc.
- **Panel**: It provide you an immediate on screen access to frequently used tools and commands. By default, some of the panels such as Color Mixer, Color Swatches, etc., appear in the right side of the Window.
- **Property Inspector:** It is a very useful panel in Flash which displays the related properties **of a** Flash document, selected object or tool. The object can be text, an image, a line, or any other shape. For example, when we draw a square on the stage and then select it, we can view and modify its height, width, on-screen position, fill color, etc., using the Property Inspector panel.
- **Timeline:** It is one of the most important components of Macromedia Flash. The timeline is used to set the sequencing and timings of various graphical objects and other elements of a Flash movie. It consists of two components, namely, **Frames** and **Layers**. Frames are the discrete, small slices of time that are combined and played back in a sequence to simulate the movement, thus creating the animation, and layers help you to organize the work, add animation and sound, etc., in a Flash movie.

38. What are tweened animations? What are its different types?

or

What are tweened animations and how can you create them using Flash?

Ans. In a tweened animation, you need to animate just the first and the last key frame—Flash automatically animates the intermediate frames to produce the desired animation sequence. Creating a tweened animation is simpler than creating a frame-by-frame animation because you need not animate each frame manually. Moreover, tweened animations are faster and smaller in size than frame-by-frame animations. Tweened animations can be classified in two types, namely, *motion tweening* and *shape tweening*.

Motion tweening

In motion tweening animation, the motion of an object is animated on the stage by setting initial and final position and then letting Flash create the intermediate movements. To understand the motion tweening in a better way, consider an example where a circle-shaped object is to be moved from one position to another. To accomplish this, follow these steps.

1. Open a new Flash document.
2. Draw a circle on the stage using the **Oval Tool**.
3. Convert the circle to a graphic symbol.
4. Click frame 20 in the timeline and insert a new key frame. Notice that now all frames from 1 to 20 are filled up with grey colour and frame 20 is filled up with a black dot indicating that it is a key frame.
5. Click frame 20 and move the circle to the right side of the stage to set its final position.
6. Right-click on frame 1 and create a motion tween by selecting the **Create Motion Tween** from the shortcut menu that appears.
7. Right-click on frame 20 and create a motion tween for this frame also. Notice that now a solid arrow appears between frames 1 and 20.
8. Click on the first frame and play the motion tweened animation.

Notice how the ball seems to move across the stage from the initial to the final position. Flash itself creates the animated frames between frames 1 and 20 to produce a smooth motion tween effect.

Shape tweening

You can use shape tweening to make one shape appear to transform into another over time. For shape tweening, you need not to convert an object into a symbol as shape tweening does not work on symbols, bitmap images or text blocks. To understand more about shape tweening, let us consider an example where an oval-shaped object is to be converted into a star-shaped object.

1. Select the first frame and draw an oval-shaped object on the stage using the **Oval Tool**.
2. Click frame 20 and insert a key frame.
3. With frame 20 selected, delete the oval, and draw a star-shaped object on the stage using the **Line Tool**.
4. Click any intermediate frame between 2 and 19 (say 2). In the **Property Inspector** panel, select **Shape** from the **Tween** drop-down list box.

5. Click on the first frame and play the shape tweening motion.

Notice how the oval-shaped object transforms into the star-shaped object. Flash itself creates the animated frames between frames 1 and 20 to produce the shape tween effect.

39. Discuss about the usage of optical storage media for storing multimedia objects.

Ans. The multimedia data especially, audio and video, either in compressed or uncompressed form, require large amount of storage space. Optical storage media offer a higher storage density at a lower cost. Optical media come in several varieties—CD-ROM, DVD, WORM (Write Once Read Many), and rewriteable optical disks. *CD-ROMs* and *DVDs* are the most popular and the least expensive type of optical disks. They have become the primary media of choice for storing audio and full-motion videos due to their sound and picture quality. In addition, they can be used as data storage device. Many software companies offer, both operating systems software and application software on CDs and DVDs. As the name implies, a CD-ROM comes pre-recorded with the data, which cannot be altered.

A typical optical disk is made up of three layers: a *polycarbonate base* through which light can pass, a *layer of aluminium*, and a protective *layer of acrylic* on top of that. A CD-ROM has one track that spirals from the centre to the outside edge. This track is divided into sectors of equal length and density. Files are stored on these particular contiguous sectors. The storage capacity of a DVD is much higher than that of a CD. In DVD, the tracks are placed closer together, thereby allowing more tracks per disk. CDs and DVDs are almost durable in normal usage and do not lose their quality with use. Other than scratching the recorded surface, CDs and DVDs are immune to most other dangers such as magnetic fields.

WORM disks, as the name suggests, can be used to read as well as to write (usually only once) data onto their surfaces. Data can be written, but cannot be erased on an optical disk. The reason is the technology used for recording. The data on such disks are recorded by using a high-power laser to create a permanent burnt-in record of data. The laser beam makes permanent impression on the surface of the disk such that the information once written can not be altered or erased. The WORM disks are mainly used in legal, stock trading management, and medical, where security of data is of utmost importance. The most common type of a WORM disk is the compact disk-recordable (CD-R). It is a thin (1.2 mm) disk made up of polycarbonate with a 120-mm diameter that is mainly used to store music or data. A CD-R disk is similar to a standard CD, but has subtle differences to enable the storage and removal of data. The disk is coated on the side with the spiral groove with a very thin layer of a special dye and subsequently with a thin, reflecting layer of silver, a silver alloy, or gold. Finally, a protective coating of a photo-polymerizable lacquer is applied on top of the metal reflector and cured with UV-irradiation.

Optical disks offer several advantages, which are discussed as follows:

- Optical disks possess large capacity to store data/information in the form of multimedia, graphics, and video files. They can store more data in less amount of space as compared to magnetic tapes and floppy or zip disks.
- The life span for data storage in optical disks is considered to be more, about 10–20 years as compared to magnetic disks, which have a comparatively lesser life span.
- Optical disks hold more data recording density as compared to other storage media; therefore, they have low cost per bit of storage.
- Optical disk is not affected by magnetic field.

- An optical disk is tougher than tapes/floppy disks. It is physically harder to break or melt.
- Due to their small size and lightweight, these disks are easily portable and stored.

In spite of these advantages, the optical disks have few disadvantages also, which are discussed as follows:

- Optical disks are not easy to write as floppy disks. One needs to use both software and hardware for writing optical disks.
- They possess slow data access speed as compared to the magnetic disks.
- The drive mechanism of optical disk is more complicated than the magnetic and floppy disks.

40. Explain in detail about rewriteable optical disk techniques.

Ans. Rewriteable optical disk, as the name suggests, behaves like a magnetic hard disk where data can be rewritten and erased repeatedly. That is, the data once written can be erased and new data can be rewritten over the old data. There are two types of rewriteable technology, namely, *magneto-optical (MO)* and *phase change*.

MO Technology

The MO systems include basic principles of both magnetic and optical storage systems. This system writes magnetically (with thermal assist) and read optically. That is, the disk recording layer is magnetically recordable and uses a weak magnetic field to record data under high temperatures. The high temperature is achieved with the help of laser beam.

- **Reading data from MO storage devices:** The MO systems use polarized light to read the data from the disk. The changes in light polarization occur due to the presence of a magnetic field on the surface of the disk. This phenomenon is known as the **Kerr effect**, where the polarity of the reflected light is altered depending on the orientation of the magnetic particles. If a beam of polarized light is shined on the surface, the light polarization of the reflected beam will change slightly (typically less than 0.50), if it is reflected from a magnetized surface. If the magnetization is reversed, the change in polarization (the Kerr angle) is reversed too. The magnetized areas, that is, pits, cannot be seen in regular light, but only in polarized light. The change in direction of magnetization could be associated with numbers 0 or 1, making this technique useful for binary data storage.
- **Recording data onto MO storage devices:** After reaching the *Curie temperature* (around 200°C), every magnetic material loses magnetization due to a complete disordering of their magnetic domains, and, as a result, loosing the data stored on them. Moreover, the material's **coercivity**—the measure of material's resistance to magnetization by the applied magnetic field—decreases as the temperature approaches the Curie point, and reaches zero when this temperature is exceeded. Therefore, it is imperative that the only change to the material, when it is heated and cooled, is the change in magnetization with no damage to the material itself. The fact that the material's coercivity drops at higher temperatures allows thermally assisted magnetic recording with relatively weak magnetic fields. Even a relatively weak laser can generate high local temperatures when focused at a small spot (about 1 micron in case of MO systems). When the material is heated, and its coercivity is low, a magnetization of the media can be changed by applying a magnetic field from the magnet. When the material is cooled to room temperature, its coercivity rises back to such a high level that the magnetic data cannot easily be affected by the magnetic fields.

The recording layer is heated by the laser to a point where its magnetic orientation is dissipated. As this spot on the disk cools, the new magnetic orientation—corresponding to the new information—is set by the magnetic head to correspond to '0' and '1' of digital signals. Normally, to rewrite data on a MO disk, it is necessary to erase all previous signals before new data can be recorded. This means either two lasers are used to record (one to erase and one to record) or the single laser must first erase the data in a first rotation and then record the data the second time. This requires either a recorder with two lasers or longer recording times for a single laser system.

Phase Change Rewriteable Optical Disk

In this kind of optical disk technology, the recording layer changes the physical characteristics from crystalline to amorphous and vice versa under the influence of heat generated from a laser beam. In crystalline state, the reflective properties are higher as compared to amorphous state. When the laser beam is shined on the surface of the disk, it heats up the spot on the disk, which crystallizes the spot. If the spot is already in crystalline state, it makes no effect on the spot. That is, it remains in the crystalline state. To change the spot into amorphous state, the laser beam heats up the spot until it melts. It then quickly cools down and changes to amorphous state.

To read the data from the disk, a low-power laser beam shined on the surface of the disk. The reflected beam is different for a crystalline state than for an amorphous state. The difference in reflectivity determines the polarity of the spot. The main advantage of phase change technology is that unlike MO technology which requires two passes to write data, it requires only one pass and no magnetic technology is required to write the data.

41. What is multimedia streaming?

Ans. Multimedia streaming is a technique where multimedia data (especially audio and video files) are constantly received by and presented to an end-user while being delivered by a streaming provider across a network or the Internet. With streaming, the client browser can start displaying the data before the entire file has been transmitted or downloaded. When the user plays a streaming media file, the file is partially downloaded and stored in a buffer before it begins to play; this process is called **buffering**. If the traffic on the Internet disrupts the flow of information, buffering may enable the file to play back with fewer breaks or interference. While streaming a file, the media player continuously monitors the network conditions and automatically makes adjustments to ensure that the user receives the best reception and playback. When the streaming media contents are being played, the statistics and information about the quality of the connection and the playback performance can also be viewed simultaneously. This information can help you determine whether you are receiving a high-quality data transmission or not.

42. Explain the use of multimedia for portable devices.

or

How multimedia is used for portable devices?

Ans Multimedia is widely used in portable devices such as mobile phones, laptops, tablet PCs, palmtops, etc. The second generation and third generation mobile telecommunications technology support multimedia. Mobile phones in the market today are not only limited to calling or sending and receiving text messages, but also contain the features and functionality of various portable devices such as digital cameras, music and video players, gaming consoles, messaging clients and personal digital assistants (PDAs). Thus, mobile phone hardware and software has become more complex. Development of wireless technologies and widespread use of portable devices have given rise to a new type of computing called **mobile computing**. A portable device (or mobile unit) uses the wireless network to access the central database that stores multimedia elements and is managed by the server(s) and usually, has a copy of DBMS software to perform local transactions. The multimedia components such as images, audio and video are all used in portable devices. The use of multimedia for portable devices is listed below.

- **Mobile entertainment:** Multimedia components such as images, audio and video can be uploaded (broadcast) and downloaded using a wireless network. The multimedia component after uploading is stored in the central database and after downloading it is stored in the portable device's memory. Mobile phones and some other portable devices allow the users create their own multimedia data by clicking pictures (image), capturing videos, and recording sounds and voices (audio). The amount and quality of multimedia content that can be stored depends on the type of portable device used. Users can store multimedia content on to these devices or can access the multimedia content stored at remote location by using an Internet connection.
- **Gaming:** With the advancement in technology, gaming experience has been enhanced a lot. Multimedia content is used by portable devices for game playing. It is used to play offline as well as online (wireless) games. Nowadays, the gaming experiences not only limited to 2D, but has extended to 3D as well. Computer graphics play a great role in game playing.
- **Music (building on ring tones):** Audio content can also be uploaded and downloaded. These music files can be used as ring tones. These may be MIDI (digital) or wave file (audio clip). Some portable devices provide facility to edit (cut, merge) the audio files.
- **Person-to-person video interactivity:** Video-conferencing allows video communication between two or more people that are far apart. It is also referred to as **video calling** or **video telephony**. Here live video is shared among two or more portable devices. Video telephony and video streaming are two of the crowning features of 3G phones, but video capability is now also showing up in 2G mobile phones

MULTIPLE CHOICE QUESTIONS

1. Which of the following is the building block of a multimedia system?
   (a) Text (b) Animation
   (c) Audio (d) All of these
2. __________ is an example of passive multimedia system.
   (a) TV documentary (b) Digital libraries
   (c) Electronic games (d) VoD
3. Which layer of multimedia architecture consists of software drivers and multimedia driver support?
   (a) Topmost (b) Second
   (c) Third (d) Last
4. __________ is a 16-bit bus standard based on IBM PC industry standard architecture.
   (a) SCSI (b) IDE
   (c) MCI (d) None of these

5. The devices through which the people view multimedia data are collectively known as ________.
   (a) Terminals (b) Video server
   (c) Media (d) Multimedia databases
6. Which of the following is not a content of multimedia data?
   (a) Format data (b) Feature data
   (c) Keyword data (d) Meta data
7. BLOB stands for ____________
   (a) Binary Large Obstacle (b) Binary Long Object
   (c) Binary Large Oriented Box (d) Binary Large Object
8. Virtual reality is also referred to as ____________.
   (a) Artificial reality (b) Synthetic reality
   (c) Both (a) and (b) (d) Synthetic virtual
9. Which of the following technique is used to compress audio?
   (a) Inter-frame encoding (b) Predictive encoding
   (c) Intra-frame encoding (d) ADC
10. Which of the following is a data file format?
    (a) RTF (b) RIFF
    (c) DIB (d) All of these

Answers. 1. d 2. a 3. c 4. b 5. a 6. d 7. d 8. c 9. b 10. d

12

Animation

1. Explain the basic concept of computer animation.

Ans. Animation is defined as a visual change in a scene with respect to time. The visual change in the scene is not only associated with the change in the position of the object, but also with its shape, color, transparency, structure, and texture. An important point about animation is that it usually signifies the hand drawn or artificially drawn sequence of images, which contrasts to the movies where actors' performances with real-world scenes are recorded. In early times, animations were made by hand drawing, every scene were drawn one-by-one on paper and then painted. This method was obviously very troublesome and time-consuming. Nowadays, the use of computer technology has made the animation process progressively simpler and more powerful. The process of drawing images and playing them back at a high speed with the help of computer software in order to create an illusion of movement is referred to as **computer animation**. The illusion of movement is created by displaying an image on the computer screen, then quickly replacing it by a new image, which is similar to the previous image, but shifted slightly.

The field of computer animation is a subset of both computer graphics and animation technologies. Computer animation is generally achieved through a series of geometric transformations – scaling, translation, rotation, or any mathematical technique – to produce a sequence of scenes. In addition, the animation can be produced by varying any of the following:

- **Camera parameters:** It involves the camera position with respect to the object, distance from the object, orientation, and focus.
- **Lighting conditions:** It involves direction and color of light, number of lights, and so on.

These days computer animation is widely used in the entertainment industry for producing motion pictures, cartoon movies, and video games. In addition, it is being used in education and training, industrial applications, virtual reality systems, advertising, scientific visualization, and many engineering applications.

2. What are the steps involved in the design of animation sequence? Explain.

Ans. In the early days, an animation sequence was created by drawing different images in different frames and then showing them at a high speed. However, these days, animations are created with the help of computers. In computer animation, the frames required for animation are generated using computers, and are then displayed on an output device at a high speed. A basic approach to design an animation sequence consists of the four stages, namely, *storyboard layout*, *object definitions*, *key frame specifications*, and *generation of in-between frames*.

i. **Storyboard layout:** The **storyboard** is an outline of the action. This stage basically defines the motion sequence of the object as a set of basic events that are to take place. For example, while creating an animation sequence of cricket play, the storyboard layout would consist of action and motion of batting, bowling, fielding, running, and so on. Depending on the type of animation to be created, the storyboard consists of a set of rough sketches, models, or even in some cases it could be verbal description or list of basic ideas of the motion.

ii. **Object definitions:** Once the storyboard layout has been prepared, the next step is to define all the objects or participants in the action. The objects are generally described in terms of their dimensions, shapes (such as polygons or spline surfaces), colors, movements, or any other additional information which can help in defining the objects. For example, while creating animation for cricket play, the object definitions could be player's dimensions, colors of their uniform, dimensions of the ball, bat, stumps, etc.

iii. **Key frame specifications:** The next step in the process of creating animation is to specify key frame specification. A **key frame** is a detailed drawing of the scene at a certain time in the animation sequence. In each key frame, the position, color, shapes, etc., of all the objects is positioned according to a particular point of time for that frame. More the number of key frames, smoother will be the animation. For complex motions, one need to specify more key frames as compared to simple, slowly varying motions. Some key frames are specified at extreme positions, where others are spaced such that the time interval between them is not too large.

iv. **Generation of in-between frames:** Once the key frames are specified, the next step is to generate intermediate frames. The total number of in-between frames required for an animation depends on the display media that is to be used. For example, film requires 24 frames per second, and graphics terminals require more than 60 frames per second. Typically, time intervals for the motion are set up such that there are three to five intermediate frames between any two key frames. In addition, some key frames can also be duplicated depending on the speed specified for the motion. For example, for a one-minute film sequence with no duplication, 1440 frames would be required, and if we put five intermediate frames between any two key frames, then 288 key frames would only be required.

3. What are the different animation principles?

or

Discuss the various animation techniques.

Ans. There are **12 basic principles of animation** which were introduced by the Disney animators Ollie Johnston and Frank Thomas in 1981 in their book *The Illusion of Life: Disney Animation*. The main aim of the principles was to produce an illusion of characters adhering to the basic laws of physics. However, these laws also dealt with more abstract issues, such as emotional timing and character appeal. The 12 basic principles of animation are described as follows:

- **Squash and stretch:** It is the most important principle of animation. Its main purpose is to give a sense of weight and flexibility to the drawn objects. Stretch and squash technique is basically used for simulating accelerating effects especially for non-rigid objects. This technique can be applied to simple objects like a bouncing rubber ball, as well as to complex constructions like musculature of a human face. For example, when a rubber ball bounces and hits the ground, it tends to get flatten on hitting the ground. This is squash principle. As soon as the ball starts bouncing up, it stretches in the direction of its movement. This is stretch principle. Another example is the stretching and squashing of a human face. When the muscles of human face are stretched or squashed to an exaggerated degree, it can give a comical effect. The most important aspect of this principle is the fact that the stretching and squashing of an object does not affect its volume. That is, no matter how an object is deformed, it should still appear to retain its volume.

- **Timing:** Timing is the most vital element of an animation. It refers to the spacing between motion frames. The more is the spacing between the frames, the faster the object will appear to move. The speed at which an object is moving gives a sense of what the object is, what can be the weight of an object and why it is moving. Timing in an animation is significant for establishing the mood, emotion, and reaction of a character. For example, the blinking of an eye can be fast or slow. If it is slow, a character seems to be tired and lethargic. However, if it is fast, a character seems to be alert and awake. Timing can also be used to communicate important aspects of the personality of a character.
- **Anticipation:** It is used to prepare the audience for the upcoming motion or action and to make such action more live and realistic. For example, a person throwing a ball has to first swing his or her arm backwards, or a dancer jumping off the floor must bend his or knees first. These are preliminary actions that are used to emphasize the object movements. Anticipation can also be used for less physical actions, such as a character looking off-screen to anticipate someone's arrival, or attention focusing on an object that a character is about to pick-up.
- **Follow through and overlapping actions:** Follow through refers to the actions that are performed at the end of the actual motion. Follow through actions emphasize the fact that characters follow the laws of physics, which state that separate parts of a body will continue to move even after the character has performed the specified action. In other words, follow through captures how parts of an object continue to move even after other parts of that object have stopped moving. For example, the arm of a person continues to move even after throwing a ball. This is a follow through action. Overlapping action is another important principle of animation. It is the tendency for parts of the body to move at different speeds and different times. For example, when a dog is running, all its body parts are moving at different rates. The timing of his legs is different from the timing of the movement of his tail, or ears. By overlapping the actions of an object's body, hair, tail, clothing, etc., you can make your animation more fluid, natural, and realistic. It is to be noted that while creating an animation sequence, an action should never be brought to a complete stop before starting another action. Overlapping maintains a continual flow between whole phrases of actions.
- **Staging:** It refers to the presentation of an idea in such a way that it is completely and clearly understood. An idea could be an action, a personality, an expression, or a mood. Its main aim is to draw the attention of the audience to the most relevant action, personality, expression, or a mood in a scene so that it is easily recognizable. Staging helps in keeping focus on what is relevant, and avoiding unnecessary details. It can be performed in several ways such as placing a character in a frame, using a light and shadow, and setting an appropriate angle and position of the camera.
- **Straight ahead action and pose-to-pose action:** These two are the basic approaches of creating animation. In **straight ahead animation**, the animator draws a scene frame by frame from beginning to end. That is, he or she first draws the first frame of the animation, then the second, and so on until the sequence is complete. **Pose-to-pose animation**, on the other hand, is created by drawing a few key frames, and then creating in-between images. The straight ahead action allows you to

create a more fluid, dynamic illusion of movement and is better for producing realistic action sequences. On the other hand, pose-to-pose allows you to create better dramatic or emotional scenes, where composition and relation to the surrounding are more important. With computers, people generally use a combination of the two techniques. That is, they first plan out the overall process using pose-to-pose approach, and then create the in-between images using the straight ahead approach.

- **Slow in and slow out (or ease in and ease out):** The basic idea behind this principle is that when the human body or other objects move, they need time to accelerate and slow down. For this reason, we add more drawings near the beginning and end of our animation sequence to emphasize the extreme poses, and fewer drawings in the middle. This makes the animation looks more natural and realistic. For example, a bouncing ball tends to have a lot of ease in and out when at the top of its bounce. As it goes up, gravity affects it and slows down (ease in), then it moves in downward direction more and more rapidly (ease out), until it hits the ground.
- **Arcs:** In real world, generally the actions tend to follow an arched trajectory. That is, all actions move in an arc. For example, when a ball is thrown or kicked, it moves along a parabolic trajectory. Thus, while creating an animation sequence, the animator should try to have motion following curved paths rather than straight line paths. This will make the animation look more natural and realistic.
- **Exaggeration:** Generally, a perfect imitation of reality makes the cartoons or animation static and dull. To make the animation lively and entertaining, the exaggeration is used. This effect is used to emphasize an action. One can exaggerate motion, for example, moving an arm just a bit too far briefly in an extreme swing. Exaggeration may also involve the supernatural alterations to the physical features of a character, or elements in the storyline itself. However, exaggeration should be employed in a careful and balanced manner, not arbitrarily. The main idea is to make something more extreme in order to give it more life, but not so much that it becomes unbelievable.
- **Secondary actions:** They are generally used to make animation look more interesting and realistic. Adding secondary actions to the main actions add more life to the scene, and can help to support the main action. For example, if a person is walking, he/she can simultaneously swing his or her arms, or keep them in the pocket, or express his/her feelings through facial expressions, and so on. The main idea behind secondary actions is to emphasize the main action, rather than taking attention away from the main action. Secondary actions are generally included at the beginning and end of the movement, and not during the action.
- **Solid drawing:** The main idea behind solid drawings is to create 3D drawings, and giving them weight and volume. It is very important for an animator to understand the basics of 3D shapes, weight, balance, anatomy, light and shadow, and other relevant characteristics. Though these days, the computer animators need to draw less images because of the facilities provided by computers, still they need to have a basic understanding of animation principles and artwork.
- **Appeal:** While creating an animation sequence, it is necessary to include something that appeals the audience. Appeal in a cartoon character is similar to charisma in an actor. An appeal can be quality of charm, design, simplicity, communication, or magnetism. It is important to note that an appealing character is not necessarily sympathetic or good – evils or monsters can also be appealing. It is basically the charm and charisma added to the character to make it real and interesting.

4. Explain in detail about the animation languages.

Ans. To handle the design and control of animation sequences, several animation functions such as a graphics editor, a key frame generator, an in-between generator, and standard graphics routines are required. Though these animation functions can be programmed using a general-purpose programming language, such as C, Lisp, Pascal, or FORTRAN, still several specialized animation languages have also been developed. These animation languages are categorized into three types, which are as follows:

- **Key frame systems:** These are specialized animation languages which are designed to generate the intermediate frames from the user-specified key frames. Originally, these systems were designed as a separate set of animation routines, but now these routines are often form a component in a more general animation package. In the simplest case, each object in the scene is defined as a set of rigid bodies connected at the joints and with a limited number of degrees of freedom. For example, for a single-arm robot, one can specify six degrees of freedom including arm sweep, shoulder spin, elbow lengthening, pitch, yaw, and roll. If we specify 3D translational and rotational for the base, then we can extend the number of degrees of freedom for this robot arm to 12. However, for a human body, one can specify more than 200 degrees of freedom.
- **Parameterized systems:** These systems allow specifying the object motion characteristics as a part of the object definitions. The adjustable parameters control such object characteristics as degrees of freedom, motion limitations, and allowable shape changes.
- **Scripting systems:** These systems allow the user to define object specifications and animation sequences based on the user-input script. With the help of the script, a library of various objects and motions can be constructed.

5. Differentiate between scene description and action description with respect to animation specification.

Ans. There are typically two main tasks in an animation specification, namely, *scene description* and *action description*. **Scene description** includes the positioning of object and light sources, defining the photometric parameters, and setting the camera parameters. **Action specification**, on the other hand, includes the layout of motion paths for the objects and camera.

6. What do you mean by morphing? How do you implement morphing animation technique? Discuss with an example.

Ans. The word *morph* has been derived from the word *metamorphosis*, which means to change shape, appearance, or form. **Morphing** is an animation technique that is used to transform (or morph) one image into another through a seamless transition. It basically allows you to dynamically blend two still images, and creating a sequence of in-between pictures such that, when played, metamorphosis the first image into the second. The basic idea behind morphing is that as the morphing proceeds, the initial image is gradually distorted and is faded out, while the final image is faded in. These days morphing is not only used in entertainment and gaming industry, but also used for enhancing many multimedia projects such as presentations, education, electronic book illustrations, and computer-based training.

Morphing can be applied to any motion or transition that involves change in shape. An animator can model morphing by transitioning polygon shapes through the intermediate frames from one key frame to another. Suppose we are given two key frames k and $k + 1$, each having a different number of edges and each of them specifying an object transformation. Before applying transition, a preprocessing step needs to be performed, where we first adjust the object specification in one of the frames in order to equalize the number of polygon edges (or the number of vertices) in the two frames. For example, suppose we need to transform a straight-line segment in key frame k into two line segments in key frame $k + 1$. Since the key frame $k + 1$ has an extra vertex, we add an extra vertex between vertex 1 and 2 in the key frame k so that the number of vertices (and edges) becomes equal in the two frames. The added vertex in the key frame k is transformed into vertex $3'$ along the straight-line path as shown in Figure 12.1.

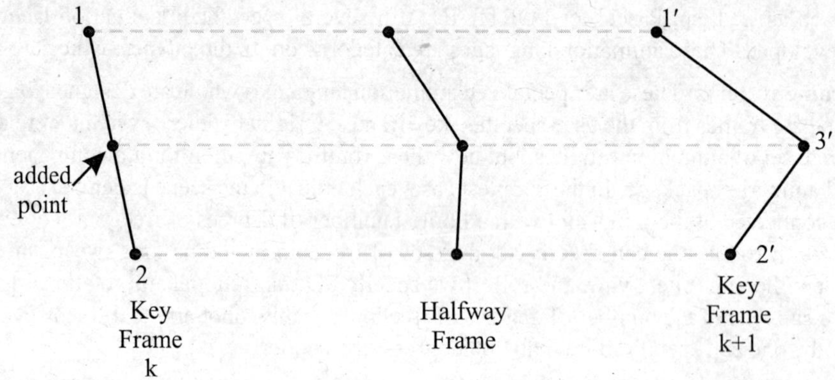

Figure 12.1 Transforming a Line Segment in Key Frame *k* into Two Connected Line Segments in Key Frame $k + 1$

Another example of morphing is the transitioning of a triangle into a quadrilateral as shown in Figure 12.2.

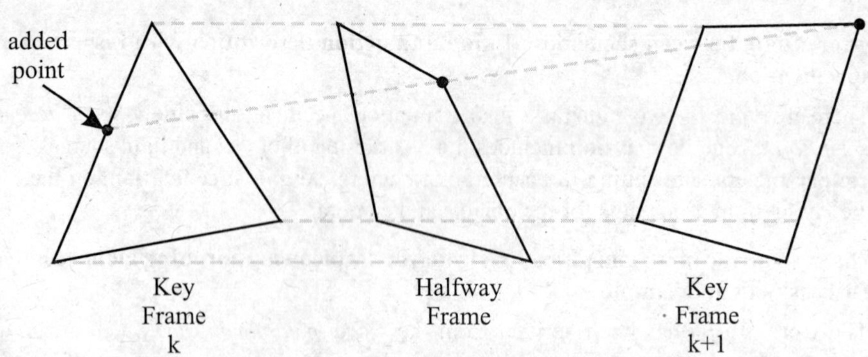

Figure 12.2 Transforming a Triangle into a Quadrilateral

Depending on the number of edges or the number of vertices to be equalized (or added) to a key frame, the general preprocessing rules can be stated as follows:

- Suppose we need to equalize the number of edges in the two key frames, and parameters L_k and L_{k+1} indicate the number of edges (or line segments) in the two consecutive frames. Then, we define

$$L_{max} = \max(L_k, L_{k+1}), \qquad L_{min} = \min(L_k, L_{k+1})$$

and compute the following two values as:

$$N_e = L_{max} \bmod L_{min}$$

$$N_s = \mathrm{int}\left(\frac{L_{max}}{L_{min}}\right)$$

These two values can then be used for performing edge equalization by following these steps:

(i) divide N_e edges of *keyframe*$_{min}$ into $N_s + 1$ sections.

(ii) divide the number of remaining edges of *keyframe*$_{min}$ into N_s sections.

To understand the preprocessing steps for edge equalization, consider an example, where $L_k = 15$ and $L_{k+1} = 11$. Therefore, $L_{max} = 15$, $L_{min} = 11$, $N_e = 4$ and $N_s = 1$. Now, we divide four edges of *keyframe*$_{k+1}$ into two sections each, and the remaining edges are left intact.

- Now suppose we need to equalize the number of vertices in the two key frames, and parameters V_k and V_{k+1} indicate the number of vertices in the two consecutive frames. Then, we define

$$V_{max} = \max(V_k,\ V_{k+1}), \qquad V_{min} = \min(V_k,\ V_{k+1})$$

and compute the following two quantities as:

$$N_{ls} = (V_{max} - 1) \bmod (V_{min} - 1)$$

$$N_p = \text{int}\left(\frac{V_{max} - 1}{V_{min} - 1}\right)$$

These two quantities can then be used to perform vertex equalization by following these steps:

(i) add N_p points to N_{ls} line sections of *keyframe*$_{min}$.

(ii) add N_p -1 points to the remaining edges of *keyframe*$_{min}$.

To understand the preprocessing steps for vertex equalization, consider the transition of the triangle into a quadrilateral as shown in Figure 12.2. Here, $V_k = 3$ and $V_{k+1} = 4$. Therefore, $V_{max} = 4$, $V_{min} = 3$, $N_{ls} = 1$, and $N_p = 1$. Now, we add one point to one edge of *keyframe*$_k$ and other edges will remain intact of keyframe$_{k+1}$.

7. How to specify object motion in an animation system?

Ans. There are several ways for specifying the motions of the object in an animation system. These are discussed as follows:

- **Direct motion specification:** This is the simplest and most straightforward method for defining a motion sequence. It is mostly used for specifying motions of objects in simple user-programmed animation sequences. In this method, firstly the rotation angles and translation vectors are explicitly specified, and then geometric transformation matrices are applied to transform coordinate positions. Alternatively, we could use an approximating Equation to specify certain kinds of motion. For example, we can approximate the path of a bouncing ball, with a damped, rectified, *sine* curve, as follows:

$$y(x) = A\ |\sin(\omega x + \theta_0)|\ e^{-kx},$$

Where A is the initial amplitude of the ball, ω is the angular frequency, θ_0 is the phase angle, and k is the damping constant.

- **Goal-directed systems:** In goal-directed systems, as the name suggests, the values of the motion parameters are determined from the pre-specified goals of the animation. These systems specify an animation in terms of the final state of the motions at the extreme positions. For example, we could specify that we want an object to "pick up" something from a particular location, or we could specify that we want an object to "walk" or "run" to a particular destination. The input directives are then interpreted in terms of motions of components that will accomplish the desired task. The motion of human body, for instance, can be defined as a hierarchical structure of submotions for the torso, limbs, and so on. Thus, if we are given a goal "run to the door", then we can calculate the motions required of the torso and limbs to accomplish this task.

- **Kinematics and dynamics:** An animation sequence can also be constructed by describing kinematics and dynamics. **Kinematics** refers to the positions and velocities of points, whereas, **dynamics** takes into account the physical laws that govern kinematics. Thus, a **kinematic description** takes into account the motion parameters (such as position, velocity, and acceleration) of an object without giving any reference to the forces that cause the motion. Moreover, kinematic specification of a motion can also be given by simply describing the motion path. This is done by using spline curves. On the other hand, in **dynamic description**, we specify the forces that produce the velocities and accelerations. Some of the examples of forces that affect the object motions include electromagnetic, gravitational, frictional, and other mechanical forces. The description of object behaviour in terms of the influence of forces is known as **physically based modelling**.

  It is also possible to invert both kinematics and dynamics. These approaches to modelling are referred to as inverse kinematics and inverse dynamics. In **inverse kinematics**, the initial and final positions of objects are specified at a particular point of time and motion parameters are computed by the system. In **inverse dynamics**, from the given initial and final positions of objects and type of motion required, one can obtain the forces.

8. Describe the different techniques used in animation control mechanisms.

Ans. Animation control mechanisms employ different techniques, which are discussed as follows.

- **Full explicit control:** It is simplest technique of controlling an animation, where the animator is completely responsible for controlling the animation. In this technique, the animator explicitly provides the position and attributes of every object in a scene by means of scaling, translations, rotations, and other attribute-changing operators. He/she can also provide the key frame information and interpolation methods to be used between the key frames. The interpolation can be given either explicitly or interactively by means of input devices such as mouse, joystick, data glove, etc.
- **Procedural control:** This technique is based on the communication between various elements in order to determine their properties. Procedural control is a significant aspect of several other control mechanisms. The main advantage of this technique is that the procedural interaction among elements can be used to generate motions that would be difficult to specify through explicit control. However, the main drawback is that it requires the animator to be a programmer.
- **Constraint-based systems:** In real world, most of the objects do not move in a linear path, rather, their motion is influenced by the other objects with which they are in contact. For example, consider an animation in which a ball rolls up and hits another ball. This causes the second ball to roll away. The speed of the second ball entirely depends on the force with which it is hit by the first ball. If the first ball is made to move more slowly, the rolling away of the second ball will be delayed. Thus, the motion of the second ball is constrained by the speed of the first ball. Consider another example of a pendulum swinging from a pivot. It always follow a to-and-fro motion around a fixed

axis. Such motions can be modeled by constraints. Specifying an animation sequence using constraints is generally much easier to do as compared to that of explicit control.

- **Tracking live action:** This technique helps in generating the trajectories of objects in the course of animation. Tracking can be done in several ways. The traditional way of performing tracking is rotoscoping. In this technique, a film is made in which people or animals play the role of characters in the animation. Then the animators enhance the backgrounds and replace the human actors with equivalent animated characters by drawing over the film. This technique provides exceptionally realistic motion. Another technique of tracking live action is to attach any kind of indicator, say sensor, to key points on a person's body. Now, one can get the locations of corresponding key points by tracking the positions of the indicators. For example, one can attach small lights at key locations on a person, and then positions of these lights are recorded from different locations (or directions) to give a 3D position for each key point at each time.
- **Actors:** An **actor** in an animation is a small program that is invoked once per frame to determine the characteristics of some object in the animation. During the execution, an actor may control the behavior of other actors by sending messages to them. For example, one can create an animation sequence for the construction of a train by allowing the engine actor respond to some predetermined set of rules (for instance, move along the track at a fixed speed). Moreover, the engine actor can also send the message to the first compartment of the train "place yourself on the track by attaching your front end to the back end of the engine." All the compartments can then send the similar message to their subsequent compartments, thus allowing the compartments to follow the engine.

MULTIPLE CHOICE QUESTIONS

1. The __________ is an outline of the action.
   (a) Object definitions (b) Key frame specifications
   (c) Storyboard (d) In-between frames
2. Which of the following is not an animation technique?
   (a) Anticipation (b) Actors
   (c) Timing (d) Arcs
3. _________ refers to the presentation of an idea in such a way that it is clearly understood.
   (a) Staging (b) Exaggeration
   (c) Solid drawing (d) Squash
4. Which of the following is a type of animation language?
   (a) Scripting systems (b) Key frame systems
   (c) Parameterized systems (d) All of these
5. _________ is an animation technique that is used to transform one image into another.
   (a) Transformation (b) Scaling
   (c) Morphing (d) Kinematics
6. Which of the following is one of the main tasks performed in an animation specification?
   (a) Scene description (b) Action description
   (c) Both (a) and (b) (d) Tracking live action

7. Which is the simplest technique of controlling an animation?

   (a) Procedural control (b) Full explicit control
   (c) Actors (d) Constraint-based systems

Answers. 1. c 2. b 3. a 4. d 5. c 6. c 7. b

Index

A

B

C

D

E

F

S

T

U

V

W

X

Y

Z